Global Tourism

Global Tourism
The next decade

Edited by William F. Theobald

BUTTERWORTH
HEINEMANN

Butterworth-Heinemann Ltd
Linacre House, Jordan Hill, Oxford OX2 8DP

 A member of the Reed Elsevier plc group

OXFORD   LONDON   BOSTON
MUNICH   NEW DELHI   SINGAPORE   SYDNEY
TOKYO   TORONTO   WELLINGTON

First published 1994
Reprinted 1994
Paperback edition 1995

British Library Cataloguing in Publication Data
Global Tourism: The Next Decade
  I. Theobald, William F.
  338.4791

ISBN 0 7506 2353 5

Library of Congress Cataloging in Publication Data
Global tourism: the next decade/edited by William F. Theobald.
  p.   cm.
  Includes bibliographical references and index.
  ISBN 0–7506–2353–5
  1. Tourist trade.   I. Theobald, William F., 1934–
  G155.A1G49   93–32527
  338.4'791—dc20   CIP

Printed and bound in Great Britain by Clays (St Ives) plc

Contents

Foreword

Tourism is one of the world's largest and fastest-growing industries and thus demands the comprehensive analysis and consideration that this book offers. As Secretary-General of the World Tourism Organization (WTO), it is gratifying for me to see that the substantial approaches to tourism development and global issues addressed in these pages uphold, and in fact, parallel much of the work of the WTO.

As the only intergovernmental organization for the development and promotion of tourism, the WTO is responsible for collecting data on tourism flows and working throughout the world for the sustainable development of tourism. In 1992, our statistics show that international tourist arrivals grew by 4.6 per cent to 476 million, and international tourism receipts by 6.8 per cent to US$279 billion. If most other industries had experienced this same level of growth, the economies of the main generating countries probably would not have been affected by recession, and tourism would have grown even faster.

That same year, 1992, was also the year of the Earth Summit in Rio de Janeiro, which was held in June. That conference had deep significance for the future of tourism, especially given the WTO's forecast of 3–4.5 per cent average annual growth in international tourism over the remainder of this decade, and into the twenty-first century. By the year 2000, international tourist arrivals will have jumped by 50 per cent to approximately 650 million, if not more.

With such tremendous growth forecasted and, in fact, already occurring, careful planning, development and management are essential for the preservation of a clean, safe environment. And a clean environment is a key prerequisite for the continued prosperity of the tourism industry and, of course, most if not all other industries.

Codes of conduct, environmental audits, tour operator–destination partnerships to repair the damage caused by overdevelopment, campaigns for clean beaches, development of environmental indicators, carrying capacity management – these are all possible ways to ensure a sustainable, long-term global tourism industry. Therefore, this book is both a substantial and important contribution to these efforts.

Antonio Enriquez Savignac, Secretary-General
World Tourism Organization
Madrid, Spain

Preface

This book is the result of a need for such a collection, which the editor personally experienced when attempting to teach a seminar in tourism where no traditional source books were available. It is intended for anyone who is or will be engaged in the tourism industry, regardless of their particular field of interest. The work is planned on original lines because the editor has found in his experience as teacher and author that the needs of students and practitioners, whether in university or graduate school, in government or in the private sector, are not met by the usual 'Introduction to Tourism' book. Rather, the need is for a new view of the subject which ordinary textbooks tend to separate.

This volume draws together the insights of twenty-nine observers commonly concerned with the effects of tourism on contemporary society. The chapters represent various viewpoints from leading educators and practitioners from such disciplines as anthropology, economics, environmental science, geography, marketing, political science, psychology, public administration, sociology and urban planning.

The purpose of this book is to present critical issues, problems and opportunities facing the tourism industry. Tourism problems are complex and interrelated and they suggest a myriad of crises, such as overcrowding of tourist attractions, overuse and destruction of natural resources, resident–host conflicts, loss of cultural heritage, increased crime and prostitution, inflation and escalating land costs, and a host of other political, socio-cultural, economic and environmental problems that may be brought about or exacerbated by tourism development.

The approach taken by this book does not focus on a particular subject, but rather the exploration of issues facing those involved in the tourism domain. The scope of the book provides each chapter as a mini-treatise on tourism, from an *international* perspective. Individual chapters scrutinize, reflect upon and question the changes and transformations needed. Each chapter provides an exploration of concerns, issues, assumptions, values and perceptions, and the reasoning for a view taken by individual authors. The issues raised in the book will hopefully bring about much needed thought, discussion, reflection, argumentation and, perhaps, debate.

It would be patently absurd to claim that this book encapsulates all that might or should be said about tourism. It should be discerned, however, that an attempt has been made to present the viewpoints of both those who look with optimism at tourism and those who scrutinize it with some scepticism. It has not been a goal to prove any individual point of view as the 'right' one, but rather to examine the phenomenon of tourism as fully as possible. Now, let me turn to those special individuals whom I sincerely wish to recognize and thank.

It would not have been possible to undertake this project without the love, support and total commitment of my wife, Sharon. Thank you for for being by my side through the years.

As editor I wish to acknowledge the contribution of Brian Archer, who not only provided encouragement to undertake this project, but also recommended it to the publisher, Butterworth-Heinemann. Thanks are also extended to my colleagues at the Universities of Surrey (UK) and Waterloo (Canada) for the many opportunities they provided which helped expand my view of tourism as an international phenomenon.

Acknowledgement is made of both the World Tourism Organization (WTO) and the Travel and Tourism Research Association (TTRA), who granted permission to reproduce selected portions of previously published materials. The editor is indebted to Antonio Enriquez Savignac, Secretary-General of the WTO, who generously agreed to write the Foreword to the book.

Appreciation is extended to B. Frederique Samuel, one of the editor's doctoral students at Purdue University, for his contribution, editing four of the chapters and compiling the contributor biographies; to Siming Chu for his interpretative and editing skills, and to Bonnie Snyder for her direction of the voluminous facsimile and postal communications between the editor and contributing authors.

The editor wishes to thank Kathryn Grant, Publishing Director (Business Books) at Butterworth-Heinemann for her enthusiastic support of the idea underlying this book and her cogent suggestions throughout its compilation. In addition, the publisher's editorial staff are acknowledged for their help with the completed manuscript.

Finally, a specific note of appreciation is extended to the contributors to this volume for their wholehearted efforts in bringing their knowledge, ability and experience to the task at hand. It was an exhilarating experience working with them.

William F. Theobald
Purdue University
West Lafayette, Indiana

Contributors

John Ap is a certified town planner and is currently an Assistant Professor of Tourism at the Hong Kong Polytechnic Institute. Formerly, he was a planner with the Wollongong City Council and a project manager with the Tourism Commission of New South Wales (Australia). A native of Australia, he has an undergraduate degree from the University of New South Wales and graduate degrees from the Wollongong University and Texas A & M University (USA). Mr Ap's research interests include tourism impacts, service quality in the hospitality industry, and tourism/recreation planning. He is the author of two articles in the *Annals of Tourism Research*.

Brian Archer is Pro-Vice-Chancellor at the University of Surrey (UK), where he was Head of the Department of Management Studies for Tourism and Hotel Industries. Before 1978, he was Director of the Institute of Economic Research at the University College of North Wales, Bangor. With degrees in economics (London), geography (Cambridge) and a doctorate from the University of Wales, he is a Fellow of the Tourism Society, and of the Hotel, Catering and Institutional Management Association. Professor Archer is the author of several monographs, a large number of reports and several hundred articles. His principal research interest is in the economics of tourism, and he has conducted research and consultant assignments in more than forty countries and has presented at over thirty conferences.

Chris Cooper is Senior Lecturer in Tourism Management at the University of Surrey (UK). Formerly, he worked in market planning for a major tour operator and retailer in the UK. He has a doctorate in geography from the University of London. Dr Cooper is the author of many articles and conference papers in tourism, and in addition, is editor of *Progress in Tourism, Recreation and Hospitality Management*, an international research review annual.

Graham M.S. Dann is Reader in Sociology at the University of the West Indies (Barbados). A native of Edinburgh, he has a doctorate from the University of Surrey (UK). Dr Dann is the author of six books and over fifty refereed articles, and is an associate editor of *Annals of Tourism Research*. A founder of the International Academy for the Study of Tourism, his research interests in tourism focus principally on motivation and the semiotics of promotional literature.

Thomas Lea Davidson was, until his death, Principal and CEO of Davidson-Peterson Associates, Inc., a company he founded with Karen Ida Peterson. A full-service marketing research and strategic planning consulting company based in York, Maine (USA), they specialize in the travel, tourism, accommodations, meetings and conventions, entertainment and recreation marketplace. Formerly, he was Executive VP of Davidson-Lasco, and Oxtoby-Smith, Inc. He was an adjunct faculty member at several universities including Northwestern and Connecticut (USA) where he was also Associate Director of Graduate Studies in Business. Mr Davidson was a member of the editorial board of the *Journal of Travel Research*, and the US Department of Commerce Task Force on Assessment Research Methods (Performance Accountability). A past national chairperson, board member and committee chair of the Council of American Survey Research Organizations (CASRO), he also chaired the Certification Committee of the Association of Travel Marketing Executives.

H.W. (Bill) Faulkner is Associate Professor of Marketing at Griffith University (Australia). Former positions held included: inaugural Director of the Australian Bureau of Tourism Research; Director of Research and Policy Development at the Australian Department of Sport, Recreation and Tourism, and; senior researcher in the Bureau of Transport Economics. Dr Faulkner has a doctorate from the Australian National University, and has taught and conducted research there and at the University of Wollongong, as well as at other institutions.

Donald Getz is Associate Professor of Tourism and Hospitality Management at the University of Calgary (Canada). Formerly, he was with the Department of Recreation and Leisure Studies at the University of Waterloo (Canada), and an urban and regional planner. He is active as a festival volunteer organizer and strategic planner, and is a consultant of managing and marketing events. Dr Getz's academic interest in festivals and event tourism originates from his doctoral research in the Spey Valley of Scotland (UK), where both traditional and new events acted as tourist attractions and community focal points. He is on the educational foundation of the International Special Events Society, and contributed to the first research symposium at the annual conference of the International Festivals Association. The author of *Festivals, Special Events and Tourism* (1991), he is also co-editor of a new international journal, *Festival Management and Event Tourism*.

Alison Gill is Associate Professor at Simon Fraser University (Canada) where she teaches graduate level courses in community tourism development and tourism systems in the School of Resource and Environmental Management. She also teaches tourism courses in the university's geography programme and is a member of the Center for Tourism Policy and Research. Dr Gill's research interests are closely aligned to the study of single industry and small community development processes and issues. She is currently specializing in research related to planning and development processes in resort communities.

Frank M. Go is Head, Department of Hotel and Tourism Management, Hong Kong Polytechnic. Formerly, he was Director of the Tourism and Hospitality Management Concentration, Bachelor of Commerce Programme, Faculty of Management at the University of Calgary (Canada); and a faculty member of the School of Hospitality and Tourism Management, Ryerson Polytechnical Institute, Toronto (Canada). Dr Go is the co-author of *Competitive Strategies in the International Hotel Industry*, and co-editor of the *World Travel and Tourism Review*, Volumes I and II. He served as the 1991 chairperson of the New Horizons Conference on Tourism and Hospitality Education, Training and Research, and co-edited its proceedings.

Donald E. Hawkins is Professor of Travel and Tourism, Director of the International Institute of Tourism Studies and Research Professor of Medicine in the School of Medicine and Health Sciences at the George Washington University (USA); he is also President of Hawkins and Associates, Inc., a consulting, information and decision support group specializing in tourism development, marketing, policy analysis, strategic planning, investment and training. Dr Hawkins is editor of the Van Nostrand Reinhold reference series in tourism and commercial recreation management; co-editor-in-chief of the *World Travel and Tourism Review*, founding editor of the *Journal of Leisure Research*, and serves on the editorial boards of the *Journal of Travel Research*, *Tourism Management*, *Journal of Travel and Tourism Marketing*, and the *Runzheimer Report on Travel Management*. He is a Fellow of the International Academy of Hospitality Research, and the International Academy for the Study of Tourism.

Myriam Jansen-Verbeke is a professor of Tourism Management in the Department of Marketing Management, Rotterdam School of Management at the Erasmus University of Rotterdam (The Netherlands). Formerly, she was Lecturer at the Catholic University of Nijmegen where she received her doctorate. With a master's degree in geography from the Catholic University of Leuven (Belgium), and a post-graduate diploma at the London School of Economics in urban geography, she teaches physical planning issues of tourism and recreation. Dr Jansen-Verbeke's research activities and publications have been mainly focused on urban tourism. She has been a Visiting Professor at the Free University of Brussels (Belgium), the University of Lodz (Poland), and in the ERASMUS

programmes: Ghent (Belgium), Wageningen (The Netherlands), Dundee
(UK) and Tours (France). She serves on the editorial boards of *Recreatie
& Toerisme* (NL), *Journal of Sustainable Tourism* (UK), *International Journal
for Event Tourism* (Canada); is resource editor for *Annals of Tourism Research*; and a reviewer for *Tourism Management*.

Josef A. Mazanec is Professor at the Vienna University of Economic and
Business Administration (where he received his doctorate), and Director
of the Institute for Tourism and Leisure Studies. He has been a member
of the Austrian delegation to the European Association of Advertising
Agencies (1971–81); and a Visiting Scholar at the Sloan School of Management, MIT (US). Dr Mazanec's main research interests include models of consumer/tourist behaviour, strategic planning, tourism and
hospitality marketing, multivariate methods and decision support systems.
A member of the International Academy for the Study of Tourism, he is
a resource editor for the *Annals of Tourism Research*.

David Mercer is Senior Lecturer in the Department of Geography and
Environmental Science at Monash University (Australia) where he has
been teaching for twenty years. He holds degrees from Cambridge and
Monash Universities. Dr Mercer's research interests are environmental
policy, tourism impacts, recreation planning and indigenous land rights.
He has published seventy academic papers, and has authored and edited
seven books. They include: *Leisure and Recreation in Australia*; *Outdoor
Recreation: Australian Perspectives*; *A Question of Balance: Natural Resources
Conflict Issues in Australia* (and with Elery Hamilton-Smith); *Recreation
Planning and Social Change in Urban Australia*; and is currently completing
work on a new volume, *Controversies in Australian Environmental Policy*.

Michael Morgan is Senior Lecturer in tourism marketing at Bournemouth
University (UK), where he is Course Tutor of the BA Honours Degree in
Leisure Marketing. Formerly, for fifteen years, he was in marketing and
operations management for the Sealink cross-channel ferry operator. He is
also a consultant to the Southern Tourist Board, analysing the effectiveness
of the Board's tourism brochures. Mr Morgan's interest in beach resorts
began during his time with Sealink at Weymouth (which claims to be the
original sea bathing resort form the time of George III). With two articles
published in *Leisure Management* and *Tourism Management*, he is currently
completing work on an undergraduate textbook on Marketing for Leisure.

Peter E. Murphy is Professor and Head of Tourism Management Programme, School of Business at the University of Victoria (Canada), where
he teaches several courses in tourism. He received his doctorate from
the Ohio State University where his dissertation focused on consumer

behavior modelling. Dr Murphy has been engaged in research in tourism for the past seventeen years; and his focus has been community participation in the development of local tourism involving the concept of sustainable development from both an environmental and business perspective. The author of several articles and two books: *Tourism in Canada: Selected Issues and Options*, and *Tourism: A Community Approach*, he has been a consultant to the provincial government and various local communities regarding tourism development, and on monitoring needed for a more balanced and sustainable tourism business.

Philip L. Pearce is Foundation Professor of Tourism at James Cook University of North Queensland (Australia). With degrees in psychology and education from the University of Adelaide (Australia), he received his doctorate from Oxford, examining the social and environmental perceptions of overseas tourists. Dr Pearce has authored two books on tourism, and over fifty academic articles on visitor and community studies of tourism. He is also editor of the *Journal of Tourism Studies*, and is a founding member of the International Academy for the Study of Tourism.

Stanley C. Plog is founder of Plog Research, Inc. a Los Angeles (USA) based company specializing in worldwide travel research studies for airlines, hotel chains, cruise lines, rental car companies, resort destinations, tour operators, and a variety of other travel-related groups. He received his doctorate from Harvard University. Dr Plog is the author or co-author of five professional books, the most recent being *Leisure Travel: Making It A Growth Market ... Again!* He has been keynote speaker at conferences throughout the world, has contributed to a variety of social science and professional travel journals, and is an editor of the *Journal of Travel Research*.

Linda K. Richter is Professor of Political Science at Kansas State University (USA) where she teaches in the areas of public administration, public policy, gender politics and developing nations. She has lectured and conducted field research on tourism policies in nineteen nations throughout Asia and the Pacific Basin. Dr Richter has contributed over forty articles and book chapters on tourism issues, and is author of *Land Reform and Tourism and Tourism Development Policy-Making in The Philippines* (1982); *The Politics of Tourism in Asia* (1989), and; co-author of *Tourism Environment* (1991). She is an associate editor of *Annals of Tourism Research*, a member of the US National Travel and Tourism Advisory Board, and the International Academy for the Study of Tourism.

Regina G. Schlüter is Professor at the John F. Kennedy University in Buenos Aires (Argentina), and serves as Director of the Center for

Tourism Studies and Research. She is a graduate of the same university in demography and tourism, and received her doctorate in social psychology. Formerly, she was Associate Dean and Director of the School of Demography and Tourism. Dr Schlüter is the author of several articles in various journals in Argentina, the UK, USA, Canada and Brazil. She has written several books: *Turismo y Sexo: Una Aproximación al Estudio de la Prostitución y el Turismo en Argentina* (1985); *Turismo y Parques Nacionales: Una Perspectiva* (1987), and; *Social & Cultural Impact of Tourism Plans and Programs in Latin America* (1991).

Valene L. Smith is Professor of Anthropology at California State University, Chico (USA). She is the editor of *Hosts and Guests: The Anthropology of Tourism* (1977, 1989), and senior editor of *Tourism Alternatives: Potentials and Problems in the Development of Tourism* (1992). Dr Smith serves on the editorial board of the *Annals of Tourism Research* for which she has edited three special issues: 'Tourism and Development: Anthropological Perspectives'; 'Domestic Tourism' and 'Pilgrimage and Tourism: The Quest in Guest', and is preparing a fourth special issue, 'Antarctic Tourism'. She edited a special issue on 'Careers in Tourism' in *Practicing Anthropology*, and serves on the editorial board of *Tourism Recreation Research*.

Edmund Swinglehurst, who regards himself as an archivist, was born in Chile and educated in the UK. He has worked and travelled in South America and in Europe for over forty years. He joined Thomas Cook in 1953 after studying painting in Paris. Mr Swinglehurst is the author of *The Romantic Journey* (1974); *The Victorian and Edwardian Seaside* (1978) with his wife Janice Anderson; *Cooks Tours* (1982); *The Midi* (1986); *Italy* (1987), and *Viva Espana* (1989).

Gordon D. Taylor is a tourism consultant since his retirement in 1988 from Tourism Canada where he was Manager, Special Research Projects. Formerly, he was Director, Research and Planning for the Manitoba Department of Tourism, Recreation and Cultural Affairs; and a Research Officer with both the Canadian Parks Service and the British Columbia Provincial Parks. During the past fifteen years, he has served as Adjunct Professor of Geography at Carleton University (Canada). Mr Taylor was the president of the Travel and Tourism Research Association in 1976, and is currently a member of the Board of Directors of the Canada Chapter, TTRA. He has edited the proceedings of the TTRA Canada conference on 'Sustainability: Impossible Dream or Essential Objectives?' and has published articles in *International Tourism Reports* and *Tourism Report*.

William F. Theobald is Professor and Chairman of both the Interdisciplinary Graduate Program in Travel and Tourism, and the Leisure

Studies Division at Purdue University (USA) where he teaches recreation and tourism management. Formerly, Professor and Head of the Recreation and Leisure Studies Department at the University of Waterloo (Canada), he has also served as a Visiting Professor at the George Washington University (USA) and the University of Surrey (UK). Dr Theobald's research interests are tourism planning and development. He has contributed to a variety of social science and professional journals, and is author of *The Female in Public Recreation (1976); Evaluation of Recreation and Park Programs* (1979) and *The Evaluation of Human Service Programs* (1985). He has served as an associate editor or reviewer for *Tourism Economics*, the *Journal of Leisure Research* and *Leisure Sciences*, and has conducted numerous studies in tourism planning and development for private corporations and various branches of government.

Carlton Van Doren is Professor in the Department of Recreation, Park and Tourism Sciences at Texas A&M University (USA). His doctorate is from Michigan State University in geography, and he holds undergraduate and graduate degrees in geography from the University of Illinois (USA). Dr Van Doren has chaired more than twenty doctoral and thirty Master's committees in his twenty-four years at Texas A&M. More than half of his students are now teaching courses in tourism or employed by institutions involved in tourism. He is co-author of the recent North American edition of *Travel and Tourism: A North American–European Perspective*. The co-founder of *Leisure Sciences*, he was the first editor of the *Journal of Leisure Research*, and is currently an associate editor of the *Journal of Travel Research*, and resource editor of *Annals of Tourism Research*.

Jan van Harssel, a native of The Netherlands, is Associate Professor in the Institute of Travel, Hotel and Restaurant Administration at Niagara University (USA). He holds a master's degree in tourism and travel administration from the Graduate School of Management and Urban Professions in New York City, and a doctorate from the University of Vermont (USA). Dr van Harssel serves as Chairperson of Niagara University's annual Tourism Industry Symposium series. He has written numerous articles on travel and older adults, and is the author of *Tourism: An Exploration*.

Turgut Var is Professor, Department of Recreation, Park and Tourism Sciences at Texas A&M University (USA). He holds degrees in business administration from Claremont Men's College (USA), an MBA in finance from the University of Chicago (USA), and a doctorate in accounting from the University of Ankara (Turkey). Dr Var has been active in the hotel industry and has been recognized as a Fellow of the Academy of

Hospitality Research and a Certified Hotel Administrator of the American Hotel/Motel Association. He is author of over fifteen books and eighty articles including *Managerial Accounting, Financial Accounting* and *Tourism Encyclopedia*. He is currently editor-in-chief of *Texas Tourism Trends*; editor of *Journal of Academy of Hospitality Research, Journal of Travel Research*, and *Journal of Tourism Marketing*; and an associate editor of *Annals of Tourism Research*.

Stephen Wanhill is Professor of Tourism at the University of Wales, Cardiff (UK). Formerly, he was Professor of Tourism and Head of Department at the University of Surrey (UK). He was a Parliamentary Specialist Adviser on Tourism in the UK House of Commons during 1985–9. Dr Wanhill has worked on development projects in eighteen countries and lectured in ten. He has published on tourism projects, investment incentives and the impact of tourism in *Tourism Management* and the *Service Industries Journal*. He has also contributed chapters to *Tourism Marketing and Management Handbook*; *Managing and Marketing Services in the 1990s*; *Perspectives on Tourism Policy*, and *Managerial Economics: Applications to Hotel Operation*.

Peter W. Williams is Director of the Centre for Tourism Policy and Research at Simon Fraser University (Canada) where he teaches graduate level courses in tourism policy, planning and development in the School of Resource and Environmental Management. Dr Williams is particularly involved with research addressing issues of sustainability in tourism development. His research interests, however, are centred on issues related to growth management strategies in tourism settings and behavioural dimensions of tourism product development.

Stephen F. Witt is Lewis Chair of Tourism Studies in the European Business Management School at the University of Wales, Swansea (UK). He holds master's degrees from the Universities of Leeds, and Warwick (UK), and his doctorate is from the University of Bradford (UK). Dr Witt has published numerous papers in academic journals, especially on tourism demand forecasting and the economics of tourism. His books include: *Portfolio Theory and Investment Management* (1983); *Practical Business Forecasting* (1987); *Practical Financial Management* (1988); *Tourism Marketing and Management Handbook* (1989); *The Management of International Tourism* (1991), and *Modelling and Forecasting Demand in Tourism* (1992). He serves on the editorial boards of *Tourism Management*, the *Journal of International Consumer Marketing* and the *Journal of Euromarketing*.

Andreas H. Zins is Assistant Professor at the Institute for Tourism and Leisure Studies at the Vienna University of Economics and Business

Administration (where he received his doctorate). He lectures in marketing, business administration and the statistical analyses for social sciences. Dr Zins is active in research in tourist behaviour, computer-assisted interviewing and in theme parks. He has served as Project Manager of the National Austrian Guest Survey since 1988.

Part One

Clarification and Meaning:
Issues of Understanding

Tourism has grown significantly since the creation of the commercial airline industry and the advent of the jet airplane in the 1950s. By 1992, it had become the largest industry and largest employer in the world. Together with this growth there have emerged a number of extremely critical issues facing the industry in terms of the impacts it has already had on destination areas and their residents, and the future prospects for people and places into the twenty-first century.

One of the major issues in gauging tourism's total economic impact is the diversity and fragmentation of the industry itself. Theobald (Chapter 1) suggests that this problem is compounded by the lack of comparable tourism data since there has been no valid or reliable means of gathering comparable statistics, either at the national, regional or local levels. This is due to a lack of uniformity in both defining industry terminology and reporting similar, therefore comparable data.

The origin and derivation of travel and tourism definitions are provided and the major developments that occurred between 1936 and 1993 whose objectives were to reduce or eliminate the incomparability of gathering and utilizing tourism statistics are chronicled.

Davidson (Chapter 2) questions the common practice, especially as suggested in the literature of referring to tourism as an industry. He contends that such a designation may not be correct, and that tourism is not an industry at all. He states that much of the current misunderstanding, resistance and even hostility plaguing proponents of tourism may be due to its mistakenly being called an industry.

Three arguments for tourism's designation as an industry are: it needs to gain the respect it now lacks among other competing economic sectors; it needs sound, accurate and meaningful data in order to assess its economic contribution; and it needs to provide a sense of self-identity to its practitioners.

As in Chapter 1, Davidson similarly decries the difficulty in defining terms, tourist and tourism among others. He suggests that rather than a production activity or product, tourism should be viewed as a social phenomenon, an experience or a process. Therefore, defining tourism as an industry is incorrect and demeaning to what it really is.

Throughout the literature, one of the major positive benefits ascribed to tourism is its potential for promoting international understanding and world peace. While there is general agreement of the contribution of tourism toward these ends, little empirical evidence is available to substantiate this claim. If the tourism industry and its proponents are to maintain their credibility, attempts to measure its impact and verify the relationship between tourism and world peace are necessary.

Var, Ap and Van Doren (Chapter 3) examine the relationship between tourism and world peace from two perspectives, political and socio-cultural. The results of a cross-national study of the relationship between tourism and world peace have revealed that tourism is viewed as positively contributing to both economic development and peace, but that the strength of that relationship is tenuous. This finding suggests that the role of tourism as a contributor to world peace is uncertain and may not be perceived by respondents as being as critical as most tourism proponents believe.

Plog (Chapter 4) suggests that, in addition, there are a number of other major issues facing the tourism industry. He questions why tourism has escaped criticism for its destruction of culture and the environment.

Culture is destroyed by forcing certain 'native' people to give up part of their own identity and adopt uniform rules of behaviour around tourists. The environment is destroyed by overdevelopment and subsequent overuse of tourism resources. Specific examples of environmental degradation are cited, including air and water pollution as well as loss of animal and fish habitat, thereby interrupting the food chain.

Common action by all parties involved in tourism is needed in order to halt destruction of tourism resources. Government, industry, academics and other interested individuals must join together in order to change current practices. As a starting point, the author proposes a set of guidelines that might be followed in order to protect the integrity of both tourist destinations and their residents' culture.

For many people, much time and effort is expended in looking back to a previous time in their lives, perhaps to try to recapture a past that for them was happier or more rewarding than what the future might hold. The past has always been more orderly, more memorable, and most of all, safer.

In the final chapter in this section, Dann (Chapter 5) states that tourism is the nostalgia industry of the future. He suggests that tourism has employed nostalgia for its own financial advantage. A strong connection between nostalgia and tourism is explored, especially tourist resources such as hotels and museums. In addition, it is pointed out that tourists often have a strange fascination for tragic, macabre or other equally unappealing historical sites. Nostalgia is grounded in dissatisfaction with social arrangements, both currently and with the likelihood of their continuing into the future. Natives in Third World countries living for generations in one village would not be able to comprehend the concept of nostalgia. On the other hand, today's dislocated Western tourist often travels in order to experience nostalgia.

Tourism collateral literature and publicity which are based upon nostalgic images of the past promote glamour and happiness, provide something to be envied, and return love of self to the reader. Nostalgia is big business, and when it is associated with the world's leading industry, tourism, it offers unlimited financial possibilities.

1 The context, meaning and scope of tourism

William F. Theobald

Background

Travel has existed since the beginning of time when primitive man set out, often traversing great distances, in search of game which provided the food and clothing necessary for his survival. Throughout the course of history, people have travelled for purposes of trade, religious conviction, economic gain, war, migration and other equally compelling motivations. In the Roman era, wealthy aristocrats and high government officials also travelled for pleasure. Seaside resorts located at Pompeii and Herculaneum afforded citizens the opportunity to escape to their vacation villas in order to avoid the summer heat of Rome. Travel, except during the Dark Ages, has continued to grow, and throughout recorded history, has played a vital role in the development of civilizations.

Tourism as we know it today is distinctly a twentieth-century phenomenon. Historians suggest that the advent of mass tourism began in England during the industrial revolution with the rise of the middle class and relatively inexpensive transportation. The creation of the commercial airline industry following the Second World War and the subsequent development of the jet aircraft in the 1950s signalled the rapid growth and expansion of international travel. This growth led to the development of a major new industry, tourism. In turn, international tourism became the concern of a number of world governments since it not only provided new employment opportunities, but it also produced a means of earning foreign exchange.

Tourism today has grown significantly in both economic and social importance. The fastest growing economic sector of most industrialized countries over the past several years has been in the area of services. One of the largest segments of the service industry, although largely unrecognized as an entity in some of these countries, is travel and tourism. According to the World Travel and Tourism Council (1992), 'Travel and tourism is the largest industry in the world on virtually any economic measure including: gross output, value added, capital investment, employment, and tax contributions'. In 1992, the industry's gross output was estimated to be $3.5 trillion, over 12 per cent of all consumer spending. The travel and tourism industry is the world's largest employer, with almost 130 million jobs, or almost 7 per cent of all employees. This industry is the world's leading industrial contributor, producing over 6 per cent of the world gross national product, and accounting for capital investment in excess of $422 billion in new facilities and equipment. In addition, it contributes almost $400 billion in direct, indirect and personal taxes each year.

However, the major problems of the travel and tourism industry that have hidden or obscured its economic impact are the diversity and fragmentation of the industry itself. The travel industry includes: hotels, motels and other types of accommodation; restaurants and other food services; transportation services and facilities; amusements, attractions and other leisure facilities; gift shops and a large number of other enterprises. Since many of these businesses also serve local residents, the impact of spending by visitors can easily be overlooked or underestimated. In addition, Meis (1992) points out that the tourism industry involves concepts that have remained amorphous to both analysts and decision-makers. Moreover, in all nations, this problem has made it difficult for the industry to develop any type of reliable or credible tourism information base in order to estimate the contribution it makes to regional, national and global economies. However, the nature of this very diversity makes travel and tourism ideal vehicles for economic development in a wide variety of countries, regions or communities.

Once the exclusive province of the wealthy, travel and tourism have become an institutionalized way of life for most of the world's middle-class population. In fact, McIntosh and Goeldner (1990) suggest that tourism has become the largest commodity in international trade for many world nations, and for a significant number of other countries it ranks second or third. For example, tourism is the major source of income in Bermuda, Greece, Italy, Spain, Switzerland and most Caribbean countries. In addition, Hawkins and Ritchie (1991), quoting from data published by the American Express Company, suggest that the travel and tourism industry is the number one ranked employer in Australia, the Bahamas, Brazil, Canada, France, (the former) West Germany, Hong Kong, Italy, Jamaica, Japan, Singapore, the United Kingdom and United States. Because of problems of definition which directly affect statistical measurement, it is not possible with any degree of certainty to provide precise, valid or reliable data about the extent of world-wide tourism participation or its economic impact. In many cases, similar difficulties arise when attempts are made to measure domestic tourism.

The problem of definition

It is extremely difficult to define precisely the words *tourist* and *tourism* since these terms have different meanings to different people, and no universal definition has yet been adopted. For example, *Webster's New University Dictionary* (Soulchanov and Ellis, 1984) defines tourism as 'traveling for pleasure; the business of providing tours and services for tourists', and a tourist as 'one who travels for pleasure'. These terms are inadequate synonyms for travel, and their use as such adds further confusion when the field of travel is variously referred to as the *travel industry*, the *tourism industry*, the *hospitality industry* and most recently, the *visitor industry*.

Why is so much attention given to these definitions? According to Gee, Makens and Choy (1989), the concern is both from an academic and a practical perspective. 'First, travel research requires a standard definition in order to establish parameters for research content, and second, without standard definitions, there can be no agreement on the measurement of tourism as an economic activity or its impact on the local, state, national or world economy.' Therefore, comparable data are necessary requisites, and identical criteria must be utilized in order to obtain such data. For example, in North America, the US Census Bureau and US Travel Data Center's annual travel statistics consider only those trips taken that are 100 miles or more (one-way) away from home. However, Waters (1987) argued that this criterion is unreasonably high, and proposed instead in his annual compendium on travel that similar to the US National Tourism Resources Review Commission's guidelines, distances of fifty miles or more are a more realistic criterion. On the other hand, the Canadian government specifies that a tourist is one who travels at least twenty-five miles outside his community. Therefore, each of these four annual data sets is quite different, and which (if any) contains the most accurate measurement of tourism activity?

The United Nations was so concerned about the impossible task of compiling comparative data on international tourism that they convened a Conference on Trade and Development which issued guidelines for tourism statistics (UNCTAD Secretariat, 1971). The ensuing report suggested that the functions of a comprehensive system of national tourism statistics could serve:

(a) To measure from the demand side the volume and pattern of foreign (and domestic) tourism in the country (as well as outgoing tourism) . . .
(b) To provide information about the supply of accommodation and other facilities used by tourists . . .

(c)   To permit an assessment to be made of the impact of tourism on the balance of payments and on the economy in general . . .

Therefore, accurate statistical measurement of travel and tourism is important in order to assess its direct, indirect and induced economic impacts; to assist in the planning and development of new tourist facilities and resources; to determine current visitor patterns and help formulate marketing and promotional strategies, and to identify changes in tourist flows, patterns and preferences.

The derivation of definitions

Etymologically, the word *tour* is derived from the Latin 'tornare' and the Greek 'tornos', meaning 'a lathe or circle; the movement around a central point or axis'. This meaning changed in modern English to represent 'one's turn'. The suffix *-ism* is defined as 'an action or process; typical behaviour or quality,' while the suffix *-ist* denotes 'one that performs a given action'. When the word *tour* and the suffixes *-ism* and *-ist* are combined, they suggest the action of movement around a circle. One can argue that a circle represents a starting point, which ultimately returns back to its beginning. Therefore, like a circle, a tour represents a journey that it is a round-trip, i.e., the act of leaving and then returning to the original starting point, and therefore, one who takes such a journey can be called a tourist.

There is some disagreement as to when the word *tourist* first appeared in print. Smith (1989) suggests that 'Samuel Pegge reported the use of "tourist" as a new word for traveller c.1800; England's *Sporting Magazine* introduced the word "tourism" in 1911'. Feifer (1985) proposes that the word tourist 'was coined by Stendhal in the early nineteenth century [1838]'. Mieczkowski (1990) states that 'The first definition of tourists appears in the *Dictionnare universel du XIX siecle* in 1876', defining tourists as 'persons who travel out of curiosity and idleness'. Kaul (1985) argues that even though the word *tourist* is of comparatively recent origin, nevertheless invaders were commonly referred to as tourists in the hope that one day they would leave. In addition, Kaul points out that:

> In the 17th and early 18th centuries, the English, the Germans and others, traveling on a grand tour of the continent, came to be known as 'tourists.' . . . In 1824, Scott, in *San Roman's* stated thus, 'it provoked the pencil of every passing tourist.'

Leiper (1979) relates that the word *tourism* appears to have first been used in England to describe young male British aristocrats who were being educated for careers in politics, government and diplomatic service. In order to round-out their studies, they embarked upon a customary three year grand tour of the European continent, returning home only after their cultural education was indeed completed. According to Inskeep (1991), the first guide book for this type of travel was Thomas Nugent's *The Grand Tour*, published in 1778. Far from the traveller of 1778, today's tourist tends to connote a singularly negative image, one who is a bargain hunter, who travels en masse, and according to Eliot (1974), is one who is sought out for his cash, but despised for his ignorance of culture.

In addition, tourism has been variously defined (or refined) by governments and academics to relate to such fields as economics, sociology, cultural anthropology and geography. Economists are concerned with tourism's contributions to the economy and the economic development of a destination area, and focus on supply/demand, foreign exchange and balance of payments, employment and other monetary factors. Sociologists and cultural anthropologists study the travel behaviour of individuals and groups of people, and focus on the customs, habits, traditions and life styles of both hosts and guests. Geographers are concerned with the spatial aspects of tourism, and study travel flows and locations, development dispersion, land use and changes in the physical environment.

It is generally recognized that there are two different types of tourism definitions, each with its own rationale and intended usage. Burkart and Medlik (1981) suggest that there are *conceptual* definitions which attempt to provide a theoretical framework which identify the essential characteristics of tourism, and what distinguishes it from similar, sometimes related, but different activity.

Examples of such a conceptual definition would include that proposed by Jafari (1977), who states that 'tourism is a study of man away from his usual habitat, of the industry which responds to his needs, and of the impacts that both he and the industry have on the host socio-cultural, economic, and physical environments'. In addition, Mathieson and Wall (1982) conclude that 'Tourism is the temporary movement of people to destinations outside their normal places of work and residence, the activities undertaken during their stay in those destinations, and the facilities created to cater to their needs.'

There are also *technical* definitions which provide tourism information for statistical or legislative purposes. The various technical definitions of tourism provide meaning or clarification that can be applied in both international and domestic settings. This later approach, technical definitions, can be seen in the actions taken to help standardize comparative international tourism data collection.

Finally, Leiper (1979) postulated that there are three approaches in defining tourism: economic, technical and holistic. Economic definitions view tourism as both a business and an industry. Technical definitions identify the tourist in order to provide a common basis by which to collect data. Holistic definitions attempt to include the entire essence of the subject.

Dimensions of travel

Although technical definitions such as suggested above should be applicable to both international and domestic tourism, such definitions are not necessarily utilized by all countries with respect to domestic tourism. However, most have adopted the three elements of the international definition: (1) purpose of trip; (2) distance travelled, and (3) duration of trip. In addition, two other dimensions or elements are sometimes used to define travellers. One that is used frequently is (4) residence of traveller; and one that is more infrequently used is (5) mode of transportation.

1 *Purpose of trip:* The notion behind this tourism dimension was to include the major components of most travel today. However, there are a number of destination areas that only include non-obligated or discretionary travel in defining tourists. They only view leisure travellers as tourists, and purposely exclude travel *solely* for business purposes. However, one might well argue that business travel is often combined with some amount of pleasure travel. In addition, business travel to attend meetings or conferences should be included since it is considered to be discretionary travel rather part of the normal, daily business routine.

2 *Distance travelled:* For statistical purposes, when measuring travel away from home (non-local travel), a number of national, regional and local agencies use total round-trip distance between place of residence and destination as the distinguishing statistical measurement factor. As indicated earlier, these distances can and do vary from zero to 100 miles (0–160 kilometers). Therefore, attractions that are less than the minimum prescribed distance(s) travelled are not counted in official estimates of tourism, thereby creating both artificial and arbitrary standards.

3 *Duration of trip:* In order to meet the written criteria for defining travellers, most definitions of tourists and/or visitors include at least one overnight stay at the destination area. However, this overnight restriction then excludes many leisure-related one-day trips which often generate substantial business for attractions, restaurants and other recreation resources.

4 *Residence of traveller:* When businesses attempt to identify travel markets and associated marketing strategies, it is often more important for their business to identify where people live than to determine other demographic factors such as their nationality or citizenship.

5 *Mode of transportation:* Used primarily for planning purposes, a number of destination areas collect information on visitor travel patterns by collecting information on their mode of transportation: air, train, ship, coach, auto or other means.

Finally, according to Williams and Shaw (1991):

Each national tourist organization may record different types of information. For example, duration of stay, mode of travel, expenditure, age, socioeconomic group, and number of accompanying persons are all important aspects of tourism but these are not recorded in all tourist enumerations.

Major definition developments

The growth of world receipts from international tourism that occurred between the two World Wars led to the need for a more precise statistical definition of tourism. An international forum held in 1936, the Committee of Statistical Experts of the League of Nations, first proposed that a 'foreign tourist' is one who 'visits a country other than that in which he habitually lives for a period of at least twenty-four hours'. In 1945, the United Nations (which had replaced the League of Nations) endorsed this definition, but added to it a maximum duration of stay of less than six months. Other international bodies have chosen to extend this to one year or less.

A United Nations Conference on International Travel and Tourism held in Rome in 1963 and sponsored by IUOTO, the International Union of Official Travel Organizations (now the WTO, World Tourism Organization) recommended that a new word, 'visitor', be adopted which would define a tourist as 'any person visiting a country other than that in which he has his usual place of residence, for any reason other than following an occupation remunerated from within the country visited'. Visitors included two distinct categories of travellers: (1) tourists – temporary visitors staying at least twenty-four hours in the country visited, and whose purpose was for leisure, business, family, mission or meeting; and (2) excursionists – temporary visitors staying *less* than twenty-four hours in the destination visited and not staying overnight (including cruise ship travellers). Since 1963, most world nations have accepted the definitions of *visitor*, *tourist* and *excursionist* that were proposed by the Conference and many of the revisions made subsequently.

At their 1967 meeting in Geneva, the United Nations (UN) Statistical Commission recommended that a separate class of visitor be established. Tourists stay at least twenty-four hours, but since some visitors take excursions then return back to their place of residence the same day, they were to be called, 'excursionists'. This group included daily visitors with purposes other than employment, cruise passengers and visitors in transit. Excursionists could be easily distinguished from other visitors since there was no overnight stay involved.

The definition of the term *visitor* defined in 1963 refers only to international tourism. However, although it is more difficult to measure, it is quite obvious that it is also applicable to national (domestic) tourism as well. For example, in 1980, the WTO's Manila Declaration implicitly extended the definition to all tourism. According to BarOn (1989), the Working Party on Tourism Statistics of the WTO Commission for Europe agreed that recommendations on domestic tourism, although narrower than international tourism, were nevertheless compatible. These definitions have undergone subsequent refinements, and it would appear that the WTO/UN definition of tourism should have created a uniform basis for collection of standardized tourism data. Although the majority of countries utilize these definitions, unfortunately, not all adhere to them.

Incomparability of tourism statistics

The principal difficulty in measuring the extent of tourism demand is the basic incomparability of tourism statistics. Such incomparability exists not only when attempting to compare data from various nations but also creates problems when regions, provinces, states or cities within a country attempt to compare with one another data on tourism demand. At the international level, there are a number of reasons for this incomparability.

The definitions of a *tourist* and a *visitor* vary, especially so at frontiers where statistics are collected. Not all countries have adopted the United Nations Statistical Commission's definitions, while others use their own definitions. Even when the UN definitions are utilized, data collection methods vary widely so that some countries may not gather information on the purpose of visit or whether or not the visitor will be (or has been) remunerated. In addition, although most countries gather statistical data at their frontiers, others rely on information provided by hotel registrations. In his case, even though the same definitions may be used, the two data sets are not comparable.

Some countries do not even count the arrivals of foreign nationals from bordering countries, especially if there is a unique or special relationship between the countries. Often, in some world nations visitors who are travelling for business or other similar purposes are not regarded as tourists, and therefore they are not recorded as such. In addition, students who spend most of the academic year studying abroad in foreign countries are also often overlooked in compiling statistical data.

Excursionists and other day visitors are included in the statistical data of some countries, but are excluded in others. Special situation visitors such as cruise ship passengers are often not counted in some countries since they are considered to be transients. Flight crews and other visitors in transit are often treated likewise.

Frechtling (1992) suggests that of the 184 nations in the world, 166 report tourism data to the World Tourism Organization each year, and

Of these 166 countries, four do not have a measure of international visitors or tourists. Thirteen countries have no recent measure of international tourism receipts, and 46 do not estimate international travel expenditures. More than one-half (84) have no measure of international departures, and two-thirds (113) do not count visitor nights in all accommodation establishments.

At the sub-national level, similar situations also exist. For example, in the United States, there is no standard definition valid throughout the country. As a result, definitions of tourism vary from state to state. Gee, Makens and Choy (1989) suggest that in Florida, 'a tourist is an out-of-state resident who stays at least one night in the state for reasons other than necessary layover for transportation connections or for strictly business transactions'. In Alaska, 'a tourist is a nonresident travelling to Alaska for pleasure or culture and for no other purpose'. Massachusetts defines a tourist as 'a person, not on business, who stays away from home overnight'. For Arizona, 'a tourist is a nonresident traveller in the state, while a traveller is used to identify Arizona residents travelling within the state'. In Utah, 'a tourist will participate in some activity while in the state, while a traveller simply passes through on their way to another state'. Finally, in Nevada, 'tourists are residents of states other than Nevada who visit the state or stop somewhere in the state while en route through and without regard for trip purpose'.

The confusion in terminology is by no means limited to the United States. A review of any of the statistics published by the UN/WTO points up the innumerable footnotes to the data indicating national variations, differences in data collection methodology, and significant diversity in terminology standards. Indeed, one of the important tasks of the WTO is to work systematically to improve and help develop definitions and classifications of tourism that are of world-wide application and that emphasize both clarity and simplicity in their application.

Common measures of tourism

In June 1991, 250 individuals representing nineteen countries participated in a landmark meeting co-sponsored by the World Tourism Organization and Tourism Canada held at Ottawa, Canada. The International Conference on Travel and Tourism Statistics had three primary aims:

1 Development of a uniform and integrated definition and classification system of tourism statistics.
2 Implementation of a strict methodology for determining the economic impact of tourism and the performance of various sectors of the industry.
3 Establishment of both a means of dialogue between governments and the tourism industry and a coherent work programme for collecting tourism statistics and information.

The conference was successful in agreeing on approaches to standardize tourism terminology and industrial classifications, as well as indicators of market growth, economic impact and overall industry development. All delegates to the conference endorsed the concepts, measures and definitions that were proposed in the resolutions that came out of the meetings. In 1993, the United Nations accepted the report of the WTO and adopted the recommendations of the UN Secretariat's Statistical Division pertaining to tourism statistics.

One of the principal findings that came out of the conference resolutions (World Tourism Organization, 1991) recommended that tourism be defined as:

> the activities of a person travelling to a place outside his or her usual environment for less than a specified period of time and whose main purpose of travel is other than the exercise of an activity remunerated from within the place visited . . .

In addition, tourism was further defined as the activities of people travelling for leisure, business and other purposes to places outside their usual environment and staying for no more than one consecutive year.

Basic tourism units

As indicated by Figure 1.1, for a given country, three basic forms of tourism were first identified, then defined as: (1) *domestic tourism* –

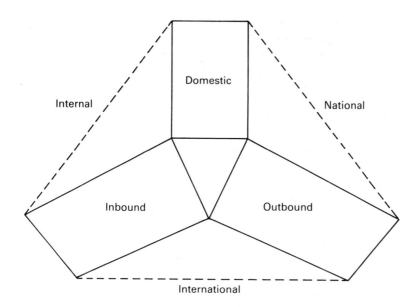

Figure 1.1 Forms of tourism. (Source: World Tourism Organization)

comprised of residents visiting their own country; (2) *inbound tourism* – comprised of non-residents travelling in a given country; and (3) *outbound tourism* – comprised of residents travelling in another country. These forms can be combined in a number of ways in order to derive the following categories of tourism: (a) *internal tourism* – involves both domestic and inbound tourism; (b) *national tourism* – involves both domestic and outbound tourism; and (c) *international tourism* – involves both inbound and outbound tourism. It should be noted that although this figure refers to a country, it could be applied to any other geographic area(s).

Basic tourism units refer to individuals/households that are the subject of tourism activities and therefore can be considered as statistical units in surveys. 'Travellers' refer to all individuals making a trip between two or more geographic locations, either in their country of residence (domestic travellers) or between countries (international travellers). However, as can be seen in Figure 1.2, there is a distinction made between two types of travellers: *visitors* and *other travellers*.

All travellers who are engaged in the activity of tourism are considered to be 'visitors'. The term 'visitor' then becomes the core concept around which the entire system of tourism statistics is based. A secondary division of the term 'visitor' is made into two categories:

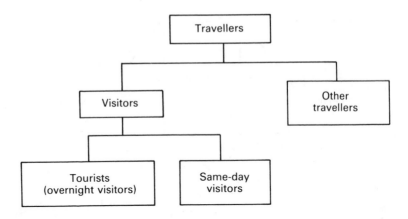

Figure 1.2 Traveller typology. (Source: Travel and Tourism Research Association)

1   'Tourists (overnight visitors)'.
2   'Same-day visitors' (formerly called 'excursionists').

Therefore, the term 'visitor' can be described for statistical purposes as 'any person travelling to a place other than that of his/her usual environment for less than twelve months and whose main purpose of trip is other than the exercise of an activity remunerated from within the place visited'.

Classification of tourism demand

An extended classification system of tourism demand delineating the main purpose(s) of visits or trips by major groups was developed (see Figure 1.3), based upon that first proposed by the United Nations (1979). This system was designed to help measure the major segments of tourism demand for planning and marketing purposes. The major groups include:

1   Leisure, recreation and holidays.
2   Visiting friends and relatives.
3   Business and professional.
4   Health treatment.
5   Religion/pilgrimages.
6   Other (crews on public carriers, transit and other or unknown activities).

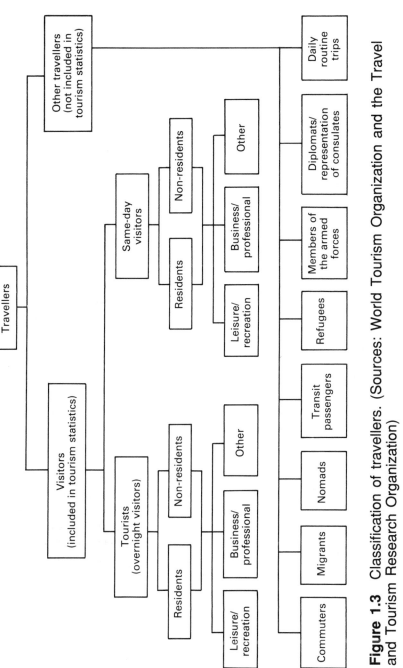

Figure 1.3 Classification of travellers. (Sources: World Tourism Organization and the Travel and Tourism Research Organization)

Other measures of tourism demand enumerated in the recommendations were:

(a)   duration of stay or trip;
(b)   origin and destination of trip;
(c)   area of residence or destination within countries;
(d)   means of transportation;
(e)   tourism accommodation.

Each of the demand measures were defined, and where possible, examples of each were indicated.

Paci (1992) argued, however, that not only tourism demand be considered, but more importantly, tourism 'must seek to more clearly delineate a supply-based conceptual structure for its activities because that is the source of most national economic statistics'. When incorporated into supply-based statistics, the relationship and relative importance of tourism to other economic sectors can be more easily recognized. The Ottawa Conference also recommended the adoption of the WTO's, Standard Industrial Classification of Tourism Activities (SICTA). Paci pointed out that such a system would not only foster and provide for greater comparability among national tourism statistics, but would also 'provide statistical linkage between the supply side of tourism and the demand side'.

Classification of tourism supply

Tourism expenditure data are some of the most significant indicators used to monitor and evaluate the impact of tourism on an economy and on the various representative tourism industry segments. The Conference has defined *tourism expenditure* as 'the total consumption expenditure made by a visitor or on behalf of a visitor for and during his/her trip and stay at a destination'.

It has been proposed that tourist expenditures be divided into three broad categories, depending upon the specific periods of time the visitor makes those expenditures. The first, advance spending that is necessary to prepare for the trip (trip purpose); second, expenses while travelling to, and those at the travel destinations (trip location) and; third, travel-related spending made at home after returning from the trip (trip conclusion).

It has been recommended that tourism consumption expenditures should be identified by a system of main categories, and should include:

1 Packaged travel (holidays and pre-paid tour arrangements).
2 Accommodations (hotels, motels, resorts, campgrounds etc.).
3 Food and drinking establishments (restaurants, cafes, taverns etc.).
4 Transport (airplane, rail, ship, bus, auto, taxi etc.).
5 Recreation, culture and sporting activities.
6 Shopping.
7 Other.

Summary

For too long, the tourism industry, both international and domestic, has had difficulty making statistical comparisons with other sectors of the economy. In all nations, this has led to difficulty in developing a valid, reliable and credible information or data base about tourism and its contribution to local, regional, national and global economies.

A number of individuals throughout the world who are involved in the travel and tourism industry have long recognized the interdependent nature of travel and tourism statistical systems at all levels of government. Further, they realized the need for ongoing reviews and revisions of both concepts and working definitions of travel and tourism used internationally. The Ottawa Conference recommendations (which were subsequently adopted by the United Nations Statistical Commission) laid the foundation for new, expanded and modified international definitions and standards for travel and tourism. Those principles and guidelines provide for the harmonious and uniform measurement of tourism among world nations.

It would appear that since an international UN/WTO definition of tourism now exists, there is a universal basis for the collection of standardized data on tourism. However, although there has been significant progress in reaching consensus on what constitutes international tourism, there is no such consensus on domestic tourism terminology. Therefore, caution must be exercised since a clear distinction must be made between basic definitions of tourism and those elements which describe tourists themselves, and their demographic and behavioural characteristics. Since the tourist is the principal component of tourism, it is therefore unrealistic to develop uniform tourism data without first deciding the types of variables and the range of phenomena that should be included in data collection efforts.

Finally, the Ottawa Conference further recommended the development and implementation of a system of performance measures and indicators which could help measure trends and provide forecasts for the industry as a whole, thereby maximizing the tourism contribution to national benefits.

The World Tourism Organization will be largely responsible for reviewing and revising the definitions, classifications, methodologies, data collection and analysis of international tourism proposed by the conference. However, the ultimate success or failure of gathering and utilizing comparable tourism statistical data lies with their acceptance and implementation by the entire world community.

References

BarOn, Raymond, (1989) *Travel and Tourism Data: A Comprehensive Research Handbook on the World Travel Industry*, London, Euromonitor Publications, p. 19

Burkart, A.J. and Medlik, S. (1981) *Tourism: Past, Present and Future*, Heinemann, London, p. 39

Eliot, E. (1974) Travel, *CMA Journal*, 2 February, p. 271

Feifer, Maxine, (1985) *Tourism in History: From Imperial Rome to the Present*, Stein and Day Publishers, New York, p. 2

Frechtling, Douglas C. (1992) International Issues Forum: World Marketing and Economic Research Priorities for Tourism, *Tourism Partnerships and Strategies: Merging Vision With New Realities*, Proceedings of the 23rd Travel and Tourism Research Association Conference, Minneapolis, 14–17, June p. 20

Gee, Chuck, Y., Makens, James C. and Choy, Dexter, J.L. *The Travel Industry*, 2nd edn, Van Nostrand Reinhold, New York, pp. 10–11

Hawkins, Donald E. and Ritchie, J.R. Brent (eds) (1991) *World Travel and Tourism Review: Indicators, Trends and Forecasts*, vol. 1, CAB International, Wallingford, England, pp. 72–3

Inskeep, Edward (1991) *Tourism Planning: An Integrated and Sustainable Development Approach*, Van Nostrand Reinhold, New York, p. 6

Jafari, Jafar (1977) Editor's Page, *Annals of Tourism Research*, **V**, Special Number, October/December, p. 8

Kaul, R.N. (1985) *The Dynamics of Tourism*, volume 1: *The Phenomenon*, Sterling Publishers Private Limited, New Delhi, India, p. 2

Leiper, Neil (1979) The Framework of Tourism: Towards a Definition of Tourism, Tourist, and the Tourist Industry, *Annals of Tourism Research*, **6**(4), 391, 394

Mathieson, Alister and Wall, Geoffrey (1982) *Tourism: Economic, Physical and Social Impacts*, Longman, London, p. 1

McIntosh, Robert W. and Goeldner, Charles R. (1990) *Tourism Principles, Practices, Philosophies*, 6th ed., John Wiley and Sons, New York, p. 18

Meis, Scott (1992) International Issues Forum: response, *Tourism Partnerships and Strategies: Merging Vision With New Realities*, Proceedings of the 23rd Travel and Tourism Research Association Conference, Minneapolis, 14–17 June, p. 17

Mieczkowski, Zbigniew (1990) *World Trends in Tourism and Recreation*, Peter Lang, New York, p. 20

Paci, Enzo (1992) International Issues Forum: Common Measures of Tourism, *Tourism Partnerships and Strategies: Merging Vision with New Realities*, Proceedings of the 23rd Travel and Tourism Reseach Association Conference, Minneapolis, 14–17 June, p. 10

Smith, Stephen L.J. (1989) *Tourism Analysis: A Handbook*, Longman Scientific and Technical, London, p. 17

Soukhanov, Anne H. and Ellis, Kaethe (eds) (1984) *Websters 11 New Riverside University Dictionary*, Houghton Mifflin, Boston, p. 1221

UNCTAD Secretariat (1971) Conference on Trade and Development, *Guidelines for Tourism Statistics*, United Nations, New York, p. 6

United Nations (1979) Statistical Division, *Provisional Guidelines on Statistics of International Tourism*, Statistical Papers, Series M, No. 62, United Nations, New York

Waters, Somerset (1987) *Travel Industry World Yearbook: The Big Picture* (annual), Child and Waters, New York, p. 21

Williams, Allan M. and Shaw, Gareth (eds), (1991) *Tourism and Economic Development: Western European Experiences*, 2nd edn, Belhaven Press, London, p. 11

World Tourism Organization (1983) General Assembly, Definitions Concerning Tourism Statistics, *Report of the Secretary-General on the Execution of the General Programme of Work for the Period 1982–1983: Addendum (C.3.5)*, New Delhi, 3–14 October, pp. 7–9

World Tourism Organization (1991) *International Conference on Travel and Tourism Statistics: Ottawa (Canada), 24–28 June 1991, Resolutions*, Madrid, World Tourism Organization, p. 4

World Travel and Tourism Council (1992) *The WTTC Report*, 2nd edn, Belgium, Brussels, pp. 2–12

2 What are travel and tourism: are they really an industry?

Thomas Lea Davidson

Introduction

Common practice, at least among those who are involved in the development and marketing of tourism, is to refer to (travel and) tourism as an industry. In fact, considerable effort has been devoted to creating the impression that tourism is a legitimate industry worthy of being compared to other industries such as health services, energy or agriculture. The importance of tourism is underscored by referring to it as 'one of the top three industries in most states', 'largest or next to largest retail industry', or 'largest employer (industry) in the world'.

The intent of this chapter is to suggest that this designation may not be correct. In fact, I will contend that tourism is not an industry at all. At best, it is a collection of industries. Furthermore, I will suggest that referring to tourism as an industry may be a major contributor to the misunderstanding, resistance and even the hostility that often plague proponents of travel and tourism as worthy economic forces in a modern economy.

Background

By way of preface, let us consider why so much effort has been devoted toward making tourism an industry. Historically, tourism has not been taken seriously by economists, economic developers, even government. Tourism is seen as fun and games, recreation, leisure, unproductive. Under this view tourism is just the opposite of the traditional work ethic. Residents see tourists as crowds, enemies of the environment, undesirable – the 'ugly visitor' from wherever he or she may have come. Too bad that tourists spend money or there would be no redeeming virtue to hosting tourists in one's community.

This negativism culminated in the early 1970s when petrol sales were banned on Sunday as a way to address the fuel crisis. Although this ban crippled tourism, it was not viewed as critical – except by the businesses whose customers could not, or would not, come.

In response, those in the business of tourism undertook to gain respect by defining tourism as an industry and then by measuring the economic impact of the tourism industry in terms that were comparable to those used for other industries. 'Industry' was a positive term connoting work, productivity, employment, income, economic health – all attributes that tourism wanted but did not have.

Tourism as an industry

Under this 'industry' view, the tourism industry is composed of a clearly defined grouping of firms that are perceived to be primarily in the business of selling to or serving tourists. Hotels, restaurants, transportation and amusements are examples of the types of firms that comprise the tourism industry. The United Nations identifies seven industrial areas while the US Travel Data Center includes some fourteen types of businesses as defined by the Standard Industrial Classification (SIC) system.

What are the advantages of designating tourism as an industry? Let me suggest three.

1 First is the **need to gain respect**, respect based on understanding the contribution that tourism makes to economic health. Tourism has an image problem. It is not really perceived as a legitimate part of economic development. For some, tourism is not even a legitimate part of government and in today's budget crises, not worthy of funding. If tourism can argue that it really *is* an industry worthy of being considered on the same terms as other recognized industries, then the image of and the support for tourism will improve.
2 Second is the **need for a sound framework to tabulate, analyse and publish data about tourism** – data that are accurate, meaningful and believable. Historically, economists have used the 'industry' as the basis for measurement and study. If tourism wants to be measured and studied seriously, it follows then that tourism must be an industry. Only by treating tourism as an industry can tourism be compared to other industries in the world economy.
3 Third, there is a **need among some in 'tourism' for a format for self-identity**. Being part of an industry is a clear and easy way to achieve identity and the self-esteem that goes with identity.

Tourism is beset by many outside pressures: world events; budget problems and mounting deficits; recession; the staggering need for funds to support education, health care, social needs and crime prevention; and the maturing, competitive tourism marketplace. In this environment, a great effort has been devoted to legitimizing tourism as a key industry in today's service economy. In great measure, these efforts have been successful. But, is this 'success' really positive? Or has the 'industry' label actually hurt the cause that this designation is supposed to champion. To answer this question we need to define what an industry is, use this definition as a framework to look at tourism, and then consider the ramifications of the difference.

What is an industry?

We can look to two sources for an answer:

1 Economics defines an industry as being a group of independent firms all turning out the same product. Whether or not two products are 'the same' is defined in terms of their substitutability expressed as the cross-elasticity of demand. In lay terms, the more that the purchase of Product A replaces (can be substituted for) the purchase of Product B, the more A and B are the same and hence in the same industry.
2 The second source for definitions are the Standard Industrial Classification (SIC) manuals. Such publications suggest that the SIC system was developed to classify establishments by the type of activity in which they are engaged. To be recognized as an industry, a group of establishments must share a *common primary activity* and be *statistically significant in size*.

It is clear that the focus of 'industry' is:

• Individual business establishments grouped together.
• The revenue *received* by these economic units.
• Producing and selling a common product, i.e., the product of one firm is a substitute for the product of any other firm in the same industry.

And it is equally clear that the 'manufacturing' sector provides the framework for this focus. Thus, to the extent that tourism is an industry, economists and others will position tourism in terms of these factors – individual businesses, revenues of those businesses, and a common product.

But just what is tourism?

But what is travel and tourism? Do they fit this industry mould? To answer these questions we need to define a tourist and tourism and then relate this phenomenon to an industry as defined above.

Clearly, there is confusion and controversy surrounding the definitions of travel and tourism. Are they the same or are tourists only seeking pleasure while travellers may also be on business? How far must one travel from home to be a tourist/traveller? Does paying for a room make one a tourist? . . . And so forth.

From the viewpoint of economic development and/or economic impact, a visitor – nominally called a tourist – is someone who comes to an area, spends money and leaves. We employ an economic framework to be comparable with the concept of 'industry' which is an economic term. The reasons for the visit, length of stay, length of trip, or distances from home are immaterial.

Thus, we define a tourist as *a person travelling outside of his/her normal routine – either normal living or normal working routine – who spends money.* This definition of visitor/tourist includes:

- People who stay in hotels, motels, resorts or campgrounds.
- People who visit friends or relatives.
- People who visit while just passing through going somewhere else.
- People who are on a day trip (do not stay overnight).
- An 'all other' category of people on boats, who sleep in a vehicle of some sort, or who otherwise do not fit the above.

For purposes of this definition a resident (or someone who is not a tourist) is defined as a person staying more than thirty days.

Note that visitors/tourists can:

- Be attending a meeting or convention.
- Be business travellers outside of their home office area.
- Be on a group tour.
- Be on an individual leisure/vacation trip – including recreational shopping.
- Be travelling for personal or family-related reasons.

In today's world there are three problems with this definition:

1 Some people travel considerable distances to shop, especially at factory outlets. They may do so many times a year. They are difficult to measure. Technically they are not tourists; their shopping has become routine.

2 Some people maintain two residences – a winter home and a summer home. The stay in either one usually exceeds one month and these people are *not* classified as tourists. Again, their travel is routine. However, short-stay visitors to their homes whether renting or not *are* tourists.

3 When people live in an area just outside of a destination and have friends or relatives visit them, how are these visitors classified when they visit the destination? Actually, the problem here is not whether they are tourists – those visiting friends or relatives clearly are. Rather, the question is which area gets the credit? Or, how should the people they are visiting be classified? Again, while measurement is difficult, the destination area should be credited for money spent therein.

Tourism, then can be viewed as:

- A social phenomenon, *not* a production activity.
- The sum of the expenditures of all travellers or visitors for all purposes, *not* the receipt of a select group of similar establishments.
- An experience or process, *not* a product – an extremely varied experience at that.

To underscore this view of tourism, let us focus on the economic impact of tourism on the economic health of a community. The best measure of this economic impact is not the receipts of a few types of business. Rather, the economic impact of tourism begins with the *sum total of all expenditures by all tourists*. Yes, this impact includes some of the receipts of accommodations, restaurants, attractions, petrol (gas) stations – the traditional tourism-orientated businesses. (We might note that these are vastly dissimilar businesses.) However, it also includes retail purchases that often amount to more than the money spent for lodging. These include services (haircuts, car repairs), highway tolls in some countries, church contributions, and so forth. In fact, visitors spend money on just about everything that residents do. Thus, any and every 'industry' that sells to consumers is in receipt of cash from tourism. Clearly, the criteria of similar activity or common product or production process are *not* met in tourism!

Further, the requirement of substitution is not met either. More often than not, most of these expenditures go together as complementary or supplementary purchases. Thus, food is not competitive with lodging. A visitor buys both.

Seen this way, travel and tourism – the movement of people outside their normal routine for business, pleasure or personal reasons – is much, much more than an 'industry' in the traditional sense. As an economic force, it is the impact of everything the visitor/tourist spends. Thus, we really have an expenditure-driven phenomenon, not a receipts-driven one.

So what? Why raise the issue at all?

With so much effort to sell tourism as an industry, specifically an 'export industry', what is the purpose of questioning this designation? Are not many of these people just going to fight for their viewpoint? Won't this conflict be a problem?

These are legitimate questions. However, I believe that there are several important – and negative – ramifications in attempting to make tourism an industry when, in fact, it is not an industry in the traditional sense. Let me comment on three such negative ramifications.

The first negative ramification comes from the disbelief that is created. Somehow, whether it is conscious or subconscious, people know that tourism does not fit the traditional definition of an industry. This disbelief tends to discredit the arguments supporting the importance of tourism and the level of support that tourism and tourism growth deserve. How often do we hear economic development proponents say that tourism is not an industry and therefore, not economic development?

In essence, this ramification says that when people recognize – correctly – that tourism does not fit the classic definition of an industry, then they discredit the argument that tourism deserves the benefits that accrue to a legitimate industry.

The second negative ramification is more subtle. It says that the attempt to define tourism as an industry has led to attempts to employ traditional methods of measurement and analysis to the study of tourism. But traditional methods just do not work well. One result has been inaccurate results that often understate the size, impact or benefits to a community of the tourism phenomenon. Let me offer two examples:

1   The issue of business receipts *vs.* total tourism expenditures. Receipts of specific businesses are the traditional method for measuring an industry. Usually, the total receipts of all of the relevant business units are summed. Yet few businesses receive all of their receipts from tourists and few consumer businesses receive no money at all from tourists. Thus, tourist expenditure is the better measure of the size, scope, and impact of tourism.
2   The issue of substitute/competitive goods *vs.* supplementary or complementary goods. Traditionally, members of an industry compete on some level for the same money. If a visitor stays tonight in Hotel

A, he or she does not spend tonight in Hotel B, and hotels are an industry. However, many expenditures of tourists are complementary. When spending the night in Hotel A, the tourist travels, eats, pays for entertainment and may buy a gift to take home. Taking one action does not necessarily exclude taking another action. It is more probable that all are done during the course of the stay.

The third negative ramification relates directly to the disadvantage tourism faces for public funding. When tourism – an industry composed of individual business firms seeking their own benefit – comes up against education, public health, crime prevention, infrastructure repair or development etc. (all seen as serving society as a whole), the problem before the appropriations committee is clear. Why should government use limited funds to support one industry – and a 'frivolous' one at that – when there are so many social ills that demand attention? As an industry, tourism is often seen as self-serving when, in fact, it is a key ingredient in the economic health of the community. Thriving tourism can be key to attending to these other issues.

Thus, the question raised by this issue is, 'Does the "industry" designation make it harder to argue – and win – the broader implication?' Frankly, as one who has been intimately involved in these confrontations, I believe that it does. The net of this argument is that to truly understand, measure, analyse and sell tourism we need to go beyond traditional thinking. We need to 'think outside of the box'.

- If we are to study tourism to expand it or to control it, is it not better to have an accurate understanding and definition?
- If we are to communicate the value of tourism, is it not more effective to reflect the totality of tourism and not just champion a few industries?

In sum, I believe that *defining tourism as an industry is incorrect*; and further, *this definition demeans what tourism really is.* Tourism is a social/ economic phenomenon that acts both as an engine of economic progress and as a social force. Tourism is much more than an industry. Tourism is more like a 'sector' that impacts a wide range of industries. Tourism is not just businesses or governments – it is people. Supporting rational tourism growth and development needs to be viewed in this broader context.

Given today's economic conditions, environmental concerns, evil, turmoil and strife, positioning tourism properly takes on added importance. Maybe now is the time to rethink the 'industry' classification and find a way to communicate more clearly just how important tourism's health is to our economy.

3 Tourism and world peace

Turgut Var, John Ap and Carlton Van Doren

I have watched the cultures of all lands blow around my house and other winds have blown the seeds of peace, for travel is the language of peace.

Mahatma Gandhi

Introduction

Among the positive benefits attributed to the social and cultural impacts of tourism are the promotion of goodwill, understanding and peace between people of different nations (D'Amore, 1988; D'Amore and Jafari, 1988; International Union of Tourist Organizations, 1974; World Tourist Organization, 1980). The role of tourism as an ambassador and vehicle of international understanding and peace has been recognized by international bodies such as the United Nations. In 1980, the World Tourism Conference in Manila declared that 'world tourism can be a vital force for world peace'. Recognition of the role and importance of the development of world peace through tourism was also declared through the 'Columbia Charter', which was prepared at the First Global Conference: Tourism – A Vital Force for Peace, held at Vancouver in 1988.

Many world leaders and statesmen have also recognized this benefit and attribute of tourism. President John F. Kennedy called attention to the world significance of tourism and stated:

Travel has become one of the great forces for peace and understanding in our time. As people move throughout the world and learn to know each other, to understand each other's customs and to appreciate the qualities of the individuals of each nation, we are building a level of international understanding which can sharply improve the atmosphere for world peace. (Kennedy, 1963)

While there is general recognition of the contribution of tourism towards world peace, there has been very little research on this subject. In the limited research that has been carried out, researchers have suggested that tourism helps promote mutual understanding and therefore, peace (Rovelstad, 1988). In another study it was found that one of the main motivations for overseas travel by Americans is to learn more about the people and culture in foreign countries (Skidmore and Pyszka, 1988). This motivation provides a conducive setting to developing harmonious relations and peace. However, the real question – Does tourism enhance peace? – has not yet been answered nor demonstrated through empirical research. World peace is an intangible attribute and its impact resulting from tourism is a difficult concept to measure. While it is generally recognized that peace is a pre-condition for tourism, some have suggested that the relationship between tourism and peace is tenuous. For example, it has been stated that:

> The universal desire for peace and the desire to see tourism as an avenue for cross-cultural understanding which is a prerequisite to such goals, have long been expressed. Unfortunately, such expressions of desire and hope have never been actually pursued beyond ritual occasions . . . Thus, at this stage, 'Tourism as a vital force for peace', remains at best a futuristic statement. (Din, 1988)

A similar sentiment was expressed by Barlow (1988), who indicated that: 'tourism has a long way to go before it is universally accepted as a force that helps mankind reach a state of peace and harmony'. However, if the tourism industry and its supporters are to maintain its credibility and continue to espouse world peace as a positive attribute of tourism, attempts to measure its impact and verify the relationship between tourism and peace will be necessary. This raises a serious question – is the promotion of world peace a realistic attribute of tourism, or is it a mere platitude?

The purpose of this chapter is (1) to examine the relationship between tourism and world peace, and (2) to discuss the findings and implications of a cross-national study on this issue.

Defining and measuring peace in the tourism context

According to the Webster dictionary, peace is defined as:

> 1: a state of tranquillity or quiet: as (a) freedom from disturbance (b) a state of security or order within a community provided for by the law and customs. 2: freedom from disquieting or oppressive thoughts or emotions.

3: harmony in personal relations. 4: a pact or agreement to end hostilities between those who have been at war or in a state of enmity.

This definition highlights the diverse nature and concept of peace. Within the context of tourism, peace applies to the concept of harmonious relations. Despite existence of this definitional concept of peace, the majority of research and literature on peace has focused upon its concept as an absence of war (Boulding, 1978; Newcombe, 1984). Peace is more than the absence of war, and consideration of peace as a positive concept within the context of tourism, it is believed, will lead to a better understanding of the meaning of peace.

This role of tourism and peace can be viewed from two perspectives, namely, socio-cultural and political. A typical socio-cultural perspective is embodied in comments such as:

> tourism has been recognized to be an instrument of social and cultural understanding by the opportunity offered to bring different people in contact and to provide facilities for acquisition and exchange of information about the way of life, cultures, language and other social and economic endowments of the people as well as a chance for making friendships and achieving goodwill. (Kaul, 1985)

The socio-cultural perspective is the predominant viewpoint which has been advocated. It focuses upon tourism as a cultural ambassador and the fact that tourism provides an opportunity for people to understand each other's customs and to exchange information and ideas. An absence of research on this aspect of tourism was acknowledged by one author who commented that:

> Empirical description and insightful analyses of various combinations of these situational pressures and cultural norms are greatly needed to increase our knowledge of social relationships and to determine what steps could be taken to increase the likelihood that touring will, indeed, contribute to understanding and comity among nations. (Sutton, 1967)

Even after two decades, this call for 'empirical descriptions and insightful analysis . . . that touring will indeed contribute to understanding and comity among nations' have virtually gone unheeded. The fact that there has been very little research is no doubt attributed by the intangibility and subjective nature of peace.

The political perspective on tourism and world peace focuses upon tourism as a promoter of national integration and international understanding, goodwill and peace (Kaul, 1985; Matthews, 1979). This perspective acknowledges the importance of tourism as a means of establishing and improving political relations with other countries. An example that illustrates this point well was evidenced by the manner in which the People's Republic of China opened its doors to the Western world in the 1970s. Tourism has been an important avenue by which the People's Republic of China has established links with other countries. Furthermore, it has been pointed out that: 'Political stability, improved relations between nations and international peace accelerate travel and tourism. World travel is a fundamental expression of international co-operation' (Kaul, 1985).

Three levels of international relations that are generated by world tourism have been identified (Matthews, 1978). First, at the non-governmental level private citizens of different nations come into contact and experience cultures different from their own: 'A kind of private international relations develop: [which] can, of course, be altered by government action' (Matthews, 1978: 91). Secondly, there is a public level of international relations which relates to government-to-government dealings on matters essential to the industry, for example, agreements on air transport, immigration and custom procedures and double taxation treaties. Finally, there is a corporate sector – government level of international relations where tourism is found in the interaction of national government with foreign private investment. Examples of these corporations include airlines, banks, hotels and tour operators.

In examining the perceptions of individuals towards tourism and world peace it is the first level – 'private' international relations – that is suggested as the appropriate means for examining this relationship. Critics may argue that it is incongruous to seek individual perceptions of a 'group' concept such as peace. In other words, peace is viewed as a condition that applies to groups not individuals, hence it is not practical to attempt to measure accurately individual responses to a group condition. However, this argument is based upon the concept of peace as an absence of war or hostilities in which group action is generally involved. Consideration of the individual's perception on tourism and peace is being based upon the positive concept of peace as a harmonious relationship. This may occur at an individual-to-individual or group level or at any of the other two levels of international relations which have been identified. There has been very little research on the positive social, cultural and political impacts of tourism and its role in contributing towards world peace. Research does, however, exist on the negative social and cultural aspects of tourism (Chesney-Lind and Lind, 1986; Farrell, 1982; Mathieson and Wall, 1982; O'Grady, 1982), which challenges the validity of the time-honoured belief that tourism promotes understanding between people of different nationalities. Despite this attention on the negative impacts of tourism it has been suggested that tourism can bring understanding and prosperity if it is properly planned, organized and managed (Bloomstrom et al., 1978; deKadt, 1979).

The literature on the perceived impacts of tourism forms a basis upon which to develop measures to identify the relationship between tourism and world peace. Knowledge of people's perceptions will be investigated to ascertain whether there are any variables that may enable a better description of this relationship. In support of this approach some researchers have indicated that cross-national comparisons appear useful in identifying common parameters and establishing norms in terms of perceptual differences in the attitudes of people (Liu et al., 1987).

One of the positive social impacts perceived by host populations which relates to world peace is that tourism promotes understanding of different people through cultural exchange. Two studies provided empirical data indicating that 50 per cent or more of those interviewed agreed that tourism brought positive benefits through cultural exchange (Belisle and Hoy, 1980; Liu et al., 1987). Through cultural exchange an understanding and appreciation of people from different cultures may be obtained and in doing so, remove any misconceptions or prejudices between resident and tourist. In a study of American international travellers it was found that the main motivation for international travel was to be exposed to another culture and thus learn about other people and cultures (Skidmore and Pyszka, 1988). But, in another study on mass tourists from Japan visiting Singapore, it was found that stereotypic images may in fact be reinforced rather than be broken down (Hassan, 1975). Nevertheless, findings from most studies offer support to the role of tourism in breaking down cultural barriers.

In the development of measures to quantify the contribution of tourism upon world peace, it has been advocated that: '[we] think in terms of a positive definition of peace' (D'Amore, 1988). In following this line of thought two related aspects of tourism come to mind. One is the promotion of cultural exchange as a means of breaking down the barriers between peoples of different nations. The other is the development of greater understanding between individuals or people of different nations resulting from this exchange. It is suggested that these two aspects of tourism are necessary conditions that enable peace to exist and flourish. Thus, they can be used as variables to quantify the relationship between tourism and peace.

Findings of a cross-national study on tourism and world peace

In an exploratory attempt to examine the relationship between tourism and world peace, a cross-national study was conducted in six countries (Australia, Canada, England, Korea, Turkey and United States of America). Details of the study will not be reported here and can be found elsewhere (Var et al., 1988). Rather, attention is primarily focused upon the main findings and their implications.

Background

A college/university student sample was used in this study because students are at a stage of life where there is a greater propensity for travel and convenience for administration of the survey. A total of 1064 responses were obtained and the demographic characteristics of this sample appear representative of a student population (that is, predominantly in the 20–24 years age group and of single marital status). Moreover, within the past five years nearly 60 per cent had travelled to a foreign country with an average of 2.6 countries being visited.

A two-part questionnaire was devised for this study. The first part consisted of fifteen statements, each representing a variable relating to an impact of tourism, including peace. The three statements used to measure the peace variables were, 'I believe that tourism promotes cultural exchange': 'I believe that tourism brings greater understanding of people from different cultures' and 'I believe that tourism promotes world peace'. Respondents were asked to check their response to each statement on a scale that ranged from one (strongly agree) to five (strongly disagree).

The second part of the questionnaire sought classification information from the respondent. Classification of respondents was made with respect to six variables: (1) formal training or education in the tourist industry; (2) work experience in the tourist industry; (3) ethnic background; (4) bilingualism; (5) existence of relatives in a foreign country; and (6) have visited a foreign country. Differences in perceptions were postulated between those who possessed an attribute and those who did not. For the first two variables it was expected that the greater the knowledge of the industry, developed either through formal training and education or work experience, the greater the appreciation and awareness of the role of tourism in promoting world peace. Thus it is suggested, respectively, that: those with formal training in the tourist industry will have a more positive and different perception of tourism and world peace than those who do not; and those with work experience in the tourist industry will have a more positive perception of tourism and world peace than those who do not.

Differences in perceptions are also postulated on the basis of ethnicity and related attributes. The ethnic background of a respondent, their ability to speak a second language and, existence of relatives in a foreign country are independent variables which were also included for measurement. Generally speaking, those who are ethnically different from the dominant racial group of the country they live in, are likely to have some close affinity and relationship to their ethnic origins. This affinity is often maintained through use of the respondents' native tongue in the home situation and close contact with relatives who remain in the native homeland. Thus it is considered that minority ethnic groups will have greater awareness and understanding of different cultures and therefore be more appreciative of the positive role of tourism in developing that understanding. Accordingly, it is also considered that those who come from a different ethnic background than the dominant ethic group in the country will have a more positive perception of tourism and world peace than those who do not; those who speak a second language will have a more positive perception of tourism and world peace than those who do not; and those who have relatives in a foreign country will have a more positive perception of tourism and world peace than those who do not.

It has been often quoted that travel brings greater understanding between peoples of different nations. To test this idea, the respondent was asked if he or she had visited a foreign country. As a result of this travel experience one would expect that the respondent would develop a better awareness and understanding of the country visited and its people. Therefore, they should have a greater appreciation of the role of tourism in promoting world peace. Hence, those who have visited a foreign country will have a more positive perception of tourism and world peace than those who have not.

Main findings

Overall perceptions toward tourism

Responses to the fifteen tourism statements are presented in Table 3.1. Strongest support was shown for the economic and peace variables where, in the majority of cases, agreement was indicated by over 80 per cent of the respondents. For a number of responses to some of the statements, a neutral position was selected. Such responses pertained primarily to the environmental and awareness variables. The environmental factors and the exploitation of worker groups variable are generally considered to be sensitive issues, and the large block of respondents (ranging from 20 to 34 per cent) who chose the neutral response is not surprising. A high neutral response (33 per cent) was selected for the world peace variable, which indicates a degree of uncertainty for some respondents. Based on the mean score responses, the respondents generally viewed tourism as contributing positively to economic development and peace.

In order to determine how valid the three variables used to describe the peace construct were, the results were analysed by a statistical technique called factor analysis. No significant results were found to confirm the validity of this construct.* However, the positive influence of

---

* For those statistically minded, the eigenvalue for the three variables used to interpret the peace factor was 0.55. This falls well short of the accepted cut off of 1.0 for a factor to be considered significant.

Table 3.1 Combined responses to statements

Statement – I believe that tourism ...	Agree	Neutral	Disagree	Mean scores[a]
Economic				
1 Contributes to national economy	85	11	4	1.9
2 Contributes to economic growth	88	10	2	1.8
3 Promotes infrastructure development	80	16	4	2.0
4 Creates employment opportunities	92	6	2	1.7
5 Exploits certain 'worker' groups	23	34	43	3.2
Environmental				
6 Conserves natural and historic environments	58	23	19	2.5
7 Preserves social and cultural environments	51	30	19	2.6
8 Leads to deterioration of environment	25	32	43	3.2
9 Disrupts small communities and towns	38	27	35	2.9
Peace				
10 Promotes cultural exchange	84	12	4	2.0
11 Promotes cross-cultural understanding	80	13	7	2.0
12 Promotes world peace	53	33	14	2.5
Awareness				
13 Benefits outweigh costs	61	30	9	2.4
14 Public unaware of benefits	54	25	21	2.6
15 Greater awareness needed	77	20	3	2.0

[a] 1 = Strongly agree; 5 = Strongly disagree.
$n = 1.064$

tourism upon the economy was confirmed.[†] Thus the variables used for the economic construct are validated and tourism may be viewed primarily as an economic activity that has positive impacts.

Perceptions towards tourism and peace by nation

Figure 3.1 presents the mean scores to the peace variables for each nation and it shows that cross-national differences exist for the variables indicated.[‡] When examining the cross-natural differences from a statistical viewpoint it is found that the differences are not very strong.[§] This means that the variables used may serve as common parameters in measuring this impact of tourism.

In general, it was found that those educated and trained in tourism, those with work experience in the tourist industry, those who speak at least two languages, and those who have visited a foreign country have a more positive perception of tourism.

The world peace variable 'I believe that tourism promotes world peace' showed the most number (4) of statistically significant differences.[¶] More specifically, (i) those with formal training in the tourist industry have a more positive and different perception of tourism and world peace than those who do not have formal training; (ii) those with work experience in the tourist industry have a more positive and different perception of tourism and world peace than those who have not worked in the tourist industry; (iii) those who speak at least two languages have a more positive and different perception of tourism and world peace than those who only speak one language; and (iv) those who have visited a foreign country have a less positive and different perception of tourism and world peace than those who have not visited a foreign country. This latter finding ran contrary to the original postulation that foreign travel experience would lead to a more positive perception between tourism and world peace.

Ethnicity and existence of relatives in a foreign country did not figure at all as being indicators with significant differences.

[†] The four variables – contributes to the national economy, contributes to national growth, promotes infrastructure development, and creates employment opportunities – constitute the economic factor with an eigenvalue of 2.0 and 39 per cent of the variance explained.
[‡] These differences were statistically significant for all three variables at 0.0001 when the mean scores were analysed using analysis of variance. Duncan's multiple range test was also conducted on the scores to identify similarities of responses by nation and it was found that Australians and English showed similarity of responses. They generally showed less agreement to the variables than the other nations which comprised another grouping.
[§] The mean square error for the Duncan's multiple range test ranged form 0.450 to 0.809 and the (ω^2) values with a range from zero to unity for the variables indicate the amount of variance explained in the analysis of variance is low. These squares ranged from 0.03 to 0.09.
[¶] The statistically significant differences are based upon statistical analyses which measure for mean differences between two or more groups, where appropriate (that is, *t*-Test and analysis of variance). The differences reported are significant at 0.05.

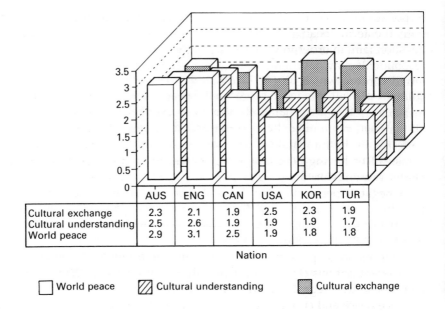

	AUS	ENG	CAN	USA	KOR	TUR
Cultural exchange	2.3	2.1	1.9	2.5	2.3	1.9
Cultural understanding	2.5	2.6	1.9	1.9	1.9	1.7
World peace	2.9	3.1	2.5	1.9	1.8	1.8

Nation

☐ World peace   ▨ Cultural understanding   ▧ Cultural exchange

Figure 3.1 Mean scores on peace construct by nation
(1 = strongly agree, 5 = strongly disagree)

Discussion

The results of this exploratory study reveal that tourism is viewed as contributing positively to economic development and peace. The strength of that positive contribution of tourism is higher for the economic aspects than the peace aspects. This was further confirmed by a statistical analysis of the results (through factor analysis) where the variables comprising the economic factors were found to be significant in terms of their validity. However, the peace construct variables did not produce a significant result which indicates that the validity of the variables, being representative of peace, cannot be verified. These findings suggest that the role of tourism as a contributor to peace is tenuous and may not figure as prominently in the perceptions of the respondents as commonly thought by tourism advocates.

More investigation into the specific social and cultural attributes of tourism will be necessary in order to quantify it as a common parameter and justify peace as an attribute of tourism. While two of the variables of the peace construct, the promotion of cultural exchange and contribution to cross-cultural understanding, indicated a relatively high level of agreement, the world peace variable showed a high degree of uncertainty, with one-third (33 per cent) of respondents providing a neutral response. This uncertainty probably arose from a definitional problem with the term 'peace'. No definition of peace was indicated on the questionnaire in order to prevent bias with the survey instrument. Many respondents may have associated peace as an 'absence of war'. The preferred concept which would be most appropriate in the context of this study is that of 'harmony and harmonious relations'. Refinement in measurement of this variable will be necessary and it is suggested that all the related concepts and meanings of the particular attribute need to be tested in the future.

Instead of having a more positive perception of tourism and world peace, respondents who had recently visited a foreign country had a more negative perception than those who had not visited a foreign country. This result concerning perceptions of respondents with foreign travel experience lends support to the finding in a previously mentioned study that tourism, particularly mass tourism, seldom generated strong intercultural relationships and reinforces stereotypic images between peoples of different nations (Hassan, 1975). The findings of both the Singapore and this study suggest that contrary to popular belief, tourism may not enhance peace and cultural understanding. It has been indicated that the quality of communications between hosts and tourists possibly plays an important yet unknown influence upon the nature of cultural exchange and understanding which result (Mathieson and Wall, 1982). Thus, if intercultural communication is limited and the tourist had a bad experience in a foreign country, it is likely to reinforce a negative image of the role of tourism. Another possible explanation may be found from the results of a study of international travellers, where it was noted that the degree of intercultural communication may also depend upon the motivations of the traveller (Fisher and Price, 1989). It suggests that intercultural communication for travellers seeking new cultural and educational experiences are different from those who primarily seek rest and relaxation. The response could also depend upon the respondent's role as a tourist, that is, as a mass tourist, individual mass tourist, explorer, or drifter (Cohen, 1972). Further research on foreign travel experience upon the perceptions of travellers is required to develop a better understanding of its influence. Areas of investigation should examine the influence of intercultural communication, the degree of contact with the host population and the nature of the travel experience (especially mass versus individual and do-it-yourself tourism) upon cultural exchange and understanding.

The results indicate that education and work experience in the tourist industry, and an ability to speak at least a second language, provides a greater awareness and appreciation of tourism and its role. Implications for the industry are that if it is to promote and espouse the social and cultural attributes of tourism, it must generate a greater level of awareness of the impacts and contribution of tourism upon society. Programmes also need to be developed to improve the nature of cross-cultural exchange and understanding between hosts and tourists. The responsibility rests not only upon local tourism officials in the host community, but also on the intermediaries, such as travel agents, to provide detailed information to prospective clients about the host culture and how to enhance experiences between host and guest. The industry cannot rest on its laurels and rely upon platitudes in order to legitimize its role in society.

Conclusion

Doubts about the claim that tourism engenders peace and promotes peace have been raised. For example, Brown (1989) stated, 'The idea that tourism can promote peace is indeed a noble, as well as fashionable one – but does it work?' Other questions about the tourism and peace relationship which need to be addressed are does tourism expand because a condition of peace exists, or, as it has been assumed does tourism enhance peace? Perplexing questions, indeed. However, as long as the advocates of tourism espouse world peace as an attribute of tourism, this claim needs to be ventured cautiously and further research is still necessary to justify it. Otherwise, it remains a mere platitude.

References

Barlow, M. (1988) Tourism, peace, and conflict: a geographer's perspective. In *Tourism – a Vital Force for Peace* (eds L. D'amore and J. Jafari), Color Art Inc., p. 108
Belisle, F. and Hoy, D. (1980) The perceived impacts of tourism by residents – a case study in Santa Marta, Columbia. *Annals of Tourism Research*, **VII**(1), 83–101
Bloomstrom, R., McIntosh, W. and Christie-Mill, R. (1978) The positive side of tourism development: principles for identifying and developing the cultural resource potential. *Journal of the Mulga School of Business Administration* (Special Issue – International Tourism Congress: 'New Perspectives and Policies', Turkey)
Boulding, K. (1978) *Stable Peace*, University of Texas Press. Newcombe, H. (1984) Survey of peace research. *Peace Research Institute Reviews*, **IX**(6), 5–72
Brown, F. (1989) Is tourism really a peacemaker? *Tourism Management* **10**(4), 270–1
Chesney-Lind, M. and Lind, I. (1986) Visitors as victims: crimes against tourists in Hawaii. *Annals of Tourism Research*, **XIII**(2), 167–91
Cohen, E. (1972) Toward a sociology of international tourism, *Social Research*, **39**(1) (Spring)

D'Amore, L.J. (1988) Tourism – the world's peace industry. *Journal of Travel Research*, **27**(1), 35–40

D'Amore, L. and Jafari, J. (eds) (1988) *Tourism – a Vital Force for Peace*, Color Art Inc, Montreal, Canada

deKadt, E. (1979) Social planning for tourism in the developing countries. *Annals of Tourism Research*, **VI**(1), 36–48

Din, K. (1988) Tourism and peace: desires and attainability. In *Tourism – a Vital Force for Peace* (eds L. D'Amore and J. Jafari), Color Art Inc., p. 80

Farrell, B. (1982) *Hawaii: The Legend That Sells*, University Press of Hawaii

Fisher, R. and Price, L. (1989) The relationship between international travel motivations and post-cultural attitude change. Faculty working paper, College of Business Administration, University of Colorado, Boulder, Colorado

Hassan, R. (1975) International tourism and intercultural communication. *Southeast Asian Journal of Social Sciences*, **3**(2), 25–37

International Union of Tourist Organizations (IUOTO) (1974) Tourism – its nature and significance. *Annals of Tourism Research*, **1**(4), 105–12

Kaul, R.N. (1985) *Dynamics of Tourism*: vol. 1 *The Phenomenon*, Sterling Publishing Co., New Delhi, pp. 5, 51

Kennedy, John F. (1963) *The Saturday Review*, 5 January. Cited in Sutton, Jr, W.A. (1967), p. 223

Liu, J., Sheldon, T. and Var, T. (1987) Resident perception of the environmental impacts of tourism. *Annals of Tourism Research*, **14**(1), 17–37

Mathieson, A. and Wall, G. (1982) *Tourism: Economic, Physical and Social Impacts*, Longman, London and New York

Matthews, H.G. (1979) *International Tourism: a Political and Social Analysis*, Schenkman Publishing Co., Cambridge, Mass.

O'Grady , J. M. (1982) *Tourism in the Third World: Christian Reflections*, Orbis Books, New York

Rovelstad, J.M. (1988) World awareness and perceptions among university business majors. Paper presented at the First Global Conference: Tourism – a Vital Force for Peace, Vancouver, Canada

Skidmore, S. and Pyszka, R. (1988) Americans as international travelers. Paper presented at the First Global Conference: Tourism – a Vital Force for Peace, Vancouver, Canada

Sutton, Jr, W.A. (1967) Travel and understanding: notes on the social structure of touring. *International Journal of Comparative Sociology*, **8**, 218–23

Var, T., Ap, J. and Van Doren, C. (1988) Tourism and peace. Paper presented at the First Global Conference: Tourism – a Vital Force for Peace. Vancouver, Canada, 16–19 October

World Tourist Organization (1980) Manila Declaration on World Tourism. In Kaul, R.N. (1985) *Dynamics of Tourism*: vol. I *The Phenomenon*, Sterling Publishing Co., New Delhi, pp. 245–51

4 Leisure travel: an extraordinary industry faces superordinary problems

Stanley C. Plog

'They're all the same, these brochures . . . same picture, same caption on every one . . . Paradise. It bears no resemblance to reality, of course.'

'Doesn't it?'

'Six million people visited Hawaii last year. I don't imagine many of them found a beach as deserted as this one, do you ? It's a myth. . . .'

'Tourism is wearing out the planet . . . The footpaths in the Lake District have become trenches. The frescoes in the Sistine Chapel are being damaged by the breath and body-heat of spectators. A hundred and eight people enter Notre Dame every minute: their feet are eroding the floor and the buses that bring them there are rotting the stonework with exhaust fumes. Pollution from cars queuing to get to Alpine ski resorts is killing the trees and causing avalanches and landslides. The Mediterranean is like a toilet without a chain . . . In 1987 they had to close Venice one day because it was full. In 1963 forty-four people went down the Colorado river on a raft, now there are a thousand trips a day. In 1939 a million people travelled abroad; last year it was four hundred million. By the year two thousand there could be six hundred and fifty million international travellers, and five times as many people travelling in their own countries. The mere consumption of energy entailed is stupendous.'

'My goodness,' said Bernard.

'. . . It's no coincidence that tourism arose just as religion went into decline. It's the new opium of the people, and must be exposed as such.'

(David Lodge, *Paradise News*, Viking Penguin, New York, NY, 1991)

Author David Lodge's cutting, sarcastic dialogue seems to run against the grain of what the majority of us know and believe about leisure travel. Most travel professionals and government officials feel that tourism is, at least, benign and, at best, one of the most positive contributors to local and regional economies ever conceived. It seems that everyone wants tourists – and the more of them the better. They spend hard cash, solve local unemployment problems by hiring relatively unskilled workers, and developers and their financial backers pump millions of dollars into the economies of growing destinations. So ingrained is this conviction that the Travel and Tourism Research Association chose as the theme for its 1991 annual conference, 'Building Credibility for a Credible Industry'. A nice thought, if it can be sustained. And it has been for decades, with such homey beliefs as, 'Bring more tourists: they take nothing but pictures and leave nothing but footprints.'

Unfortunately, as footsteps grow with the increases in leisure travel, so do problems. And the problems are deep, severe and difficult to reverse. Even more unfortunate, most professionals in the travel industry do not know that these difficulties exist.

The purpose of this chapter is to raise the level of consciousness about some of these problems so that problem situations, old or about to happen, can be reversed or 'nipped in the bud'. Based on more than twenty-five years of travel research, this author has some firm convictions.

Unplanned and uncontrolled tourism can have three distinct consequences. These include:

1   *Physical deterioration of destination facilities.* As tourism increases at a destination, it carries along an unwelcome guest – the possibility of excessive commercial development. What was once quaint, unique and unspoiled now may become a bit run down, seedy around the edges and present a gaudy and overly commercial picture to the outside world. To use a good New Zealand word, the place has become 'tatty'. A fresh coat of paint will not help because trinket shops have replaced local artisans since the 'natives' long ago could not meet the accelerating demand for their goods. And, mass produced souvenirs cost less than products requiring hand work so even the local artisans may not benefit from the growth in travel. The process is so gradual and year-to-year changes so imperceptible that almost no one notices the advancing 'age' of the area. But happen it does, almost with the certainty of the tides.

2   *Destruction of the environment.* The image of tourism as a pure and 'clean' industry (in contrast to 'dirty' ones, such as heavy manufacturing) has led local and national governments throughout the world to establish its development as a priority over creating a heavy industrial base. Yet, deeper difficulties lie below the surface. Too many tourists visiting the same place at the same time can create environmental havoc. Native lands are torn up to make room for commercial development. Sewerage treatment and management, a costly part of the infrastructure, may be inadequately planned and funded, resulting in untreated wastes entering local streams, lakes or oceans. Road development cannot keep up with demand and crowded streets now create a smog problem.

Hawaii most often gets cited as a prime example where hundreds of species of plants and animals have become extinct as a result of tourism pressures. David Lodge's novel chooses a Hawaiian locale to make its point. Every day, worldwide, twenty plants or animal species become extinct, according to current estimates. No guess has yet been given as to what portion of that total is the result of tourism.

3 Destruction of local cultures. Foreign companies exploiting the resources of Third World countries often have been criticized for contributing to the loss of many unique cultures throughout the world. In their efforts to establish standard work rules similar to what they have at their home plants, they obliterate pagan beliefs of the natives and establish Western standards of morality, dress and social behaviour, according to the critics. Old traditions are abandoned in favour of a more homogenized and uniform view of how one should act and treat others, even in the nuclear family.

This picture of world-wide industrialization obviously overlooks the positive contributions of economic development. But, a more important question is why has tourism escaped similar criticism for its unending destruction of local and regional cultures throughout the world? In major sections of Latin America, parts of Africa, areas of the Pacific and, yes, even the Hawaiian islands, old cultural patterns and social unity have been pushed aside. To feed, house and make tourists happy, relatively universal standards for how to treat and serve guests are established and all locally hired help ('natives') must conform to these new rules of behaviour. Natives learn that there is a proper way to act and to defer to others. Nothing else is acceptable. In so doing, they give up part of their own identity and often part of a valuable ancient heritage or tradition that contributes to pride, self-confidence and feelings of self-worth. More fundamental, long stable, family relationships can undergo destructive change. Whereas the culture may previously have been based on a male-dominated household, tourism relies on service jobs for which, most often, women are chosen. The wife, daughter, or sister in the family frequently ends up in a higher status positioning, earning more than her husband, brother, or father who continue to work in long-held, native jobs. Known patterns of interacting that form the core of stable relationships get torn apart. And, the anomie of a corporate culture offers no clearly defined set of social values as a substitute for lost belief systems. Thus, local cultures not only can be lost, but family stability is eroded. Crime, drugs, prostitution and other Western social ills often follow.

But, tourism need not always cause problems, as we shall see. And it has generally made a very positive contribution to making this a better world in which to live. It is just that its positive impact is declining at a time when its negative consequences are accelerating.

A rising chorus of criticism

When travel providers produce collateral materials describing their products, the pictures of idyllic settings, friendly people, great food and fabulous accommodations can lull even local planners to sleep. And, promotional hype reinforces how fabulous it is to live in this paradise setting. Everything seems serene and secure in this wonderful world of leisure travel. But, everyone concerned with the field must wake up and pay attention to the mounting chorus of criticism aimed at the very heart of leisure travel.

In the United States CBS's '60 Minutes', ABC's '20/20', several of NBC's news 'magazine' shows and various PBS programmes and series have all aired stories spotlighting the destructiveness of leisure travel. *National Geographic* has also produced TV specials and coffee table books about how we have destroyed, and continue to destroy, some of the world's prettiest spots – the places with beauty sufficient to entice people to travel thousands of miles to see.

Numerous magazines, particularly news weeklies and daily newspapers in the US, increasingly carry stories about how once pristine travel destinations now exist only in the mind's eye. Pollution, overdevelopment and excess commercialism, all brought about by too many visitors, various writers conclude, have combined to cause severe environmental problems in some parts of the world. These writers typically state that drastic action may be required to reverse the damage – including controlling the flow of tourists.

One does not have to be an extremist to support the position that uncontrolled tourism growth has severe negative consequences. The development plan for the delicate Galapagos islands ultimately calls for 25,000 visitors a year, but 50,000 already tromp across nesting grounds and breeding areas yearly. So, why develop a plan, if it will not be enforced? In various parts of Central Africa, elephant herds and lion prides have been reduced not only by hunting (mostly illegal, at present), but also by tourism. More than fifty tour vehicles may gather around a single lion, whose hunting, breeding and nursing habits now get interrupted by a lack of privacy. Tourist roads not only interfere with delicate local botanical and ecological systems, but dust storms created by the tour vehicles, all of which seem to leave lodges at the same time (for morning and afternoon photo safaris), frighten elephants, lions and other game animals to retreat into smaller and smaller enclaves trying to avoid this onrush of civilization. Even something as innocent as scuba diving and snorkeling has unwanted consequences. Australian giant clams, prized worldwide by divers, have become an endangered species. And, diminution in their numbers has a further consequence. Starfish now multiply unimpeded by their natural enemy, and they, in turn, have killed thousands of acres of coral reefs. On the California coast scuba diving has also nearly wiped out an entire ecological system. Prized abalone, mussels and clams feed on sea urchins. With a dramatic decline in these molluscs, the sea urchin population has grown geometrically. They attack the roots of giant sea kelp, resulting in the destruction of millions of acres of kelp forests. These, in turn, are home to hundreds of varieties of fish, which now disappear. Thus, entire food chains can be lost by uncontrolled acts of well-meaning visitors. Steps are now being taken to reverse these trends (entrepreneurial divers now hunt sea urchins since these are a prized delicacy in Japan).

The list goes on. The *Wall Street Journal*, hardly a travel-writer's home, has recounted how acid rain, caused by visitors' cars travelling to ski resorts, is killing off alpine forests. World-wide attention now focuses on Brazil, not only because it has pursued a policy allowing millions of acres of rain forest to be churned up for agricultural land and new cities, but a lack of concern about the garbage and raw sewerage dumped into the Amazon by uncaring local tour operators has also caused a firestorm of protest.

Some travel writers, seemingly willing to bite the hand that feeds them, have jumped into the fray with articles critical about what they believe contributes to a decline in some of the world's best vacation spots. Surprisingly, their frankness extends even to airline in-flight magazines. *Scanorama* (SAS), which produces some of the freshest and most honestly reported articles, has written about problems along the Great Barrier Reef.

The natural cycle of destination destruction

Tourists are the beginning and the end in a cycle of growth and decline. The more venturesome travellers initiate the process by 'discovering' unknown areas and experiencing their pristine beauty. They tell their friends about their newly found experiences who then also travel to the destination. They, in turn, tell others and, like the ripple effects of a pebble thrown in a pond, each new visitor passes on the word to an ever-widening circle of experience seekers. Rapid growth, which typically has not been foreseen by local officials, often occurs in an unplanned and uncontrolled manner. The stage is now set for the development of grand resorts which use bulldozers to create a new environment that achieves a desired ambience and also to maximize the use of the land. High-rise hotels provide scenic views for the largest number of people possible. Beautiful scenery, long a primary reason for people visiting the area, typically will gradually disappear with increased development. More important, a tawdriness can creep in as small entrepreneurs see opportunities to open shops and sell T-shirts, plates, mugs and other trinkets emblazoned with pictures of local attractions or statuettes of famous people and landmarks. Whatever the cause or reason for this gradual decay, a once pristine and unique spot has lost much of its charm – and reason for existence.

Just when everything seemed so rosy to local travel providers – uninterrupted growth had been going on for years – tourists begin casting votes on the changes in the only manner they know how – with their feet. They gradually select other places to visit, as the word spreads, year after year. They do not like what they now see when they visit. The destination has lost the charm written about in travel brochures and tourism books. Crowds of people have replaced once deserted streets, the 'natives' no longer seem as friendly and relaxed, and the environment shows obvious signs of abuse and misuse. In short, it is not as nice as it used to be, so why not go somewhere else? The present author has provided elsewhere a more complete explanation of what is an almost inexorable cycle, when it is unplanned, pointing to these and other reasons as to why interest in leisure travel in North America in particular is declining (Plog, 1991).

It may be difficult for many readers in parts of the world other than North America to understand how such a decline can really be significant. Is it not true that Europeans, Asians and Latin Americans are pursuing leisure travel at increasing rates year after year? Yes, but . . . their patterns of travel are about fifteen years behind those of Americans and Canadians. Deprived since the Second World War of the wealth to travel internationally, and the very high expense associated with foreign travel, non-Americans stayed close to home. But, since the mid-1980s, these conditions have changed dramatically. New wealth in various continents, and more favorable monetary exchange rates for some nations, have provided grand opportunities to experience travel pleasures previously only read about. People from these continents are now exploring the world at large. But, they, too, will gradually become disenchanted with places that are long past their prime. Then they will also cut back on the amount of leisure travel they pursue. Whatever needs to be changed in the world of tourism should occur long before universal disdain for travel sets in.

Another force also will impede leisure travel growth in the future. Its impact is small, but not imperceptible at present. Local citizens in these once magnificent destinations are awakening to the fact that the areas in which they live no longer feel like home. Tourists crowd their favourite places to meet or play, much of the scenic beauty has been lost and the visitors do not seem to be paying their own way as judged by the fact that taxes have gone up, not down. In short, tourism has not provided all of the benefits that politicians and travel providers promised and, instead, many unforeseen negatives have occurred. From London to Niagara Falls, Maine to the Caribbean, and Pacific isles to quaint villages in Europe, a rising chorus of protest by local citizens threatens to curtail tourism because of its unwanted by-products. Unless the citizens affected by tourism are included as permanent contributors to the planning process, their protests will grow even more shrill and effective in the future.

A different kind of beginning

The mounting conflict between tourism and the environment need not be that way. And, in fact, it was not always so. Leisure travel came of age as a protector of the environment, and it could play that role again.

Yellowstone became the world's first national park in 1872. The Cavalry had to be called in to get rid of squatters in Yellowstone, and it set in motion a debate that has yet to be resolved. How much land can the government take from private owners for public use? And, why does it even have the authority to violate private rights of ownership? The US Congress established the National Park System in 1916, another first for park development. It became a model for other nations to follow. The US Park Service now manages forty national parks, dotting the land from East to West, and as far North as Alaska to the Keys of Southern Florida. Alarmed at the rapacious appetite for land by the logging and mining interests, and their indiscriminate destruction of almost anything they touched, early conservationists adopted and extended the philosophy of John Muir. They pushed to set aside areas of natural beauty from these large, special interest groups. These special lands (parks), it was decided, were for the people – to visit and enjoy. Tourists became the saving souls for these unspoiled areas because they would not destroy the scenic beauty. They would come only to view the mountains and forests, not tear them down. Rights were granted to railroads to bring in visitors, and thousands of miles of new tracks were soon put in place. Even more squatters had to be removed by the army, but the natural affinity between tourism and environmental protection was born. From that point forward, leisure travel typically has been viewed in the most positive light possible. Tourism, as an alternative to commercial development, is a message so powerful that billions of tax dollars in the United States have been poured into acquiring lands, developing them and managing their use – all for the benefit of people who travel.

The closely intertwined relationship between tourism and the national parks ultimately depends upon the continued goodwill of citizens throughout the United States. The original concept that these national lands belong to the people and that access should be easy and inexpensive results in a dependence on the public largesse. User fees do not support the operation of the parks. Thus, tax dollars must be set aside each year to continue operating the system. Will the public always support the idea? Should urban types who never venture into rustic surroundings be called upon to contribute to other people's pleasures? But, with 250 million visitors annually, the National Park Service has a large constituency and has a more secure – and environmentally protected – future than many other naturally beautiful destinations around the world. As the system increasingly attracts larger numbers of foreign visitors, who often discover that the timberlands and hinterlands of the United States offer more beauty and excitement than its cities, the Park Service also develops a new constituency. And, national policy-makers now tend to view tourism to the US from foreign lands as offering a positive contribution to the US balance of payments.

Unfortunately, the tide is turning. But, travel industry executives, planners and academicians are only slowly awakening to the new realities. Travel and tourism will be cast more and more as villains, rather than helpmates, by the myriad of people whose livelihood does not depend directly on the travel industry. Environmentalists, who often seem to want everything to be left untouched, will find new allies in local citizens who have become fired up over the destruction of their local communities. When that happens, tourism can receive a severe setback because hastily implemented controls are likely to be poorly thought out and inconsistently implemented.

Tourism continues to be the best alternative to heavy industrial development, in most situations. But, it, too, requires controls. The profit motive has overtaken the protectionism philosophy in far too many situations with the result that large corporate conglomerates now run many public tourism facilities worldwide.

As the tide turns . . .

The discussion thus far has focused primarily on the destruction of the physical environment at destinations. In other words, too many tourists in the same spot at the same time can obliterate not only what was once natural and beautiful, but also the local sense of community and identity that previously had existed for the area's residents. But a 'flip side' also exists to this portrait of the impact of travel, one which also is not pleasant. The social character and sense of a community can be altered radically.

When a place loses its quaintness and charm, and its sense of natural-ness, it no longer can attract visitors at the rate it once did. Since it competes with destinations which are not as advanced in this destructive cycle, visitors can go elsewhere for their leisure trips and bypass what was once a very popular spot. Word-of-mouth works two ways: it can help a destination to grow or accelerate the trend towards decline. For tourists, a loss of previously attractive destinations is relatively insignifi-cant: they can simply choose another place to visit. With local residents, however, their loss is much more severe and permanent. Their 'home' has been destroyed in ways they do not fully understand and for which they lack the capability and unity of action to restore what they once possessed. Social and economic costs are far too high for the destination to reverse the decades of change to revert back to a simpler, more pris-tine era. And, new residents who have since moved in, attracted by jobs offered through tourism growth, have permanently changed the social character of the destination. Thus, developing a plan for common action becomes almost impossible. As the tide turns against a destination, from glory days to dreary days, the process can be relatively quick. Travel fits in an economic climate that is much more competitive than was previ-ously the case, and the new socio-economic realities can contribute to a very rapid fall from grace of the travel spot.

A number of new factors in North America point to the fact that des-tinations cannot count on automatic growth in the future . . . at least in terms of the numbers of US visitors.

1   The growth rate for the number of domestic passengers enplaned has been declining steadily since 1985, reaching negative growth by 1989. Thus, problems in the air travel industry are not just a result of recessionary forces.
2   About as many people are flying today as can maximally fly, judging by the growth curve for the number of persons who have flown in the past year. About one-third of the population takes a trip by air in any given year. Given the economics of the cost of travel, not many more than that number can be expected to fly annually.
3   The savings rate has fallen during the past decade from about 6 per cent of salaries to 3 per cent, leaving less money accumulated in interest-bearing accounts for discretionary spending. This has been changing somewhat in recent years, rising to slightly over 4 per cent, but any increase in savings will temporarily subtract from the amount that can be spent on leisure travel.

4 Baby boomers married late, following a free-spending style of life in their earlier years. As a result, they have less equity at their disposal than did their parents at comparable ages. Thus, 'boomers' now have to set aside more money for the costs associated with starting a family, buying a home and equipping it with furniture and other belongings.
5 People are living longer today, passing on their money less quickly to their children. That, too, subtracts from the ability to enjoy the little luxuries of life, such as leisure travel.
6 In the United States the federal government has been gradually cutting back on benefits to all citizens because of the pressures of an unbalanced budget. And, Social Security faces continuing future funding problems, particularly as the population lives longer. The number of persons on Social Security has been rising dramatically in the past fifteen years. Less money will be available for retirees to travel during their golden years.
7 Leisure travel has become more expensive and takes a bigger bite out of budgets, leading to a decline in the ability to travel. During the decade of the 1980s, the cost of living rose 51 per cent while the cost for travel rose 94 per cent.
8 The average length of a trip has been decreasing since 1985. The number of days available for vacation has not declined (nor has it risen) in recent years, but now people more often stay closer to home and spend much of their free time around the house.

More important than all of the above, perhaps, is the fact that travel is less fun than it used to be. As destinations have declined in their attractiveness, the trip seems less rewarding. And, there is less felt need to return to that or any other place the following year. This feeling of *ennui* about travel may have developed slowly, but its cumulative effects become relatively permanent and difficult to overcome. Add to this the distaste for the journey itself – getting to and from the place one wants to visit – the potential for systematic decline becomes even stronger. Long drives to airports because of traffic, parking that seems miles away, crowded and noisy air terminals, airline flights that are densely packed and taxi drivers at the other end who too often seem bent on 'ripping off' their unsuspecting prey, add to a feeling of frustration and irritation with the whole process of travel. The interactive effects of all of these forces combine to accelerate this downturn.

The pattern pictured here describes North America. But the rest of the world, which has lagged behind the economic growth of North America until the 1980s, has been rapidly catching up in its standard of living. In many cases, foreign growth exceeds the United States and Canada which have been facing economic decline of some sort since 1987. Thus, total travel in the world should increase at healthy rates up to the end of this century because of the new travel binge occurring in Europe, the Far East and Latin America. However, two consequences arise out of the world-wide travel boom:

1 Many destinations will self-destruct even more rapidly because of increased pressure from the rapidly accelerating tourism growth in other nations.
2 Interest in travel will also decline among these world populations for the same reasons that have been true in North America.

After a while, travel will seem to be less fresh, exciting or rejuvenating. It is only a matter of time, and the travel industry should unite to work against these dire circumstances, and as soon as possible.

A need for common action

To protect the world for tourism, and protect the world from tourism, a common set of goals, evolving into specific plans for different regions, is desperately needed. Otherwise, some of the most scenic, natural and unique areas in the world will lose all of the qualities that set them apart from the common and the ordinary. This fact applies to current leisure destinations and ones that are in the process of developing.

Achieving such a goal is difficult in any industry, but even more so in the very fractionated field of leisure travel. In spite of its huge size (the largest industry in the world, according to the American Express/WEFA studies), travel remains the most fractionated of all major industries. Most analysts and professionals take their perspective from the emergence of mega-airlines in North America that have gobbled up small rivals to take a commanding presence on the scene. However, all other sections of the industry remain fractionated to the point that small businesses and 'mom and pop' operations constitute a majority in many situations. This 'Balkanization' of the industry makes pleas for common action extraordinarily difficult because so many players are involved, each of whom has competing goals and agendas. For example:

• In 1983, it was widely predicted that the total number of travel agencies would decline in the United States as mega-agencies took over. However, the number since that time has grown from 23,700 to more than 32,000, at the time of writing. Currently, the average agency size is $2.35 million, based on continuing surveys by Plog Research. Using an average commission base of about 13 per cent on total sales means that a typical agency survives on a little over $300,000 per year in commission revenue. Thus, travel agencies generally fit in the small business category.

- The major rental car firms (Hertz, Avis, Budget and National) were supposed to slug it out among themselves for dominance throughout the country – and the world. Instead, small independents continue to start up and survive (as General, Alamo, Dollar, Thrifty, American International, Enterprise, Snappy, Value etc.). Some of these have grown in size so as to take important market share points away from the majors.
- Although hotel chains merged and changed hands at a relatively rapid pace in the 1980s, new companies also began operation. At present, more than 160 significant hotel chains can be identified in North America, in contrast to only ten major domestic airlines serving the United States and Canada. Each year, more than 11,000 advertisers place ads in the 15 lb (6.5 kg) Hotel and Travel Index directory.
- Although the cruise line industry is supposed to have gone the way of the airlines by now, the number of mergers has not yet equalled the number of new lines in operation. Miami alone can boast of being the headquarters for nineteen cruise lines.
- Perhaps the epitome of this fractionation in travel is tour operators. A dozen or so major companies count their revenues in tens of millions of dollars annually. But, hundreds of other companies provide specialized tours to religious groups, ethnic populations, college and university alumnae, upscale markets, ecotourism seekers, and soft and hard adventure lovers.

To sit down together and develop common goals undoubtedly would seem to cut against the grain for most of the people in these groups, particularly since other diverse interests will come into play. Gaming interests now dominate the revenue intake at some of the prettiest spots in the world. And local attraction operators (deep sea fishing, scuba diving operations, ski lift operators etc.) also have different goals than retailers. Most of these simply want more and more visitors to help their businesses grow, regardless of the impact on the physical and social environments where they work and live. These and other small businesses, which compete daily for a place in the sun, obviously have a difficult time seeing beyond the necessity of meeting next week's payroll, getting the rent money, or making certain they have a profit at the end of the year.

But, come together we must – for the common good. These efforts will happen, even without pressure from outsiders. Sometimes it will be on a small scale when a particular destination faces the reality that it must improve its product or face extinction because visitors have been declining in recent years. Occasionally, it will occur on a larger scale as more enlightened executives at airlines, cruise lines or other travel providers recognize that they must protect the broad base of leisure travel that has been nurtured so carefully for decades.

Whenever a new plan is developed, it must be two-sided. It needs to include a set of rules for how a destination is to be developed and/or protected over time, and a code of conduct for leisure travellers to ensure that they leave the destinations they have visited relatively undisturbed. Ecotourism, in its purest form, demands that travellers to unspoiled locales must actively contribute to the preservation and improvement of places they visit, either through diligent work while they are there or through the contribution of fees to help with maintenance and upkeep. This side of the equation is the easiest, i.e., controlling the behaviour of visitors. Codes of conduct can be printed, widely circultated (along with explanations as to why they are necessary), and enforced through adequate supervision at the destination. The Audubon Society (1990) has adopted perhaps the best set of guidelines for its members, which also provides an excellent starting point for other groups to consider. In brief, this code states:

1   Biotas shall not be disturbed.
2   Tourism to natural areas will be 'resource-sustainable'.
3   Sensibilities of other cultures shall be respected.
4   Waste disposal shall have neither environmental nor aesthetic impacts.
5   The experience a tourist gains in travelling with Audubon shall enrich his or her appreciation of nature, conservation, and the environment.
6   The effect of an Audubon tour shall be to strengthen the conservation effort and enhance the natural integrity of places visited.
7   Traffic in products of certain wildlife and plant populations shall not occur.

Although the task for protecting a destination seems almost insurmountable, it must occur – and quickly before the irreversible patterns of destruction obliterate many more pristine areas.

This author has developed a code for leisure destination development to protect their futures as they grow over the years, particularly in the early planning stages (Plog, 1991). It sets guidelines which can be followed by existing tourist areas or ones that are in the process of development. In brief, it indicates that there is a necessity to:

1   *Protect* what is natural and beautiful for the benefit of 'natives' and tourists.
2   *Reduce* density – do not overcrowd an area with too many hotels, tourist shops, or visitors.
3   *Enhance* the feeling of seclusion and privacy to preserve the feeling

of the area and the psychology that travellers want, i.e., a retreat and escape from the cares of the world.

4 *Seek* quality throughout since it entices visitors to stay longer, brings them back time after time, and ensures a longer life for the area.

5 *Emphasize* diversity – the more activities that are available, the greater the likelihood that something will be of interest to each visitor each day.

6 *Restore* the natural and the historical to retain the sense of heritage, continuity and community.

7 *Value* local culture and traditions to protect local populations, their heritage and culture.

8 *Institute* height limits (buildings usually no taller than three storeys) to protect vistas and other scenic views.

9 *Negotiate* for open areas to provide the 'breathing room' that enhances every project.

10 *Gain* community acceptance so that the local populations are the ones who benefit most from tourism (this is their home), in partnership with commercial enterprises.

These words together form the acronym *PRESERVING* to signify that progress can only be achieved through active and concerted efforts in developing a final plan. *Preserve, protect* and *plan* for the future constitute the three Ps of making leisure travel better for everyone in the future.

How distant these goals are is anyone's guess. However, first steps must be taken to make the public more conscious of the impact of both the negative and positive aspects of leisure travel. Academic conferences on ecotourism and related themes are now becoming more popular. These efforts are extraordinarily useful, but the push now must be to involve commercial interests in these conferences and related programmes. Only when local entrepreneurs and major corporations become convinced that their futures may be in jeopardy will there be an opportunity to make significant changes since they control the development funds. The relationship between groups interested in ecology and commercial tourism interests should be one of working together and not confrontation or hostility. Conflicts and battles growing out of the environmental movement have been the norm, without much thought given as to how various interests can work together. An educational approach should be the prime goal – including public and commercial travel interests. All must recognize that, unless something is done rather quickly, travel will decline in the future. The greatest impact in the shortest period of time can be achieved by professional planners in various governmental agencies who have responsibility for the futures of the areas they serve. Since planners can dictate the direction of development – and re-development – their potential for positive impact can be enormous.

Awareness of the problems and the need for solutions are just developing. Hopefully, such awareness will accelerate over time leading to more positive, long-term actions. Finger pointing and mutual blaming must be avoided since these always interfere with solutions.

Unfortunately, even if the PRESERVING acronym forms a model for what should be done at a resort or destination, there will be great disagreements about the specifics. Obtaining compromise can be difficult. For this reason, planning directors and officials, by necessity, are central in the process. They alone can force compromise and accommodation. Otherwise, almost everyone involved will feel that he or she has the right answers, the right solutions . . . much in the manner of René Descartes's insightful observation that:

> Good sense is of all things in the world the most equally distributed, for everybody thinks he is so well-supplied with it, that even those most difficult to please in all other matters never desire more of it than they already possess.
>
> *Le Discours de la méthode* (1637)

References

Audubon (March 1990), Audubon Society, New York
Lodge, D. (1991) *Paradise News*, Viking Penguin, New York, NY, pp. 63–4
Plog, S.C. (1991) *Leisure Travel: Making It a Growth Market . . . Again!*, John Wiley and Sons, New York, NY

5 Tourism: the nostalgia industry of the future

Graham M.S. Dann

A lot of intellectuals these days are griping about nostalgia, saying that our obsession with the past is inhibiting our ability to create a unique culture of the present. But me, I think nostalgia is OK.

(Schoemer, 1992)

INTRODUCTION

Today a great deal of time and energy is dedicated to looking backwards, toward capturing a past which, in many ways, is considered superior to the chaotic present and the dreaded future. This world of yesteryear is a safe environment. It is secure. It is orderly. The way we were is surely an improvement on the way we are, or are ever likely to be. Perhaps that is why currently the media and advertisers appear to emphasize so much that old time religion, golden oldies, conservation and heritage. It may also explain the evident popularity of country and western music, the honky tonk, sepia tints, soft focus, Vintage Clothing Patterns, Laura Ashley prints and Bugsy. How else can one account for the anachronistic presence of a Nostalgia Book Club (with its free pamphlet on the life of Judy Garland and its bulletin 'Reminiscing Time'), Radio Yesteryear (with its swing bands, Jack Benny comedy shows and serials from the 1930s and 1940s) (Davis, 1979) or the Best of the Beeb (with its cassettes including *Dad's Army, Yes, Minister* and *The Archers*, and videos featuring *Fawlty Towers*)?

In Britain there has been a massive revival in preserving the past. Recently, for example, Urry (1991) notes that the British Isles boast of at least half a million listed buildings, over 5500 conservation areas and 12,000 museum type venues. The latter have witnessed a 150 per cent increase in the past two decades and half of them have emerged in the past sixteen years. The National Trust (with 1.5 million members in 1987) is said to be the largest mass organization in the UK with 4.2 million persons annually visiting its properties. Relatedly, more people in Britain patronize museums, galleries and heritage centres than ever they do the theatre or cinema, and a similar statistical pattern can be observed among tourists as well. In fact, the quest for the quaint and the pursuit of patrimony have reached such epidemic proportions that it has even been suggested that the UK no longer manufactures goods, but heritage, and that it might be more appropriate to appoint a national curator instead of a Prime Minister (Urry, 1991: 109–10). No small wonder that, in such a climate, the Conservative party managed to be elected in 1992 for a fourth successive term.

A similar scenario may be found elsewhere. In the Republican dominated USA, for example, where the national register of historic places contained 1200 entries in 1968, some seventeen years later this number had risen to 37,000. Baltimore's Harbor Place alone manages to bring in 29 million visitors a year (Urry, 1991: 108, 119).

Thus, whatever is depicted – from glass blowing to candlestick making – and wherever it is portrayed – from Wigan Pier to Sydney's Darling Harbour – the one thing that unites this ever increasing bricolage of yearning is the realization that it represents big business, very big business (Davis, 1979: 118). Moreover, when the nostalgia industry is linked to the world's number one enterprise – that of tourism – such an alliance has limitless pecuniary possibilities.

It is the purpose of this exploratory essay to examine some of this nostalgia-tourism connection with reference to:

1   Hotels ('the tourist in his castle, the rich man at his gate').
2   Museums and other emporia ('sales of the centuries').
3   Infamous sites ('milking the macabre').
4   Dirty dumps ('where there's muck there's brass').

Finally, there is a brief discussion on the mechanics of promoting the past by projecting it into the future. The complementary sociological counterpart to this treatment can be found in 'Tourism and nostalgia: looking forward to going back' (Dann, 1992).

1 The tourist in his castle, the rich man at his gate

This distorted line from an otherwise well-known hymn has been irreverently changed to depict the inversion that takes place when tourism offers its protégés the luxury of being a King or a Queen for a day (Gottlieb, 1982), where:

To live for a short time surrounded by gracious deferring servants may have powerful appeal among those seeking escape from 'egalitarian affirmative action norms' as well as those middle class, do-it-yourself capitalists who are ready to pay for a week or two of being treated as visiting potentates. Sleeping in a castle or château and surrounded by a covey of fawning attendants, are, for more than we may appreciate, a dream realized. (Buck, 1978: 110)

But how can this transformation take place in a contemporary era which obliterates divisions based on class, gender and race? Only by imaginatively reverting to a period where the distinctions between lord and serf were most pronounced, and then by drawing them into the present and future. In such a manner, the de-differentiation of postmodern society becomes suspended or bracketed and one begins to live 'as if' it did not exist.

In the case of some Indian hotels (e.g. the Lake Palace at Udaipur, Rambagh Palace at Jaipur and Umaid Bhawan Palace at Jodhpur cf. Sigman, 1991), such romanticization becomes possible because the establishments either were, or still are, abodes of the maharajahs. In this way these Mogul style pavilions, with their vast marble bathrooms and banqueting halls, can be retained, along with the sculptured grounds and retinue of turbaned waiters. All the tourist has to do is to pay the necessary $200 a day and then sink into palatial luxury.

Sometimes, aristocrats, while living on the premises, may be reduced to taking in tourist lodgers, in order to maintain the upkeep of their properties and to avoid the clutches of the tax man. Such is the case of the thousand-year-old Château Loriol in France, where the proprietors entertain bed and breakfasters so as to stave off inevitable bankruptcy. The *nouveau riche* visitor from within the four-poster can then stay 'awake for a few minutes listening to the quiet and just enjoying the feeling of history' (O'Sullivan, 1990).

More often than not, however, the tourism industry assumes the corporate responsibility for renovating a hotel in the style of its erstwhile glory. Thus the restored Manila Hotel, originally opened in 1912, harks back to the former era by having a 258-page history book, and an archives room with memorabilia depicting illustrious guests. At the same time, it retains its marble floors, mahogany doors and old-fashioned service (Deans, 1990).

The Ritz Carlton (Naples, Florida), on the other hand, emphasizes its links with the past by spending $2 million on art and antiques, along with its displayed collection of 200 oil paintings, Persian carpets and nineteenth-century crystal chandeliers. The public rooms are done out like the interiors of London clubs, the lounges have butlers, and tea and scones are offered from a silver service. Reportedly, one guest was so taken in by the gracious old worldliness of the place that he recalled his grandparents' wedding on the premises. Yet the hotel was not opened until 1985 (List, 1990)!

Then there is the case of the legendary Raffles Hotel in Singapore which recently spent more than $100 million in renovations in order to restore as closely as possible the atmosphere and décor of 1915. Today, each of the 104 suites, with oriental throw rugs, wicker furniture and silver ice buckets, is reached through open air courtyards and attended by three bellhops apiece. This former haunt of Somerset Maugham, Rudyard Kipling and Noel Coward, manages to capture something of its heyday with its turn-of-the-century theatre and memento-stuffed museum. Only the prices are different. Now an original Singapore Sling is sold at over $10 a shot and a good top-of-the-list bottle of wine served in the ornate Raffles Grill costs $1675 (McArthur, 1992).

Meanwhile, over in Amarillo, at the Big Texan Restaurant and Ranch, the rooms come complete with bar-style swinging doors, large brass beds, murals of ranch scenes and mounted steer horn lamps. Diners are entitled to free 72-ounce steaks (massive even by Texan standards!), provided, of course, they can eat them within the hour (Simmons, 1990). But even if they cannot manage this light repast, at least they have been transported back to the mythical days of mighty John Waynesque heroes who could.

A few hundred miles away, one finds another relic from the past, whose advertisement reads as follows:

> Stay aboard the Hotel Queen Mary and chart your course to the best Southern Californian attractions. Indulge in the romance of the Queen's original first-class staterooms . . . Dance in the same lounge where celebrities rocked to the roll of the ship before rock 'n roll. (Walt Disney, Inc., 1991)

Here the legends of the Queen Mary are enhanced by their quaint Mother Country connection.

It is therefore not surprising to find the epitome of nostalgia located in the British manor house, set amid such dreamlike places as Bowston-on-the-Water and Stow-on-the-Wold. In one of these stately homes in a nearby county, a Canadian travel writer thus describes his luxurious stay:

> I supped my champagne (G.H. Mamm, Cuvée René Lalou, 1982), leaned back in my chaise longue . . . and contemplated the scene. Elegant, but casually elegant, people nibbling at their raspberries and cream – by the side of the outdoor pool . . . Ah yes, that pool. It has a little niche in history. Narrow your eyes a little and your imagine you see a beautiful auburn-haired girl emerge from it, naked, cavort happily around the deck and run smack into a tall, balding gent in a tuxedo. The girl was Christine Keeler, a sometime model, and the man was John Profumo . . . And that first meeting at Cliveden in Berkshire . . . set in motion an affair that turned into a scandal

that finally toppled the Tory government of Harold Macmillan . . . But that's a story from the 1960s. This is 1990 and Cliveden is no longer the home of Profumo's friend Lord Astor. Now it's a hotel. But what a Hotel! (Smyth, 1990)

The author then goes on to describe the sixty bedroom, 324-year-old mansion situated in 376 acres, where guests pay £310 a night. For this small sum they are met by a liveried chauffeur in a Rolls–Royce, they enjoy the comforts of a king size bed, an emperor size bathroom and a dictator size drawing room, while all the time surrounded by oil paintings, sculptures and other *objets d'art*. No wonder that at Cliveden one has a butler, whereas in 'a lesser establishment you would call him the hotel manager'.

Here the journey back into the past occurs in two stages. First there is a brief stop at the naughty 1960s, a reflection on the lifestyle of the aristocracy, and how this in turn was embroiled at the highest level of British politics. Afterwards there is the deep plunge into the gracious seventeenth century of the stately home, where power and affluence were still as synonymous as they are supposedly rejected at present. The upmarket tourist is permitted to enter this world of the past continuous, while never, of course, being able to appropriate it.

2 Sales of the centuries

Safely ensconced in his Berkshire castle, Smyth (1990) is further able to meditate on the temporal transformation of the British countryside; on

> weavers' cottages [that] are now weekend retreats for London stockbrokers and doctors, barns and stables [that] are now self-catering apartments, the mill that's now a museum, the jail that's an art gallery . . .

In this connection, MacCannell observes that:

> In modern society 'symbols' of the past are collected in museums when they are small enough and when they are too large they are left outside in parks and called 'monuments'. Some, as in the case of the paddle boat, San Francisco's cable cars and large old homes, are restored and kept functioning as 'living reminders' of the past. (1976: 88)

Just as 'almost everywhere and everything from the past may be conserved' (Urry, 1991: 105), so too can it be retained by making it a spectacle, a commodity or a service. Part of this process is museumization, the freezing of heritage and the selling of the frozen product.

In some instances, the content of the package is simply a romantic gaze at a slice of history, whether remote or proximate, as for example in Frannies Teddy Bear Museum, with its sentimental $2 million collection of 1600 furry pieces so evocative of childhood (MacDonald, 1990).

There is also San Antonio's Alamo shrine with relics from the days of Davy Crockett, Jim Bowie and William B. Travis. Nearby, in Ripley's 'Believe it or Not' Museum, sightseers can behold the stuffed remains of the first monkey in space, or even a pair of fleas dressed as bride and groom (*Toronto Star*, 1990).

Sometimes the museum is dedicated to a famous, or better still, infamous person, whose legendary exploits (exploitation?) permit voyeurs to engage nostalgically in a reactionary political discourse which would otherwise be quite unacceptable if voiced among their liberal peers. The Malacanang Presidential Palace Museum in Manila, for instance, would seem to cater to such a mindset, for here are displayed 1700 pairs of shoes belonging to Imelda Marcos, along with her bullet-proof bra. Yet, in spite of, or even because of, her intimate association with the late dictator of the Philippines, this representative (though arguably inadequate) sample of footwear (symbolizing the downtreader?) manages to attract 500 visitors a week (Bragg, 1991).

On other occasions, the museum becomes an emporium actually retailing nostalgia, thereby allowing the tourist to purchase trophies from the past as 'souvenirs' or memories. The Cumberland General Store in Homestead, Tennessee, for example, has an exhaustive collection of artefacts including spittoons, jews' harps, bowler hats, goose quill pens, along with such books as 'Be Your Own Chimney Sweep' or 'Learning to Play the Community Fiddle'. What is so attractive about these memorabilia is that they 'all evoke images of a simpler lifestyle, of the days when people were self-sufficient' (Kroll and Kroll, 1990).

However, perhaps the biggest 'sale of the century' is the Presley business where 'you can't travel 50 miles on any interstate, it seems, without passing an Elvis car museum, an Elvis memorabilia shop, or an "Elvis pelvised here" plaque' (Cohn, 1991). According to CBI TV, the late King's annual worth is $210 million, and, if present trends continue, by 2001 this figure should easily top the one billion dollar mark. At Graceland alone, the family home and grave of the nostalgia monarch (purchased in 1957 for $100,000), there are on average as many as 4000 visitors a day (almost 1.5 million per year) who are fed through the mansion in groups of twenty on a conveyor belt (Cohn, 1991). Certainly, Elvis is much better dead than ever he was alive.

By way of partial summary and explanation, Urry observes:

> We have seen a spectacular growth in the number of museums in western countries. This is clearly part of the process by which the past has come to be much more highly valued in comparison with both the present and the

future ... And the attraction of museums increases as people get older –
thus the 'greying' of the population in the west is also adding to the number
and range of museums. (1991: 128)

3 Milking the macabre

It was previously noted that tourists have a particular fascination with
notorious characters, whether these be drawn from the distant or close
past. Nostalgia, it would seem, knows no limits, to the virtual extent that
the worse the experience the more appealing the attraction (cf. Urry,
1991). Hence the success of the Gestapo Prison Museum in Berlin, the
Japanese Prison of War Museum in Singapore, the Auschwitz visitor
centre in Poland, the Inquisition Museum in Lima, Peru, the sea wall
prison in Panama City, Los Angeles' cemetery tour, Palermo's skeleton
filled catacombs and the Bloody Tower in London.

Such celebration of atrocity may, of course, be simply explained in
terms of morbid curiosity, in a similar fashion to the gathering of contemporary ghouls to witness a car crash, a fire or some other disaster –
the 'thank God it's not me' syndrome. Yet, however valid this interpretation for present day events, it does not appear to account fully for
a fascination with an ignominious past. More likely in this connection is
nostalgia's ability to filter out unpleasant experiences by first of all concentrating upon them, recognizing them as safe and dead (Urry, 1991:
109), and then going on to hanker after what is left. Thus the good old
days of the 1930s somehow manage to omit the depression, the 1940s the
war and the 1950s McCarthyism (Davis, 1979: 109, quoting M. Marty),
once the symbols of those eras, along with their monuments and shrines,
have been acknowledged, visited and deleted. At the same time, one
should recognize that the sources of nostalgia are most evident at those
points in the past which pose the greatest threats to continuity and identity
(Davis, 1979: 107).

Seen in this light, one can begin to appreciate that:

> Every country in the world has its macabre tourist attractions – Madame
> Tussaud's Chamber of Horrors in London, Lizzie Borden of Fall River,
> Mass., who gave her mother forty whacks with an axe, or Salem, also in
> Massachussetts, where witches were burned at the stake. (MacDonald, 1991)

One example is provided by MacDonald (1991) in Jamaica's (in)famous
Rose Hall, which manages to attract 100,000 tourists annually. According
to Gray (1991), this haunted property has recently been restored to its
original grandeur at a cost of $2.5 million. It was the home of one Annie
Palmer, an English woman who allegedly murdered her three husbands

(successively holing them up in their own bedrooms), and thereafter taking countless slave lovers before eventually being slain herself by one of them. After visiting the place and listening to various accounts, Gray reckoned 'it was easy to believe the story that the white witch of Rose Hall, as her neighbours called her, was still on the premises'. Thus, even though he would also have been exposed to the version which found Mrs Palmer to be an upright and respectable lady (MacDonald, 1991), he preferred to go along with the more sensational variant, even to the point where he could almost sense her presence. Otherwise, of course, Rose Hall would simply have been another Great House, another instance of 'dog does not bite man'.

A second example of touring the terrible can be found in the KGB's infamous Lubyanka headquarters in the heart of Moscow. Here 'post-*glasnost*' visitors may now on twice-weekly three-hour tours view the windowless cells where prisoners were once tortured, the office of former KGB and Soviet chief Yuri Andropov, suitable references to Kim Philby and George Blake, and all sorts of captured spy paraphernalia ranging from poison pellets hidden inside eyeglasses to drop boxes disguised as sticks and stones, cameras concealed inside pens and watches, and a stun gun masquerading as a flashlight. When tour guide KGB Lieutenant Valery Vozdvizhinsky is asked about his former colleagues' participation in Stalinist purges, he simply states that they were acting under orders, and when quizzed about Soviet spy hardware, he replies 'I believe such devices are in the museums of our counterparts around the world'. The 300 interrogation chambers have been closed since 1962, but six unused cells remain 'just in case' (McKinsey, 1992).

A third illustration of milking the macabre can be found in Bodie, the remains of a late nineteenth century California gold mining town. According to the publicity pamphlet, Bodie

> was second to none for wickedness, badmen and the worst climate out of doors. One little girl, whose family was taking her to the remote and infamous town, wrote in her diary, 'Goodbye God, I'm going to Bodie'. The phrase came to be known throughout the west. Killings occurred with monotonous regularity, sometimes becoming almost daily events. The fire bell, which tolled the ages of the deceased when they were buried, rang often and long. Robberies, stage holdups, and street fights provided variety, and the town's 65 saloons offered many opportunities for relaxation after hard days of work in the mines. The Reverend F.M. Warrington saw it in 1881 as a 'sea of sin, lashed by the tempests of lust and passion'. (California Department of Parks and Recreation, 1988: 3)

Today, thousands of visitors drive on unpaved roads to this remote ghost town. They can walk along Bonanza Street, Maiden Lane and Virgin Alley, and other haunts of the ladies of the night, view the town jail from which a vigilante group extricated and hanged Joseph de Roche, enter the only Protestant church, which was heavily vandalized and from which a painting of the ten commandments ('thou shalt not steal') was purloined, and see the remains of the schoolhouse which was burned down by one of its pupils.

But what is so attractive about Bodie and its badmen, which now has a Friends of Bodie society to ensure its preservation? Perhaps it is nostalgia for the pioneering days of the goldrush era when everyone theoretically had the possibility of getting rich, and the myth of equality of opportunity which freezes out the seedier side of reality by making a spectacle of it (in much the same way as the nostalgic movies *Bonnie and Clyde* and *Butch Cassidy and the Sundance Kid* had done so successfully before). Seen in this perspective, 'tourism becomes the new gold mine'. As Cernetig (1991) goes on to observe à propos the goldrush of 1896:

> There isn't much easy gold left in the Klondike field. Today the real pay dirt is the tourists who roll into Dawson. It's the past, not gold or grubstaked miners, that has become the no.1 industry in Dawson City. 'Nowadays we sell nostalgia', Dawson Mayor Peter Jenkins says.

4 Where there's muck there's brass

This old Yorkshire saying (with its early nostalgic counterparts in the song 'My Old Man's a Dustman' and the once popular TV show *Steptoe and Son*), suggests that money can be made from junk, discarded refuse, the unclean and unwholesome, something which the tourism industry has realized for decades.

Thus, MacCannell (1976: 57) remarks that

> In Paris at the turn of the century, sightseers were given tours of the sewers, the morgue, a slaughterhouse, a tobacco factory . . .

all of which could be somehow viewed as 'muck' bringing forth 'brass'. For him, functioning establishments, occupations, transportation networks and public works figure prominently as tourist attractions because they represent alienated leisure (MacCannell, 1976: 51–7). Hence the significance of the morgue, where

> This final display of working class stiffs illustrates, as well as any other example, how the display of even a horrible object normalizes it. (MacCannell, 1976: 72)

In Britain, Urry (1991) points to several other instances where money can be made from the industrial past. As examples he gives the Wigan Pier Heritage Centre in Lancashire, Quarry Bank Mill in Cheshire, Black Country World near Dudley, the Birmingham Canal, the Gloucester Docks, the Salford Quays, a Chemicals Museum in Widnes, a Living Dockyard in Chatham, a Pencil Museum in Keswick and the Big Pit in South Wales. Just one of these, the Albert Dock in Liverpool, welcomes as many as 3 million visitors a year, while on the drawing board are planned a Rhondda Heritage Park (which will include the Lewis Merthyr Coalmine), and a Roman Centre (Diva) in Chester, complete with Roman coins and Roman food. According to Urry (1991: 104–7), there are now 464 UK museums displaying industrial material, and matters have even reached the stage where locations such as Bradford, which formerly sent its holidaymakers to Morecombe, have now become major tourist attractions in their own right. Furthermore, such is the business potential of these projects, that now the private sector has taken over in exploiting the various ways of representing history and of commodifying the past. Interestingly also, the proportion of the service class patronizing these centres is about three times that of manual workers (from whom the majority of these ventures originated).

As an explanation for this fascination with the often heroic and backbreaking work of *others*, Urry reckons that it is closely bound up with the post-modern breaking down of boundaries, particularly between the front and backstage of people's lives, or what he terms 'a post-modern museum culture' in which almost anything can become an object of curiosity for vistors. Coterminously, the process is facilitated by a parallel rapid de-industrialization (especially in the north of England, South Wales and Central Scotland), and hence a sense of loss of 'certain types of technology (steam engines, blast furnaces, pit workings) and of the social life that had developed around those technologies' (Urry, 1991: 107). Clearly, a rosy future lies ahead for 'factory tourism', and plants producing cars, planes, processed food, submarines etc. can all be opened up for public gaze. At present, the English Tourist Board calculates that up to 6 million people visit a factory each year, and this figure will soon reach 10 million. In becoming an object of sightseeing, the factory has been museumized (Urry, 1991: 131–2).

Discussion

As the end of a century and, perhaps even more important, a millennium, approach, academic interest as well as popular curiosity appear to be increasingly preoccupied with rediscovery and reassessment of the past. (Buck, 1979: 2)

This brief overview has highlighted four areas where the tourism industry has successfully employed nostalgia to its own financial advantage. Now is the time to examine the mechanics of the operation.

In the first place, it should be noted that nostalgia is not simply an antiquarian feeling or mindless yearning. Rather, it is 'a positively toned evocation of a lived past in the context of some negative feeling toward present or impending circumstance' (Davis, 1979: 18). In other words, nostalgia relates to and is grounded in dissatisfaction with current social arrangements and concern over their continuation into the future. It is therefore to be expected, rather than anomalous, that tourism's largest shrines to nostalgia, Disney World and Disneyland, are located in two of the most future-oriented states of the union (Davis, 1979: 119–21) and that EuroDisney has recently opened close to one of that continent's most progressive capitals. As Urry observes:

> Indeed the way in which all sorts of places have become centres of spectacle and display and the nostalgic attraction of 'heritage' can both be seen as elements of the postmodern. (1991: 93–4)

Alternatively stated, remote Third World villagers living for generations in one place would be baffled by nostalgia. It is the dislocated Western traveller of today who experiences nostalgia to its fullest, and who, incidentally, travels precisely on account of such disorientation (cf. Davis, 1979: 50). Thus 'a daily allowance of nostalgia can be a tonic to the ills of the here and now' (Schoemer, 1992: 59).

The second point to note is the way the past is promoted by tourism, like the discourse of any other form of advertising:

> knows no present, and only speaks of the future with reference to the past. This allows viewers and readers to project themselves into new situations which often permit the carrying of personality equipment and nostalgia rewarding experiences into the future. (Dann, 1988: 8)

Hence, that tourism publicity which is based on nostalgic images has to sell the past to the future (Berger, 1983: 139). In so doing, it promotes glamour and happiness (rather than pleasure); it provides something enviable; it steals love of self and offers it back to the client to be consumed (Berger, 1983: 132).

Thirdly, the evocation of the past as a promise to the future, contains elements which lead to that future. They are drawn out of time into an eternal moment where both time and space become incorporated synchronically into the structure of myth. The promotion therefore takes away the present out of real time and replaces it with the metaphysical time of the advertisement, and history becomes appropriated by memory or projection, in order that consumers can fill the void by identifying themselves with the product (Williamson, 1983: 152–5). Thus the hazy nostalgic picture of the brochure creates an aura of the collective past which we are called upon to remember, and to which by future action we can become transported in one magical moment (Williamson, 1983: 156–60). McLuhan was therefore surely correct when he relatedly observed that in this way the media can travel into the future with one eye cocked on the rearview mirror (Davis, 1979: 135).

Seen in the above light, the ancient and glamorous hotel of yesterday becomes the 'old green grass of home' of tomorrow. The associated lifestyles of the rich and famous become envied and enviable, only satiated (we are led to believe) when we become those regal occupants disdainfully looking out of the picture at our longing and hopeless admirers. Museums and emporia are now no longer viewed simply as showcases containing trophies of a bygone era. They are to be entered and possessed, and their booty is to be paraded as a symbol of the good life ahead. Even the macabre world of Robbie Burns' 'ghoulies and ghosties and long-leggedy beasties' becomes attractive, to the extent that it replaces the monotony and alienation of the present with an exciting future agenda drawn from the past. Murder and mayhem, the wildness of the wicked west, hangmen and other horrors, become forthcoming heroes whose exploits symbolically reverse present day justice toward favouring the mythical underdog. Finally, the lure of the beachcomber, the satanic mills and the grease and grime of yesteryear point us in a counter-direction to the clinical clean and green of today. After all, and in spite of the rhetoric of ecotourism, the natural after which we hanker is often warm and earthy.

Through the calligraphy and iconography of tourism's promotional literature, the holiday is thus transformed into its original meaning – a holy day in which we venerate the past; a vacation becomes a rest from and a suspension of the present; and a trip . . . well, a trip is a trip down memory lane . . . and a voyage into the well-charted waters of the future.

References

Berger, J. (1983) *Ways of Seeing*. British Broadcasting Corporation and Penguin, London and Harmondsworth

Bragg, R. (1991) Strange encounters and weird stories around the world. *Toronto Star*, 9 November

Buck, R. (1978) Toward a synthesis in tourism theory. *Annals of Tourism Research*, 5(1): 110–11

Buck, R. (1979) Bloodless theatre: images of the old order Amish in tourism literature. *Pennsylvania Mennonite Heritage*, 2(3): 2–11

California Department of Parks and Recreation (1988) *Bodie State Historic Park*
Cernetig, M. (1991) Tourism becomes a new gold mine. *Globe and Mail*, 3 July
Cohn, N. (1991) Two for the show. *Sunday Times*, 24 March
Dann, G. (1988) The people of tourist brochures. Paper presented to the First
    Global Conference: Tourism – a Vital Force for Peace, Vancouver, 16–19
    October
Dann, G. (1992) Tourism and nostalgia: looking forward to going back. Paper
    prepared for the international congress *Le tourisme internationale entre tradition
    et modernité*, co-hosted by the Centre d'Etude Tourisme et Civilization of the
    University of Nice and the working group on tourism of the International
    Sociological Association, November
Davis, F. (1979) Yearning for yesterday. A sociology of nostalgia. Free Press, New
    York, p. 119
Deans, B. (1990) Manila Hotel a 'mirror to passing generations'. *Globe and Mail*,
    20 October
Gottlieb, A. (1982) Americans' vacations. *Annals of Tourism Research*, 9: 165–87
Gray, B. (1991) Jamaica: for mature audiences. *Globe and Mail*, 9 November
Kroll, B. and R. Kroll (1990) Tennessee store practical fun. *Toronto Star*, 3
    November
List, W. (1990) Putting on the Ritz. *Globe and Mail*, 24 November
McArthur, D. (1992) Raffles Hotel reborn. *Globe and Mail*, 18 January
MacCannell, D. (1976) The tourist. A new theory of the leisure class. Macmillan,
    London
MacDonald, J. (1990) Travel trends. *Toronto Star*, 17 November
MacDonald, J. (1991) Jamaica's white witch certainly was no lady. *Toronto Star*,
    2 November
McKinsey, K. (1992) KGB open to tourists in the 'new' Moscow. *Toronto Star*, 8
    February
O'Sullivan, B. (1990) Zagging around France and missing a château. *Toronto Star*,
    10 November
Schoemer, K. (1992) Thoroughly modern madrigals. *Mademoiselle*, February, pp.
    59–60
Sigman, D. (1991) Exploring the splendour of the Rajahs. *Globe and Mail*, 16
    November
Simmons, J. (1990) Where's the beef? At this Texas eatery. *Toronto Star*, 24
    November
Smyth, M. (1990) Away from it all. *Toronto Star*, 27 October
Toronto Star (1990) San Antonio offers a multi-faceted experience. Disover USA
    Winter Sun, advertising feature section, November 22
Urry, J. (1991) *The Tourist Gaze*. Sage, London
Walt Disney, Inc. (1991) Hotel Queen Mary. *San Francisco Examiner*, 14 July
Williamson, J. (1983) *Decoding Advertisements. Ideology and Meaning in Advertising*.
    Marion Boyars, London

Part Two

Results and Residuals:
The Issue of Impacts

Throughout recorded history, tourism has impacted in some way everything and everyone that it touched. Ideally, these impacts should have been positive, both in terms of benefits to destination areas and their residents. These positive impacts should include results such as improvements in local economic conditions, social and cultural understanding and protected environmental resources. In theory, the benefits of tourism should produce benefits far in excess of their costs.

Initial studies of tourism impacts dealt mainly with economic aspects since they were more easily quantifiable and measurable. In addition, it was presumed that the income derived from tourism could make up for any negative consequences of tourism. However, over-emphasis on economic benefits has often led to adverse physical and social consequences.

Due to the rising concern for the environment, the concept of 'sustainable tourism development' (defined as the protection and conservation of an area's ecology in order to maintain its useful life over a long period of time) has emerged. Archer and Cooper in Chapter 6 review the key elements of the positive and negative impacts of tourism, including economic, political, socio-cultural, environmental and ecological impacts.

Careful planning and management, including the understanding of an area's carrying capacity is essential in order to avoid exploitation and potential destruction of physical and personal resources. The authors conclude that what is needed to avoid the negative impacts of tourism is a shift away from short-term to longer-term thinking and planning, and a recognition that exploitation of places and people is not only unethical but unprofitable (in the long run) as well.

Swinglehurst (Chapter 7) traces the socio-cultural impacts of tourism beginning in eighteenth-century England to the present. From the advent of the 'grand tour', there has been little social or cultural contact between the more affluent traveller and the ordinary people of the countries they visited. A traveller's friends were cultural equals, but others with whom he came in contact were servants, innkeepers, boatmen and other peasants. Communication began to change late in the nineteenth century when wealthy tourists began to recognize the plight of the poor in the countries they visited. Paternalism and a sense of largesse caused many wealthy tourists to contribute to local schools, libraries and hospitals to help improve the lives of the impoverished and uneducated.

With the advent of the jet airplane and mass tourism, a new era of tourism had begun, and the age of travel hedonism arrived. Recently, a reversal of roles between tourists and natives has occurred when comparing tourism values. In the past, natives were regarded as carefree, fun-loving children while tourists were considered as seekers of knowledge and enlightenment. Today, however, it appears to be the other way round. The cultural gap between these two worlds is closing since the tourist and the resident are exchanging ambitions and ways of life. While tourists seek escape, residents try to learn how they can satisfy the demands for the good life they imagine the tourist has achieved.

In Chapter 8 Pearce extends the issue of tourist–resident impacts by offering the proposition that social impact effects may be *real*, since objective data can be found to verify their existence, or may be *perceived*, views held by the community that life is different. Perceived views are equally as important as real views because if residents believe an impact does exist (regardless of whether or not it is true), their behaviour will be altered.

The effects of the tourist–resident interaction process appear to have maximum social and psychological impacts on residents when the destination areas are small, unsophisticated and isolated. These impacts may be either powerful, direct interpersonal encounters, or more subtle, indirect influences. Conversely, these impacts are lessened, the larger, more urbane and urban the destination area.

After reviewing the literature on social impacts of tourism and the variety of models that have been developed to better explain this phenomenon, the author presents five emerging solutions to combat social impact problems. Tactics proposed for reducing the decline of tourist–resident social contacts include: better education and training; incorporating community perspectives in development; increasing resident opportunities; establishment of local equity and management committees, and increased research and monitoring of social impacts.

The rather uneasy relationship between contemporary western tourism development and native peoples is explored by Mercer in Chapter 9. His examination of the Aboriginal, 'outback' population of northern and central Australia focuses on the social appropriateness of tourism development from the native Aboriginal viewpoint. Two case studies are presented, both dealing with the concepts of control and choice. Control relates to whether native populations control their own destinies when negotiating decisions regarding tourism development on their land. Choice relates to their having the freedom to choose to negotiate, or simply to refuse to do so.

Growing Aboriginal militancy related to what they viewed as their basic rights had come up against the Western practice of eminent domain, i.e., government gaining control of individual (or group) owned land 'for the good of the many', through a legal process often including condemnation. This practice, together with other denials of land ownership, led to what some writers termed 'the invasion and theft of the Aboriginal nation'.

The key problem facing native peoples including Aboriginals today is how they can achieve the most benefits derived from tourism without being overrun and overwhelmed by the excesses that tourism itself can cause.

In the final chapter in this section, Chapter 10, Richter deals with the political role of gender, as it relates to tourism. Gender differences in tourism throughout history are reviewed, areas of tourism research which have politically important gender issues are explored, and trends in political organizations and tourism that may affect emerging gender distinctions are presented.

As an employment and ownership sector, a rationale is provided for prostitution, and arguments for sex tourism are explained. Examples of gender differences in marketing, souvenirs and attractions are also provided. Marketing linking tourism with sex is rampant throughout the industry, souvenirs continue to promote women as sex objects, and destination attractions remain male-dominated preserves.

The bulk of the financial control of both the private and public tourism sectors lies in the hands of men. Rightly or wrongly, women have always been perceived as particularly appropriate for 'front line' tourism positions due to their assumed greater social and hospitable skills. However, women holding public office have consistently demonstrated a disproportionate concern for areas such as health, social welfare and concern for the environment, which the tourism industry has tended to downplay or ignore. Thus, if women achieve greater access to management and public policy positions, their greatest impact may well be in those tourism areas where they have traditionally had the least control or influence.

6 The positive and negative impacts of tourism

Brian Archer and Chris Cooper

Introduction

Tourism, both international and domestic, brings about an intermingling of people from diverse social and cultural backgrounds, and also a considerable spatial redistribution of spending power which has a significant impact on the economy of the destination area. Early work on the impact of tourism upon destinations focused primarily on economic aspects. This was not only because such impacts are more readily quantifiable and measurable, but also there was a pervading climate of optimism that these studies would show that tourism was of net economic benefit to host destinations. In many cases, this was indeed true. Yet tourism, by its very nature, is attracted to unique and fragile environments and societies and it became apparent that in some cases the economic benefits of tourism may be offset by adverse and previously unmeasured environmental and social consequences.

The benefits and costs of tourism accrue to two quite distinct groups of people. On the one hand, the visitors themselves receive benefits and incur costs in taking holidays. On the other hand, the resident populations of the host region benefit from tourism (not only financially) but at the same time incur costs of various types. Since it is not possible to deal adequately with both aspects within the limited scope of a single chapter, attention will be devoted to the positive and negative effects of tourism from the point of view of the host country or region.

The general issues central to any discussion of the positive and negative impacts of tourism must include notions of carrying capacity and also of how impacts can be assessed. Carrying capacity is a relatively straightforward concept – in simple terms it refers to a point beyond which further levels of visitation or development would lead to an unacceptable deterioration in the physical environment and of the visitor's experience (Getz, 1983; O'Reilly, 1986). Any consideration of tourism's impact must recognize the pivotal role which carrying capacity plays by intervening in the relationship between visitor and resource.

The impact made by tourism therefore depends upon the volume and profile characteristics of the tourists (their length of stay, activity, mode of transport, travel arrangement etc.). In this respect, a number of authors have attempted to classify tourists according to their impact on the destinations (see, for example, Smith, 1977). The character of the resource (its natural features, level of development, political and social structure etc.) is equally important as it determines the degree of its robustness to tourism and tourism development (Mathieson and Wall, 1982).

A range of variables, therefore, needs to be taken into account in any determination of the impact of tourism. Yet determining such impacts also raises a number of issues. In economics, impact methodology has a long pedigree but the measurement of environmental and social impacts has not progressed anywhere near as far. Indeed, in all forms of impact analysis, it is important to distinguish tourism-induced events from other agents of change; ensure that secondary and tertiary effects are considered; and have a view as to what the situation was before tourism intervened. All of these points are problematic and the tendency is therefore to simplify and narrow the scope of investigation to 'contain' the research into a manageable outcome (Mathieson and Wall, 1982).

In part, the difficulty of quantifying the environmental and social impacts of tourism has delayed the development of impact methodologies. But the rising tide of environmentalism has caught up with tourism and has lent support to the view that in some cases the economic benefits of tourism are more than outweighed by the environmental and social costs of tourism. Concepts such as 'sustainable tourism development' and 'the responsible consumption of tourism' are seen as the answer, along with the enhanced planning and management of tourism. These issues are discussed later in this chapter. However, the issue of management is closely related to the notion of carrying capacity as a destination can be 'managed' to take any number of visitors. Simply by 'hardening' the environment and managing the visitor, large volumes can be accommodated without an unacceptable decline in the environment or the experience. The question must therefore be asked, management for whom? In pluralistic societies, the conflicts and tensions between the stakeholders in tourism – tourists, developers, planners, environmentalists – will in the end determine levels of tourist development. After all, tourism takes place within political and social contexts. It is, however, heartening that the current pressure for sustainable/responsible tourism will give a different emphasis to the continuing debate amongst the various groups in society and may change the perceived balance between the positive and negative effects of tourism in the future.

Economic effects

The economic advantages and disadvantages of tourism have been extensively documented (see, for example, Archer, 1977; Bryden, 1973; Eadington and Redman, 1991).

The economic impact of tourism

International tourism is an invisible export in that it creates a flow of foreign currency into the economy of a destination country thereby contributing directly to the current account of the balance of payments. Like other export industries, this inflow of revenue creates business turnover, household income, employment and government revenue.

The generation process does not stop at this point however. Some portion of the money received by the business establishments, individuals and government agencies is re-spent within the destination economy thereby creating further rounds of economic activity. These secondary effects can in total considerably exceed in magnitude the initial direct effects. Indeed any study purporting to show the economic impact made by tourism must attempt to measure the *overall* effect made by the successive rounds of economic activity generated by the initial expenditure. The process has been documented with attention drawn to the strengths, weaknesses and limitations of the various approaches (see, for example, Archer and Fletcher, 1991).

Domestic tourism has somewhat similar economic effects upon the host regions of a country. Whereas, however, international tourism brings a flow of foreign currency into a country, domestic tourism redistributes domestic currency spatially within the boundaries of a country. From the point of view of a tourist region within a country, however, domestic tourism is a form of invisible export. Money earned in other regions is spent within the host region creating additional business revenue, income, jobs and revenue to local government. The process of secondary revenue, income and employment generation within the host region is then the same as for a national economy. The principal difference during these secondary stages, however, is that individual regions within a country are usually less economically self-contained and hence a far greater proportion of the money is likely to leak out of the regional system into other regions. The secondary effects in individual regions are far lower in magnitude than for the national economy as a whole.

Moreover, tourism seems to be more effective than other industries in generating employment and income in the less developed often outlying regions of a country where alternative opportunities for development are more limited. Indeed, it is in these areas that tourism can make its most significant impact. In such places many of the local people are subsistence farmers or fishermen and if they become involved in the tourism industry their household incomes increase by a relatively very large amount. The growth of tourism in such areas may provide also a monetary incentive for the continuance of many local crafts, while the tourist hotels may create a market for local produce. Indeed, the introduction of a tourism industry into such areas can have a proportionally very much greater effect on the welfare of the resident population than the same amount of tourism might have on the more developed parts of the same country.

The development of tourism, especially in a previously underdeveloped part of a country, requires the existence of an infrastructure, as well as hotel accommodation and other facilities specific to tourism. In many cases these utilities are economically indivisible in the sense that, in providing them for the tourism industry, they at the same time become available for the use of local people. Thus in many countries, highways and airfields, constructed primarily to cater for tourism, now provide an access to wider markets for many locally produced goods. Unfortunately, in a lot of cases, however, the local people still receive little direct benefit from these developments. This in essence is a problem of both physical and economic distribution, i.e. of the extent to which, and the speed at which, these facilities should be made more generally available.

As tourism continues to grow in a region it makes increasing demands upon the scarce resources of that area. Land in particular is required and in consequence land prices rise. Farmers and other local landowners are encouraged to sell, with the result that, although they may obtain short-term gains, they are left landless with only low-paid work available. Indeed much of the benefit from higher land prices may accrue to speculators who buy land from the previous owners before it has been scheduled for development. These problems can be overcome, however, if either the land is acquired at an early stage by the government for a fair market price or if the land is rented rather than sold to the developers. Market forces do not necessarily ensure that development keeps pace with demand. There is a need for realistic planning and the effective enforcement of planning regulations to reduce possible conflicts of interest and, where appropriate, to conserve unique and unusual features for the enjoyment of future generations of visitors and residents alike. This is a lesson that has been learned rather late in many developed countries.

Superficially at least the economic 'benefits' of tourism seem self-evident. Yet in recent years several writers have expressed reservations about the nature and size of the benefits attributable to tourism and have become increasingly sceptical about the potentialities of tourism as a tool for development and growth and as a means of maximizing the welfare of the indigenous population.

The problem is essentially one of resource allocation and of whether or not the development of a tourism industry offers the optimum usage of the resources available – in other words an assessment of the costs and benefits of tourism development *vis-à-vis* alternatives.

Cost–benefit analysis

In cost–benefit terms, the economic benefits gained by a recipient country from tourism have been outlined above. Against these benefits have to be offset the economic costs involved. Apart from the purchase of import requirements, the earnings of expatriate workers and the overseas expenses incurred by the foreign companies concerned during both the construction and operating phases of the development, none of which benefits the resident population, the country itself incurs considerable costs internally. The real cost to society of employing resources and factors of production in any one sector, including the construction and operation of hotels and other associated tourism services, is the value of the output which could have been obtained from their use in other sectors of the economy. Since capital and skilled labour are rarely, if ever, abundant in such countries, the development of a tourism industry requires some of these scarce resources to be diverted from their alternative uses. Admittedly, some factors of production might otherwise be unemployed, in which case their use in tourism involves no real cost to society, but in most cases the opportunity cost incurred is the value of the production lost in other sectors.

Whether or not tourism creates greater net benefits to society than other forms of development depends primarily upon the nature of the country's economy and what alternative forms of development are practicable. Also, in the interests of diversification it is sometimes considered desirable to promote several forms of development even though one or more of these may offer relatively lower net benefits.

Issues requiring further research

Despite the plethora of economic analyses undertaken during the past twenty years, economists have not displayed any noticeable propensity to work jointly with specialists from other disciplines in multi-disciplinary teams. Their contribution to such work has normally consisted of analyses undertaken in parallel but not jointly with other specialists.

- A more balanced view of the economic effects of tourism demands a deeper understanding of the human issues surrounding the impact made by tourism. This requires joint work by economists, sociologists, political scientists and others. In particular, economists should work more closely with sociologists in analysing and quantifying the social costs and benefits of tourism
- The long-term advantages and disadvantages of tourism can be better understood if economists work more closely with environmentalists as well as specialists in the various humanities. At present economists are not contributing fully to the current debates on sustainable, alternative and responsible tourism, discussed later in this chapter,
- The economic analysis of tourism will be improved if more economists apply their efforts to improving the methodology of existing techniques rather than merely replicating them in a succession of case studies. There is an especial danger that replication of economic impact studies in isolation will simply fuel the call for development in destinations and omit considerations of other costs.

In addition to the economic costs and benefits already mentioned, tourism also imposes political, cultural, social, moral and environmental changes upon the host country. Although such costs are rarely quantifiable in money terms, they must be taken into account in the process of decision-making. Tourism, however, is not alone in generating such 'costs' and it is likely that other forms of development may create far more adverse side-effects which more than offset any advantages they may possess over tourism in purely economic terms. Analysing such effects is properly the province of experts in each field, but it is appropriate here to share some thoughts to stimulate future discussion.

Political effects

The political costs and benefits of tourism

Whereas the virtues of international tourism have been extolled as a major force for peace and understanding between nations (World Tourism Organization, 1980, 1982), the reality is often far removed from this utopian image. Long-haul travel between developed and developing countries is increasing annually and is bringing into direct contact with each other people from widely different backgrounds and with very contrasting life styles and levels of income. Where these disparities are very great the political as well as the socio-cultural consequences may be severe.

In extreme cases international tourism has imposed a form of 'neo-colonial' type development upon emerging nations. Quite simply, this neo-colonialism takes power from the local and regional levels and concentrates it into the hands of multi-national companies. These companies will negotiate only at the national level and expect any 'problems' to be solved by national governments, otherwise investment will be withdrawn. At the operational level, the higher paid, more 'respectable' posts in hotels and other establishments are sometimes occupied by expatriates who possess the necessary expertise and experience, while the lower paid, more menial jobs are frequently reserved for the indigenous population. It is possible that such apparent discrimination can foster resentment and can sour international relationships. In extreme cases such development can even inhibit the growth of a national consciousness in a newly independent country.

Domestic tourism, on the other hand, can act as an integrating force strengthening national sentiment. Peoples in outlying areas are traditionally more preoccupied with local village affairs and in consequence sometimes prove easy prey to separatist agitators. If, by travel to other parts of the same country, such people can begin to experience pride in their national heritage, a sense of a national unity may help to prevent regional fragmentation.

In the more developed countries, visits to national historical monuments, stately homes and ancient battlefields form a significant motivation for domestic travel and similar developments are already taking place in other parts of the world. In many developing countries students and groups of schoolchildren travel to other regions of their homelands and such movements of people can do much in the long run to strengthen the political unity of a country. Provided that the individual characteristics and identities of the various regions are not submerged and lost, such travel can benefit both tourists and residents alike.

Unfortunately, contact between peoples of different backgrounds is not always beneficial and may in some cases generate additional cultural, social and moral stresses. While the mixing of people from different regions of a country can produce a better understanding of each other's way of life and a better appreciation of problems specific to particular regions, it can at the same time create misunderstandings and even distrust.

Issues requiring further research

So far political scientists have contributed relatively little to the analysis of tourism and most of the work in this field has been concerned with the situation in particular countries. One noteworthy exception is a paper by Mathews and Richter (1991) which reviews the efforts made by political scientists to apply their special disciplines to the study of tourism. These authors examine first the ways in which many important aspects of tourism involve some of the central concepts of political science, and secondly the contribution which political science can make to the study of tourism. Two major issues in tourism can be addressed by political scientists.

- A fuller understanding of the human impact of tourism upon destination areas can be achieved only by a much greater integration of the work of political scientists with specialists in other disciplines and with tourism practitioners. At present too many political scientists work in a self-imposed isolation and in consequence fail to take into account or misinterpret some of the favourable (and unfavourable) human effects of tourism which lie outside their own expertise and experience.
- Knowledge of the impact of tourism upon many aspects of human life and organization can be improved if more political scientists are willing to use their expertise to study tourism as an independent variable affecting areas of concern in public administration, comparative politics, political theory, international relations and national politics (Richter, 1983). Many of these fields are virgin territory for aspiring young researchers – will they heed the call? Specific work is needed in a variety of areas but particularly welcome would be:
  — studies examining the influence of tourism upon the roots of power in communities and the implications for community-based investment and the integration of tourism into the community;
  — work examining the stage of destination life cycle at which community involvement is most appropriate, and the stages at which communities are most vulnerable to external political and commercial decision-taking; and
  — further examination of policy impact analysis within a tourism context.

Socio-cultural effects

Some socio-cultural costs and benefits

Wide cultural differences occur between different countries and sometimes between different regions within the same country. Indeed the existence of such differences may be one of the principal stimulants of a tourism industry. In some developing countries such traditional cultural behaviour patterns of particular groups of people form one focus of the tourism industry. Sometimes, however, differences in physical appearance and, perhaps more importantly, differences in cultural behaviour between visitors and residents, are so great that mutual understanding is replaced by antipathy.

The problem is exacerbated because tourists are, by definition, strangers in the destination. Their dress codes and patterns of behaviour are different from the residents, and often different from those that the tourist would display at home: inhibitions are shed and the consequent problems of prostitution, drugs, gambling and sometimes vandalism ensue. As strangers, tourists are also vulnerable and fall victim to robbery and crimes perpetrated by the local community who may see these activities as a way to 'redress the balance'.

When the cultural distinctions between the residents and tourists from more prosperous countries and regions are strongly marked, local culture and customs may be exploited to satisfy the visitor, sometimes at the expense of local pride and dignity. Here the issue of staged authenticity is an important one where the host destination is able to convince tourists that festivals and activities in the 'front region' of the destination (public areas such as hotel lobbies or restaurants) are authentic and thus they protect the real 'back region' (resident's homes and areas where local life continues) (MacCannell, 1973). One of the problems of 'alternative tourism' is that the tourists are encouraged to penetrate this 'back region'. With good management and planning, however, tourism can provide an impetus for the preservation of ancient cultures, but too often the local way of life degenerates into a commercially organized effigy of its former self. The traditional dances and the skilled craftwork give way to cheap imitations to satisfy the needs of the visitor and to obtain money with the least possible effort. In some cases this is merely an initial response, and later tourism can stimulate high quality revivals of crafts in particular.

In primitive and isolated areas, the arrival of too many visitors can even cause local people to leave their settlements and move to new areas where they can remain undisturbed. To combat this in vulnerable areas such as North American Indian reservations 'governing rules' for visitors have been formulated. In more developed areas, in extreme cases tourism has disrupted completely the way of life of the local people. The institution of the National Park system in some parts of Africa, although justifiable on the grounds of wildlife conservation and tourism, has in some cases seriously affected the hunting and nomadic existence of the local people. The problem is not confined however, to developing countries. In Canada, for example, the creation of parks for outdoor recreation and domestic tourism at Forillon and Gros Morne necessitated the eviction of a number of previous residents and in consequence aroused considerable local opposition.

Insufficient research has been carried out so far to disentangle the social and cultural side-effects of tourism development. Where the cultural and socio-economic backgrounds of the tourists are very different from those of the local population, the results of their intermingling may be favourable but it can be explosive. The so-called 'demonstration effect' of prosperity amidst poverty may create a desire among local people to work harder or to achieve higher levels of education in order to emulate the way of life of the tourists. On the other hand, in many cases the inability of the local people to achieve the same level of affluence may create a sense of deprivation and frustration which may find an outlet in hostility and even aggression.

The merit of social intercourse between tourists and the indigenous population as a means towards fostering better understanding and goodwill between nations has been extolled as a major social benefit obtained from tourism. While this is true in many cases, particularly in those countries where tourists are still comparatively rare, it is certainly not true in many countries where tourists' tastes and habits have proved offensive to particular sectors of the local population. Because of factors such as these, some writers have rejected the term 'demonstration effect' and substituted for it the phrase 'confrontation effect'.

Perhaps the most significant and one of the least desirable byproducts of this 'confrontation' is the effect on the moral standards of the local people. In extreme cases, crime, prostitution, gambling and drug traffic may be imported into the holiday areas from other regions. Many of the social conventions and constraints imposed upon tourists in their home areas are absent when they visit another region, and in consequence their moral behaviour can deteriorate without undue censure. As a result, many local people find that by catering to the needs of their visitors they themselves can achieve a relatively high level of prosperity. While the credit or blame for developments – such as red light districts – can be attributed more to the growth of international tourism than to an increase in domestic tourism, the latter must bear its share of the responsibility.

A critical issue here is the form of contact between host and guest. In the 'enclave' tourism model, so berated by proponents of 'alternative forms of tourism', contacts are controlled and minimal, mainly confined to 'culture brokers' who speak both languages and understand both cultures. It is when the tourist penetrates into the daily lives and homes of the hosts that real exposure of cultural and social differences between the two groups emerge, and problems may occur.

Tourists have been blamed for assisting the spread of venereal disease and AIDS in many countries, but their contribution is probably very small in relation to the part played by the local population. Indeed, visitors themselves do not always emerge unscathed from their interaction with the local community (Petty, 1989). Poor hygienic conditions in many tourist resorts create suitable conditions for the spread of various intestinal diseases, typhoid, cholera and hepatitis. Lack of forethought and igno-rance result in cases of severe sunstroke and skin cancer. Inappropriate

precautions result in infection by the AIDS virus, which already affects
up to 40 per cent of the population of some countries in Africa. Governments, tour operators, airlines and resort operators have a duty to visitors and residents alike to provide adequate information to ensure that
these risks are known and minimized.

Many of the other socio-cultural problems associated with tourism
are related to the degree of intensity of tourism development. Although
difficult to measure, there is a relationship between tourism density and
the growth of local resentment towards tourism. The flow of tourists into
a region increases the densities at which people live and overcrowds the
facilities which tourists share with the local population. Overcrowding
reduces the value of the holiday experience and creates additional strain
for the resident population.

In extreme cases local people may be debarred from enjoying the natural
facilities of their own country or region. Along part of the Mediterranean,
for example, almost half of the coastline has been acquired by hotels
for the sole use of their visitors, and in consequence the local public is
denied easy access to the sea.

Issues requiring further research

The literature on the socio-cultural effects of tourism is quite extensive,
although the majority of the contributions are concerned with specific
cases in particular countries. Among the more general papers are useful
articles by Hasan Zafar Dogan (1989) and Graham Dann and Erik Cohen
(1991).

Dogan provides an interesting analysis in which he shows how the
reactions of the host community to the influx of tourists and the changes
which tourism brings have been quite diverse, ranging from an active
resistance to the complete acceptance and even adoption of the tourists'
culture patterns. He shows how the choice of strategies, deliberate or
otherwise, to cope with the changes depends upon both the nature of the
socio-cultural characteristics of the host community and the magnitude
of the changes themselves. His conclusion is that even a previously
homogeneous community that adopts a particular response to tourism
will itself become diversified and groups will emerge within the community exhibiting very different responses to tourism developments.

Dann and Cohen are concerned with the contribution which the
discipline of sociology can make to the understanding of the tourism
phenomenon. Different perspectives on tourism have been adopted by
sociologists and in consequence this has led to the emergence of a variety
of approaches. Dann and Cohen believe that 'some of the best work in
tourism has been eclectic, linking elements of one perspective with those
of another, rather than opting for an exclusive point of view'.

Two major issues require the attention of sociologists:

- There is a need for many more multi-disciplinary studies where sociologists can contribute the insights of their discipline to the study of particular aspects of the tourism phenomenon or to the analysis of tourism in specific countries and regions. Here there is a clear need for work to examine the social carrying capacity of destinations; work which must be closely linked to community-based models of tourism planning.
- The quantification of the socio-economic costs and benefits of tourism requires the joint efforts of sociologists and economists. At present this work is being carried out almost entirely by economists, who are not always in the best position to identify all of the phenomena requiring quantification or the appropriate weightings to apply to each.

Environmental and ecological effects

The environmental and ecological costs and benefits of tourism

Excessive and badly planned tourism development affects the physical environment of destinations. In many areas the uncontrolled commercial exploitation of tourism has produced unsightly hotels of alien design which intrude into the surrounding cultural and scenic environment. In such cases the architectural design has been planned to meet the supposed wishes of the visitor rather than to blend into the local environment. The effects, moreover, are not solely scenic, since the waste and sewage from these developments are often discharged in an unprocessed form and pollute the rivers and seas of the holiday areas.

Poor and ill-conceived forms of tourism development also destroy irreplaceable natural environments, the true and long-term benefits of which may not have been properly evaluated. Thus for example marshlands and mangrove swamps, which provide both outlets for flood control and also the basic ingredients for local fishing industries, have been drained to create tourist marinas. Water resources needed by local farmers and villages have been diverted for the use of tourists hotels and golf courses and, in some mountainous areas, forests have been depleted to create ski slopes with much resultant soil erosion, flooding and, in a recent case, mudslips causing substantial loss of life and damage to property.

Furthermore, the tourists themselves are often guilty of helping to destroy the surrounding environment. In many areas tourists sometimes ignorantly, sometimes deliberately, damage crops and farm equipment, frighten farm animals and bestrew large quantities of garbage over the countryside. From one mountain alone in Great Britain during the summer months, almost a ton of litter a day is brought down from the summit, while from the New Forest in southern England approximately 25,000 empty bottles are retrieved each year.

In other areas wildlife has been severely disturbed, coral reefs have been despoiled and alien forms of plant life have been introduced into delicate ecosystems on the shoes and clothing of visitors.

Lest the picture appear too bleak, it should be remembered that tourism, both domestic and international, is at the same time a positive force in helping to conserve the environment of the holiday regions. Many of the disadvantages mentioned above can be offset by high quality planning, design and management and by educating tourists to appreciate the environment. Tourists are attracted to areas of high scenic beauty, regions of historical and architectural interest and areas with abundant and interesting wildlife. Some of the money spent by tourists in the region, in particular the revenue received from entry fees, can be used to conserve and improve the natural and man-made heritage (as is the case for example, in the Kenyan game reserves).

The extent and nature of the environmental and ecological damage done by tourists is related to the magnitude of the development and the volume of visitors, the concentration of usage both spatially and temporally, the nature of the environment in question, and the nature of the planning and management practices adopted before and after development takes place.

The literature abounds with good and bad practices. What is possible in any one instance depends upon the nature of the destination area and the aims and objectives of the host community. Unfortunately, in the past too little attention has been given to the wishes of the local population. Decisions are taken too often by politicians and planners in terms of their perception of the national rather than the local interest. In this their views are often influenced by the opinions of financiers and developers whose primary concern is the financial return on their investment.

In recent years, however, many academics have increasingly devoted their efforts towards the environmental problems in destination areas created by the rapid expansion of world tourism and the opening up of new tourist areas. This has resulted in the growth of new terminologies, some of which confuse rather than clarify the issues.

Environmental issues

There is obviously a need for research to examine the environmental impact of tourism. In particular, environmental indicators should be developed for use in cost–benefit analysis and also to allow environ-mental standards to be devised at destinations to assist consumers in their choice. Already, the WTO has embraced this concept and commis-sioned work in the field. It is therefore implicit in this trend that plan-ning for tourism will be undertaken. Here the 'planning in' of the environmental , social and cultural context of tourism at the destination (in terms of using local architectural styles etc.) is vital. In other words, the relationship between tourism and the environment is mediated by planning and management. These tourism planning and management techniques exist and are well tried in many areas. What is necessary is for the barriers to planning and management, which exist in many areas, to be removed to allow the existing techniques to be applied effectively. A major stumbling block here is the privatization of many public tourist agencies and the deregulation of planning in some Western nations. A future issue to consider will be the development of new financing mod-els to ensure continuity of funding for privatized agencies who perform a regulatory role.

A critical issue in the 1990s therefore will be the relationship of tourism and the environment. The environment is moving into centre stage in the debate, as evidenced by the discussion on tourism in the 1992 Rio de Janeiro Earth Summit. Here, while the excesses of tourism development were identified, the alliance of tourism with environmentalists to sensitize tourists to the issues was also recognised. It is this issue which forms the next section of this chapter.

Sustainable development and responsible consumption of tourism

This chapter has reviewed the key elements of the positive and negative impacts of tourism. As mentioned in the introduction, it is only in recent years that the negative 'downstream' effects of tourism on environments, societies and vulnerable economies have been set more fully against the tangible economic gains. Add to this the rise of environmentalism and 'green' consciousness in the mid to late 1980s, and the stage was set for a reassessment of the role and value of tourism. In part, this is also a reflection of the growing maturity of both the tourist as consumer and the tourism industry itself. In the early decades of mass tourism, short-term perspectives prevailed as the industry and public agencies attempted to cope with burgeoning demand. In the 1980s and 1990s growth rates have slowed and tourists are increasingly questioning some of the ex-cesses of tourism development. In response, longer planning horizons are being considered and new forms of tourism advocated as industry and governments slipstream behind public opinion and media attention given to these issues.

One of the most valuable results of this reassessment has been the belated discovery of the relevance of the sustainable development concept to tourism (see for example Farrell and Runyan, 1991; Pigram, 1990). As with many service industries, some of the most important ideas and innovations come from outside the industry or the subject area. The concept of sustainable development has a long pedigree in the field of resource management and, at last, is becoming an acceptable term in tourism. The Brundtland Report puts it simply as 'meeting the needs of the present without compromising the ability of future generations to meet their own needs' (World Commission on Environment and Development, 1987). The concept of sustainability is central to the reassessment of tourism's role in society. It demands a long-term view of economic activity, questions the imperative of continued economic growth, and ensures that consumption of tourism does not exceed the ability of a host destination to provide for future tourists. In other words, it represents a trade-off between present and future needs. In the past, sustainability has been a low priority compared with the short-term drive for profitability and growth, but, with pressure growing for a more responsible tourism industry, it is difficult to see how such short-term views on consumption can continue long into the 1990s. Indeed, destination 'regulations' are being developed in some areas and already the band-wagon for sustainable development and responsible consumption is rolling. Public agencies are issuing guidelines for acceptable development (see, for example English Tourist Board, 1991); tourism consumer groups are growing in number and influence (Botterill, 1991) and guides to responsible tourism are available (Anscombe, 1991; Wood and House, 1991). As a philosophical stance or a way of thinking, it is difficult to disagree with the concept of sustainable tourism development and responsible consumption of tourism. But a little knowledge is a dangerous thing and some commentators have oversimplified the complex relationship between the consumption and development of tourism resources. This is particularly true of the so-called 'alternative' tourism movement which is lauded by some as a solution to the ills of mass tourism. Indeed, the tenor of much of the writing about alternative tourism is that any alternative tourism scheme is good while all mass tourism is bad. Butler (1990) provides a useful characterization of the two extremes, while Wheeler (1991, 1992) provides telling criticism of alternative tourism. There is, of course, a case for alternative tourism, but only as another form of tourism in the spectrum. It can never be an alternative to mass tourism, nor can it solve all the problems of tourism.

A variety of issues emerges from these trends. It is important to disseminate cases of good practice in sustainable/responsible tourism, and

to draw out generalities from these cases. In this way, responsible behaviour may pervade the provision and consumption of tourism and
displace the more extreme calls for 'politically correct' tourism development. It must be recognized that the relationship of economics to
environmental and social issues and policies in tourism is a complex one.
Often economic policy is determined at the regional or national level, yet
the impact of that policy is felt at local level on environments and societies
(Hough and Sherpa, 1989). Good models of community participation and
planning in tourism are still rare and those that exist should be given
greater prominence (Haywood, 1988; Murphy, 1985). But it must also be
recognized that tourism takes place in many different social and political
contexts and what works in one place, may need adaptation for another.
This also applies to the borrowing of concepts and techniques from other
subject areas and industries. Nevertheless, tourism has much to learn
from others. In particular, techniques of environmental management,
visitor planning and management, and studies of visitor/environment
relationships are well developed in the recreation literature, and are just
as applicable to tourism (Cooper, 1991). In particular, recreational managers are much more advanced in their use of the notion of 'capacity'
than are tourism planners (Barkham, 1973).

Perhaps the central issue emerging from this section is the gradual
shift from short-term to longer-term thinking and planning in tourism –
it is no longer acceptable for the industry to exploit and 'use up' destinations and then move on. In addition there is an urgent need for tourism
to sharpen up its terminology (alternative? responsible? soft tourism?), to
think clearly about the implications of sustainable/responsible initiatives
and to develop a code of business ethics.

Conclusions

Over the past twenty years, both the planning and marketing of tourism
have been primarily orientated towards the needs of the tourist and the
provision of interesting tourist experiences. This attitude has its basis
first in the need of developers and operators to attract large numbers of
visitors and hence ensure an adequate financial return on their investments and operations, and secondly in the desire of politicians and
planners to maximize the financial benefits from tourism for their country or region. For both parties the primary concerns have been how
many tourists will come, how can we attract more and what facilities and
services will they require?

Fortunately the climate of thought is changing, albeit slowly. Increasingly politicians and planners are becoming aware of the longer-term

social, economic and environmental consequences of excessive and badly planned tourism expansion. It is crucial if the adverse effects are to be prevented or remedied that politicians and planners should become *less* preoccupied with increasing the number of visitors (and indeed with volume as a yardstick of success) and devote more consideration to the long-term welfare of the resident population.

Key questions to be considered are:

- First, how many and what type of tourists does the resident population of an area wish to attract?
- Secondly, what is the optimum number of tourists that the area can support in terms of its physical, environmental and social carrying capacity?
- Thirdly, how can these tourists contribute to the enhancement of the life styles of the residents?

Planning for the resultant impact necessitates a careful definition of the respective responsibilities of the public and private sectors. Planning should be designed to maximize the economic and social benefits of tourism to the resident population, while at the same time mitigating or preferably eliminating the adverse effects. In the past most of this type of planning has been remedial – it has taken place after much development has occurred. In the future planners must take a more proactive role in controlling the nature of such development in terms of stricter building and design regulations, controlled access to vulnerable sites and attractions, strict transport regulations, especially in core areas, and the use of entry fees, barriers and designated routes for vehicles and pedestrians alike.

Tourism creates both positive and negative effects in the destination country or region. Thoughtful policy-making and planning can do much to minimize or even remove the negative effects. Tourism can be a very positive means of increasing the economic, social, cultural and environmental life of a country. The major issue now is can politicians, planners and developers rise to the challenge and create a truly responsible tourism industry – one which brings long-term benefits to residents and tourists alike without damaging the physical and cultural environment of the destination region?

References

Anscombe, J. (1991) The gentle traveller. *New Woman*, June, pp. 51–3
Archer, B.H. (1977) *Tourism Multipliers: The State of the Art*, University of Wales Press, Cardiff

Archer, B.H. and Fletcher, J.E. (1991) *Multiplier Analysis in Tourism*, Cahiers du Tourisme, Centre des Hautes Études Touristiques, Université de Droit, D'Economie et Des Sciences, Aix-en-Provence

Barkham, J.P. (1973) Recreational carrying capacity. *Area*, **5**(3), 218–22

Botterill, T.D. (1991) A new social movement: tourism concern, the first two years. *Leisure Studies*, **10**(3), 203–17

Bryden, J.M. (1973) *Tourism and Development*, Cambridge University Press, Cambridge

Butler, R. (1990) Alternative tourism: pious hope or Trojan Horse? *Journal of Travel Research*, Winter, pp. 40–5

Cooper, C.P. (1991) The technique of interpretation . In *Managing Tourism* (ed. S. Medlik), Butterworth-Heinemann, Oxford, pp. 224–30

Dann, Graham and Cohen, Erik (1991) Sociology and tourism. *Annals of Tourism Research*, **18**(1), 155–69

Dogan, Hasan Zafar (1989) Forms of adjustment: socio-cultural impacts of tourism. *Annals of Tourism Research*, **16**(2), 216–36

Eadington, William R. and Redman, Milton (1991) Economics and tourism. *Annals of Tourism Research*, **18**(1), 41–56

English Tourist Board (1991) *The Green Light, a Guide to Sustainable Tourism*, ETB, London

Farrell, B.H. and Runyan D. (1991) Ecology and tourism. *Annals of Tourism Research*, **18**(1), 26–40

Getz, D. (1983) Capacity to absorb tourism: concepts and applications for strategic planning. *Annals of Tourism Research*, **10**(2), 239–63

Haywood, K.M. (1988) Responsible and responsive tourism planning in the community. *Tourism Management*, **9**(2), 105–18

Hough, J.L. and Sherpa, M.N. (1989) Bottom up versus basic needs. *Ambio*, **18**(8), 434–41

Mathews, Harry G. and Richter, Linda K. (1991) Political science and tourism. *Annals of Tourism Research*, **18**(1), 120–35

Mathieson, A. and Wall, G. (1982) *Tourism Economic, Physical and Social Impacts*, Longman, London

MacCannell, D. (1973) Staged authenticity: arrangement of social space in tourist settings. *American Journal of Sociology*, **79**, 586–603

Murphy, P. (1985) *Tourism, A Community Approach*, Routledge, London

O'Reilly, A.M. (1986) Tourism carrying capacity. *Tourism Management*, **7**(4), 254–8

Petty, Richard (1989) Health limits to tourism development. *Tourism Management*, **10**(3), September, 209–12

Pigram, J. (1990) Sustainable tourism policy considerations. *Journal of Tourism Studies*, **2**(3), 2–9

Richter, Linda K. (1983) Tourism politics and political science: a case of not so benign neglect. *Annals of Tourism Research*, **10**(3), 313–35

Smith, V. (1977) *Hosts and Guests: an Anthropolgy of Tourism* University of Pennsylvania Press, Philadelphia

Wheeler, B. (1991) Tourism's troubled times. *Tourism Management*, **12**(2), 91–6

Wheeler, B. (1992) Is progressive tourism appropriate? *Tourism Management*, **13**(1), 104–5

Wood, K. and House, S.L. (1991) *The Good Tourist*, Mandarin, London
World Commission on Environment and Development (1987) *Our Common Future*, Oxford University Press, New York
World Tourism Organization (1980) *Manila Declaration on World Tourism*, WTO, Madrid
World Tourism Organization (1982) *Acapulco Document*, WTO, Madrid

7 Face to face: the socio-cultural impacts of tourism

Edmund Swinglehurst

Any meeting of people has a rub-off effect on those involved in the encounter. In some cases, when the two people have a similar cultural background and a knowledge of each other's language, the communication is verbal. In most cases it is a silent dialogue of the kind described by Martin Buber the philosopher – a communication by look, gesture and general manner of behaviour. This most universal kind of communication is particularly related to travellers and the natives of the regions they visit, for the impact of their meeting is usually brief and superficial.

In spite of this, however, travellers carry away powerful images of places they visit and the native resident receives a strong impression of the traveller and his ethos. One has only to read the opinions of travellers of the period of the Grand Tour to glean a fairly vivid impression of a traveller and his attitudes and perhaps an idea, though distorted by the traveller's prejudices, of the land he travelled in.

The eighteenth century in England was the era of the landed gentry and the *parvenu* gentry, families who had benefited from the redistribution of Church and royalist lands since the time of Cromwell and other families who were becoming rich on slavery and the West Indian trade. These new rich families with little cultural heritage of their own were eager to demonstrate their support for the classical and Renaissance traditions of Europe. It was they therefore who became the Grand Tour clientele, sending their sons round Europe accompanied by a tutor who was supposed to help young men to complete their education.

Of all the countries of the Grand Tour it was Italy that commanded most of their attention, for Italy was the home of both Classical and Renaissance culture. This aspect of it was communicated by cultured English travellers, who probably stayed in the villas of other wealthy Englishmen or the British Embassy. One of these was Edmund Burke, who wrote to a friend in 1791, 'It is a sort of Native Land to us all; as our earliest ideas are from antient (sic) Italy, and some of our pleasantest amusements from the modern.' The modern amusements were no doubt opera and the *commedia dell'arte*.

The effect of the cult of Italian culture on the tourist was to engender in him an intellectual snobbery which was reflected in Dr Johnson's famous comment that, 'A man who has not been in Italy is always conscious of an inferiority, from his not having seen what it is a man should see.' The grand objective of travel in his opinion was to see the shores of the Mediterranean, but he did not mean literally the beaches, which are the attraction for tourists today, that came later.

In the quotes from Burke and Johnson one finds two of the fundamental socio-cultural effects of tourism until recent times. On the one hand admiration for the treasures of the past, and on the other a feeling of superiority felt by those who travelled over those who had not.

The common people

At the time there was little real contact between the well-off English traveller and the ordinary people of the countries they visited. Their friends were people of the same cultural level as themselves, and the others whom they met were servants, postillions, innkeepers, boatmen etc. Contacts with the plebs did not inspire the same feelings as those with people of the traveller's standing, as Samuel Sharp's 'Letters from Italy' reveal. 'Give what scope you please to your fancy and you will never imagine half the disagreeableness that Italian beds, Italian cooks, Italian post-horses, Italian postillions and Italian nastiness offer to an Englishman in an autumnal journey; much more to an English woman.'

Thus early on in the days of European tourism, in which the English were pioneers, one sees three attitudes to travel which are still prevalent today, securely established. Though these attitudes prevailed throughout the nineteenth century they also became modified and changed by other factors. The eighteenth century English traveller it seems was basically a chauvinist; he was convinced of the superiority of his race and he was aggressive when travelling on the Continent because he was unused to it, having rarely set foot outside his fortress island.

Most of his vitriol was reserved for the French, whose rivalry in the Atlantic trade was a thorn in the flesh to English merchants. 'They have not even the implements of cleanliness,' complained Tobias Smollett in 1766. When he complimented Dr Johnson on his dictionary and told him of the French failure to produce one as good – Johnson replied, 'Why what would you expect of fellows that eat frogs?'

The Napoleonic Wars did little to improve an Englishman's opinion of the French, but the French Encyclopédistes did. Jean Jacques Rousseau, actually born in Geneva, coined the famous phrase, 'Man is born free and everywhere he is in chains', and was the founder of the idea of the goodness of natural man and thus the inspiration for the love of Nature which imbued the Romantic spirit of the nineteenth century. Romanticism was the mainspring of nineteenth century travel, the socio-cultural *raison d'être* for tours to the Alps, to lakeland regions and to anywhere where there were ruins of the past, and if the ruins were covered in ivy or lay alongside gorges or near waterfalls, so much the better. The cult of nature came to a head in Switzerland and was enhanced by the English traveller's vision of the country's legendary love of freedom. 'Oh happier Switzerland,' wrote Ann Seward in 1785, 'as yet tis thine. To see bright Liberty triumphant shake Her radiant Aegis on thy craggy shrine.'

Natural beauty and freedom – what better ideals than these for a nation that had defeated Napoleon and was helping to liberate the countries of the old Spanish Empire?

Cooks tours

The English travellers flocked to Europe with a new confidence in themselves, and among them were a new class of travellers, the Cooks tourist.

Thomas Cook had begun his tourist business by taking his fellow workers on excursions to get them away from the demon drink. As his skill as an excursion agent grew he began tours to Europe in 1855 and found new clients among the new middle classes that the industrial affluence of Britain was creating. By the 1860s Cooks tourists were flooding into Europe and, in particular, to Switzerland and Italy where they were regarded as a plague by the well-to-do English who regarded these countries as their private playground.

Cornelius O'Dowd, Her Majesty Queen Victoria's Consul in Italy, expressed their feelings, 'Some unscrupulous man had devised the project of conducting some forty or fifty persons, irrespective of age and sex, from London to Naples and back for a fixed sum,' he wrote, 'anything so uncouth I never saw before.' The old snobbery of travel was raising its head once again, as it would continue to do for the next hundred years, though with diminishing force.

Thomas Cook had started something which would have a shattering effect on the socio-cultural aspects of travel. He had removed travel from the realm of privilege for the educated and affluent classes of society and put it within the reach of all. Not quite all, but that would come.

Tourist communications

The early tourists of the eighteenth and nineteenth centuries had no ambition to communicate with the people of the countries they travelled in. In fact, judging from the evolution of Thomas Cook's tours one might assume that most tourists wished to be protected from contact with the peoples of the countries they travelled; they were surrounded by servants, they travelled in reserved trains and on private steamers, and even as the cult for romantic nature began to wane, they seemed to want to be protected from the countries as well.

Charles Dickens, instead of waxing lyrical about Switzerland's craggy mountains, notes 'The land of wooden houses, innocent cakes, thin butter soup and spotless little inn bedrooms with a family likeness to dairies'; Mark Twain, in *A Tramp Abroad*, says bluntly, 'Switzerland is simply a large, humpy, solid rock, with a thin skin of grass stretched over it.'

Things were changing; the tourist of the late nineteenth century was beginning to cease to be awed by the scenery which had once impressed the world when travel was still a novelty. Even Ruskin, the great lover of Italian culture and especially of Venice, wrote, 'whereas Rogers say "There is a glorious city in the sea," a truthful person must say, "There is a glorious city in the mud." '

The late nineteenth century traveller was beginning to sound suspiciously like the one that would invade Europe in ever-increasing numbers in the twentieth.

Two-way communication

The rich – and to native people of poor countries all travellers were rich – English and American travellers may have looked upon the tourist world they travelled in as a vast showplace and may have communicated their opinions to their fellow countrymen, but what communication was there between themselves and the host population?

At first examination of the records one might think there was none, but here we should stop and consider that silent dialogue of which Buber wrote. Whatever impression the early travellers recorded of their journeys abroad, these were mainly gained from observations seen through the glass of prejudice. Apparently unappetizing food, low standards of living and bad manners are often a matter of ignorance of the circumstances of the country that arouses these reactions in a tourist's mind. These are opinions of prejudiced minds lacking in understanding, but on the other hand the native's view of the tourists was just as mistaken. Because the standards of living and education of tourist and native were so different, a correct view of each other was almost impossible.

In some respects the socio-cultural gap was too great to bridge, but in others communication between tourist and native, between the advanced industrial nations of the north of Europe and America and the impoverished nations of the Mediterranean region was beginning to occur. The tourist visitors could not help being aware of the conditions of life among the people of the places they visited – the condition of the poor in Naples and Palermo, in Cairo and Damascus – while in part encouraging them to congratulate themselves on the state of education and the application to work in their countries, poverty also aroused humanitarian feelings. Tourists were free with their largesse and contributed generously to such projects as the Cooks Luxor Hospital and the grants to schools and libraries which would enable the poor and illiterate to strive for the standards achieved in Britain and America. On the whole the tourists treated their servants better than their local masters. The conditions which they found in the country they visited aroused in tourists the kind of paternalism which was developing in the industrial ambience of their own countries. If this was a bit patronizing, the local people seemed unaware of it.

To the native the tourist was a godsend; he provided work, was generous with his money and his sympathies could be easily enlisted by manipulating his sense of guilt at being so much better off than the native. Not the ideal platform for communication but better than none.

To the people who lived in tourist regions the tourist was someone as far removed from them as their local ruler. The idea that society could change, that it was possible to move from one class to another, never occurred to them. That would come later. However, they observed the behaviour of the tourists and some began to emulate them; there was some social cachet in behaving like the milord *inglese*.

The tourists did not behave well according to our present ideas. They carried shotguns and aimed at every animal in sight; they scratched their names on the frescoes in Italian churches, in Greek temples and Egyptian tombs; they chipped pieces off ancient ruins. It did not occur to them that these neglected stones had any value to the people who made no effort to maintain them.

The native people watching the tourists took in their behaviour and set about providing the tourists with the souvenirs they sought. Then, as they became aware of the value of their ruins, they began to care for and protect them. Thus tourists had a socio-cultural effect on archaeology and the preservation of ancient monuments, albeit an indirect one.

Until the Second World War this tourist interaction between visitor and host country went on unnoticed. There were not enough people involved to make it worthwhile to record the effects of the tourists on the populations of the countries they visited, but a change was taking place which would have its effect later.

Mass tourism

After the Second World War the idea that everyone who worked should have a holiday with pay finally arrived. There had been talk of this in the British Parliament since the turn of the century. When it happened it transformed a market of about two million potential tourists into one of over twenty million. Gradually, encouraged by travel agents, the mass began to move. They streamed across the Channel to escape from the austerity of their own country to France, Switzerland, Northern Italy and Northern Spain – the limit of a journey by rail for a week or fortnight's holiday.

When jet aircraft released the turbo-prop fleets of European airlines for charter, the boundaries were extended to the southern shores of the Mediterranean. A new era of mass travel had begun, and a new and powerful socio-cultural effect on both tourist and native population.

At first the tourists tended to follow the same pattern of life as their predecessors. They travelled ostensibly to see the historic sights and the beauty spots; Italy and Switzerland were high on everyone's list of priorities. In the 1950s proportionately higher numbers of tourists arrived here and in France than elsewhere but the air travel of the 1960s opened up the coasts of Spain.

The total numbers of tourists were rising rapidly, as shown below:

	1948	1970
Austria	149,041	6,157,888
France	2,028,000	6,971,000
Italy	1,590,033	10,066,571
Switzerland	1,683,217	5,879,636
Spain	456,000	7,000,000

Spain – with its undeveloped coast and low cost of living – was however outstripping the rest, and what was more it was heralding an entirely new era in the socio-cultural aspects of travel. The accent from now on would be not on culture and scenery but, as the *Sunday Times* put it, 'SEA, SAND, SUN and SEX'. The age of travel hedonism had arrived.

Spain

The rapid rise of tourism in Spain, a country which had been lagging behind the socio-cultural developments in the rest of Europe, provides a classic example of the effect of mass tourism.

From 1950 to the 1960s main tourist means of arrival was the train. Special chartered trains arrived in Barcelona and their passengers spread along the Costa Brava and went by ship to the Balearic Islands. From 1960s onwards they arrived in ever-increasing numbers and the development of the Spanish 'Costas' got under way.

Earlier tourists had always visited the famous inland historic centres, Madrid, Segovia, Seville, Grenada; the tourists from 1950 onwards headed for the coasts. Here they found villages where the inhabitants still earned their living from fishing and subsistence farming. Simple people, used to a hard life, religious and conservative in their manners and mores. The arrival of millions of visitors from the more liberal countries of northern Europe at first alarmed them and then gradually began to effect a change in their way of life. Brief bathing costumes – which at first scandalized the natives of the seaside villages, and even provoked threats of arrest – were accepted, so was the familiar behaviour of young men and women unaccompanied by the chaperones who still survived in Spanish society. Magazines showing scantily clad women, at first prohibited, began to appear at newspaper kiosks. The hotels began to reduce the amount of olive oil and garlic in their cuisine and develop what came to be known as the international menu.

Young Spaniards observing the behaviour of the visitors began to copy it; a socio-cultural age gap rapidly became noticeable in Spanish society. The visitors on their side were perplexed at what they found in Spanish society; they were too young to know about Victorian England and it amazed them that a society that worried about bathing costumes should also be a society with open café prostitution and brothels. Spain was the arena for the first mass confrontation between two cultural attitudes, one based on liberal values for all, including women, and one dominated by males, the army and the Catholic Church. The encounter was a good-humoured one because most of the Spaniards involved in the new tourist industry which was spreading round their coasts were enjoying the money that was reaching them and a new freedom. Poor fishermen were becoming launch pilots and casting off their faded denims and donning colourful shirts; drivers of ancient cars were becoming owners, on credit, of new buses; shopkeepers selling meagre and ancient haberdashery were filling their shops with colourful souvenirs. Moreover the males were enjoying the adulation of romantic ladies from northern Europe and America who had read Hemingway and thought that every Spaniard was a matador.

Everyone was having a good time, and that became the main reason for a holiday.

And the rest . . .

The Spanish effect was being felt in other parts of the Mediterranean too, and as the jet aircraft flights became cheaper, in other parts of the world. The effect was more than a surface change in manners and mores, for it gave the natives of holiday countries a taste of freedom which began to spread into other levels of their lives.

Mediterranean countries had largely remained in the social world of Britain's early nineteenth century. Society was divided into the rich and their circle, and the poor. There was no middle class such as that which had formed in Britain towards the end of the century and which provided Thomas Cook with his Continental tourists. The arrival of mass tourism awoke in the hard-working Mediterranean poor the notion that they were being exploited. One way in which this was brought home to them, and which shows an amusing insight into how ideas change through tourist communication, was a result of the preponderance of female over male visitors. The local young men, anxious to take the young visitors dancing at night, were irked at being prevented from doing so owing to their long working hours. The result was a protest to their employers, threats of strike etc., which led to a change in their work schedules.

This is only one example of similar changes brought about by the grass roots communication between tourists and natives of tourist countries. The desire for freedom for personal reasons also led to a more ideological demand for freedom which spilled over into every aspect of social life, including politics. In countries where political, religious and social beliefs are considered essential to the unity of the State, the liberalism of tourist attitudes is not welcome. On the other hand tourist foreign exchange is, and this dichotomy is one of the unresolved problems of the socio-cultural aspect of tourism in many countries today.

Culture or philistinism?

In examining the socio-cultural effect of tourism we have so far taken this to mean the effect on the general cultural basis of a society, its manners and mores and not its culture in the sense of aesthetics. Culture in this sense was, of course, one of the main motives for travel from the time of the Grand Tour until the time of mass travel.

Classical history, Bible history, Egyptian history, the Renaissance were the motivation of most tours and the claim to consider oneself a cultured person. The arrival of mass travel made the pursuit of pleasure the main motivation for a holiday. To some this seems like a new philistinism, an indifference to the bases of Western civilization and a dedication to a thoughtless hedonism, the cult of the sun, drink and souvenir shopping. Instead of lecture tours of ancient ruins it appears that more and more tourists are deriving their entertainment from theme parks, oceanariums, centre parks and Disneyland. Certainly the early tourists had none of these distractions. They read their Baedekers, ate large meals and wrote their journals or made water-colour sketches.

Times have changed and the purely cultural aspect of travel is fading, or is it? In terms of the total number of world tourists the numbers who visit the Uffizzi or the Acropolis have increased enormously since the time of the Victorian tourist. So much so that most historic monuments have to be protected from the tramp of their feet and even from the carbon dioxide they exhale. In France tourists may only visit a copy, but a splendid copy, of the Lascaux caves, in Rome the newly-restored Sistine Chapel is visited by limited numbers.

Interest in cultural things is therefore growing, and helps to establish further an interest in conservation and further archaeological exploration. But a section of the travelling public is not interested, which section is not always easy to define; there are those who enjoy the Acropolis and Disneyland.

One of the noticeable characteristics of tourists as a whole is that those of European origin – once the cultured tourist *par excellence* – tend to be more given to hedonist holidays than overseas visitors to Europe who seek enlightenment from a study of the roots of Western civilization. Perhaps this says something about Western civilization itself.

Whatever the meaning of the phenomenon of the changes in the socio-cultural evolution of tourism, one can safely say that the effect of mass tourism in Europe has been repeated all over the world and changes of one kind or another will go on as face-to-face communication increases from the 500 million travellers of today to the billion forecast for the twenty-first century.

What lies ahead?

Until the 1950s Europe was still the main destination of world travellers, but as the figures (of OECD countries) given in Table 7.1 show, there has been a spectacular growth in travel to other parts of the world since then. Some of the growth, as in the case of the United States, has been due to cross-border travel from neighbouring countries, but most of it is the result of more and cheaper long-haul air services.

Table 7.1 Growth in world travel

	1948	1968	1991
North America			
USA		7,334,327	36,523,904
South America and the Caribbean			
Jamaica	53,470	189,040	1,340,516
Peru	5708	79,065	316,871
Africa			
South Africa	67,098	226,899	1,709,554
Australasia			
Australia	26,171	147,878	2,370,400
Asia			
Hong Kong	15,247	364,065	6,032,081
Japan	6310	352,832	3,532,651

Figures from Tourist Offices and the OECD.

The socio-cultural effect has varied considerably, according to the cultural and economic status of the regions involved. In the USA and Australia, for example, the effect of mass tourism from other countries of a similar socio-cultural background has been negligible except economically. The desire to encourage tourism has led to more investment in tourist amenities and attractions. Many of these have resulted in the enhancement of natural attractions: improved services in national parks, development of sea areas rich in natural life, walking and climbing facilities in mountain regions etc.; but others have been based on the construction of artificial environments: Disneyland, heritage theme parks, wild animal parks, Center Parcs etc. The latter development illustrates the growing demand among modern tourists for imitation in preference to the real thing. In Center Parcs, for example, the tourist – or rather holiday-maker as there is very little travel involved – can at any time of the year enjoy summer temperatures amid streams and waterfalls surrounded by tropical vegetation, all in a sealed environment. In these conditions the tourist can enjoy the perfect conditions of his expectations without the hazards of the real world.

This new trend in travel enjoyment has a parallel in the visual reality of the video world and seems to agree with the view that tourism is, in fact, a form of escape from the real world, at least as far as the leading industrial countries of the Western world are concerned. This direction of a modern tourist's inclination was noted some years ago in the very thorough, though politically orientated book, *The Golden Hordes* by Louis Turner and John Ash, who wrote, 'In an affluent and highly organized industrial society, work tends to lose its dignity and personal significance, and the individual seeks to discover his identity and sense of purpose in his leisure time.'

While this is going on in advanced industrial countries, something different is occurring in the tourist destination countries of the Third World. In these countries the individual wants to emulate the industrial success which enables people to be tourists. There is therefore a desire bred in natives of tourist countries to visit and learn from countries that produce the well-off tourists.

Comparing modern tourism values with the rather earnest ones of the Victorian era, one is aware that something dramatic has happened, a kind of reversal of roles of tourist and native. For hitherto it was the latter who were regarded as the insouciant children of nature with a carefree, fun-loving attitude to life, and the tourists who, Baedeker in hand, were the seekers after knowledge and enlightenment; whereas today it seems that it is the other way round.

Here perhaps lies the irony of the socio-cultural effect of mass travel; the cultural gap between different worlds is gradually closing, tourist and host native are exchanging ambitions and ways of life, while the tourist from the industrial world seeks escape, the native travels to learn how he can satisfy the demands for the good life that he imagines the affluent tourist has achieved.

Sources

Martin Buber, *Silent Dialogues*
Edmund Burke, Letter to Friedrich Ludwig Wilhelm Meyer, 1791
Charles Dickens, *The Uncommercial Traveller*, 1861
Dr Samuel Johnson, *Boswell's Life of Johnson*, 1776
Cornelius O'Dowd (real name Charles Lever), *Blackwood's Magazine*, 1863
Jean Jacques Rousseau, *Contrat social*, 1792
John Ruskin, Letter to Charles Eliot Norton, 1859
Samuel Sharp, *Letters from Italy*, 1767
Tobias Smollett, *Travels through France and Italy*, 1766

Reference

Turner, L. and Ash, J. (1975) *The Golden Hordes. International Tourism and the Pleasure Periphery*, Constable, London

8 Tourist–resident impacts: examples, explanations and emerging solutions

Philip L. Pearce

Conceptual background

The amount, and increasingly, the sophistication of research pertaining to tourist–resident impacts is impressive. It would not be difficult, for example, to cite over 200 articles relating to this area of tourism interest. Conceptually, it is valuable to sort out the intersecting and overlapping research areas of most relevance. At the broad level there is considerable research on the economic, environmental and social effects of tourism which all have general implications for tourist–resident impacts. These areas clearly overlap and may be seen as a set of interlocking envelopes. The topic of tourist–resident impacts is subsumed within the topic area of the social impacts of tourism, but some tourist–resident contacts have clear economic and environmental components, thus placing tourist–resident research at the core of the interconnected themes. Superimposed upon these frames of reference is the distinction between tourist–resident impacts deriving directly from tourists dealing with residents versus tourism the phenomenon influencing resident attitudes and feelings (Figure 8.1).

The present review will concentrate specifically on tourist–resident interaction with a focus on the impacts of this interaction on the residents. Unlike many other reviews of this area, however, some note of the effects of the contact on the tourists themselves will be made.

It is critical to note at the outset that social impacts effects may be *real* in the sense that objective data can be collected to verify their existence (e.g. length of time spent in doing one's shopping) or *perceived* (e.g. the view that there is more crime in the community and life is less safe than

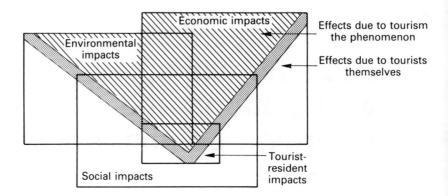

Tourism studies

Figure 8.1 Tourist–resident impacts set within the framework of the social, environmental and economic impacts of tourism and consisting of both broad tourism and specific tourist influences

in the past). From the point of view of assessing community feeling, *real* and *perceived* impacts are equally important. If residents believe an impact exists, then their behaviour will be altered irrespective of the accuracy of the perception. Nevertheless it is valuable to comment on whether impacts are objectively verifiable or subjectively felt, since the tactics for preventing and dealing with social impacts may be different in the two cases. For example, perceived impacts may be changed by the processes of education and community information whereas this is less of an option for objectively verifiable impacts (such as restricted access to a recreation site).

The importance of tourist–resident impacts

Tourist–resident impacts are important not simply from an ethical point of view but also because the international evidence indicates that when negative impacts are ignored there can be some major economic and political repercussions. This *community backlash* may include:

• A loss of support for the authorities/councils which promote tourism.
• An unwillingness to work in the tourism industry.
• A lack of enthusiasm in promoting the tourism product by word of mouth.

- A hostility to the tourists themselves which can be manifested in overcharging, rudeness and indifference to the tourists' holiday experiences.
- Delays in the construction of tourism development because of community protests.

These negative consequences of poor tourist–resident contact have major implications for tourism development in a region. They represent the combined effects of all the smaller consequences of social interaction transformed into political and economic power through community action. It is important to be aware of them, but it may not be possible to alter them quickly, because they represent the culmination of a complex web of community dissatisfaction. In short, while they are highly un-desirable for tourism development purposes, they can best be influenced by understanding the underlying interactions and effects on which they are based.

Variability in tourist–resident studies

Tourist–resident interaction is a specific but diverse example of cross-cultural interaction. Typically, tourists stay in the visited communities for very short and carefully structured periods of time. Their travel motivations set them apart from other inter-cultural sojourners and their affluence compared to the locals is pronounced. These characteristics generate at least two unique features of tourist–host intercultural liaison. First, tourists, as opposed to immigrants, students and foreign workers, do not have to adapt to the local community. For example, tourists are granted immunity from many local legal and cultural restrictions and can traverse the landscape in a small cultural bubble of their own nation-ality (Urry, 1990). Although tourists may experience culture shock, this experience is often confined to the initial stage of that process (Furnham and Bochner, 1986), and may indeed be stimulating and exciting to the traveller, since it can fulfil sensation-seeking motivations. Secondly, the tourists' affluence, even when they are relatively young drifter-nomads (Cohen, 1968) or backpackers (Riley, 1988; Pearce, 1990), locates them in a peculiar sociological niche, that of strangers or outsiders (Simmel, 1950) who are able to observe and scrutinize the visited community. In this review it will be argued that the effects of tourist–resident contact are mediated by the tourists' affluence, motivation, transience and socio-logical status in the host community.

It is important in the context of this chapter to avoid cliches and superficial generalization about the tourist–resident interaction process.

There are many types of tourists with specific motivational and attitudinal profiles. Some of these visitors are intensely interested in interacting with residents while for others the local people are little more than a part of the scenery. Additionally the size and technological sophistication of the host community plays a crucial role mediating the impact of tourism and the nature of the resident–host contact and while the present review seeks generality in the collated results of research, the specific contexts and communities studied must always limit the generalizations which can be made.

Effects

Direct contact influences for isolated and poor communities
Direct contact between tourists and the local people of Third World and poor communities often generates discord, exploitation and social problems.

The simple process of tourists observing or watching the local people can have profound effects. Certain cultural and economic day-to-day activities of ethnic groups seem to appeal to tourists and are promoted as tourist attractions. For example, Smith (1978a) demonstrated that tourists in Alaska walked along the beaches as fishermen and hunters returned to butcher their kill. Smith observed that the locals resented the tourists photographing their activities and in time erected barricades to prevent access to the would-be photographers. In a final attempt to regain their privacy taxis were hired to haul the seals and other game to the Eskimos' homes, where the slaughtering could proceed.

From studies in Tonga, Urbanowicz (1977, 1978) noted that tourists from large cruise ships produced crowded conditions in the small towns and that Tongan children sometimes begged from the visitors at major tourist attractions.

Such observations are not limited to tiny Pacific islands (cf. Cohen, 1982). For instance, the Seychelles islands, promoted to tourists as 'islands of love' because of their traditionally uninhibited sexual standards, now have 'rampant' and 'ferocious' rates of venereal disease (Turner and Ash, 1975). Similarly Bangkok and the Phillipines have reputations for prostitution and the availability of drugs in response to the needs of European, Japanese, American and Australian tourists (Cohen, 1988).

For some small, technologically unsophisticated communities direct contact with tourists, if the latter come in small, manageable numbers, can be psychologically beneficial to the hosts. For example, Sofield (1991) notes that with skilful management the traditional Vanuatu ceremony, the naghol – an event which involves young men leaping from a high tower with a vine rope attached to their ankles – has been strengthened by the commercial importance attached to the event. Restricting the numbers of visitors and requiring certain codes of behaviour seem to be important factors affecting the outcome of direct tourist–host contact (cf. Boissevain, 1979).

Indirect contact effects for isolated and poor communities

Many of the social and psychological contact effects on the local people are of a less direct nature and not all such effects are negative. One of the strongest arguments for the view that tourism can provide social benefits to Third World or technologically unsophisticated communities, is that it can revitalize ethnic arts and traditions. Thus Waters claims, somewhat eulogistically:

> this cultural renaissance is taking place all the way from the grass roots at the village level to the top councils of national governments ... With a modest amount of help, the native craftsman practising a dying art finds a new demand for his product and then employs young apprentices, thus teaching his trade to a new generation. (1966: 116)

One feature of selling local culture to the tourists is often overlooked. Many cultures attach enormous symbolic and spiritual importance to their ceremonies and art objects. Furthermore, an adequate interpretation of these symbolic meanings may require considerable anthropological knowledge on the part of the consuming tourist. Without an understanding of the cosmological significance of cultural activities such as Aboriginal corroborees or Indonesian burials, tourists will merely see these events as 'quaint' or 'pretty' customs (Altman, 1988; Crystal, 1978). This not only trivializes the local event, it also wastes an opportunity for tourists to appreciate the ethnocentrism of their own culture. Worst of all, the more extreme forms of tourist exploitation of local cultural products may make a sacrilege of former religious symbols by marketing them *en masse* (Mackenzie, 1977). This may literally endanger the lives of women and young children of the ethnic groups for whom such objects are traditionally taboo and where sighting these items should be punished by death.

Increasing economic dependence upon tourism may alter the job structure and roles of a community, sometimes creating more new jobs for women than men (cf. Petit-Skinner, 1977). Furthermore, many of these jobs are menial and underpaid, which promotes local frustration and alienation (Kent, 1977). The combined effects of such negative tourist influences have led researchers to postulate empirical indices of tourist–host friction. For example, Hills and Lundgren (1977) proposed an irritation index, which they described as a composite of the myriad forms of friction tourists produce for their hosts. While the researchers did not adequately specify how to evaluate and measure the tourist impact, they did specify some common sources of irritation. They note that in the Caribbean, shop attendants serve tourists first and locals last; inflation due to the tourist presence makes locals pay more for food; access to beaches is cut off by tourist hotels; local commuting time increases; and the crowding of beaches and parks makes traditional, spontaneous cricket games dangerous.

Direct contact effects for technologically advanced communities

One of the major studies of the impacts of tourism to have been conducted in the past few years is the Hawaiian Statewide Tourism Impact Core Survey (Community Resources Inc., 1989). In a special section of the report entitled 'Daily life and attitudes towards visitors' the complexities of resident attitudes to tourists are revealed. Twenty-five per cent of the 3900 residents studied felt that favourite recreation areas had been 'taken over' by tourists in the past five years, yet the very parks and beaches reported to be crowded with tourists were also the residents' favourite places for interacting with tourists. Additionally, 80 per cent of residents said this visitor contact was usually pleasant. Younger residents were more likely to report positive behaviours towards tourists (friendly talks, giving directions) although younger residents in general were somewhat more likely to express anti-visitor sentiments.

The issue of traffic congestion was one direct effect of the tourist presence which was widely reported by different sections of the Hawaiian resident community. In total 83 per cent of all residents reported that traffic was worse than five years ago with 71 per cent in the high density area reporting that it was a big problem in their lives.

The research concludes from its detailed findings that popular opinion about tourism impact in the region should not be confused with residents' views – conventional wisdom was in fact mistaken in several instances, for example tourism industry personnel did not differ appreciably from general residents in their attitudes. The study also attempted to integrate the findings of the report – that is, the mix of seemingly contradictory positive and negative attitudes to tourists and their effects – by suggesting that there is a hierarchy of community needs which explain attitudes to visitors. According to this view jobs are a top priority for individual and community survival. In Hawaii tourism has played a major role in meeting that need for many communities. When the basic needs are met, attention turns to other needs or to the negative tourism side-effects which once seemed less important. Accordingly, the overall view of Hawaii may well be composed of regional views which place different emphases on these community needs, hence producing a blurred total view.

The stimulating detail of the Hawaiian study did not extend to attitudes towards different types of visitors. In an Australian study of a small but high density tourism environment, Ross (1990) notes that some negative perceptions of visitors may develop even when the host culture is relatively affluent. In his analysis of residents in the tropical city of Cairns, he observed that visitors from the United States and, to a lesser extent, domestic Australian visitors, were not as well liked as the more polite Japanese and European visitors. As in the Hawaiian study, the actual detailed research findings did not conform to conventional wisdom, with an expected anti-Asian attitude not confirmed by the data.

Pearce (1980a) and Pi-Sunyer (1978) have noted how quickly local stereotypes of international visitors can emerge and negatively influence the quality of the host-resident encounter. These stereotypes are readily applied when the outgroup is easily identified and their behaviours are distinctive or culturally different, thus promoting prejudice and attributions to nationality rather than to individual personality. Nevertheless, there is a broad consensus that international contact promotes goodwill and that the direct interpersonal encounters soften or modify harsh images of the contact parties (Amir, 1969).

One further perspective on this positive networking of the world's travellers and their hosts is provided in the work on tourism as an industry promoting world peace (d'Amore, 1988). One of the important challenges of future tourism research is to identify those factors that will promote the best social and cultural outcomes of the direct contact between hosts and guests. It would appear that pre-contact mutual education about the social and cultural practices of both societies is one of the promising avenues for engendering more positive attitudes in tourist–resident encounters (Furnham and Bochner, 1986).

Indirect contact effects for technologically advanced societies

A further note in this section on the tourists' impact on local communities concerns the indirect influences of the tourist presence in advanced societies. The maintenance of great houses, the continued existence of zoos, national parks and wildlife reserves all owe some measure of their success to tourist incomes. For many aspects of cultural life, then, the indirect effects of tourists when they visit affluent countries assist the local people (Murphy, 1985).

Nevertheless a number of countries seem to hold a set of assumptions that the impacts of tourism are likely to be negative. For instance, Turner and Ash (1975) observed that Intourist, the Russian travel organization, exerted enormous control over foreign tourists' experiences. Implicit in this structuring of the tourists' experience is the notion that direct tourist–host contact would be prejudicial to the correct perspective of one or both contact parties. Similarly Ritter (1975), in discussing the attitudes of Islamic countries towards foreign tourists, observed that Saudi Arabia, Libya, Iraq and a number of southern Arab states were frankly not interested in having non-Islamic visitors. Again it appears that tourists are viewed as agents of cultural change, with the dress of women, the use of alcohol and the mixing of the sexes being particularly sensitive areas of potential influence (Ahmed, 1992).

Researchers have focused considerable attention on the issue of the costs incurred by local communities to support tourism. For example, fire services, health facilities, roads, water and sewerage facilities are often strained by the increased visitor numbers (Haywood, 1988; Long et al., 1990). In a study typical of this field Allen, Long, Perdue and Kieselbach (1988) report findings from twenty rural communities in Colorado. They found that perceptions of the quality of community life were positively related to the size of the rural community and that only some aspects of community life appear to be sensitive to changes in tourism development. In their rural communities, tourism growth influenced environmental issues, public services (fire, police, roads) and the social opportunities (amount of community contact and participation in organizations), but had little impact on recreation, education and medical facilities. The development of taxation schemes to reflect the true costs of tourism to the community in these economic and environmental terms is now being realized as well as the need to plan for tourism growth in all community and local government development plans (Dredge and Moore, 1992).

Summary: tourist impact on the local people

In summary, tourists appear to have maximum social and psychological impact on their hosts when the host communities are small, unsophisticated and isolated. This impact may be a powerful one, either in direct interpersonal encounters or in subtle, indirect influences on the visited community. When the receiving society is technologically more advanced and the affluence gap between tourists and hosts narrower, the contact experience has less impact. In such instances, tourists may develop friendships with the hosts, and the visitors can sustain local social institutions as well as promoting pride in the visited community. The negative effects are not restricted to interpersonal friction, but also include indirect stress to the hosts through environmental degradation and infrastructure costs.

This overall assessment may appear somewhat negative and, indeed, it must be remembered that tourism can still be compared favourably with many other industries as a source of economic growth with only some social and environmental impacts. This view is confirmed by some studies where residents recognize the impacts of tourism but still support its development compared to other industries (Kinhill Cameron

McNamara, 1990). Furthermore, it must be noted that many studies fail to disentangle the effects of tourism on residents from the effects of growth in general. There is a clear need for more comparative studies like the Colorado research which seek to distinguish tourism impacts from effects due to general increases in population or the parallel growth of other industries (e.g. residential and condominium development).

The effects of intercultural contact on the tourists

There are two views concerning the effects of the travel experience on the tourists themselves. On the one hand international travel is said to promote tolerance and understanding of other cultures. Another view is that 'we travel not that we may broaden and enrich our minds, but that we may pleasantly forget they exist' (Huxley, 1925). This perspective considers the tourist experience to be shallow and inconsequential and hence very unlikely to leave any lasting impression on the traveller.

Social psychological studies of tourist attitude change

An early study of the effects on tourists of intercultural contact is pro-vided by Smith (1955, 1957). Young Americans who spent a summer touring Europe were sent a mail questionnaire, both before and after their travels. Smith reported few attitudinal changes on the scales used, and concluded that deeply rooted attitudes were not affected by the travel experience. For the few subjects who did change their attitudes, Smith argues, following interviews with the travellers, that the change that took place was due more to peer conformity pressures than to some functional personality need of the individual. The brief European ex-cursion had fostered some contacts with the hosts, since most travellers exchanged correspondence and gifts. A follow-up study revealed that in a few cases these relationships persisted for up to four years, but only where intense personal relationships had been established (Smith, 1957).

Another study more directly concerned with assessing tourists' attitudes to the visited nationality was conducted amongst British tourists visiting either Greece or Morocco (Pearce, 1977a). The tourists studied were young members of cheap package tours on two- to three-week tours of either country. A set of questions concerning their travel motivations revealed that they were predominantly interested in relaxing, drinking and having a good time with fellow-travellers in novel, sunny settings, and that they were not particularly motivated by a desire to meet the local inhabitants and study their culture. A group of control subjects who were interested in travel but could not join these particular groups for time-scheduling reasons were used to assess test sensitization and measurement effects in the questionnaire.

Both the travellers to Greece and to Morocco changed their perceptions of the host communities, with the Greeks being evaluated more favourably and the Moroccans less favourably. Additionally, the travellers also saw their own countrymen more positively following their holidays. The finding that tourists can make some small-scale re-evaluations of their own countrymen after travelling abroad parallels findings for students living abroad, who also alter their perceptions of home (Herman and Schild, 1960; Riegel, 1953; Useem and Useem, 1967).

Other kinds of impacts on the tourists may also be discerned. Tourists are subject to particular health risks while travelling and contact with local people may have long-range effects on the tourists' physical well-being (Turner and Ash, 1975). There are also reported cases of psychiatric breakdown amongst tourists (Prokop, 1970). In studies of German tourists visiting Innsbruck, Prokop found several instances of tourist depression, alcoholism and other mental health problems, as recorded by the Innsbruck hospitals. He attributed these behaviours to the high incidence of drinking among the travellers, and argued that the release from day-to-day pressures precipitated the tourists' self-doubts and depression. It is apparent that the advertising images of stress-free holidays are considerably misplaced.

Further evidence that travelling can create problems is provided in the work on life stress by Holmes and Rahe (1967). In scaling stress-related events in an individual's life span from 0 (no stress) to 100 (maximum stress), holidays were given a score of fifteen. This was comparable to such events as changes in working conditions, troubles with one's boss and mortgage stresses. The figure of fifteen may also be an underestimate for international travel where the tourist has to cope with an unfamiliar culture. Europeans typically report that travel is more stressful than do Americans, presumably because they experience more foreign culture contacts by travelling in other European countries (Harmon et al., 1970).

The origins of the social stresses for the tourist in his contact with the local people are numerous. The tourist has problems in locating and orientating himself in the new environment (Pearce, 1977b), and this alone has implications for the travellers' sense of security and emotional well-being (Lynch, 1960). In New York special maps are available to warn tourists of the 'safe, dangerous at night and dangerous all day' areas of the city (Downs and Stea, 1977).

While the tourist is occasionally treated as a special kind of stranger in the community and is helped more by the local people (Feldman, 1968; Pearce, 1980b), the social interaction between tourists and locals is another potent form of stress. The question of language is paramount here. Many tourists find that their inability to communicate with the local people is enormously frustrating, and language difficulties may generate considerable stress when sickness occurs, travel plans go astray or luggage and money are lost (Furnham and Bochner, 1986). The solution for many tourists is to confine their travels to countries where their own language is understood fairly readily or use guides to limit the effects of culture shock (Pearce, 1984).

There are also subtle differences in non-verbal communication between different cultures. For example, the gestures of the locals may confuse the tourist. To the American visiting Sardinia it may be a considerable source of confusion to find that the OK gesture is interpreted as a symbol of homosexuality (Morris et al., 1979). Even the basic nodding of the head for agreement and disagreement has subtle variations. While it is apparent that many universally applicable gestures and emotional expressions exist (Argyle, 1975), some features of interaction with the hosts are likely to be subtly different for the tourists; for instance the use of space may differ. Watson and Graves (1966) found that Americans tend to think Arabs pushy and threatening because of the latter's preference for more direct, closer and intimate interaction. While specialized training procedures may help to overcome these difficulties (Collett, 1971), most tourists are probably unaware of these non-verbal cues until they are confronted with dramatic breakdowns in their interactions.

Some host cultures, finding their visitors to be difficult and socially unskilled from their own perspective, have started to produce pamphlets outlining some of the local cultural rules and norms that tourists should follow. For example, Fiji suggests that visiting Australians should not tip the local people, should learn the correct greeting rituals, should appreciate the polite and reciprocal bonds of friendship, and should not confuse lack of clothing with promiscuity (Fiji Visitors' Bureau, 1975). This kind of educational material is also often contained in guidebooks but the extent to which tourists follow these specific prescriptions is unknown.

Explanation

In trying to understand and order the kinds of studies reviewed above, stage or step models have been popular. For example, Smith (1978b) saw the development of tourism in terms of distinct waves of tourist types; the seven categories, in order of expanding community impact, are shown in Figure 8.2.

Smith's model was directed at cross-cultural contact issues and her pioneering book *Hosts and Guests* contained several studies where social impacts on local communities were directly related to the expansion of tourism. At about the same time as Smith's work was gaining attention from anthropologists encountering tourists in the cultures the researchers had come to study, Doxey (1975) proposed an irritation index or 'irridex' to assess host–guest interactions and relationships. Doxey's scale

Type of tourist	Number of tourists	Community impact
1 Explorer	Very limited	
2 Elite	Rarely seen	
3 Off-beat	Uncommon but seen	
4 Unusual	Occasional	Steadily
5 Incipient mass	Steady flow	increasing
6 Mass	Continuous influx	
7 Charter	Massive arrival	

Figure 8.2 Smith's (1978b) seven categories of tourist

has four steps; euphoria (delight in the contact), apathy (increasing in-difference with larger numbers), irritation (concern and annoyance over price rises, crime, rudeness, cultural rules being broken) and finally antagonism (covert and overt aggression to visitors).

Another stage development model relating to tourism was proposed by Butler (1980). In this model the impacts of tourism are not the direct focus of attention. Instead the model is concerned with the more general issue of the evolution of tourist areas (marketing issues, organization and ownership of the tourist services and attractions), although the attitudes of residents and community support for tourism are discussed as a part of the larger process. Butler sees tourist areas as evolving through the stages of exploration, involvement, development, consolidation, stagnation and then either decline or rejuvenation. In the consolidation stage he sees the emergence of social impacts:

> The large numbers of visitors and the facilities provided for them can be expected to arouse some opposition and discontent among permanent residents. (Butler, 1980: 8)

The stagnation phase where peak numbers of visitors have been reached is seen as follows:

> Capacity levels for many variables will have been reached or exceeded with attendant environmental, social and economic problems. (Butler, 1980: 8)

Stage-based models of individual and social processes invite a number of criticisms, many of which can be directed at these tourism-related models. All three models have poor demarcation between the stages or steps. It is also unclear whether shifting from one stage to another precludes the continued existence of the previous stage. For example, just as children who have moved from crawling to walking may also still crawl, is it the case that tourism communities that have moved from development to consolidation will retain and exhibit many of the features of the development phase or are they necessarily superseded? Additionally, stage models prompt the question of whether or not the order of the stages is invariant. The Doxey and Smith models appear to assume this point but Butler notes that some tourism destinations (he cites the major Mexican resort of Cancun) may move directly into a higher level stage without the proceeding steps. A related question concerns the speed of progression through the resort development or tourism growth stages. Does it matter, in terms of community impact, how quickly the environment has been developed for tourism or is it simply a matter of which stage of development has been reached? Further, in the final stages of the Doxey and Butler models is it the whole community which becomes hostile to tourism or are there only sections of the population who suffer and complain about the social impacts? And finally, one must query whether the whole process of social impacts and tourism evolution as outlined is inevitable, leaving individuals and local groups powerless to confront the forces of economic change and gain.

These questions are more than curious asides to the developing literature on tourism and community effects. One needs to question whether or not the models advanced in the tourism literature to date are really post-hoc descriptive devices or whether they have predictive possibilities. One can conclude that the models discussed are incomplete and simply do not meet the challenges raised in these critical questions. Similarly, despite being widely quoted in the tourism textbooks as the definitive sources on the matters of social and community impact, the evidence to support these models is virtually non-existent (cf. Murphy, 1985).

Nevertheless work on the social impacts of tourism has continued throughout the past decade and while the models reviewed above have been formally cited they have been effectively bypassed. Studies conducted in the 1980s may be summarized under a new banner – a segmentation approach to tourism's social impacts. This work has the following characteristics. It describes in detail resident reactions to the impacts of tourism. In this work, lists of critical social impacts have been constructed, factor analysed, employed in different countries and related to the demographic characteristics of respondents. Typical examples of this approach include the work of Brougham and Butler, 1981; Liu and Var, 1986; Liu, Sheldon and Var, 1987; Long, Perdue and Allen, 1990; Milman and Pizam, 1988; Murphy, 1981, 1985; Sheldon and Var, 1984. Across these studies there is recurring evidence that older residents are more affected by tourism impacts than younger residents, those working in the tourist industry have more positive attitudes and those living closer to the tourist zone have more negative attitudes towards tourism, as do those individuals with higher daily contact with tourists.

This line of work offers several promising directions for an under-standing of tourist–resident interaction. It appears to suggest that atti-tudes towards tourism and tourists follow some kind of fundamental equity function (Bryant and Napier, 1981). For example, business leaders, those working in the industry and those with economic investment in the area are more positive towards tourism (Murphy, 1985), although the Hawaiian study noted earlier found little evidence of such differences in that community. The costs to benefit ratios are clearly different for such groups than for the elderly and for those living in maximum contact with tourist zones where crowding, pollution and local services are heavily strained by the visitor pressure.

While equity considerations appear to underlie much of the work done in the past decade in the segmentation category of tourism's social im-pacts, there remains a need to model or portray the general attitudes towards tourism held by residents. It is apparent from the studies of Brougham and Butler and others that there is an organization of people's attitudes to tourism which results in consistent findings in segmentation analysis. One can express this same point in a different language system, one familiar particularly to European psychologists – there appear to exist social representations of the tourism industry within communities (Farr, 1987; Moscovici, 1984). Moscovici defined a social representation as 'the elaborating of a social object by the community for the purpose of behaving and communicating' (1963: 251). He argued that social representations are more than public attitudes towards, or opinions of, certain objects or issues. Social representations are like theories or sys-tems of knowledge which include values, ideas and guides for behaviour which allow communities to make sense of their social world. Farr (1987) points out that social representations as discussed by Moscovici can be seen as involving a social construction of reality and emphasize social groups rather than individuals, as in the classic psychological work on attitudes and opinions. This allegiance with traditions in sociology and anthropology leads to a focus on the media and literature of a community as the sources of information on social representations rather than the exclusive use of surveys of individuals within a community. Examples of such social representations for the tourist industry would be 'Tourism as a new source of employment' or tourism as a 'vulture destroying cultures' (cf. Brougham and Butler, 1981; Greenwood, 1978).

This review of the literature on tourism's social impacts can be sum-marized by suggesting that a new model for understanding social impacts can be empirically explored. This new model rejects the previous stage models of tourism impacts and advances a joint equity–social representational view of tourism. In this new approach resident reactions to future tourism developments should depend on a cost–benefit style accounting of the effects of tourism which residents have experienced. This accounting, together with information presented in the media, is likely to predispose sections of the community to sharing one of several social representations of tourism. Those likely to be suffering from the costs of tourism should be predisposed towards social representations such as 'tourism – an environment destroyer', 'tourism – just for the rich' and 'tourism – taking over our town'. Where the equity calculations are more even-handed social representations such as 'tourism – dangerous, needs managing', 'tourism – OK if controlled', are more likely to result. Finally, where personal gains outweigh costs, social representations should include 'tourism – our future', 'tourism – town saviour', 'tourism – tomorrow's industry'. One large-scale empirical study of an Australian tourism city, Carns, through interviews with over 500 residents, found clear support for the equity–social representation explanation of tourism (Pearce et al., 1991). The greater use of this model in interpreting existing data, such as the comprehensive Hawaiian study of tourist–resident relationships, should enhance our future understanding and promote better resident–host management solutions.

Emerging solutions

Five tactics for arresting the decline of tourist–resident attitudes can be proposed. These tactics follow the most promising explanations of the decay of tourist–resident attitudes outlined earlier and concentrate on the social representation and equity issues in tandem.

Education and tourism

Since many of the negative tourist–resident impacts of tourism are perceived impacts, that is judgements made by individuals about others, then it follows that mistakes and errors of interpretation are possible. A community which receives more detailed education in the field of tourism will be better able to analyse the impacts that are specifically tourism-related with a rounded appreciation of both the negative and positive consequences of development. Murphy (1985), a leading international figure in tourism social impact analysis, strongly argues that tourism is better received when the community has been more adequately informed about the industry.

Accordingly, non-trivial information campaigns about tourism, about tourist habits and cultural differences offer one line of attack for improving tourist–resident relationships.

Incorporating community perspectives

It must be recognized that the community or the groups which represent community interests are not necessarily experts in tourism planning. Their right to comment on proposals should, however, not be ignored, since the very act of expressing opinions is often therapeutic and constructive.

Nevertheless, their view is but one of a number of the necessary inputs to the planning process. In particular, attention should be given to allowing whole communities to compare two or three alternative proposals for development in a region or location, at least at the broad concept stage. This procedure is well suited to:

- very large developments; and
- regional plans.

Much psychological research exists showing that people make better decisions and judgements in situations involving a comparison of alternatives (Zube, 1980). A format for environmental evaluation which permits communities and individuals to *vote* on alternative proposals is recommended. Additionally, faced with specific models of alternative developments for a region, communities can provide a list of requirements which they strongly feel must be met by developers. Such approaches give specific advance warnings to the industry of community concerns. For large-scale private developments, it would be an appropriate step prior to the formal submission of a development application.

The general theme of incorporating community perspectives in tourism development can be divided into a number of subgoals or themes. These themes each represent important guidelines in forecasting, preventing and managing social impacts. It has been suggested that social impacts will be lessened if:

- Overall development goals and priorities are in harmony with those of the residents (including attending to urgent growth problems before more tourism work proceeds).
- The promotion of local attractions is subject to resident endorsement.
- Native people and/or ethnic groups are closely involved with the development process to respect their social needs.
- There is broad-based community participation in tourist events and activities.
- Destination areas adopt or refine themes and events that reflect their history, location and geographic setting.

Principle of increasing resident opportunity

One of the common factors underlying a host of social impacts of tourism is the restriction of the local people's opportunities for recreation, shopping and easy living. For example, in Australia the national tradition of expecting free access to beaches, national parks and scenic environments needs to be respected in the design and layout of new facilities. The corollary is that tourism developments which enhance the social and leisure world of communities by considering their needs in resort and attraction development planning should be well received.

Community equity and management committees

Control of tourism facilities through ownership by community groups (particularly aboriginal or ethnic sub-groups) as well as by substantial community representation on management committees represent other techniques of limiting negative social impacts.

One recommended guideline is that of trying to maximize local capital, entrepreneurial ability and labour in tourism developments. Following the social representation perspective it can be argued that where residents have the impression that tourism is in the hands of outsiders more negative attitudes will follow. If local capital and labour are not appropriate a *local* social monitoring committee may be usefully employed.

Research and monitoring

Allied to the preceding recommendation is the thorough use of the academic research community to identify local social impacts in advance of tourism growth in a region. As in the environmental/biological field, research and monitoring of key social impact indicators or warning signs would also serve a useful function in respecting community interests and providing data on likely flashpoints of public dissatisfaction. The techniques and skills exist to undertake this monitoring of social impacts.

Particular research issues which need addressing are:

- Building up a data base of tourist–resident interaction in similar communities where different types of developments have occurred.
- Monitoring social impacts over time in *high pressure* communities. This would address such questions as do tourist–resident interactions improve over time or do the social impacts of tourism persist and in turn cause problems for the economic viability of the development.

Finally, it is notable that the topic of tourist–resident impacts has its own pattern of academic and tourist industry interest. While the

120   *Global Tourism*

academic interest has been relatively constant, private sector attention is more varied with the community concerns receiving more at the development and rejuvenation phases of growth rather than in the consolidation or maintenance phase. Nevertheless tourist–resident interaction, despite these fluctuations of attention, is likely to be a critical tourism issue for the next decade and beyond.

References

Ahmed, Z.U. (1992) Islamic Pilgrimage (Hajj) to Ka'aba in Makkah (Saudi Arabia): an important international tourism activity. *Journal of Tourism Studies*, 3(1), 35–43

Amir, Y. (1969) Contact hypothesis in ethnic relations. *Psychological Bulletin*, 71, 319–42

Allen, L.R., Long, P.T., Perdue, R.R. and Kieselbach, S. (1988) The impact of tourism development on residents' perceptions of community life. *Journal of Travel Research*, XXVII(1), 16–21

Altman, J. (1988) *Aborigines, Tourism and Development: the Northern Territory Experience*, Australian National University North Australia Research Unit, Darwin

Argyle, M. (1975) *Bodily Communication*, Methuen, London

Boissevain, J. (1979) The impact of tourism on a dependent island, Gozo, Malta. *Annals of Tourism Research*, 6, 76–90

Brougham, J.F. and Butler, R.W. (1981) A segmentation analysis of resident attitudes to the social impact of tourism. *Annals of Tourism Research*, 8, 569–90

Bryant, E.G. and Napier, T.L. (1981) The application of social exchange theory to the study of satisfaction with outdoor recreation facilities. In *Outdoor Recreation Planning, Perspectives and Research* (ed. T.L. Napier), Kendall Hunt, Dubuque, IA, pp. 83–98

Butler, R. (1980) The concept of a tourism area cycle of evolution: implications for management of resources. *Canadian Geographer*, 24, 5–12

Cohen, E. (1968) Nomads from affluence: notes on the phenomenon of drifter-tourism. *International Journal of Comparative Sociology*, XIV, 1–2, 88–103

Cohen, E. (1982) Thai girls and Farang men: the edge of ambiguity. *Annals of Tourism Research*, 9, 403–28

Cohen, E. (1988) Tourism and AIDS in Thailand. *Annals of Tourism Research*, 15(4), 467–86

Collett, P. (1971) Training Englishmen in the non-verbal behaviour of Arabs. *International Journal of Psychology*, 6, 209–15

Community Resources Inc. (1989) *1988 Statewide Tourism Impact: Cor Survey Summary*, Department of Business and Economic Development, Tourism Branch, Hawaii

Crystal, E. (1978) Tourism in Toraja, Sulawesi, Indonesia. In *Hosts and Guests* (ed. V.L. Smith), Blackwell, Oxford

D'Amore, L. (1988) Tourism – the world's peace industry. *Journal of Travel Research*, 27(1), 35–40

Downs, R. and Stea, D. (1977) *Maps in Minds*, Harper and Row, New York

Doxey, G.V. (1975) A causation theory of visitor–resident irritants: methodology and research inferences. In *Proceedings of the Travel Research Association Sixth Annual Conference*, San Diego, California, pp. 195–8

Dredge, D. and Moore, S. (1992) A methodology for the integration of tourism in town planning. *Journal of Tourism Studies*, 3(1), 8–21

Farr, R.M. (1987) Social representations: a French tradition of research. *Journal for the Theory of Social Behaviour*, 17(4), 343–69

Feldman, R. (1968) Response to compatriot and foreigner who seek assistance. *Journal of Personality and Social Psychology*, 10, 202–14

Fiji Visitors' Bureau (1975) *Advice to Visiting Australians*, Fiji Visitors' Bureau, Suva

Furnham, A. and Bochner, S. (1986) *Culture Shock*, Methuen, London

Greenwood, D.J. (1978) Culture by the pound: an anthropological perspective on tourism as cultural commoditization. In *Hosts and Guests* (ed. V.L. Smith), Blackwell, Oxford

Harmon, D.K., Masuda, M. and Holmes, T.H. (1970) The social readjustment rating scale: a cross-cultural study of Western Europeans and Americans. *Journal of Psychosomatic Research*, 14, 391–400

Haywood, K.M. (1988) Responsible and responsive tourism planning in the community. *Tourism Management*, 9, 105–18

Herman, S. and Schild, E. (1960) Contexts for the study of cross-cultural education. *Journal of Social Psychology*, 52, 231–50

Hills, T.L. and Lundgren, J. (1977) *The Impact of Tourism in the Caribbean – a Methodological Study*, Department of Geography, McGill University, Montreal

Holmes, T.H. and Rahe, R.H. (1967) The Social Readjustment Rating Scale. *Journal of Psychosomatic Research*, 11, 213–18

Huxley, A. (1925) *Along the Road*, Chatto and Windus, London

Kent, N. (1977) A new kind of sugar. In *A New Kind of Sugar: Tourism in the Pacific* (eds B.R. Finney and K.A. Watson), The East-West Center, Honolulu

Kinhill Cameron McNamara (1990) *Tourism Development Plan for Townsville and Environs*, Kinhill Cameron McNamara, Brisbane

Liu, J.C. and Var, T. (1986) Resident attitudes to tourism in Hawaii. *Annals of Tourism Research*, 13, 193–214

Liu, J.C., Sheldon, P. and Var, T. (1987) Resident perception of the environmental impacts of tourism. *Annals of Tourism Research*, 14, 17–37

Long, P.T., Perdue, R.R. and Allen, L. (1990) Rural resident tourism perceptions and attitudes by community level of tourism. *Journal of Travel Research*, 28, 3–9

Lynch, K. (1960) *The Image of the City*, MIT Press and Harvard University Press, Cambridge, Mass.

Mackenzie, M. (1977) The deviant art of tourism: Airport art. In *The Social and Economic Impact of Tourism on Pacific Communities* (B. Farrell, ed.), Center for South Pacific Studies, University of California, Santa Cruz

Milman, A. and Pizam, A. (1988) Social impacts of tourism on Central Florida. *Annals of Tourism Research*, 15, 191–204

Morris, D., Collett, P., Marsh, P. and O'Shaughnessy, M. (1979) *Gestures: Their Origins and Distribution*, Jonathan Cape, London

Moscovici, S. (1963) Attitudes and opinions. *Annual Review of Psychology*, 14, 231–60

Moscovici, S. (1984) The phenomenon of social representations. In *Social Representations* (R.M. Farr and S. Moscovici, eds), Cambridge University Press, Cambridge, pp. 3–10

Murphy, P.E. (1981) Community attitudes to tourism: A comparative analysis. *International Journal of Tourism Management*, **2**, 189–95

Murphy, P.E. (1985) *Tourism: A Community Approach*, Methuen, New York

Pearce, P.L. (1977a) The social and environmental perceptions of overseas tourists. Unpublished D.Phil. thesis, University of Oxford

Pearce, P.L. (1977b) Mental souvenirs: a study of tourists and their city maps. *Australian Journal of Psychology*, **29**, 203–10

Pearce, P.L. (1980a) A favourability–satisfaction model of tourist's evaluations. *Journal of Travel Research*, **14**(1), 13–17

Pearce, P.L. (1980b) Strangers, travellers and Greyhound bus terminals: studies of small scale helping behaviours. *Journal of Personality and Social Psychology*, **35**, 935–40

Pearce, P.L. (1984) Tourist–guide interaction. *Annals of Tourism Research*, **11**, 129–46

Pearce, P.L. (1990) *The Backpacker Phenomenon: Preliminary Answers to Basic Questions*, James Cook University of North Queensland, Townsville

Pearce, P.L., Moscardo, G.M. and Ross, G.F. (1991) Tourism impact and community perception. *Australian Psychologist*, **26**, 147–52

Petit-Skinner, S. (1977) Tourism and acculturation in Tahiti. In *The Social and Economic Impact of Tourism on Pacific Communities* (B. Farrell, ed.), Centre for South Pacific Studies, University of California, Santa Cruz

Pi-Sunyer, O. (1978) Through native eyes: tourists and tourism in a Catalan maritime community. In *Hosts and Guests* (V.L. Smith, ed.), Blackwell, Oxford

Prokop, H. (1970) Psychiatric illness of foreigners vacationing in Innsbruck. *Neurochirugie und Psychiatrie*, **107**, 363–8

Riegel, O.W. (1953) Residual effects of exchange of persons. *Public Opinion Quarterly*, **17**, 319–27

Riley, P. (1988) Long term budget travellers. *Annals of Tourism Research*, **15**, 313–28

Ritter, W. (1975) Recreation and tourism in Islamic countries. *Ekistics*, **236**, 56–69

Ross, G. (1990) Do we really dislike the Japanese? Resident reactions to various cultural groups of tourists. *Mina*, **1**(6), 16–19

Sheldon, P. and Var, T. (1984) *Resident Attitudes to Tourism in North Wales Tourism Management*, **5**, 40–8

Simmel, G. (1950) *The Sociology of Georg Simmel* (translated by H. Woolf), Free Press of Glencoe, New York

Smith, H.P. (1955) Do intercultural experiences affect attitudes? *Journal of Abnormal and Social Psychology*, **51**, 469–77

Smith, H.P. (1957) The effects of intercultural experience: a follow-up investigation. *Journal of Abnormal and Social Psychology*, **54**, 266–9

Smith, V.L. (1978a) Eskimo tourism: micro models and marginal men. In *Hosts and Guests* (ed. V.L. Smith), Blackwell, Oxford

Smith, V.L. (ed.) (1978b) *Hosts and Guests*, Blackwell, Oxford

Sofield, T. (1991) Sustainable ethnic tourism in the South Pacific: some principles. *Journal of Tourism Studies*, **2**(1), 56–72

Turner, L. and Ash, J. (1975) *The Golden Hordes. International Tourism and the Pleasure Periphery*, Constable, London

Urbanowicz, C. (1977) Integrating tourism with other industries in Tonga. In *The Social and Economic Impact of Tourism on Pacific Communities* (B. Farrell, ed.), Centre for South Pacific Studies, University of California, Santa Cruz

Urbanowicz, C. (1978) *Tourism in Tonga: Troubled Times*, In *Hosts and Guests* (V.L. Smith, ed.), Blackwell, Oxford

Urry, J. (1990) *The Tourist Gaze*, Sage, London

Useem, J. and Useem, R. (1967) The interfaces of a binational third culture: a study of the American community in India. *Journal of Social Issues*, **23**, 130–43

Waters, S.R. (1966) The American tourist. *Annals of the Academy of Political and Social Science*, **368**, 109–18

Watson, O.M. and Graves, T.D. (1966) Quantitative research in proxemic behaviour. *American Anthropologist*, **68**, 971–85

Zube, E. (1980) *Environmental Evaluation*, Brooks/Cole, Monterey, California

9 Native peoples and tourism: conflict and compromise

David Mercer

The main aim of this chapter is to explore a number of themes concerning the often uneasy relationship between contemporary Western tourism developments and the native Aboriginal population in 'outback', northern and central Australia. This is large subject area about which we now have a considerable body of expert opinion which is currently being added to at a very rapid rate. Unfortunately, much of the research is necessarily contradictory in its conclusions, a reflection of the varied ideological nature of the research assumptions, methodologies and interest group orientations of the investigators. Two internationally outstanding national parks provide the main case studies. These are Kakadu National Park and Uluru (formerly Ayers Rock), in the Northern Territory. Visitors to these parks have increased by almost 240 per cent in the past ten years, a situation that has engendered the negotiation of some innovative, 'joint' managerial strategies, incorporating elements of both Aboriginal and Eurocentric viewpoints. The 'success' of this joint management approach is currently a topic for some considerable debate in Australia, as is the related question of the extent to which it is possible to reconcile Aboriginal, conservation and tourism interests in the one place (Head, 1992).

Even though the focus here is directly on Australia, many of the ideas are also relevant to other national settings where tourism has recently brought together peoples from vastly different cultural and economic backgrounds. The discussion is of particular significance to other, federated states, such as Canada and the United States, where the goals and policy orientation of the national government may sometimes be in conflict both with minority native peoples and one or more sub-national levels of government. An obvious comparison is with Canada, where the pressures for several kinds of resource developments north of the 60th parallel have highlighted basic concerns about quality of environment and the rights and welfare of northern Canadian peoples of Indian or Inuit ancestry (Lynge, 1987). The key problem being addressed revolves around the question of whether or not contemporary tourism development in north and central Australia can be said to be socially appropriate from the Aboriginal viewpoint. What might be called the 'sub-plot' relates to the contradictory role of the modern capitalist state in both encouraging big tourism developments on the one hand and yet at the same time having to take special care to appease the growing demands of native peoples and environmentalists who may be opposed to such projects. Both themes highlight the inherently political nature of tourism and tourist developments and underscore Prosser's (1992) argument that there are a number of key ethical questions at the core of discussions about tourism as an 'industry', both internationally and in specific national settings. Recent land rights' decisions in favour of Aboriginal interests in both Canada and Australia suggest that in the future in those countries, at least, we can certainly expect a more forceful representation of Aboriginal interests where tourism developments are mooted (Mercer, 1993).

'Invasion' and 'levelling'

In common with such countries as South Africa, Fiji, New Zealand, Canada and the United States, Australia is a modern polygeneric nation. This term is used by Willmot (1987) to refer to that relatively small group of nations made up of human groups with markedly varied origins and race memories. Frequently, this includes people of Aboriginal descent. By contrast, indigenous societies such as Japan, Nigeria and, to a lesser extent, Britain and France, are ethnically much more homogeneous. In the past, polygeneric societies 'failed' and became 'indigenous' either by a process of genocide or by miscegenation. But today, Willmot argues that

> the old process of forgetting or replacing memory with mythology is no longer possible. By the time societies become literate and this literacy becomes popularly based the forgetting of origin memories is not possible. (1987: 17)

Part of the argument here is that this situation raises a number of important issues for tourism planning in such societies.

Moorehead (1966) entitled his epic account of the eighteenth century European 'invasion' of the South Pacific, *The Fatal Impact*. The same title could equally be used to describe the contemporary tourist incursion into many areas long settled by 'primitive' peoples. Globally, tourism's reach is now virtually total. From Antarctica to Amazonia, from the Sahara to the deepest recesses of central Asia, there is scarcely a part of the world that has not been affected to some degree by the modern tourism phenomenon. As but one aspect of 'modernity', tourism of course takes many different forms. Goulet (1977) has presented a persuasive argument for regarding 'tourism' – along with education, medicine, agriculture etc. – as yet another medium for technology transfer. Thus, in addition to novel transport and image technologies, less affluent peoples in tourist regions frequently come to experience new food and refrigeration, construction, management, recreational and finance technologies, to mention but a few developments. Native peoples in some parts of Africa and central Australia, for example, are now routinely exposed to the spectacle of high speed car rallies or the sight of photographic teams on extravagant advertising assignments. As well, in addition to the well-publicized, mass tourism air travel/hotel package vacations to places as diverse as Tibet, Cameroon, Vietnam or Peru, a growing number of 'adventure tour' companies are now continually seeking out and promoting new, exotic frontiers for rafting, ballooning, four-wheel drive or trekking expeditions. Frequently these, too, bring visitors from affluent, Western societies directly into contact with primitive native peoples (Singh and Kaur, 1986). In short, as Turner and Ash (1975: 130) put it, 'the individual who visits the havens of the antique, the ethnic and the pristine is, unwittingly, instrumental to the expansion of high technology and the uniformity it imposes'.

Acceleration of this levelling process is now particularly apparent in the tourism industry because of the increasing level of international domination by what Ascher (1985: 15) calls transnational tourism corporations (or TTCs). Ownership of air transport operations, hotel chains and tour operator companies is now highly concentrated and becoming more so. This has enormous implications for the geography of tourism. It means, for example, that through such media as advertising, hotel construction activities and package tours, TTCs can – if they so wish – manipulate demand to favour certain countries over others. But there are also other forces at work. In recent years the popular tourist destinations of Europe and the Middle East have both experienced a relative decline as favoured vacation venues, especially for affluent North American and Japanese tourists, because of the increased incidence of terrorist attacks (Wells, 1986). Inevitably this, together with the worsening pollution and congestion problems, especially in Europe, is having the effect of compounding tourist pressures in the 'pleasure periphery' of Africa, South-East Asia, South America and – of particular interest to the present discussion – Australia.

Analysts are deeply divided over the question of the relative costs and benefits of tourism in less affluent countries or among marginalized ethnic groups in rich nations. The overwhelming impression one gains from the literature is that, economically, tourism is, on the whole, a 'good thing', holds out enormous developmental promise and should be vigorously promoted. It appears this is the way most political and business leaders certainly view the tourism phenomenon. Indeed, the unanimous outcome of the joint Unesco/World Bank seminar, held in Washington in December, 1976 (DeKadt, 1979: 399) was that 'tourism can make a substantial contribution to the economic and social development of many countries'. The only qualifications were that attention should be paid to the precise tourism product that was being marketed and that any development should be carefully managed to fit in with a national plan. The symposium did spend some of the time discussing the distributional impact of tourism on 'life chances and welfare', but by and large the emphasis was on the positive rather than the negative effects.

Since the Washington seminar there has appeared a growing body of empirical evidence that the so-called 'benefits' of tourism are often greatly outweighed by the substantial long-term social and environmental costs incurred. Indeed, Ascher (1985: 10) comments that 'The time has long gone when international tourism was considered an obvious and easy means of contributing economically to the advancement of developing countries.' Recent studies from many different countries have underscored the often disastrous consequences of unplanned tourist developments for certain sections of the host societies. As the Colombian journalist Enrique Caldera has described it, international tourism is all too often 'poison in a luxury package' (quoted in Goulet, 1977). As the closest tourist destination to the affluent North American market, it is hardly surprising that the Caribbean traditionally has been the main focus of empirical studies highlighting some of the more pernicious effects of tourism. But as high-speed air travel has progressively induced tendencies towards the 'global village', there has been a widespread diffusion of comparable academic investigations over the past fifteen years or so to include such far-flung territories as the Canadian Arctic, the Pacific island nations, the Indian subcontinent, Africa and some of the poorer regions of Europe (Britton and Clarke, 1986). Tourism's 'reach' has also become particularly pervasive in the past decade because of the unprecedented expansion of large new tourist markets in Western Europe and Japan, as well as North America. This process will accelerate within the next few years when the next generation of 'super jumbo' jets becomes fully operational and new markets open up in such countries as Taiwan and South Korea.

Three kinds of tourism 'impacts' have been alluded to so far: economic, social (or cultural) and environmental. Much of the literature on tourism distinguishes these impacts for analytical purposes. But one of the main arguments here is that such separation is misplaced. 'Economic' impacts, for example, invariably have important distributional effects which are ultimately 'social' in their consequences. Further, the 'environmental' destruction of, say, an Australian Aboriginal sacred site can have significant cultural ramifications. It also has to be continually recognized that 'tourism' is frequently merely one part of the total development process that invariably affects many newly 'opened up' areas. As will become apparent in the Australian case studies to be discussed below, road construction and energy and water supply for mineral exploration or pastoral development, for example, often provide the initial, modern infrastructure upon which a fledgling tourist industry rapidly builds.

Australia – the tourism boom

Australia currently has one of the highest tourist growth rates in the world and, at a time when many of Australia's traditional export industries are in serious economic difficulty, both the federal and individual state governments clearly see tourism as a major growth area that should be vigorously promoted. From small beginnings in the 1930s when Australia played host to only 23,000 visitors, the industry now generates around $7.3 billion annually, or 10 per cent of the country's total foreign earnings. With 1.8 million arrivals in 1987, international visitor numbers were 27 per cent higher than the total for the previous year. Moreover, 1987 was a landmark in that it was the first year that overseas arrivals had exceeded the number of Australians who left the country to holiday overseas. 1987 witnessed a 50 per cent increase in Japanese visitors alone and a 32 per cent growth in the size of the American market. These are the two most rapidly expanding markets. Indeed, the current planning horizon is for one million Japanese visitors by the end of the century. A record 2.35 million people from overseas visited on a short-term basis in 1991 and some of the more optimistic predictions have suggested a total of 4 million visitors by the turn of the century. There is concern in many quarters that this potential flood-tide needs to be carefully monitored and controlled by means of a National Tourism Strategy but so far, despite the rhetoric, there have been few signs that the competing states are prepared to subordinate what they see as their individual economic interests to the good of the nation as a whole.

Once in the country, the favoured destinations are the two major cities of Sydney and Melbourne, the Gold Coast and the Barrier Reef (both in Queensland) and northern and central Australia. Essentially, the Northern Territory is the main drawcard for tourists to the north, though northern Queensland and northern Western Australia are also becoming increasingly popular. Currently, about 13 per cent of jobs in central

Australia are in the tourism industry. This is approximately double the national average. However, few of these jobs are held by Aborigines who, as we shall see, do not, as a rule, find many of the available occupations attractive. In 1986–7, 762,000 international and domestic tourists visited the Northern Territory and spent almost $(Aus) 300 million. This is a 15 per cent increase on the 1985–6 figures. Recent projections by the Northern Territory Development Corporation have suggested that as many as one million tourist trips could be taken in the Northern Territory by 1993. The Territory contains two major tourist sites of outstanding international significance. These are Ayers Rock (now known as Uluru National Park), in the centre of the continent, and Kakadu National Park in the north, to the east of the Territory's capital, Darwin. In view of the significance of these two sites to the Aborigines, much of the remainder of the discussion will focus on the tourism experience at Kakadu and Uluru. But first, in order to clarify the issue, a brief comment is in order concerning the general attitude of Aborigines towards tourism and development.

In summary, the Aboriginal perspective can be summed up in two words: choice and control. They demand total control over their own lands and their own destinies so that they are able to negotiate with white Australians from a position of strength when it comes to making decisions relating to mining or tourism development proposals on their land. In particular, Aborigines affirm the right to reject any proposal for developments on their land that they consider inappropriate. They also insist on the right to refuse to negotiate, if they so choose. Earlier, we mentioned some of the key differences between Aborigines and white settlers in relation to religion and 'property'. Although it may appear strange to Europeans, there is also often considerable confusion among Aborigines as to why affluent white people should choose the tourism experience in the first place. It has been pointed out by many writers that, in their modern form, tourism and recreation presuppose a work ethic and the alternation of periods of 'work' and 'play'. Such rigid separation of time and activity has no direct correspondence in pre-industrial cultures. Such confusion inevitably means that Aborigines often start by regarding tourism with some suspicion. Whether or not they continue to support developments in a particular region invariably depends on their first-hand experience with it: the numbers of tourists involved over a certain time period, their behaviour, and so on. It also means that 'If people are puzzled as to what tourists are doing, then the task of attempting to assess their reactions and any negative impacts is problematic, to say the least' (Brady, 1985).

Corporate business interests in Australia constantly promote the view that Aborigines are opposed to any kind of tourism or mining developments on their lands, and hence, 'progress'. But there is ample evidence that this is a misrepresentation of the Aboriginal stance. Rather, what the Aborigines do fear is the possible effects of such projects on their traditional way of life, on their land and on their capacity to perform their tribal ceremonies and pass on their cultural traditions to the next generation. In theory there seems little reason to doubt that Western-style development and traditional Aboriginal life styles can co-exist reasonably harmoniously so long as due consideration is given to early planning and consultation and so long as careful monitoring of effects also takes place. Two examples will be discussed below.

Australian aborigines

Aborigines have lived in what is now known as Australia for at least 60,000 years. Early estimates put their number at about 300,000 at the time of the European invasion of the continent, in 1788. More recent archaeological evidence has suggested that 500,000, or even 600,000, is probably a more accurate estimate (Butlin, 1983). For those anthropologists who define technology narrowly, simply in terms of tools, then a case could be made for the Aborigines being relatively 'primitive' and 'backward' at the time of first European contact. But if technology is defined as 'knowledge used for practical purposes' then Aborigines were at that time – and indeed, still are in many areas – extremely knowledgable and technologically advanced (Lewis, 1992).

Spiritually there was a profound gulf between the Aborigines and the early Christian colonists. Aboriginal religion had – and indeed, still has – no concept of a heaven or hell. In common with American Indians, Aborigines have no understanding of 'property' in the white European sense. Initially, the land was territorially delimited on a clan basis, but other groups were also frequently granted permission to use the land. The bond between Aboriginal people, the plants, animals, landscape and local spirits was considered indissoluble and so land could not be 'bought' or 'sold'. What is more, the human/land link was timeless; it was established prior to birth and continued after death. It is frequently said of the Aborigines that they do not own the land, the land owns them. What might appear to European eyes a 'natural' landscape of 'wilderness' is to an Aborigine a living, social landscape. The earth's topography, it is believed, was formed by the spirit ancestors who came from the Dreamtime, or *tjukurrpa* (creation) and journeyed across the continent leaving traces in the form of hills, creeks, caves, water holes and the like. Many of these topographic features are sacred and have ritual significance. Others are considered extremely dangerous and to be avoided; others are secret. All this means that special questions are at issue in planning tourism facilities in areas of significance for Aboriginal populations because Eurocentric notions of both 'conservation' and 'development' may be incompatible with Aboriginal spirituality.

Admittedly, still only in small numbers, Aborigines can now be found in most professional occupations. However, overwhelmingly they are concentrated in poorly paid rural occupations such as stockmen or, more commonly, subsist on welfare payments. The average level of unemployment in Australia is currently around 10 per cent. Among Aborigines it is 20 per cent. They also have an infant mortality rate that is three times that of the national average, and the life expectancy for males is generally in the range 48–61 years. Many commentators highlight such statistics and argue that they point convincingly to the operation of an unofficial apartheid policy in the country. Certainly there is ample evidence of continued maltreatment and abuse of basic human rights. In 1988, for example, there was constituted a Royal Commission into Aboriginal Deaths in Custody to inquire into all aspects of the 100 cell deaths that had taken place in the previous decade. This Commission has recently presented its damning report.

Most Aborigines, even in extremely remote areas, had had at least some minimal contact with Europeans from the 1930s or 1940s onwards. Virtually no Aborigines now live the strictly defined, traditional, self-sufficient, nomadic existence that prevailed prior to European settlement, but there is a very strong national movement to revive Aboriginal languages and identity, preserve cultural sites, ceremonies, art forms and customs and encourage Aboriginal children to have continuing exposure to traditional Aboriginal skills and life styles. For example, it is not at all uncommon for Aborigines working in the rural, mining or pastoral industries, in outback national parks, or even in urban centres, to periodically rekindle their strong attachment to the land and its sacred places by going 'on walkabout' deep into the central desert, often for months at a time. Especially in the Northern Territory, recent years have also witnessed a growing 'homelands' – or 'outstation' movement – whereby Aboriginals have left the often disastrous social environment of the towns or reserves and returned in small groups to enjoy healthier and much more traditionally orientated life styles on their own lands. The 'anti-ghettoization', outstation movement has of course been facilitated by the extension of land rights' legislation since the late 1970s and the allocation of funds by the federal Department of Aboriginal Affairs. By 1981 it was estimated that in the Northern Territory alone there were 150 isolated 'homeland centres' with approximately 4000 residents.

In view of the profoundly religious significance of the land for Aboriginal people, the campaign to keep Aboriginal art and traditions alive is inseparable from the land rights and sovereignty movements. The recent 'discovery' of exciting, contemporary Aboriginal painting, music and dance by white entrepreneurs in affluent New York, Sydney and London is also indivisible from the contemporary tourist invasion of northern and central Australia, a major component of which is the cultural element. Overseas art exhibitions and performances by professional Aboriginal dance companies act as powerful advertisements for the cultural and landscape attractions of a distant and often little-known country. At a more popular level, movies such as the extraordinary box-office success story *Crocodile Dundee* bring the sights and sounds of northern Australia to a vastly bigger audience. So there is a dilemma here for Aborigines. On the one hand many white entrepreneurs consistently promote tourism and the associated cultural activities as being 'good' for Aborigines on the grounds that it generates much-needed economic benefits as well as engendering a more sensitive understanding of black culture. But from the perspective of many black radicals, their desire is for nothing less than full Aboriginal sovereignty, symbolized in a treaty, compensation for historical wrongs and autonomy to decide their own economic future (Jones, 1991).

Over the past quarter of a century a combination of positive federal government policy initiatives and growing Aboriginal militancy has led to a slight improvement in Aboriginal living standards and the limited recognition of certain basic rights such as the right to vote and the granting of inalienable freehold tenure to lands previously reserved for their use. The right to vote in national elections was only granted to Aborigines by referendum as recently as 1967 and the first significant land rights legislation was enacted by federal parliament in 1976. As a result of this legislation Aborigines were, for the first time since colonization, able to make claims to their traditional lands. But the Act made reference only to unoccupied and unalienated Crown land in the Northern Territory. Under the Australian Constitution the federal government has no power to coerce the subordinate states to enact land rights legislation and so Aborigines in the six states have had mixed success in terms of securing freehold title to their traditional lands. In one progressive state – South Australia – almost 20 per cent of the land area is now classified as Aboriginal freehold land. No other state even approaches this level of ownership. Indeed, two of the largest states have no Aboriginal freehold land at all. These are Western Australia – which, with a population of 40,000 Aborigines, is more than twice the area of Texas – and Queensland, which has 62,000 Aborigines. These are two of the most populous Aboriginal states and Queensland, in particular, is a popular and increasingly significant tourist destination. One-third of the Northern Territory is currently in Aboriginal possession but, as a 'territory', it is financed and largely administered through the Commonwealth government. In total, then, only 8 per cent of Australia consists of Aboriginal freehold land, but an additional 4 per cent is held in leasehold.

Until recently it was considered something of a heresy to talk of the European 'invasion' of the Aboriginal nation, but this is no longer the case. An important book published in the late 1980s – *The Law of the Land* (Reynolds, 1987) – makes a powerful case for the 'invasion and theft' thesis and the next few years are likely to see unremitting international and domestic political pressure being exerted on the federal government in Canberra to proclaim a treaty with the Aborigines, to grant adequate compensation for the historical genocide that has occurred and to legitimate an extensive list of outstanding land rights claims. Politics and tourism, like politics and sport, are now inextricably linked on the world stage. Earlier, mention was made of terrorist attacks in some parts of the world acting as a deterrent to pleasure travel. In Australia's 'Bicentennial Year' in 1988, some Aboriginal activists called for immediate international trade sanctions against the country until substantial claims were satisfied. Tourism would be an obvious target. In addition, there were some vocal Aboriginal demonstrations at hallmark bicentennial events in 1988 both in Britain and in Australia. As well, the Minister for Aboriginal Affairs disassociated himself from all activities celebrating European settlement and on 26 January 1988 (Australia Day) a quarter-page advertisement appeared in the *New York Times* calling on the United Nations to investigate human rights violations against Australian Aborigines and to intervene in the granting of outstanding land rights claims. The primary intent of all such actions is to draw the attention of the international community to the past wrongs perpetrated on Aboriginal Australians throughout the 200 years of European occupation.

Kakadu and Uluru National Parks

Kakadu National Park is situated about 250 kilometres east of Darwin, in the Northern Territory, at latitude 13 S. Colloquially, it is known as the 'Top End' National Park. Stage 1 of the park – an area of 6144 square kilometres – was initially proclaimed in April 1979. This is exactly one hundred years after the proclamation of Australia's first national park, Royal National Park, on the outskirts of Sydney. As such parks become gazetted in more distant parts of Australia the management problems change, with traditional Aboriginal ties to the land assuming ever-greater importance. For the fifty years prior to its proclamation as a national park Kakadu had been an Aboriginal Reserve. In view of its outstanding landscape, ecological and cultural significance, the area was listed as a World Heritage Property under the terms of the World Heritage Convention in October 1981. Kakadu was the first site to be listed in Australia. The park topography is extremely diverse, ranging from the tidal flats and lowlands which represent some of the most important, pristine, tropical wetland ecosystems in the world, through to the spectacular sandstone escarpments and high country of the Arnhemland Plateau, inland. In 1980 the wetlands were listed under the conditions of the Convention on Wetlands of International Importance. In terms of its ecological value the area is of incomparable world significance, the data on species' numbers speaking for themselves: 1000 plants, 5000 insects, 250 birds (one-third of Australia's total complement), seventy-five reptiles, fifty mammals, forty-five freshwater fish (a quarter of the Australian total) and twenty-two amphibians. New species discoveries are commonplace. It is considered, for example, that the number of insect species eventually identified may well exceed 10,000 (Gare, 1984). In February 1984, under Stage 2 of the Kakadu Plan, an additional 6929 square kilometres of largely non-Aboriginal land were added to the existing park.

Culturally, the area is no less unique. Countless rock art sites exist in the Arnhemland escarpment and outliers and some of the ochre paintings have been dated at 25,000 years before present. Many are also extremely well preserved and are certainly as old as the better known palaeolithic cave art murals of Western Europe. The paintings and rock engravings depict a priceless record of historical change over thousands of years, ranging from the geological period when Australia was joined to New Guinea, through the gradual rise in sea level, 7000 years ago, and the first arrival of European man. Long extinct animals feature prominently. Recent archaeological expeditions have also discovered the world's oldest examples of ground axes, some of the earliest known sites of human habitation in Australia and many, as yet undeciphered, stone arrangements. In its own way Kakadu is every bit as valuable to the world community as the Louvre or the Prado.

Earlier it was noted that, prior to 1979, Kakadu had been a major Aboriginal Reserve. Such official status gave *de jure* recognition to the unparalleled significance of this area to the Aborigines. Its inhospitable, rocky uplands, monsoonal wetlands and crocodile-infested rivers had long made this region a natural 'refuge' for Aborigines, and in the 1920s the area was judged to be of little value to white Australians. Then, in the 1960s, 120,000 tonnes of uranium oxide deposits were discovered in the area. Mining company and government pressure eventually resulted in the boundaries of the proposed national park being drawn in such a way as to exclude the uranium province. Mining commenced in the 1970s and a sealed road to Darwin was subsequently constructed. This connected Darwin with the main mining town of Jabiru, which is actually situated inside the national park, and greatly eased access for domestic and international tourists. As uranium mining gathered pace at Ranger, Jabilucka and Koongarra, multiple threats to what had by this stage become Aboriginal-owned territory became readily apparent.

So it was that, upon its proclamation as a national park in April 1979, the traditional owners of Kakadu agreed to lease the area to the Director of the Australian National Parks and Wildlife Service for a period of 100 years as a national park. The decision followed a lengthy period of consultation with the owners – the Kakadu Aboriginal Land Trust – through its representative body, the Northern Land Council. It was generally felt by the Aborigines that their best interests would be served by such a move. Mining and tourist pressures were set to increase enormously and the Aboriginal community felt that they did not at that stage have the necessary management skills to cope with the imminent changes. The Lease Agreement was finally signed on 3 November 1978, but not before a wide-ranging information programme had been instituted to introduce the 'foreign' park idea to the traditional owners and, most importantly, the owners had been given ample opportunity to respond to the proposal. The unique aspect of the agreement is that, in the main, it was designed to ensure that the traditional Aboriginal owners would be intimately involved in the process of park planning and management and fully consulted at every stage on any matter affecting the welfare of the Aboriginal inhabitants of the area. This made Kakadu the first national park in the country where Aborigines were allowed an official say in both the long-term and day-to-day management of the park. As we shall see, other Australian parks have subsequently replicated this model, which is also being closely monitored by several overseas countries. In addition, two states have since employed Aboriginal rangers.

In all, the Kakadu Aboriginal Land Trust consists of around 100 traditional owners and an additional 200 Aborigines with some historical affiliations to the land in that area. In the eighteenth century it is estimated that some 2000 Aborigines probably used the area on a regular basis, but prior to the proclamation of the park there were only about twenty Aboriginal families living within the reserve. The establishment of the park acted as a catalyst for indigenous people to return to 'their' homeland and by 1980 an additional 150 Aborigines had returned to Kakadu to live. That number has subsequently doubled.

From the outset the Australian National Parks and Wildlife Service paid the closest possible attention to consultative arrangements. Aboriginal rangers were recruited and trained and numerous meetings were held to discuss input to the first and second management plans. Aborigines are also represented on the park's Board of Management which oversees the implementation of the management plan. In part, Aboriginal conditions included the following:

- Protection of traditional campsites.
- Protection of sites and routes of significance to the traditional owners.
- Provision for the owners to live traditionally in the park if they so choose.

- Privacy from European intrusion at certain, highly secret sites.
- Provision for the traditional owners to 're-work' rock paintings if they so wish.

This last condition may, at first, appear rather strange, but it does serve to highlight a key difference between European and Aboriginal conceptions of cultural artefacts. To most white park planners and archaeologists Kakadu is akin to a 'museum' where the art sites should be protected at all cost. To the traditional owners, on the other hand, Kakadu is a living place. They never considered their art to be 'permanent' in a Western, conservationist sense (Mulvaney, 1975). It was to be 'experienced' rather than 'possessed' and original creations were routinely painted over, modified or touched up when travellers returned to a particular site at regular seasonal intervals. It was, genuinely, 'living' art.

Not surprisingly, the joint venture between white, park planning professionals and the representatives of an ancient, pre-literate culture has not been without its difficulties. In particular, there have been considerable problems associated with different concepts of time. Traditionally, Aboriginal consultations invariably are spread over many meetings and long periods. Yet the 'Western' capitalist time frame generally is much shorter and frequently demands 'instant' solutions. Historically, mining interests in the Kakadu region, for example, have been known to 'force the pace' of long drawn-out consultative processes. As well, there are often serious practical difficulties involved in persuading Aborigines to talk openly about the precise locations of many significant sites that whites may feel are in need of 'protection'. Traditionally, some sites are so secret that their whereabouts is only known to a select number of initiated individuals. There are also others that it is taboo to discuss because they are considered so dangerous, others that cannot be talked about in the company of women or uninitiated men, and so on. In addition, the rapid escalation of tourist numbers is presently creating special management problems at Kakadu. The discussion will now focus briefly on those pressures and some of the consequences for this particular park.

Tourist numbers at Kakadu have shown a spectacular growth in the past few years. In 1972 it has been estimated that the area experienced about 20,000 visitor days. In 1987 there were 700,250 visitor days, and the five-year period from 1982 to 1987 alone saw a 364 per cent increase in this parameter. This translates into almost 250,000 visitors at present and a 50 per cent annual growth rate. The tourist 'problem' is all the more serious when it is realized that the monsoonal climate dictates that most people must visit in the dry season, between May and October. This period coincides with the winter in populous southern Australia. A major shift is occurring in the kind of visitor. Up to 1986 the tourists were overwhelmingly private visitors, but 25 per cent now visit Kakadu as part of a commercial tour group. Moreover, about one-third of all visitors are 'local', Northern Territory residents. Inevitably, numbers of this magnitude generate all the usual management problems ranging from mounting pressures on land, water, soil, vegetation and wildlife resources through to either conscious or unconscious vandalism of Aboriginal rock art sites and intrusion into sacred or forbidden areas. The ownership of four-wheel-drive vehicles and high-powered motor-boats on the part of Darwin or Jabiru residents and other Australian tourists of course also means that formerly inaccessible parts of the park are now potentially available for recreational use. Conflicts over land and other resources are thus building up between the increasing numbers of traditional Aborigines who are choosing to return to Kakadu to live and the flood of 'foreign' visitors, many of whom have no idea how to behave towards Aborigines or their cultural heritage.

Recent research by Kesteven (1987) has found that Aborigines make a clear distinction between 'tourists' and 'visitors'. 'Visitors' include, for example:

- Scientists who visit the area for research purposes.
- Non-resident Aboriginals.
- Non-Aboriginal people who are in the district to work for or with Aboriginals.
- Non-Aboriginal people making contact with relatives.

The distinction is an important one. By and large, 'visitors' are seen as understanding 'how to behave' in the socially approved manner. 'Tourists', on the other hand, Kesteven found were regarded by the Aborigines as

> bad news. 'Tourists' wandered aimlessly, got lost and had to be rescued; they got themselves into trouble by tempting crocodiles; they transgressed on sacred sites or burial areas; even worse, they sometimes stole relics or vandalized sites. They over-fished, they couldn't be trusted with rifles ... Tourists have no commitment to the people of Kakadu or to the land. (1987: 2)

Given such antipathy it is somewhat surprising to learn that the Aborigines have not been more openly antagonistic to the tourist invasion of their ancestral lands. On the whole, the Aboriginal attitude can be characterized as one of quiet tolerance to an 'inevitable' situation. Such tolerance is fuelled, at least in part, by an understanding of some of the benefits that tourism is seen to generate. We shall have more to say about this issue later in the discussion.

The geological feature formerly known as Ayers Rock is one of the world's best known natural phenomena. Like Kakadu to the north, it is visited by well over 200,000 domestic and international tourists each year. Indeed, 12 per cent of all overseas visitors to Australia made the long trip to Uluru in 1989. Current estimates project visitor numbers to 607,000 by 1997. A sandstone monolith measuring about 4 km long by 3 km wide, it rises steeply 348 m out of the Central Australian desert in the Northern Territory. The area is extremely remote. It lies in the centre of the continent 450 km from Alice Springs, the nearest town, and some 2500 km from Sydney. This is roughly equivalent to the distance between Los Angeles and Minneapolis. The Rock has been an important spiritual site for Aborigines for thousands of years, the numerous caves and over-hangs around its perimeter having being progressively decorated with hundreds of paintings. The paintings themselves have varied origins. Some were undoubtedly originally executed for amusement, others are sacred and related to tribal ceremonies. Yet others have an educational function.

The extensive Petermann Aboriginal Reserve, which included Ayers Rock, had been originally gazetted in 1920. From 1946 onwards the impact of the automobile started being felt and tour companies began taking a growing number of tourists to the area from Alice Springs. Pressure from these operators eventually resulted in the excision of a 1200 km slice of territory from the Aboriginal reserve in 1958 to form the Ayers Rock and Mt Olga National Park, under the management of the Northern Territory Reserves Board. Aborigines were, however, not involved in any aspect of this decision, nor was any thought given at that time to the employment of Aboriginal rangers. Indeed, even though the attraction of Ayers Rock is intimately linked with the Aboriginal heritage, Aborigines were, in the early days, effectively excluded from any involvement in the very activi-ties that were seriously compromising their traditional life styles in an area of profound religious significance. In the 1950s the Northern Territory administration had a hardline policy of evicting Aborigines from the vicinity of the Rock and the access road on the grounds that too much interaction with visitors was a 'bad thing'. The favoured policy was one of Aboriginal centralization focused on the three local settlements of Ernabella, Areyonga and Docker River. The hidden agenda, though, was that overseas tourists would not want their holiday experience marred by the sight of dispirited and frequently intoxicated Aborigines. These actions have served to entrench the view in the minds of many Abori-gines and white Australians alike that nature conservation and tourism, together, represent a 'new wave of dispossession' (Toyne and Johnston, 1991). By the 1970s several facilities had been built to accommodate the rapidly growing number of tourists. In 1970 there were 30,000 annual visitors; in 1972, 50,000. By 1987 192,000 tourists were recorded (20 per cent non-domestic) and the current annual growth rate in visitors is 36 per cent. Over 50 per cent of the tourists arrive in organized groups by coach transport, a third by private car and 15 per cent by air.

In 1977, in an important historical move, responsibility for the national park was taken from the Northern Territory and transferred to the Commonwealth government, following the passing of the National Parks and Wildlife Conservation Act, 1975. October 1985 was also an important date, for it was then that the area was handed back to its original Aboriginal owners, the Mutitjulu community. This was effected through the federal, Aboriginal Land Rights (Northern Territory) Amendment Act, ownership from henceforth being vested in the Uluru–Katatjuta Land Trust. This was not a popular move with either the Northern Territory government nor the corporate tourist sector. In 1979 the Northern Territory mounted a concerted legal attack on the land rights claim and, indeed, had temporary success.

Since coming under the administrative umbrella of the ANPWS there have been a number of significant changes at Uluru. The road to Alice Springs has been sealed and a major new resort – Yulara (an Aboriginal word for howling) – has been deliberately sited on an excised area of 104 sq km, some 20 km away from the Rock. This huge resort, which was built at a cost of $250 million, contains three major hotels, an airport and a large camping ground; its positioning and development on the other side of the Rock from the Aboriginal settlements were recommended in a series of specially commissioned consultants' reports. The frenzied construction activity at Yulara has been carried out by private enterprise, assisted by substantial financial and infrastructure support on the part of the strongly pro-developmentalist Northern Territory government. The massive resort complex generates tourist expenditure of some $30 million per year. In short, the situation at Uluru now is that the Commonwealth government, through the ANPWS, has primary responsibility for careful management of the national park and liaison with the traditional Aboriginal owners – the Mutitjulu community – while the Northern Territory government is aligned very closely with commercial concerns. The juxtaposition of a busy commercial area catering to the whims of thousands of affluent tourists with Aboriginal lands clearly poses the potential for enormous social repercussions. Indeed, Hill has commented that 'No two local communities in Australia better exemplify the inequality between black and white citizens, or more starkly illustrate the social contradictions that bloom under the influence of certain kinds of tourism' (1992: 17). Yulara – or, as it is soon to be tellingly renamed, the 'Ayers Rock Tourist Resort' – is all about conspicuous Western consumption, luxury vacationing, 'Champagne Sunsets' and staged Aboriginal authenticity. The 150-strong Mutitjulu Community on the other side of the Rock could be a million miles away in terms of living conditions and aspirations for what the resort has to offer. Superficially it might appear that one of the 'benefits' of the resort for the Aborigines would be employment prospects, yet the reality is that the local people have shown very little enthusiasm for the kinds of jobs and resulting social relationships that would be involved.

The Kakadu experiment had provided the model for European/Aboriginal co-operation in park management and similar consultative procedures have been followed at Uluru, though more speedily. The first Uluru management plan, for example, was produced in a matter of weeks, rather than years as had been the case at Kakadu. Since then, traditional Aboriginal knowledge has been used extensively in the framing of new management plans. There have been successful attempts to reintroduce important plant and animal species that have disappeared, and traditional Aboriginal burning practices have also been revived. Aborigines are in the majority on the park's board of management and have also been granted sole rights to any commercial undertakings within Uluru National Park. These are, however, likely to be only minimal. Since the old campground closed in 1983 and the motels were also moved out of the park in 1984 all tourist accommodation is now located outside the park and there are no plans to change this situation. Of the twenty park rangers, eight are Aborigines. Gate receipts to the park total some $1.6 million a year but the Mutitjulu community is allocated only 20 per cent of this sum and, overall, receives only around 1.3 per cent of annual total tourist expenditure at both Uluru and Yulara.

As at Kakadu, the changed park status made the area more attractive for the Aborigines who had previously moved away from Uluru, some of whom now returned. As noted, the Mutitjulu community now2 numbers about 150 people, currently living in four main camps at Uluru and at a much higher settlement density than at Kakadu. It is possible that others may also eventually return to Uluru, but much depends on the way in which the relationship with the tourists develops. One possibility is that the 'outstation' movement will gather momentum. This would see Aborigines deserting Uluru for what are seen to be much more 'congenial' homeland locations away from the Rock. Current predictions are that the Yulara Tourist Village, outside the park, is likely to have around 300,000 visitors by 1993. Yet a 1985 survey conducted by the Central Land Council (an Aboriginal body) found that 70 per cent of Uluru Aborigines already felt that there were too many tourists at the Rock (Altman, 1987). Quite clearly this relates to the concept of 'psychological saturation' initially raised by Young (1973) and subsequently developed by Doxey (1975) with his 'index of tourist irritation'. It refers to the situation where tourist numbers at a particular location build up to such a degree that the 'hosts' are called upon to bear what they see as being an intolerable burden of social and environmental costs. It is not at all easy for an 'outsider' fully to understand this phenomenon because it often involves attempting to understand the way the world is seen from a quite different cultural perspective.

The Aboriginal perspective and the future of tourism

Typically, orthodox economists, politicians and the general public alike, assume that their belief in the work and growth ethics and the virtues of capitalism are universally shared. Yet in many ways capitalism has only very recently been forced on to traditional Aborigines; it is not an economic system that they have freely chosen. Historically, there are four main ways in which Aborigines have come into contact with the modern market economy (Altman and Nieuwenhuysen, 1979). First, mission settlements frequently provided a pool of cheap labour for employment in the remote pastoral industry. Second, large-scale mining or tourism projects – as at Kakadu and Uluru – have sometimes started up alongside existing Aboriginal reserves, thereby providing a limited number of unskilled or semi-skilled employment opportunities for Aborigines as construction workers, full- or part-time rangers and the like. Third, there is the production of Aboriginal artefacts or paintings for sale either at selected outback tourist outlets or for export. And finally, there are a few examples of direct investment of mining or other royalties and government funds into tourist-related or other business ventures. The latter approach, for example, has been adopted at Kakadu where substantial uranium royalties paid to the Gagadju Association have been partly invested in a hotel/motel complex and a store facility in the national park. Interestingly, some of the profits from these projects have in turn been used to fund the growing 'outstation' movement, mentioned earlier. Aboriginal education is also being funded from the same source.

There are growing signs that the Aboriginal community in outback Australia has great difficulty coming to terms with the kind of consumer tourism that is becoming increasingly commonplace at popular sites such as Uluru/Yulara. Altman (1987), for example, undertook an employment survey at the Aboriginal-controlled Ininti store at Uluru in mid-1985 and observed that the local Aboriginal people traditionally 'withdraw from employment at this time of the year because they find the intensity of contact with tourists too great' (1987: 34). Elsewhere he adds that 'Anangu [Aborigines] are retreating from the residential location where daily interaction with tourists occurs . . . Bush locations provide a greater insulation from tourists and greater access to both raw materials for artefact manufacture and bush foods to supplement the diet' (1987: 33).

As I have discussed more fully elsewhere (Mercer, 1991), central to Aboriginal culture are the twin notions of responsibility and caring, even for tourists who venture on to their territory uninvited. Generally Western style tourism is not conducive to enduring personal relationships though it has to be said that what might be called the 'artefact culture' can and indeed has often accommodated quite well to consumer tourism, in Australia as well as elsewhere (Craik, 1991). Artefacts can be fashioned in relative isolation, away from the tourist gaze, and contact need only be made with an intermediary. Increasingly, as we have already noted, wealthy international tourists are combing the world in search of the exotic and the 'different'. As part of this tendency, 'Aboriginality' is being heavily promoted by white interests as a major drawcard for tourism in the Northern Territory and elsewhere in northern Australia. The Aboriginal response to this marketing pressure is ambivalent, to say the least. On the one hand they strongly object to such intrusions as being stared at or photographed without their permission or having the privacy of their camps and sacred sites violated. On the other hand, at a time when the fight for land and other rights is now high on the political agenda in Australia and becoming much more visible internationally, indigenous Australians can certainly see the advantages in 'selling' Aboriginality through the medium of tourism, as well as in other ways. They also have a clear understanding of some of the welfare and educational benefits to be gained from the sensible investment of profits derived from tourism projects.

At Uluru and elsewhere Aborigines have recently begun to produce their own tourist literature which clearly presents their unique cultural perspective on their land and customs. The 'Mutitjulu Walk' and the 'Mala Walk', for example, now compete with such activities as intrusive helicopter flights over the Rock. Also, as in Arctic Canada, a few sympathetic European tour companies now also organize small-scale outback tours in company with Aboriginal guides who are thereby given the opportunity to impart some of their knowledge to the still limited but growing number of non-Aborigines who wish to learn something of the 'wisdom of the elders' (Knudtson and Suzuki, 1992). Krippendorf (1982) argues that two broad categories of tourism can be recognized. These he calls 'hard' and 'soft' tourism. Clearly, the small-scale, Aboriginal-led, educative tours are representative of a considerate and sensitive 'soft' tourism path while large-scale tourism complexes, as at Yulara, are much more typical of a 'hard' tourism orientation.

The key problem for Aborigines in central Australia at the present time is how to make the most of the benefits to be derived from tourism without being totally swamped and overwhelmed by the worst excesses of that rapidly growing phenomenon. Dillon (1987: 9) comments that 'The existence of tourism, and the inclusion of Aboriginality as a component of the tourism resource means that Aboriginality becomes a product or good to be controlled by Aboriginal people.' In this chapter we have briefly discussed two examples where, at one level, a successful partnership appears to have been negotiated to this end between native Australians and the Australian National Parks and Wildlife Service. The only problem with this arrangement is that the Aborigines have absolutely no control over the crucial element of the numbers of visitors descending on Uluru and Kakadu and little control over their subsequent behaviour. A major, on-going, educational campaign is really required to explain carefully to Australian and overseas visitors how to behave towards Aborigines in their territory. At a more fundamental level what is urgently called for in such newly developing tourist regions as Arctic Canada, Amazonia and Central Australia is what Krippendorf (1982: 135) refers to as a 'fundamental political transformation in the conception of tourism'. Joint management is ostensibly a good idea yet it must not be forgotten that it represents 'a Western cultural model, deriving from within our culture and social context' (Craig, 1992: 147). In the future there is no certainty that an increasingly radical Aboriginal movement will view joint management favourably, especially if there is little or no improvement in their material living standards and conditions in Australia as a whole.

Currently, a major ideological conflict is being played out in northern Australia between pro-developmentalist tourism interests and the Aboriginal community. The main issue revolves around the commodification of Aboriginality. The developmentalist stance is represented by such bodies as the Northern Territory Development Corporation and the Northern Territory Tourist Commission, both of which are pressing strongly for Aborigines to be much less retiring about tourism and, in effect, to 'display' themselves and regularly 'perform' traditional dances, on cue, for tourist consumption. Their 1984 report, *Initiatives for Tourism Facilities* for example, writes of the 'acute need for the provision of some means or facility to expose tourists to aspects of Aboriginal culture, life-style, way of life or mythology' (Northern Territory Development Corporation, 1984: 23). It is suggested that this be provided in certain 'Aboriginal Culture Centres' where 'daily activities such as weaving and dancing' could take place. However, as was emphasized earlier in the chapter, the political demands of Aboriginal Australia revolve around the twin themes of choice and control. At this stage it seems rather unlikely that Australian Aborigines will readily accede to external demands to speedily 'package' their Aboriginality in tune with the whims of Australian business interests or the international tourist market.

References

Altman, J.C. (1987) *The Economic Impact of Tourism on the Mutitjulu Community, Uluru (Ayers Rock–Mount Olga) National Park*. Working Paper No. 7,

Department of Political and Social Change, Research School of Pacific Studies, Australian National University, Canberra

Altman, J.C. and Nieuwenhuysen, J. (1979) *The Economic Status of Australian Aborigines*, Cambridge University Press, Cambridge

Ascher, F. (1985) *Tourism: Transnational Corporations and Cultural Identities*, UNESCO, Paris

Brady, M. (1985) The promotion of tourism and its effect on Aborigines. In *Aborigines and Tourism. A Study of the Impact of Tourism on Aborigines in the Kakadu Region, Northern Territory* (ed. K. Palmer), Northern Land Council, Darwin

Britton, S. and Clarke, W.C. (1986) *Ambiguous Alternative. Tourism in Small Developing Countries*, University of the South Pacific, Suva

Butlin, N.G. (1983) *Our Original Aggression. Aboriginal Populations of Southeastern Australia*, Allen and Unwin, Sydney

Craig, D. (1992) Environmental law and Aboriginal rights: legal framework for Aboriginal joint management of Australian national parks. In *Aboriginal Involvement in Parks and Protected Areas* (ed. J. Birckhead, T. De Lacy and L. Smith), Aboriginal Studies Press for the Australian Institute of Aboriginal and Torres Strait Islander Studies, Canberra, ACT, pp. 137–148

Craik, J. (1991) *Resorting to Tourism. Cultural Policies for Tourist Development in Australia*, Allen and Unwin, North Sydney

DeKadt, E. (1979) *Tourism: Passport to Development?* Oxford University Press, New York

Dillon, M.C. (1987) *Aborigines and Tourism in North Australia: Some Suggested Research Approaches*. East Kimberley Impact Assessment Project, Working Paper No. 14. Centre for Resource and Environmental Studies, Australian National University, Canberra

Doxey, G.V. (1975) A causation theory of visitor–resident irritants: methodology and research inferences. In *Proceedings of the Travel Research Association Sixth Annual Conference*, San Diego, California, pp. 195–8

Gare, N. (1984) Kakadu National Park – World Heritage Area and tourist destination. In *Parks, Recreation and Tourism* (ed. M. Wells), Proceedings of the 57th National Conference of the Royal Australian Institute of Parks and Recreation, Launceston, Tasmania, October, pp. 48–54

Goulet, D. (1977) *What Kind of Tourism? Or, Poison in a Luxury Package*. Working Paper Series, No. 2, Tourism Research, Department of Geography, McGill University, Montreal Canada

Head, L. (1992) Australian Aborigines and a changing environment – views of the past and implications for the future. In *Aboriginal Involvement in Parks and Protected Areas* (ed. J. Birckhead, T. De Lacy and L. Smith), Aboriginal Studies Press for the Australian Institute of Aboriginal and Torres Strait Islander Studies, Canberra, ACT, pp. 47–56

Hiatt, L.R. (1985) Aboriginal land ownership. *Current Affairs Bulletin*, **61**, 17–23

Hill, B. (1992) The soul of the place. *Modern Times*, May, pp. 16–18

Jones, R.M. (1991) Landscapes of the mind: Aboriginal perceptions of the environment. In *The Humanities and the Australian Environment* (ed. D.J. Mulvaney), Occasional Paper No. 11, Australian Academy of the Humanities, Canberra, ACT, pp. 21–48

Keller, C.P. (1983) Centre/periphery tourism development and control. Unpublished paper presented to International Geographical Union, Commission on the Geography of Tourism and Leisure, Conference on Leisure, Tourism and Social Change. Edinburgh, January

Kesteven, S. (1987) *Aborigines in the Tourist Industry*. East Kimberley Working Paper No. 14, East Kimberley Impact Assessment Project, Centre for Resource and Environmental Studies, Australian National University, Canberra

Knudtson, P. and Suzuki, D. (1992) *The Wisdom of the Elders*, Allen and Unwin, Sydney

Krippendorf, J. (1982) Towards new tourism policies. The importance of environmental and sociocultural factors. *Tourism Management*, **3**, 135–48

Lewis, H.T. (1992) The technology and ecology of nature's custodians: anthropological perspectives on Aborigines and national parks. In *Aboriginal Involvement in Parks and Protected Areas* (ed. J. Birckhead, T. De Lacy and L. Smith), Aboriginal Studies

Press for the Australian Institute of Aboriginal and Torres Strait Islander Studies, Canberra, ACT, pp. 15–28

Lynge, F. (1987) In defence of the Inuit world – saving a way of life. *The Environmentalist* **7**(3), 191–6

Mercer, D. (1991) *'A Question of Balance'. Natural Resources Conflict Issues in Australia*, The Federation Press, Sydney

Mercer, D. (1993) Terra nullius, Aboriginal sovereignty and land rights in Australia. The debate continues. *Political Geography* **12**(4), July 1993, pp. 219–318

Moorehead, A. (1966) *The Fatal Impact*, Hamish Hamilton, London

Mulvaney, D.J. (1975) *The Prehistory of Australia*, Penguin, Ringwood

Northern Territory Development Corporation (1984) *Initiatives for Tourism Facilities*, NTDC and Northern Territory Tourist Commission, Darwin

Prosser, R.F. (1992) The ethics of tourism. In *The Environment in Question. Ethics and Global Issues* (ed. D.E. Cooper and J.A. Palmer), Routledge, London and New York, pp. 37–50

Reynolds, H. (1987) *The Law of the Land*, Penguin, Ringwood

Singh, T.V. and Kaur, J. (1986) The paradox of mountain tourism: case references from the Himalaya. *Industry and Environment*, **9**(1), 21–6

Toyne, P. and Johnston, R. (1991) Reconciliation or the new dispossession? Aboriginal land rights and nature conservation. *Habitat*, **19**(3), 8–10

Turner, L. and Ash, J. (1975) *The Golden Hordes. International Tourism and the Pleasure Periphery*, Constable, London

Wells, A.L. (1986) Terrorism abroad – does it mean more travel at home? *Destinations*, **8**(8), 31–4

Willmot, E. (1987) *Australia – the Last Experiment*, Australian Broadcasting Corporation, Sydney

Young, G. (1973) *Tourism – Blessing or Blight?* Penguin, Harmondsworth

10 Exploring the political role of gender in tourism research

Linda K. Richter

Gender and tourism have something in common when it comes to political analysis: neither was taken seriously by political scientists as important subjects of political inquiry until relatively recently. Recognition of variations in political behaviour among men and women became a subject of research only after the Second World War and public policy studies of either tourism or gender issues are less than twenty years old in the United States.

Gender studies have developed a rich literature in that time. Tourism, while gradually attracting more attention by social scientists, continues to lack sustained political study. In most cases, researchers stumble onto tourism inadvertently when they are exploring something else. Surprisingly, it was the Christian Church in Asia that perhaps earlier than any other institution recognized the political importance of tourism.

Today, however, in the church and within several other forums linkages are also being made between *gender* and *tourism*. Church and peace and justice groups are looking at the issue of international tourism's impact on the exploitation of women and children, or labor, education and development issues. In each issue gender differences exist. *Annals of Tourism Research,* a refereed social science journal, is devoting a special issue to the relationships between gender and tourism. Even in women's studies and international relations texts, new connections are being made between gender and tourism. One of the best such analyses is Cynthia Enloe's *Bananas, Beaches, and Bases* (1989). It explores not only the gender differences in opportunity structure, but the substantial evolution of travel and tourism roles.

What this chapter will do is suggest areas of tourism research in which there are politically important gender issues and speculate about how trends in tourism and political organizations may affect the gender distinctions that have emerged. But first some definitional clarification is appropriate.

There are dozens of ways to define the study of politics, but one both pithy and pertinent is that of American political scientist Harold Lasswell. He said politics is 'who gets what, when and how' (Lasswell, 1936). Knowing if and how tourism differently affects men and women would seem the very essence of studying the politics of gender and tourism.

But if tourism is like almost every other policy issue to which a gender analysis has been applied, the sexes do not begin with a level playing field. Thus, to Lasswell's definition, it would be prudent to add Michael Parenti's addition 'and who already has what' (Parenti, 1977). This writer would add 'and who cares' (Richter, 1991a). The factual discussion of the topic can take us only so far; attention also needs to be given to the *perceptions, intensity* and *salience* of the issue to individuals and groups of varying resources and commitments.

The political relationship of gender to tourism is not static but rapidly evolving. The elite-driven policy sector is increasingly opening up to more claimants for influence – in gender terms that process has meant increased access to and impact on women. That represents a marked departure from the historical gender differences *vis-à-vis* tourism.

Gender differences in tourism: a historical perspective

'Until the sixteenth century to be a woman, travel, and remain respectable one had to be generally either a queen or a pilgrim' (Robinson, 1990). Travel has had a different *contextual* meaning for men than for women until very recent times. Travel meant conquest, wars, crusades, exploration, trading opportunities, hunting, trapping, fishing, commerce. Overwhelmingly, that was the public sphere of men in contrast to the global tendency to assign the private sphere of home and family to women. To the extent women participated, they did so as a vital support system for missionary work, immigration, imperial adventures, diplomatic support, or 'civilizing the frontier'.

By the nineteenth century, travel had come to be seen as a value in its own right. The Grand Tour of Europe was the capstone to an affluent young man's education. Travel was a scarce resource eagerly sought which enhanced a young man's economic and political prospects even as it broadened his tastes. It augmented a man's prestige but it diminished a woman's reputation.

For women, education generally was seen as having much less utility and was characteristically confined to music and the domestic arts. Travel was irrelevant unless it functioned to support family goals or was justified for religious pilgrimage or health considerations. Unchaperoned travel of single women until the mid-twentieth century compromised marriage prospects and was not seen as a positive reflection on the woman's intellect and sophistication, but as betraying a certain lack of modesty and propriety. In Western societies, women were seen as requiring the protection of men from the dangers posed by other men, particularly, when venturing beyond family and friends.

In general, in Asian and Middle Eastern societies, the assumptions were quite different though the solution similar. Women were considered sufficiently lusty and unreliable that family honour required their early marriage and sustained surveillance. In China, the practice of footbinding assured that affluent women would contribute to their husband's status by their absolute inability to labour, let alone travel except by palanquin! By being economically useless and dependent, they demonstrated their husbands' ability to afford such idleness.

Thomas Cook launched his famous travel-based empire in Europe intent on providing reliable, proper escorted tours for curious women eager to transcend home and hearth – albeit respectably. It would be another hundred years before the travel industry began to cope with the needs of female *business* travelers! This was true into the twentieth century.

There were always female mavericks who travelled with gusto with and without spouses and entourages. Their exploits are only beginning to be rediscovered. Most press accounts of the day viewed them with disdain as 'globe trotteresses' and dismissed their considerable insights as irrelevant. It was not until 1892 that the Royal Geographic Society admitted women. In the United States it would be over thirty more years before women were allowed in The Explorers Club. Women by that time had set up their own Society of Women Geographers (Tinling, 1989)! But for most women of means, travel adventures were not on the horizon.

Women's accounts of their travels have differed markedly from men. Women have had greater access to the women and children in other societies than have men, and their accounts, as a consequence, offer more of a sense of family customs. Men, as might be expected, were more apt to comment on political affairs, the impact of European ideas and the state of technology (Tinling, 1989).

Not just travel, but even at home the very notion of leisure time was one enjoyed by men long before women. The weekend, for example, meant far less of a change in activity for women than for men. As Rybczynski notes in *Waiting for the Weekend*: 'The proper place for proper women was the home – public leisure was exclusively a male domain' (Rybczynski, 1991).

Gender differences in employment and ownership

Men and women not only have historically been socialized to view travel from very different perspectives, but there continues to be a division of labour by gender at all levels of the travel and tourism hierarchies.

Let's consider 'who already has what'. United Nations' statistics tell us that though women do two-thirds of the world's work, they get one-tenth of the world's income and have one-hundredth of the world's property (Johnson, 1983). Comparable statistics focused on the travel and tourism industry do not exist, but inequality appears none the less to be the norm in most sectors.

The tourism sector taken as a whole (and its boundaries are still open to dispute) is small-scale. In the United States, for example, over 95 per cent of tourism-related businesses are quite small. Women dominate travel agency ownership and are a majority of travel agents (Richter, 1991b). In monetary terms, however, men control the major sectors of the tourism economy. There are few if any women owners of airlines, railroads, major destinations (except Dolly Parton's Dolly World), hotel chains (inmate Leona Helmsley's empire is an exception), car rental companies and travel magazines. Even female travel writers are scarce – Jan Morris being a notable exception and having established her reputation first as a male.

Nationalists in developing countries bemoan the perils of tourism turning their country into a nation of waiters and bellhops because of foreign control (itself largely male-controlled) (T. Barry et al., 1984; English, 1986). The real bottom of the hierarchy, however, are the chambermaids, restaurant help and laundresses. They get few tips and have the least dignified positions (Enloe, 1989). Female cooks and waitresses tend to be found in the lowest paid parts of the food sector. While cooking is historically a female task in most societies, it becomes an overwhelmingly male niche in the fancier restaurants where salaries and tips are substantial.

So while women do have *access* and *employment* disproportionately to men in the travel sector, these positions tend to be available – as indeed, they are to minorities – because they are seasonal, part-time or minimum wage. This relates to the fact that they also are in the least organized sectors of the travel labour market.

In summary, the answer to 'who already has what' is that women have the majority of the jobs at the base of the tourism employment hierarchy; men have almost all of the jobs at the middle and top.

Prostitution

One employment sector, prostitution, once almost exclusively female has become unenviably open to men and boys. While most countries have prostitution – legal or not – certain destinations have become inextricably linked with sex tourism, such as Thailand (nicknamed 'Thighland' in some circles), the Philippines, Sri Lanka and Brazil. (K. Barry et al., 1984; Holden and Horleman, 1983; Richter, 1989a; Sereewat, 1983; Thanh-Dam, 1983). The numbers are boggling, the social spillover daunting in disease, crime and neglected children. While the prostitutes remain overwhelmingly female, a growing gay market and pedophilia market exploit men and young boys (ECPAT, 1992). In any case, the *customers* are almost exclusively male. Females buying the 'escort plus' services of black males in the Caribbean are not unknown, but the sex tourism industry revolves around the fantasies of men and is owned and controlled by men. Women work for men, not vice versa, when it comes to the provision of sexual services.

Many things combine to link sexual activity with tourism. By its minimum definition, a tourist is someone staying overnight at least 100 miles from home. The anonymity of being away from friends, business associates and relatives offers opportunity for discreet extramarital sexual liaisons without the emotional, long-term commitment of an affair. It combines a sense of kinky adventure with intimacy in a strange location.

Explaining sex tourism?

Two interesting arguments are advanced by those more sanguine about sex tourism than is the present writer. Both place the responsibility not on the men but the morals and attitudes of women. One line of reasoning is that prostitution is the world's oldest profession, and that in many of the travel markets where it is most explicit, concubinage has been its national equivalent for centuries.

This argument does not face the very different conditions associated with prostitution in a touristic context. Regularly patronizing a prostitute or supporting a concubine were much less dangerous for the men and women involved, than the transient and fleeting associations now taking place. The legalization and institutionalization of prostitution in such places as Australia and Las Vegas, have in fact been a response to the robberies, murders, drug-dealing and health problems associated with unregulated prostitution. (It is also a way to tax a lucrative industry and get kickbacks from the licensing of prostitutes.)

The second argument is even more ingenious. It blames sex tourism on the women's movement! Instead of women staying in their place, they demand equality. Instead of 'free sex', as they unshackle their inhibitions they have become more picky about the men with whom they will mate! Imagine, the women's movement did not define itself the way some men wanted. Pro-choice was extended not only to abortion but to coupling! This argument was actually made in a supposedly serious research paper this writer reviewed. It purported to explain why Australian males went on sex trips to Thailand. Supposedly, they needed to do some male bonding and be with some feminine women after contending with increasingly uppity Australian women, corrupted by the women's movement!

Not only is it insulting to suggest such fragile egos in Australian men, but it is a curious argument to suggest that a bid for equality among Australian women *naturally* will result in the exploitation of other women! Nor does it appear to be a sufficient explanation for sex tourism from Japan where the women's movement is almost microscopic, or pedophilia tours from Germany where presumably the children are no more aggressive than anywhere else!

So who cares? Increasingly, groups are organizing against sex tours, the exploitation of children, and the health and safety issues attached to each. One of the most active of these groups is End Child Prostitution in Asian Tourism (ECPAT), which is moving on child prostitution issues in scores of countries. They have already had some success.

Realistically, they have their best chance of success in terms of controlling child prostitution, through stiff fines and sentences for the *customers* and *parents* of such abused children. The global network against such exploitation offers some support to governments long on good intentions but short on will. AIDS may be a more effective antidote to misplaced ardor than government action, but advertising, family fares and destination development that sells non-sexual activities are all options that more and more groups may sponsor.

Gender differences in marketing, souvenirs and attractions

Gender and marketing

Theoretically, the appeal of combining sex with tourism should be the same for both sexes, but it is not. Whether we ascribe the differences to biological propensities, socialization or opportunity structure, an industry providing a sexual ambiance and sexual favours to male clients creates a potentially hostile environment for female clients. Yet, because males control the industry and particularly its marketing and promotion, the expectations of linking sex with tourism are everywhere. Handsome, flirtatious men are not what the ads offer. It is women, alone or with other women, and often in remote natural settings or in a serving role, as in hotel and airline ads. Intact families, older people and children are not pictured in most advertisements.

In fact, advertising encouraging whole families to travel is the exception, though industry analysts predict more of this as ageing baby boomers bring children along on vacations, e.g. children's versions of Club Med or cruise activities. In general, men who bring their wives on business trips are sold romantic, second honeymoon experiences. Women, on the other hand, are promised physically pampering environments with excellent shopping! The older woman traveller has been virtually ignored in the marketing research though evidence suggests she may be a much more active and economically important element than anticipated (Hawes, 1988). This is not surprising. The industry generally has been both myopic and sexist in its assumptions about what women need and want, despite the fact that women make the majority of the decisions regarding discretionary travel (Smith, 1979; Tunstall, 1989).

As women have increasingly become more of the travel market, the industry response has adapted in some curious ways consistent with male orientation and female concerns. The general advertising has become a bit more subtle. Prostitution services have become less small-scale, more entrepreneurial. Visa and Mastercard are accepted for a dazzling array of itemized sexual services from virtually any racial and ethnic group one desires. Presumably routinizing such services will encourage less hassling of women in general, and women travelling alone in particular. It will also encourage men to patronize services *controlled* by other men. In the age of AIDS and herpes, men get some assurances that the women they buy will be inspected and presumed healthy. The women, of course, get no such protection from their clients!

Women business travellers, then, are just as likely to be interacting professionally with men who are buying the sexual favours of other women. What the male-controlled industry offers is the better protection of their female business travellers. Thus, there is greater attention to security in the issuance of keys, better locks, and more attentive service in restaurants. Hair dryers, skirt hangers and bubble baths are also more likely to be included in hotels, be it for clients or their female guests. That women still feel vulnerable is suggested by their much greater use of room service for meals.

Gender and souvenirs

Another area where gender differences emerge with respect to tourism is in the selling of memories through postcards and souvenirs. Semiotics has demonstrated that those in control show us an image of 'the other' that is congruent with the dominant group values, their expectations and their goals. For example, we can now look back with some amusement, tinged with horror, at the way early travel writings described non-Western societies. The more lurid the tales from Asia, Africa and the American frontier of cannibals, sacrifices, savages and bare-breasted maidens, the easier it was to rationalize imperial 'civilizing' adventures.

The United States was not immune. President McKinley reportedly declared in 1898 that he was annexing the Philippines 'for our little brown brothers for whom Christ also died'. This ignored the fact that the Philippines after 350 years of Spanish rule was 85 per cent Catholic already!

Travel brochures often encourage the traveller to expect friendly pampering. One widely promoted Caribbean advertisement, had a staff of black cooks, maids, bellmen, drivers, etc. with trays of food and flowers out waist deep in the ocean offering these goodies to a white couple lounging on a rubber raft. Gender was not the issue but racial and economic dependency; however in postcards, brochures and souvenirs the gender dimension, like that of race, is well worth exploring.

Under Philippine dictator Ferdinand Marcos, the tourism slogan was 'Where Asia Wears a Smile' – and the advertising promised 'a tanned peach on every beach' (Richter, 1982). Nude or scantily dressed women are the staple of many postcard shops. To its credit, the Philippines under President Aquino was one nation that dramatically changed its government marketing of tourism (Richter, 1988). Indonesia, on the other hand, sells pictures of nude tribal people (both male and female) and penis sheaths at its Biak airport shop. The exploitation of native peoples is so much easier after you take away their dignity.

In Hawaii, this is taken a step further. Authentic Hawaiians are not even pictured, but usually some generic Polynesian-cum-Filipino-Japanese mix deemed more sexy for North American and European markets. Blond, blue-eyed women are more apt to be the erotic subjects of advertising targeting the Japanese!

Even the United States permitted its government tourist office to promote one of its Caribbean territories with giant buttons saying 'TRY A VIRGIN . . . island'. Happily, it evoked an appropriately negative response when called to the attention of the Coalition on Third World Tourism and the Caribbean Council of Churches (Richter, 1989b).

In 1984, a new product hit the market with the editorial approval of the *Honolulu Star Bulletin* – 'scratch and sniff' postcards. Scratch the females pictured and they give off scents of the flowers of Hawaii. Someone once said, 'No one ever went broke underestimating the taste of the American public!' Similarly, there would not be a shortage of sexist souvenir kitsch should one try to collect it. Even Dan Quayle when Vice President was not alone in buying a little Latin American male doll with sexually explicit moving parts.

In sculpture, be it marble, wood, or terracotta, in pictures, black velvet or canvas, in virtually any medium, so-called 'airport art' flourishes. Not always, but nearly so, when human beings are the object, they are sexually explicit female renditions.

Gender and attractions

Even though women figure prominently in advertising, postcards and souvenirs, they are sadly neglected in cultural and historical tourism destinations supported by taxpayers' money. Battlefields do not celebrate those who nursed the soldiers; galleries do not provide showcases for female talent; museums may feature fashions from an era or the dresses of First Ladies, but they seldom recall the daring adventures or courage of women. Statues recall war heroes, 'forefathers' not 'foremothers', 'founders of towns' (not their invisible spouses). In the United States the Statue of Liberty, the Madonna of the Plains and monuments to the frontier woman occasionally remember women as a category, rarely the specific woman.

It was not until the 1980s that a museum of women's art was opened in Washington, DC with *private* donations. Even the most beautiful tourist site in the world, the Taj Mahal, while built as a crypt for a woman, is remembered as a testament to Emperor Shah Jahan's love! Thus, the *impact* of tourism continues to socialize generations to the importance of what men have done while women are ignored or immortalized on postcards, nutcrackers and T-shirts.

Prospects for policy changes

Will 'who gets what, when and how' change as more women enter the workplace, as the numbers of both men and women travelling accelerate? Probably. But the prospects for greater balance in gender control are mixed.

The vast bulk of the financial control of the private tourism sector is in the hands of men. That is almost equally true of the public sector. Government policymakers, be they political appointees or career bureaucrats, are overwhelmingly male. The US example illustrates this point. The executive branch is overwhelmingly male at the policy-making levels (GS 16–18). Only two of the President's cabinet officials in 1992 were female, along with 5 per cent of the members of the House of Representatives, and 2 per cent of the Senate. Forty-seven of the fifty states are headed by male tourism directors (Richter, 1985). In 1992 the present author was the only female among the fifteen members of the National Travel and Tourism Advisory Board. In March 1992, however, the first ever female United States Secretary of Commerce, Barbara Franklin, was confirmed, and a woman was also head of United States Customs. The Philippines was unusual in 1992 in having a female Secretary of Tourism and three female undersecretaries. The Aquino role model accelerated a pattern already more pronounced there: more women in the poorly paid public sector *versus* more men in the private sector, but at least the women are in positions of influence.

Women have been perceived as particularly appropriate for 'frontline' tourism positions because they are assumed to be more social, more hospitable then men. In fact, in the Philippines, the euphemism for tourism prostitute is a 'hospitality girl'. Zulfiqar Ali Bhutto, former prime minister of Pakistan, actually saw tourism as a new sector that would be ideally suited to women, whose employment and social uplift were a priority with him. For that very reason among others tourism was seen as a force of corruption and pollution among conservative forces in Pakistan and within other Islamic cultures. Christian churches in Asia, the Pacific and the Caribbean would be inclined to agree. In the Maldives, a tiny Muslim nation in the Indian Ocean, only men are allowed to work at the tourist resorts which are on separate islands physically isolated from the rest of the population (Richter, 1989a).

Ideological forces now sweeping the globe are encouraging less national planning, more devolution of power, greater privatization of industry including the privatization and deregulation of the tourist industry. These forces may create an industry more susceptible to market forces but it may deprive further those with the least influence and political access. Equity, systemic justice and the public interest, which were seldom well-served by the tourist industry before, may have an even greater struggle in the days ahead (Richter, 1991a, b).

As this writer has noted elsewhere:

> The primary reason why US tourism policy has not taken a more holistic approach to tourism is because of its fixation on tourism as a revenue-producing activity rather than as an important facet in improving the quality of life by reducing stress, enhancing education, instilling variety, and contributing to shared family experiences. While concern for revenue is reasonable since tourism generates billions in federal, state, and local taxes, such a perspective ignores the nonmonetary features of tourism policy and the not so easily quantified monetary costs of tourism development. Unlike much of the industrialized world, which also appreciates tourism's economic impact, the United States and its policy has not moved beyond the profit motive to a consideration of the role of leisure in the promotion of health, reduction of crime, reward of labor, or the importance of travel as an information medium. (Richter, 1991b)

On the other hand, the anti-incumbency fever that has gripped not only the United States but political institutions around the globe may argue for a stronger role for the ultimate political outsiders – women. However, as I have argued elsewhere, there are many reasons to assume that class, race, religious and ethnic loyalties will continue to be more salient than gender (Richter, 1990). What we do know is that women in public office have shown a disproportionate concern for social welfare and environmental issues, for the issues of health, women and children – all areas towards which the unfettered tourism industry has on many occasions been overly cavalier (Darcy et al., 1987). Thus, if women achieve more access to representative institutions and public policy positions, current research suggests they will have an impact on tourism in specifically those areas where women have had least control and influence. Stronger worker safety, wage and health laws might be anticipated.

A phenomenon as massive as tourism and a variable as basic as gender cannot be discussed thoroughly in this brief space. Clearly, however, there are numerous *evolving* dimensions of this relationship that deserve further scrutiny. Once we acknowledge that tourism has been marginalized and trivialized as a research subject and requires careful analysis, it is a logical next step to explore its impact in the context of such a basic variable as gender.

References

Barry, Kathleen, Bunch, Charlotte and Castley, Shirley (1984) *International Feminism: Networking Against Female Slavery*, International Women's Tribune Centre, New York

Barry, Tom, Wood, Beth and Preusch, Deborah (1984) *The Other Side of Paradise: Foreign Control in the Caribbean*, Grove Press, New York

Darcy, R., Welch, Susan and Clark, Janet (1987) *Women, Elections and Representation*, Longman, New York, pp. 153–4

ECPAT (1992) Children in Prostitution: Victims of Tourism in Asia. Conference Statement, End Child Prostitution in Asian Tourism, Bangkok

English, Philip (1986) *The Great Escape: an Examination of North-South Tourism*, North–South Institute, Ottawa

Enloe, Cynthia (1989) *Bananas, Beaches, and Bases: Making Feminist Sense of International Politics*, University of California Press, Berkeley, Ca.

Hawes, Douglass K. (1988) Travel-related lifestyle profiles of older women. *Journal of Travel Research*, Fall, pp. 22–32

Holden, Peter and Horlemann, Pfafflin (eds) (1983) *Documentation: Tourism, Prostitution, Development*, Ecumenical Coalition on Third World Tourism, Bangkok

Johnson, Sonia (1983) Women and the quest for justice. A speech given at Kansas State University, April 29

Lasswell, Harold (1936) *Politics: Who Gets What, When, and How?* McGraw Hill, New York

Parenti, Michael (1977) *Democracy for the Few*, St. Martin's Press, New York

Richter, Linda K. (1982) *Land Reform and Tourism Development: Policy-Making in the Philippines*, Schenkman, Cambridge, Mass.

Richter, Linda K. (1985) State-sponsored tourism: a growth field for public administration. *Public Administration Review*, November–December, pp. 832–9

Richter, Linda K. (1988) Public bureaucracy in post-Marcos Philippines. *Southeast Asian Journal of Social Science*, **15**(2), pp. 57–76

Richter, Linda K. (1989a) *The Politics of Tourism in Asia,* University of Hawaii Press, Honolulu

Richter, Linda K. (1989b) Action alert. *Contours,* **4**(4), 4

Richter, Linda K. (1990) Exploring theories of female leadership in South and South–East Asia. *Pacific Affairs,* **63**(4), 524–40

Richter, Linda K. (1991a) Political issues in tourism policy: a forecast. In *World Travel and Tourism Review* (ed. D. Hawkins and J.B. Ritchie), CAB International (UK), pp. 189–93

Richter, Linda K. (1991b) The impact of American tourism policy on women. In *Gender Differences* (ed. Mary Lou Kendrigan), Greenwood Press, Colorado, p. 161

Robinson, Jane (1990) *Wayward Women: A Guide to Women Travellers,* Oxford University Press, London, p. 152

Rybczynski, Witold (1991) *Waiting for the Weekend,* Viking Penguin, London, p. 107

Sereewat, Sudarat, (1983) *Prostitution: Thai–European connection,* World Council of Churches, Geneva, Switzerland

Smith, Valene L. (1979) Women: the taste-makers in tourism. *Annals of Tourism Research,* **6**(1), 49–60

Thanh-Dam, Truong (1983) The dynamics of sex tourism: the case of Southeast Asia. *Development and Change,* **14**, 533–53

Tinling, Marion (1989) *Women into the Unknown,* Greenwood Press, New York, p. XXIV

Tunstall, Ruth (1989) Catering for the female business traveler. In *EIU Travel and Tourism Analyst,* No. 5, pp. 26–40

Part Three

Comparative Perspectives: Management and Policy Issues

Introduction

The decades of the 1980s and 1990s have been a period characterized by a growing global trend towards privatization. This trend has occurred in part due to the break-up of the Eastern bloc countries, especially the Soviet Union, and increased foreign investment in those countries as well as in China. However, one major development issue of privatization, that of small-scale local tourist enterprises in the Third World, has largely been ignored. Smith in Chapter 11 suggests that ecotourism, one of the most discussed development concept of the 1990s, by its nature tends to support small-scale local accommodations since they are generally more ecologically sensitive than mega-resorts.

Successful privatization of small-scale local accommodations depends upon factors not necessarily common to most Third World countries including: extensive capitalization apart from tourism; common language fluency and cultural orientation between tourists and residents; broad travel organization affiliations; access to local and regional advertising media; and knowledge of business procedures.

One of the byproducts of ecotourism is the opportunity to meet local residents through home stays. Proprietorship of small-scale businesses does bring about some economic benefit to individual owners. When introduced into Third World private homes, however, tourism essentially intrudes into traditional societies where by custom, women work in the home. In addition, as guest homes become more successful, the amount of work required by family members, especially women, to operate them increases significantly.

The tourism life cycle concept and the carrying capacity concept are interrelated in a manner that is both dynamic and dependent. The life cycle concept suggests that destination areas change over time, and progress through stages from introduction to decline. Although different disciplines have various meanings for it, carrying capacity embodies the idea that there is a limit to use, after which point negative effects occur.

Williams and Gill (Chapter 12) point out that like other economic enterprises, tourism is widely recognized as a change agent. With sound management, it holds the potential for being a low user of scarce resources as well as being a sustainable industry. Like the previous chapter, the authors point out that effective carrying capacity management is central to tourism's continued growth and popularity.

A number of tourism carrying capacity management perspectives, issues and concepts are presented. Four essential assumptions are provided on which each of the perspectives is based: tourism is a catalyst for change; desired condition for tourism can be identified; these conditions are dynamic, varying temporally and geographically on economic, socio-political and environmental circumstances and management strategies can be developed that are capable of controlling both the rate and direction of change caused by tourism.

In Chapter 13 Taylor questions the overemphasis or principle concern tourism has placed on consumption rather than on the consumer. Little systematic attention has been directed in order to gain a greater understanding of the tourist and his participation patterns and travel habits. The concept of styles of travel may be useful in developing a body of knowledge about tourism consumers. Style of travel is defined as the way people perceive, organize and execute travel. Two important types of information are important when measuring styles of travel the incidence of travel, and; the way people think about the travel they take.

The use of both travel incidence and travel style data can provide a greater understanding of international tourism, and when these two data sets are examined at the same time, the fact of change will be accompanied by the direction of change. The implications of such data should not be overlooked as a means of improving knowledge of both the markets and the opportunities for increased consumer satisfaction.

Tourist typologies have primarily resulted from consumer segmentation marketing studies conducted during the 1970s which used among other variables life style criteria. According to Mazanec and Zins (Chapter 14), the Eurostyle system is a multinational life style typology which encompasses five principal dimensions of life style which help constitute sixteen different life style types.

Europanel, a group of fifteen European commercial market research institutes produced life style data originating from consumer panels in tourism-generating countries. This life style data was adopted by the Austrian National Tourist Office in order to determine the life style and guest characteristics of travellers to Austria. It was shown to be of practical value in destination marketing, with some modifications which the chapter describes.

The political events which resulted in the downfall of communism in Eastern Europe have led to substantial changes in previously established travel patterns and thereby opened this area for international tourism. In Chapter 15 Witt provides a description of Bulgaria, Czechoslovakia, the former German Democratic Republic, Hungary, Poland, Romania and the former Soviet Union as tourist destinations, and provides statistical documentation of their visitor arrivals, total tourism receipts and tourism receipts as a percentage of exports.

Although largely unexplored by Westerners, the seven Eastern European countries have an abundance of natural resources, beautiful cities, historic and cultural resources that could attract tourists. What is needed to attract these visitors is better education and training, Western capital and expertise, and improved marketing programmes. There are, however, a number of constraints that mitigate further tourism development including inadequate infrastructure, a shortage of high-quality accommodation and an overall low quality of tourist products and services. Two key additional requisites to tourism development are political stability and visitor safety.

11 Privatization in the Third World: small-scale tourism enterprises

Valene L. Smith

Privatization, especially proprietorship of small-scale local-level tourist enterprises in the Third World, is a critical developmental issue that has essentially been ignored. As a proprietary and managerial concept, privatization gained widespread attention during the 1980s, an era when some political states chose to raise cash by selling assets including their national airlines and hotel chains. It was intended these holdings should be owned by the private sector, thus transferring management of tourism to local entities. Unfortunately capital-rich foreign corporations were sometimes the successful bidders.

In the 1990s, the privatization trend is global, fuelled by the break-up of the Soviet Union, and increased foreign investment there as well as in China. The United States government is also involved, instituting new policies to privatize many facilities within the National Parks and Forests.

Third World tourism developed rapidly in the years following the Second World War because land and tax incentives encouraged Western capital to invest in the essential infrastructure to attract foreign visitors. Westerners held managerial positions, hiring and training local labour for routine services. Literature of the 1970s and 1980s cites as one of the positive benefits of tourism 'the creation of jobs and the opportunity for people to increase their income and standard of living' (DeKadt, 1979), particularly for unskilled labour with limited education. By contrast, 'Crumbs from the table? The worker's share in tourism' (Samy, 1975) was among the first studies to challenge the supposed benefits to the host population. Subsequently other authors, including dependency theory advocates, have repeatedly urged privatization and local control as remedies for leakage as well as the sir–servitude syndrome and insensitivity to local norms.

Ecotourism, the banner of the 1990s, tends to support small-scale local-level accommodations (here also termed cottages) as environmentally sensitive in contrast to mega-resorts. But are they economically viable and socially desirable? This chapter considers these socio-economic issues, and especially host–guest relations, associated with privatization in Third World or developing countries. As used here, the term 'privatization' refers to small family-operated tourist facilities such as inns and guest houses although the discussion could be also extended to cafes and craft or souvenir shops. Bryden (1973) suggested two decades ago the need to investigate the impact of renting rooms but the published literature is still virtually nil. This present analysis depends heavily on extensive fieldwork by the author in a variety of locales – remote sites or ethnic enclaves in the Western world as well as Third World settings.

Home-stays in the Western world

Tourists travelling in Western countries, including Europe, the USA and 'down under' in Australia and New Zealand have enjoyed and thus popularized a variety of home stays. Facility ambience combined with personalized hospitality has successfully generated word-of-mouth recommendations, and often repeat annual business (Hermans (1981) describes a successful Spanish *pension*). Irish country inns with fine linen nappery, Belleek china and Waterford crystal set a high (if expensive) standard of living, while an English 'B&B' is often more cosy and less costly than hotels. New Zealand farm stays are excellent opportunities to 'meet the people' and observe sheep and deer ranch operations; in Argentina, elitist visitors can perfect their polo skills on traditional *estancias*.

Successful privatization in these ventures depends on multiple factors not common to most Third World countries. Most of these Western entrepreneurs have substantial capitalization apart from tourism (represented in their homes and ranches); their tourist income is therefore usually supplemental (Mendonsa, 1983). Hosts and guests commonly share some language fluency as well as similar Western cultural orientation and background. Many proprietors belong to organizations such as the American Automobile Association and are listed in their Tour Books, or in similar overseas touring publications; they have access to local and regional advertising media and can affiliate with reservations networks that promote and/or represent their property abroad. Telephone WATTS lines, telex and fax are almost universally available for confirmation of reservations. And proprietors are knowledgeable about business procedures, the marketplace and their type of operation through organizational affiliations.

Building codes and sanitation standards exist and are generally observed. Most enterprises have powered appliances – washers/dryers (or commercial laundry services), dishwashers, freezers etc. to minimize proprietor workload. And if income warrants, they can afford to hire part-time help as needed, and thus further contribute to the multiplier effect in the local economy. Given the fact that the volume of tourism at any given time is sensitive to many natural disasters as well as civil disturbances and economic cycles, most small-scale hoteliers and businesses prosper during good times, and survive during lean periods.

Privatization in the Third World

The positive and powerful incentives favouring privatization include the following:

1 Local residents may be able to take control and manage local tourism through existing social networks, or establish ad hoc associations to help empower them as decision-makers.
2 Proprietorship confers personal community status and accesses expanded networking through membership in service organizations such as Rotary, Kiwanis, Soroptimists, Lions etc. with a voice in the wider community.
3 The psychological satisfaction of the independent entrepreneur, as 'being my own boss', often generates personal opportunities to increase earning power through responsible management and hard work.
4 Successful privatization builds business equity, to become a family legacy or a saleable retirement asset.
5 Family proprietorships can hire elderly, disabled and juvenile family members who might not otherwise be employable.

By contrast, the disadvantageous aspects of privatization include at least some of the following:

1 Opportunities for local ownership are not necessarily equally accessible. They may be linked to education, to family standing, to geographic proximity to the tourist destination site, and to the personality of the would-be entrepreneur.
2 Successful business operation is often proportionate to personal ability, appropriate training and a market. The sophistication to conduct feasibility studies is seldom found in Third World communities (or even in rural America).
3 In developing countries, social foundations are usually rooted in traditional (often familial) networks with established hierarchies. The

emergence of new business 'leaders' based on tourist income can easily be disruptive (Mendonsa 1983) and socially divisive (Smith, 1992). Long (1989), studying Huatulco, Mexico, found that non-resident, urbanized Mexicans rushed to this new seaside resort, took over the best business sites and opened their shops. Their 'know-how' and aggressive manner overwhelmed the indigenous fisherfolk who were unable to compete, and deeply resented the intrusion. The in-migration of these dominant co-nationals proved more disruptive than the initial influx of educated government planners and engineers, who were recognized as temporaries.

4 Even small-scale enterprises need start-up capital. In his study of Nazare (Portugal), Mendonsa (1983: 231) found that over two-thirds of the families initially rented out rooms in their homes and used the additional income to improve the house. Thus they increased both their capital and earning capacity, and improved their standard of living through use of the facilities themselves during the off season. However in Boracay, Philippines (Smith, 1992), new thatched houses with (imported) toilets and sinks had to be built. In both cases, however, the result has been 'a widening of the gap between those community members who already had capital or good employment and those less fortunate' (Mendonsa, 1983).

Quite apart from the social and labour aspects of small-scale local tourism is the problem of environmental impaction. It is almost a geographical truism that sites that could now successfully innovate new small-scale local guest lodges generally occur in either (1) remote locations or (2) they are highly accessible by cheap transportation (private car or public bus) and service the low-budget 'backpackers'.

The geographical isolates include islands, mountain valleys, desert oases and high latitude locales that are too far removed from tourism-generating centres to justify long-haul transport costs to serve a limited clientele. In short, the destination attraction may not be worth the price! The Trobriand Islands – favoured with some of the world's most beautiful beaches – are a case in point. No major air corridor serves their position, off the southeast coast of New Guinea. Only the elite, the affluent or the explorer spends substantially more money just to reach these tiny islets when fine beaches abound closer to home, in Hawaii, the Seychelles or the Caribbean. Further, the resource base to support tourism – culinary water, local food production and infrastructure – is limited in these island micro-states. Contaminated water supplies because of high ground water tables and lack of sewage systems are common to many low islands, including Boracay (Smith, 1992) and Belize (Hartshorn et al., 1984). Wilkinson (1989) provides an excellent discussion of the many constraints to island development. Similarly, Canada would like to develop tourism in their Far

North to generate employment but Inuit villages on the monotonous Laurentian Shield are not apt to attract mass tourism to occupy (unbuilt) large resorts. Again, for most tourists, the limited destination attractions are not worth the expensive air fare.

The second group, small-scale guest facilities, are often low-cost lodging for budget travellers, in major destinations where expensive resorts predominate. Here the issue is economic as well as ecological: does the financial return justify the investment? The author inspected a dozen guest lodges in Belize City – mostly old (or so they appear) wooden structures, much-deteriorated because of rainfall, humidity and salt air, and generally in poor repair. Because of contamination in the Belize River (Hartshorn et al., 1984), most such hostelries collect rain water from the roof into open cisterns. The buildings would not meet US codes for electrical wiring, fire escapes or sanitation. The guests, mostly Americans in their twenties and thirties, were following the La Ruta Maya circuit, travelling by public bus from Yucatan on a low-budget, either by necessity or by choice. Some of the latter individuals were obviously upscale urbanites for whom this was almost a rite of passage, testing 'survival' under hardships. 'Montezuma's revenge' (diarrhoea) had been a frequent problem. An increase in popularity of La Ruta Maya (a developmental dream of most Central American governments) raises doubts that increased tourism will 'bring significant material and social benefits to local people' or protect environmental degradation (Daltabuit and Pi-Sunyer, 1990).

Erik Cohen, one of the most respected fieldworkers in tourism, reported (1982) that 'craft' tourism (local-level small-scale accommodations) did NOT benefit the villagers in Phuket, Thailand. Even then, a decade ago, local tourism authorities were discouraging any further expansion of cottage accommodation, in favour of larger hotels. He noted that because of the workload, families sometimes hired young girls to work as maids but the wages were too small to bring any real benefit to the community. Further, these young employees felt that to work as maids was 'demeaning', and their wages created another problem: their families operated their farms on a subsistence level but the young girls had independent cash income to spend solely on themselves.

Marketing privatized resorts and destinations

Marketing tourist accommodations has become a sophisticated enterprise, and strategies for attracting visitors to these small privatized facilities needs to be considered in terms of domestic as well as international guests. Because of investment ideas initiated two decades ago, research and development concentrated on international tourism to generate foreign exchange. However, subsequent modernization now enables a substantial number of Third World residents to become short-term domestic tourists, thanks to larger income, shorter work weeks and paid vacations. This new pool of potential travellers is now being recognized as an important source of income and employment (Savignac, 1992). Further, their motivations for travel are influenced by the media, and the growing knowledge that to vacation is integral to the modern workaday world. In her Huatulco study, Long (1989) noted inland Mexicans used to drive to the 'old' community, for a day on the beach; their domestic tourism had supported a number of small restaurants and other service businesses.

Domestic tourism in India (technically no longer Third World albeit still a large economically marginal population) is increasing dramatically, straining the British-built colonial era infrastructure (Singh, 1992). Controls on further development may become necessary in selected sites such as Simla because of travel ads in Indian newspapers reading: '4 Days 3 Nights in Simla, including air fare and hotel. Rupees—'. The number of hotels (and visitors) has tripled in ten years.

Marketing cottage tourism overseas is entirely different. Some destinations, such as Boracay (Smith, 1992), become known through word-of-mouth and avant-garde books; Ambergris Cay in Belize needs no promotion because an 'inner circle' of scuba divers keep accommodations full almost year-round. By contrast, Ranck (1987) investigated remote New Guinea beach-front cottages originally built by foreigners and now operated by locals who hoped to attract foreign tourists. Britton (1987) concluded 'small scale enterprises must be provided with basic industry linkages if they are to survive . . . including access to advertising outlets, reservation facilities, and adequate transport services'.

Communication and reservations networks are expanding with enhanced quality, through the visual advantages of Geographic Information Systems added to many travel agency computer systems. Regional organizations and governments can (and probably will) eventually link most accommodations to some marketing arm; it is profitable to do so. Many small American resorts jointly maintain a single WATTS reservation line, the cost of which is minimal compared to a high vacancy factor. This system could soon serve domestic tourism in the developing world, such as India.

A basic issue, however, is to market the particular product to a suitable tourist target. What type of tourist do hosts want, and who will most benefit the receiving community? And how does the marketing agency segment the potential, to make the property sound attractive yet with truth in advertising?

Privatization: the socio-cultural impacts

One of the growing objections to mass tourism is social pollution: traffic, noise, crowding. D'Amore (1983) defines social carrying capacity as 'that point where local residents perceive on balance an unacceptable level of social disbenefits from tourism development'. By implication, privatization is presumed to disperse the concentration of tourists congregated in mega-resorts, and encourage more one-on-one interaction between hosts and guests. Indeed, one of the sales pitches of ecotourism is the opportunity to 'meet the people' through home stays. As discussed above, home/farm stays in Western countries are financially profitable and usually pleasant experiences for both owners and their visitors. However, cottage housing (or small guest lodges/inns) in the Third World may involve social and cultural impacts, including excessive workloads, differing value systems, invasion of privacy etc.

When tourism is introduced into private homes in the Third World, it essentially intrudes into *traditional* societies where women's 'work' is in the home. There, often without benefit of electricity and powered equipment including washers/dryers/dishwashers/vacuum sweepers/food processors – or even refrigerators – the landladies take on daily loads of hand laundry for bed linens, towels, etc. Hohenegg (1989) described her parent's Austrian home, opened to the public twenty years ago as a ski pension to bring in additional cash to send children to college. Through hard work, the business grew; inflation meant higher costs; they built on more guest rooms. By 1988, working almost single-handedly an ageing (and tired) woman made up 30 beds a day and served Continental breakfasts, eight months a year. The laundry now done by machine still had to be ironed and folded. In the Third World the clotheslines are pinned with handwashed linens, drying (?) in an afternoon thundershower. The author has paid for many nights' stay in guest rooms, and slept in damp sheets because the families owned only one set per bed. The alternative was to *not* wash them between guests, which also occurs. Kouris (1989) provides one of the few published reports on family labour:

> Women who operated tourist businesses, more than those who were wage earners, experienced an environment which demanded many more hours than any previous job in Drethia. Businesses serving the tourist are open between fourteen to twenty-four hours per day, seven days per week, for seven months continuously. There are no weekends, holidays or breaks for those who work in family businesses in Drethia . . . this exhaustive work schedule hits the married women hardest; they are responsible for both child and house care. Many of them do all of these jobs simultaneously, and if fortunate, they are helped by their parents.

And even in the Western world, just the titles of two journal articles suggest a similar tale: 'Inn industry no place for leisurely' (Lyke, 1990); and 'Bed and breakfast innkeepers have a labor of love' (Graebner, 1990).

In Belize the author interviewed scores of women including those working in the one Western-standard hotel as well as the landladies of the guest inns. The hotel 'maids' were outspoken in their belief that they were the advantaged ones for multiple reasons:

1   They have a set schedule for work, forty hours per week; their employment includes sick leave, maternity benefits, and after two years, paid vacation leave.
2   Uniforms are provided so no personal expense for clothing.
3   Wages are paid directly to them as discretionary income, and does not *have* to be spent 'fixing up the house' for rental purposes.
4   Their hours at home are personal without the intrusion of outsiders, and child care is available through family members who thus also share the benefit of cash employment.
5   Also deemed very important is the fact they enjoy their time at work, where they meet nice guests (who often leave tips); and they have good cleansing agents with which to work.
6   Their peers envy the 'good jobs at the hotel' where a locker room and coffee area encourages interaction with other employees, widening their group network.

The Belize landladies who were similarly interviewed complained of long workdays, isolation at home, lack of privacy and unpleasant/ demanding guests. Not infrequently menfolk took the cash income and spent it in the coffee house or at beer parties, leaving the women powerless.

In two instances, in the Seychelles and in Seoul, Korea, the author was permitted to observe on-the-job training sessions sponsored by major hotels. In Korea, the Westin offered English language sessions for better hotel guest/maid communication, and how to greet guests in the hallways and in the rooms. In the Seychelles, the Sheraton chain had purchased and renovated a former German 'Club Med-type' property, and were retraining employees for a more diverse international clientele. The quality of presentation and staff response was impressive.

Some proprietors have tried to establish guest standards. Proctor (1992) operated a small cottage-inn in Vieques, Puerto Rico. To protect her family from 'beach bums' her policy was to accept new guests only by referral and, since they had no phone, by written reservations only. Time and again, they gave up their own beds to serve the unannounced and unknown. Reluctantly they left Puerto Rico rather than continue to earn a living through lodging, especially in view of increasing numbers of 'backpackers' who drifted into the area, and were negative role models for growing children.

Riley (1988) has provided the best description to date of the international long-term budget traveller, and a life style which is apparently increasingly orientated towards alcohol, drug abuse, sexual freedom and prostitution (Smith, 1992).

In conclusion, this effort to bring together into one article some type of assessment on the issues of privatization remains incomplete. The topic is important to the future of tourism, especially as destination access widens to truly remote areas of the world and as domestic tourism increases. Substantial additional research needs to be undertaken in a variety of settings, to evaluate the impacts presented here. Further, the following guidelines are suggested for consideration, and for ultimate testing and refinement.

Privatization of small-scale local-level enterprises could be advantageous in settings in which:

1　The infrastructure is more than adequate for local needs, and can absorb additional visitors – at least seasonal or temporary guests without disruption to the local community.
2　The government is able to bring in or provide supplemental services, including health and/or disaster relief, for both the home population and the visitors, should need arise.
3　The indigenous population welcomes visitors because they provide a new interest and a break in the monotony of routine living.
4　The presence of visitors may stimulate handicraft markets and become an outlet for sale of locally made goods.
5　The visitors form an appreciative audience for cultural performances that help preserve ethnic/national heritage.
6　Both hosts and guests share a common language so that discourse is truly meaningful.
6　Hosts and guests share some mutual basis for identity – i.e. they are members of the same religious faith/sect; they share common job skills, as farmer-to-farmer, or they have mutual friends or relatives.
7　The visitors and the visited work together on a project deemed locally important – e.g. construction of a needed community centre. Shared experiences become endearing and enduring bonds.
8　The age groups are somewhat parallel, thereby reflecting peer group interests.
9　The behaviour of the guests conforms to local mores, in dress and life style.

Privatization: in perspective

Privatization of business promises social and cultural benefits as well as greater economic return to individual owners. Proprietorship of a successful business is ego-enhancing, and confers the privilege (albeit often a responsibility) to create employment for family and community members. The owner thereby becomes a power broker, and a well-run business may endure for decades, creating family and community stability. Further, through local ownership of small-scale tourism enterprises, community members *can* control at least some aspects of their visitor industry, obtain a larger share of the profits, and minimize economic leakage. Therefore this individual desire to participate in an economic mainstream, through private enterprise, should be nurtured.

Families in the Third World often seek supplemental income from tourism by converting their homes into *pension*-style housing. However, many of these small-scale enterprises are handicapped by

1   Lack of existing infrastructure, as basic as electricity, culinary water and sewage.
2   By inadequate investment capital, for example for laundry and restaurant equipment, to protect visitor health.
3   By little or no training in business management.

This effort places an undue workload on family members and especially on the women. Thus in contrast to the dialectic statements that to work as a maid or gardener is demeaning, the data presented here suggest that individuals who serve as employees for larger, better-equipped facilities (hotels and resorts) often fare better – financially and socially – than their entrepreneurial counterparts. Because of the importance of privatization, further research is clearly needed to ascertain the criteria that favour self-employment through ownership of a small-scale business *vis-à-vis* wage employment in a larger enterprise.

References

Britton, S. (1987) Tourism in small developing communities. In *Ambiguous Alternatives: Tourism in Small Developing Communities* (ed. C. Britton and W. Clark), University of South Pacific, Suva, Fiji, pp. 167–94

Bryden, J. (1973) *Tourism and Development*, Cambridge University Press, Cambridge

Cohen, E. (1982) Marginal paradises: bungalow tourism on the islands of Southern Thailand. *Annals of Tourism Research*, **9**(2), 189

Daltabuit, M. and Pi-Sunyer, O. (1990) Tourism development in Quintana Roo, Mexico. *Cultural Survival Quarterly* **14**(1), 9–13

D'Amore, L. (1983) Guidelines in planning harmony with the host community. In *Tourism in Canada: Selected Issues and Options* (ed. P. Murphy), University of Victoria Western Geographical Series 21, Victoria, BC, pp. 135–59

DeKadt, E. (ed.) (1979) *Tourism: Passport to Development?*, Oxford University Press, New York

Graebner, L. (1990) Bed and breakfast innkeepers have a labor of love. *The Business Journal Serving Greater Sacramento*, **6**:(46), 1–2

Hartshorn, G., Nicolait, L., Hartshorn, L., et al. (1984) *Belize: Community Environmental Profile*, Robert Nicolait and Associates, Belize City, Belize

Hermans, D. (1981) The encounter of agriculture and tourism: a Catalan case. *Annals of Tourism Research*, **8**(3), 462–79

Hohenegg, Lydia (1989) Personal communication.

Kouris, M. (1989) Tourism and the family in a rural Cretan community. *Annals of Tourism Research*, **16**(3), 318–32

Long, V. (1989) Social mitigation of tourism development impacts: Bahias de Huatulco, Oaxaca, Mexico. *Tourism Recreation Research*, **14**(1), 5–13

Lyke, R. (1990) Inn industry no place for leisurely. *Hotel and Motel Management*, **205**(17), 212

Mendonsa, E.L. (1983) Tourism and income strategies in Nazare, Portugal. *Annals of Tourism Research*, **10**(2), 213–38

Proctor, S. (1992) Personal communication

Ranck, S.R. (1987) An attempt at autonomous development: the case of the Tufi guest houses, Papua New Guinea. *Ambiguous Alternatives: Tourism in Small Developing Countries* (ed. S. Britton and W. Clark), University of South Pacific, Suva, Fiji, pp. 154–66

Riley, P. (1988) Road culture of international long-term budget travelers. *Annals of Tourism Research*, **15**, 313–28

Samy, J. (1975) Crumbs from the table? The workers' share in tourism. In *The Pacific Way* (ed. S. Tupouniua et al.), South Pacific Social Sciences Association, Suva, Fiji, pp. 205–14

Savignac, A.E. (1992) Message from the Secretary-General. *WTO News*, April (World Tourism Organization, Madrid)

Singh, T.V. (1992) Tourism in the mountain environment: case references from the Himalaya and Huangshan (China). Paper presented at the IGU Commission, Geography of Leisure and Recreation, Tellurdie, Colorado, 17–18 August

Smith, V.L. (1992) Boracay, Philippines: a case study in 'alternative' tourism. In *Tourism Alternatives: Potentials and Problems in the Development of Tourism* (ed. V. Smith and W. Eadington), University of Pennsylvania Press, Philadelphia, pp. 133–57

Wilkinson, P.F. (1989) Strategies for tourism in island microstates. *Annals of Tourism Research*, **16**(2), 153–77

12 Tourism carrying capacity management issues

Peter W. Williams and Alison Gill

Introduction

Paralleling tourism's rapid expansion in recent years has come a concern for managing its future growth and impacts. Tourism, like other economic enterprises, is well recognized as an agent of change. When managed properly, it has the potential of being a relatively low user of resources and a sustainable industry. When left to expand in an unbridled fashion, it has the capability of developing beyond sustainable economic, social, ecological and political limits. Central to this issue of tourism's growth has been the notion of carrying capacity management. Along with recent thinking on sustainable development, as well as appropriate and low impact tourism, the concept of carrying capacity management suggests an approach to tourism which permits growth within acceptable limits. Consequently, it is not surprising that people intuitively support the concept of carrying capacity in tourism, even though they may not fully appreciate what it entails from a management perspective.

Despite its seemingly clear and rational intent, the concept of carrying capacity as a management tool creates ongoing controversy. On the one hand, it appeals to a recognized need to limit and control tourism which may threaten the sustained use of limited resources. Simultaneously, it runs at odds with other desires for maximizing opportunities for growth, and the benefits associated with increased visitor use.

This chapter discusses the concept and application of carrying capacity in a tourism growth management context. In particular, it describes the conceptual foundations upon which most carrying capacity management approaches have been based; it explores the potential use of these principles in a tourism context; and then suggests an approach for dealing with tourism-related growth management issues.

Tourism carrying capacity management issues and concepts

Varying perspectives on carrying capacity as a tourism management tool exist. In its most traditional sense, the concept refers to the maximum number of tourists or tourist use that can be accommodated within a specified geographic destination (O'Reilly, 1986). As such, it conjures up images of a specified 'limit', 'ceiling', or 'threshold' which tourism development should not exceed. Indeed, the literature is filled with carrying capacity indicators which describe such benchmarks in volume, density or market-mix terms (Table 12.1).

Difficulties with these numerical carrying capacity indicators arise when efforts are made to link them directly to the management of specific tourism impacts. As with the case in recreation contexts, little evidence exists to suggest that by simply lowering or raising a specific carrying capacity standard, predictable changes in an area's ability to handle tourist use will occur. Instead, the key appears to lie in how change is managed.

An environmentally based perspective suggests that carrying capacity management involves maintaining a balance between physical/ environmental and visitor experiences. Carrying capacity in this context refers 'to the maximum number of people who can use a site without an unacceptable alteration in the physical environment, and without an unacceptable decline in the quality of the experience gained by visitors' (Mathieson and Wall, 1982: 21). This implies some prior designation of conditions upon which unacceptable levels of tourism impact can be judged.

Table 12.1 Sample tourism carrying capacity indicators

Threshold type	Examples
Volume	Peak, hourly, daily, weekly, yearly volumes of various types of visitors (e.g. bed nights, visits, visitor days, etc.)
Density	Number of persons/hectare for different activities at different locations (e.g. visitors/hectare of beach, tourists/ sq. m. of restaurant/shop space, etc.)
Market mix	Number of visitor units relative to resident units (e.g. visitors/resident population, visitor bed units/resident bed units, visitor utilization of public facilities/resident utilization of public facilities)

For others, tourism carrying capacity is market-driven (Butler, 1980; Plog, 1991). Critical carrying capacity thresholds appear to occur when tourist numbers approach levels which strain the capability of the destination to provide quality tourist experiences (Figure 12.1). Key indicators of encroachment upon these capacity ceilings are related to identifiable decreases in market demand. For any number of physical, economic, social, environmental, psychological or political reasons, tourists begin to display apathy towards the destination. While many factors may trigger slumps in market demand for a tourism area, it is generally assumed that desired conditions are exceeded when actual declines in visitor demand occur. As encroachment on these standards occurs, action in the form of direct and/or indirect management strategies must be implemented. Depending upon the desired conditions established by the community, actions may be taken to expand the ability to absorb tourism and rejuvenate visitor interest in the destination; or conversely constrain the detrimental dimensions of tourism activity so as to reduce tourism's effects to more appropriate levels.

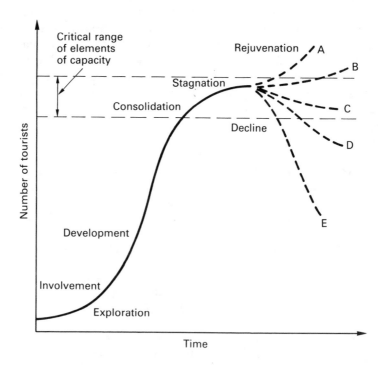

Figure 12.1 A tourism area cycle of evolution. (Source: Butler, 1980: 7)

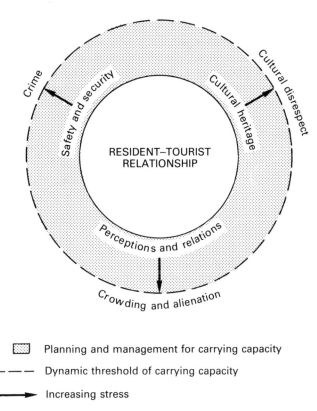

Figure 12.2 Model: socio-psychological variables.
(Source: Hawkins, 1987)

A community-based perspective suggests that carrying capacity concerns a destination area's capability to absorb tourism before negative effects are felt by the community (D'Amore, 1983; Doxey, 1975). Levels at which these impact standards are established can be based on values determined by the community on the basis of how they perceive the effects of tourism (Figure 12.2). This approach to carrying capacity management requires considerable consensus building amongst community stakeholders (e.g. residents, developers, operators, government) to determine the desired conditions for a destination area, and how tourism can be managed most effectively towards that end.

The desired conditions may change over time and in response to different planning and management approaches (Martin and Uysal, 1990). For example, an increase in the size of the police force (i.e. regulation) might assist in maintaining a safe community even with an increase in tourist numbers. In a similar fashion, an interpretive centre (i.e. education/ awareness) might assist in expanding an area's ability to manage tourism's potential impact on local cultural heritage resources.

While the preceding perspectives carry their own particular biases, they all base their rationales on four essential assumptions. They are as follows:

- Tourism in its various forms is a catalyst for change, and brings with it the potential for economic, social and environmental benefits and costs.
- Desired conditions can be identified for tourism, beyond which tourism is not sustainable for local populations, visitors, or both.
- These desired conditions are not fixed, but vary geographically and temporally depending upon local economic, social, political and environmental circumstances, as well as the understanding of tourism's influence upon local conditions.
- Management strategies can be established and implemented that are capable of controlling the rate and direction of change/impact introduced by tourism, in keeping with desired conditions.

New directions in tourism carrying capacity management

While merits to the concept of tourism carrying capacity exist, its traditional focus on attempting to determine explicit use limits have made it difficult to use in a management context. There appear to be too many complex and interrelated limiting factors that hamper its use (Figure 12.3). However, dimensions of carrying capacity research that focus on establishing desired conditions or outcomes appear to have practical value for the management of tourism. This is particularly the case if they can be incorporated into broader planning processes associated with sustainable development and growth management.

When applied within planning systems that focus on managing for desirable and acceptable change, some carrying capacity processes offer the potential of guiding the degree, rate and direction of change that occurs. Knowledge of the consequences of exceeding desired impacts can be used to direct management policies and practices in keeping with a more sustainable tourism. This implies the development of locally based management guidelines that support sustainable forms of tourism and emphasize:

- Development that reflects architectural character and style sensitive to a destination area's heritage and environment.

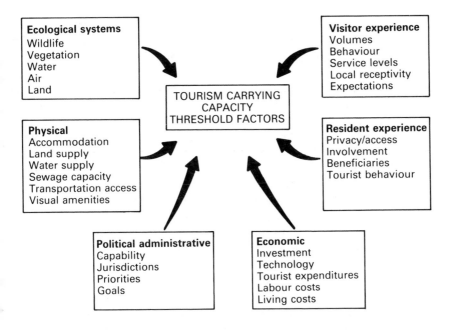

Figure 12.3   Tourism carrying capacity limiting factors

- The preservation, protection and enhancement of the quality of local resources.
- The development of visitor services that enhance local heritage and environmental resources.
- Growth that improves the quality of life for the local community (Pigram, 1990).

Systems management

In tourism carrying capacity management situations, there are frequently several groups with often divergent views to be considered. They include tourists, developers, local residents, existing and proposed businesses, and the public agencies responsible for managing the environment within which all groups must operate. Depending on the specific circumstances of each place, such as stage of tourism development, community economic conditions, or past tourist–resident encounters, the needs of one group may take precedence over those of the others in carrying capacity management decisions. It is not uncommon, for example, to see the needs of the tourist take priority over the desires of community residents during early stages of tourist development. Indeed, if communities seek to encourage and accelerate the development of the tourist infrastructure, then the goals of the developers, who seek to maximize financial return on their investments, are often met. However, while in the short term this helps stimulate growth, long-term sustainability of the tourism industry may suffer if the quality of life of residents who require affordable housing, schools and community facilities is not adequately addressed. As tourist development becomes established, the nature of the typical resident and the tourist may change, and once most of the tourism infrastructure is in place, the role of the developer diminishes. This constant change is what makes the establishment of long-term capacity limits a particularly challenging task.

In a systems management context, carrying capacity refers to desired conditions which best meet the goals of the area being managed. While sensitively managing an area's unique natural and cultural resources is frequently central to a destination's competitive advantage in the tourism marketplace, the resource base does not determine carrying capacity. Rather it is a function of the management goals and objectives established by the community. If the main objective is to stabilize population growth patterns in a community, tourism's capacity to contribute to that objective becomes the key management concern (Table 12.2). Indicators of population stabilization might include changes in migration levels or age and gender structure. If job creation is a major objective, then indicators of the types of employment change become the measure of tourism impact. The establishment of goals and objectives therefore determines which indicators of change are relevant and require monitoring. General goals give broad direction to the planning and management conditions desired. Objectives offer more precise statements of the mechanisms by which the desired conditions are achieved. A general goal might be to manage the rate and quality of development in order to achieve and maintain a diversified destination community economy. Objectives associated with this might include monitoring manufacturing and tourism development to determine whether an appropriate balance between the two land uses is being maintained, and managing residential reserve areas in an attempt to ensure that employee housing supply keeps pace with this demand.

A suggested systems approach to incorporating desired destination community conditions into management practices involves:

- Developing tourism goals and objectives which mesh smoothly with the broader comprehensive plan for a region and/or destination.
- Creating a set of performance indicators reflecting the objectives of tourism development.
- Implementing management strategies which direct tourism towards the achievement of the stated goals and objectives.
- Monitoring the performance of tourism development with respect to these indicators.

Table 12.2 Examples of community management based indicators of tourism impact

Community management objective	Indicators of impact
Population stabilization	Out-migration levels In-migration levels Age/gender structure
Employment increases	Direct job creation Indirect job creation Employment levels Job retention levels Job displacement levels Job satisfaction
Income increases	Person/household income levels Inflation levels Tax revenue levels Beneficiaries
Community viability enhancement	Infrastructure levels Public services levels Housing availability Employee housing Availability Resident attitudes
Welfare/social integration improvement	Health/social service access Services distribution Recreation activity access
Cultural enhancement	Cultural facility access Cultural event frequency Commercialization
Conservation improvement	Pollution levels Conservation practices Cultural feature damage Environment maintenance costs
Amenity enhancement	Levels of crowding density Privacy access Visual amenity satisfaction

Adapted from Getz, 1982.

- Evaluating the effectiveness of the management strategies in influencing the performance of tourism with respect to these indicators.
- Developing new tactics for tourism management based upon the monitored effectiveness of these techniques (Getz, 1982).

While similar in focus to carrying capacity management processes described earlier in this chapter, the systems approach offers a distinct perspective in that it:

- Involves no identification of an ultimate limit to the number of visitors.
- Relates tourism growth and development to its effect on destination goals and objectives.
- Employs indicators of desired conditions to trigger either the implementation of or adjustment to growth management strategies.
- Reviews and modifies goal and objective priorities as destination circumstances change.

Growth management planning

In principle, tourism carrying capacity issues can be incorporated into the comprehensive planning agenda of most tourism destinations. Key to the success of such agendas are growth management programmes. Based upon a destination's ability to provide urban services and the vision of what growth rates should be encouraged, growth management plans offer a 'guidance system' to implement that vision (Schiffman, 1989). Growth management decision guides include policy statements, capital budgets and improvement programmes. Action instruments to support identified programmes encompass public investment strategies, land-use regulations and fiscal incentives or disincentives (Table 12.3). They go beyond strictly land-use planning by incorporating other control mechanisms influencing tourism and other activities within the destination. Research in well-established tourism destinations suggests that growth management planning programmes can be effective management tools in addressing tourism impact issues. However, there appear to be few comprehensive applications of these approaches.

While many tourism-dependent communities (e.g. Stowe, Vermont; Lake Tahoe, California; Park City, Utah in the United States; Languedoc-Roussillon, France; S'Agaro, Spain; Cancun, Mexico; Niagara-on-the-Lake, Ontario, Canada) exhibit components of growth management approaches, these techniques are most fully developed in two contemporary tourism destinations. Both Aspen/Pitkin County, Colorado in the United States and Whistler, British Columbia in Canada exhibit what may be considered 'state of the art' growth management planning in North American tourism settings. While growth management approaches were introduced

Table 12.3 Growth management tools and techniques

Growth management tools	Growth management techniques
1 Policy and assessment	By-law requirements
	Comprehensive plans
	Regional plans
	Fair share low-cost housing
	Information services
	Employment/resident balances
2 Impact analyses	Fiscal impact
	Social impact
	Cost–benefit analysis
	Environmental impact
	Carrying capacity analysis
3 Regulatory systems	
3.1 Environment controls	Environmentally sensitive areas
	Special planning areas
	Pollution controls
3.2 Development right transfers	Development rates and location
3.3 Restrictive covenants	Concession in landowners
	Initial land title documents
3.4 Zoning uses	Conventional zoning
	Conditional zoning
	Planned unit development
	Special permits (e.g. historic districts)
3.5 Other zoning tools	Minimum floor areas/lot sizes
	Height restrictions
	Population density
	Performance standards
	Geographical constraints
3.6 Quota systems	Development/building permits
	Utility connections
3.7 Short-term tools	Moratoria
	Creative foot-dragging
	Negotiation and permit review
	Off-site levy charges
4 Capital expenditures	Land banking
	Development rights purchases
	Capital programming
5 Revenue systems	
5.1 Exactions	Land/money dedications
	Capital facility dedication
	Low/moderate income housing allocations
5.2 Tax and fee systems	Urban and rural service areas
	Utility fees
	User rates
	Local improvement areas
	Development districts

Source: Schiffman, 1989.

in these communities in response to tourism impact control problems largely associated with rapid growth during the early stages of expansion, the strategies and mechanisms employed have proved to have real merit over the long run. In keeping with the guidance system approach, both communities have introduced policies and supporting instruments in the form of regulatory, capital expenditure and investment, as well as fiscal growth management programmes. In essence they represent tourism carrying capacity control mechanisms.

Key elements of growth management in tourism settings

In tourist environments, there are distinctive features which must be considered in growth management. These include the diversity of stakeholders; the evolutionary stage of the tourist community; and the critical importance of maintaining a high quality resource base. Further, there is a need for constant adjustments to meet the needs of a changing environment. What strategies are implemented typically represent the meshing of political and social requirements with technical and administrative realities (Pigram, 1990).

One of the most important characteristics is the diversity of the destination's stakeholders. Community involvement in establishing desirable conditions is perhaps the single most important element of growth management. Developing appropriate mechanisms to incorporate divergent views is critical for successfully establishing appropriate resident/ visitor relationships. A basic distinction can be made between residents and visitors, but in reality there are much finer distinctions with respect to attitudinal differences towards development. In many tourist towns, there is a significant second-home resident population as well as seasonal employees. Each of these resident groups has very different needs in terms of housing and service amenities. While input into the planning process from permanent residents can be accomplished through traditional means such as public meetings, incorporating the viewpoints of these other community groups is more problematic. Alternative mechanisms, such as more informal small group meetings, have been used in some instances (e.g. Whistler, BC and Park City, Utah). In conjunction with this process, active community information and publicity programmes (e.g. via radio talk shows, newsletters etc.) are often necessary to ensure that the perspectives of more transient and/or recent residents of the community can be incorporated into the growth management process.

In addition to residents' attitudes, it is also important to conduct surveys of visitors in order to understand why they have decided to visit the destination and how well their expectations are being met; and, what can be done to make their stays more enjoyable. Maintaining a balance between the needs of tourists and those of all residents is critical. As many residents of tourist towns choose to live there because of perceived life style and amenity factors, programmes designed to allow local use of tourist-focused attractions, facilities and services through more favourable resident pricing structures can be employed to reduce friction between residents and visitors.

A second feature which must be considered is the stage of development of the destination. Resort communities are extremely dynamic in character. In the early phases of development, a high investment in tourist facilities and infrastructure is necessary to reach a 'critical mass' of attractions, services, facilities and visitors in order that the destination can sustain a tourism economy. Unfortunately, tourism demand is frequently unpredictable and subject to such problems as seasonality and aggressive competition. Development activities often entail considerable investment risk. Consequently, encouraging investment is often the primary objective in the early stages of development and destinations have often compromised the needs of the resident community to achieve this. While in the short term this seems an appropriate course of action, there may be negative repercussions at a later date. Examples of this can be found in most tourism towns that have evolved without an employee housing policy. While the cost of providing employee housing acts as a disincentive to early investors, failure to do so has created serious problems in many communities once land values have increased (i.e. developers and local businesses have frequently been required to pay disproportionately high rates to help rectify employee housing shortages).

Many tourism regions are resource-dependent. Maintaining the quality of their resources (natural and cultural) is critical to the continued success of their tourism industry. As a consequence, resource management standards and guidelines are frequently higher than those necessary in other settings. For instance, the capability of the sewage and water systems must be able to meet the peak loadings which characterize service use in many tourist communities. Similarly building and landscape design guidelines frequently reflect more stringent aesthetic goals. Identification of the desired conditions to be associated with an area's critical tourism resources is also important in establishing priorities in the event of conflicting goals. For example, in the Lake Tahoe region of California and Nevada, highest priority is given to the lake water clarity and quality, as it is the resort's most essential tourist resource. Establishing desired conditions for the resource base is an essential step in growth management. This includes consideration of natural, cultural and scenic resources in surrounding areas which may not necessarily lie within a municipality's borders, but still affect the overall quality of the area. It is important to decide how residents and visitors feel about the desired quality of such resources prior to determining what kind of management will be necessary.

Conclusions

Research suggests that traditional approaches to carrying capacity management have met with limited success in practical settings. This situation exists primarily because of:

- Unrealistic expectations (i.e. a technique exists which can provide a magic number which identifies 'how much is too much').
- Untenable assumptions (i.e. a direct relationship between tourism use and impact exists).
- Inappropriate value judgements (i.e. conflicts between the views of 'experts' as opposed to destination stakeholders concerning what conditions are appropriate for an area).
- Insufficient legal support (i.e. the lack of a formally recognized institutional process to ensure that management objectives are achieved).

Given the inability of traditional carrying capacity management techniques to overcome these barriers, an alternative approach is suggested. Its focus shifts from past concerns over establishing use limits, to issues of identifying environmental, social and economic conditions desired by a community, and the creation of growth management strategies for managing tourism's carrying capacity challenges.

References

Butler, R.W. (1980) The concept of a tourist area cycle of evolution: implications for management of resources. *The Canadian Geographer*, **14**(1), 5–12

D'Amore, L.J. (1983) Guidelines to planning in harmony with the host community. In *Tourism in Canada: Selected Issues and Options* (ed. Peter E. Murphy), University of Victoria, Victoria, BC

Doxey, G. (1975) A causation theory of visitor–resident irritants: methodology and research inferences. In *Proceedings of the Travel Research Association Sixth Annual Conference*, San Diego, California, pp. 195–8

Getz, D. (1982) A rational and methodology for assessing capacity to absorb tourism. *Ontario Geography*, **19**, 92–101

Hawkins, A.E. (1987) A Carrying Capacity Model for Resort Planning and Management with Preliminary Application to Whistler, Canada. Unpublished

Master of Natural Resources Management Research Project, Simon Fraser University, Burnaby, BC

Martin, B.S. and Uysal, M. (1990) An examination of the relationship between carrying capacity and the tourism lifecycle: management and policy implications. *Journal of Environmental Management*, **31**(4), 327–33

Mathieson, A. and Wall, G. (1982) *Tourism: Economic, Physical and Social Impacts*, Longman, London

O'Reilly, A.M. (1986) Tourism carrying capacity. *Tourism Management*, **7**(4), 254–58

Pigram, J.J. (1990) Sustainable tourism – policy considerations. *Journal of Tourism Studies*, **1**(2), 2–8

Plog, S.C. (1991) *Leisure Travel: Making It a Growth Market . . . Again!* John Wiley and Sons, New York

Schiffman, I. (1989) *Alternative Techniques for Managing Growth*, Institute of Government Studies, University of California at Berkeley, Berkeley, California

13 Styles of travel

Gordon D. Taylor

Introduction

Tourism has long been concerned with consumption and not with consumers. Traditionally standard measures have been person-trips, person-nights, numbers of visits, expenditures per day and per trip. In other words, measures of consumption and of economics. Much less systematic attention has been directed towards the consumer and the social science interest in tourism. Most tourism executives, managers, planners and developers pay respect to the adage 'know thy consumer'. Little consistent effort has been directed in research and in academia towards a basic understanding of the consumer and to the development of a systematic way of collecting information that would be applicable universally.

If a thorough examination of the phenomenon of tourism is to be attained, it will be necessary to examine the place of the consumer. A body of consumer knowledge based upon empirical evidence must be developed. In order to provide a sense of direction to this development a number of questions that require answers can be hypothesized.

1   What proportion of the population of a country travels and how frequently?
2   How is this proportion changing over time, if it is indeed changing?
3   Who are becoming travellers and who are ceasing to be?
4   Is the proportion of travellers in a population uniform by sex, age, education, income and other standard socio-demographic measures?
5   For those people who do travel, do they all think about travel the same way or can succinct groups in the population be described based upon this thought process?
6   If such groups can be described, are they unique to individual countries or do they occur on a wider basis?
7   Are these groups constant or do they change over time?

As a way of organizing the thinking that is necessary to answer these questions and of ordering the data that are required in any analysis, the concept of styles of travel can be useful. This concept is seldom used in the study of tourism. It is defined for the purposes of this chapter as the way people perceive, organize and execute travel. Two streams of information are included within this definition:

1 The incidence of travel
2 The way people think about the travel that they do.

Empirical data from a number of sources will be examined in order to:

1 Determine the incidence of travel in at least two countries and indicate the type of information that can be derived from incidence data.
2 Describe and classify segments of travellers based upon the thought process.
3 Examine changes, if any, that may have taken place over time.

The chapter will also examine the implications of these two measures of style of travel as indicators of changes that may be occurring for tourism as a business. The need for international standards in the collection of these data will also be stressed.

Incidence of travel

Introduction

Incidence of travel is quite simply the proportion of the population of an area that travels. This definition is all-encompassing and for many purposes it would be enlightening and worthy of study. For practical purposes some restrictions will be needed. People under a certain age do not make independent travel decisions; they travel because of the decision of a parent or other authority figure. Hence an age restriction should be used. In the two examples that will be cited minimum ages of fourteen years in one case and fifteen in the other were used. An age limitation in the mid-teens would seem appropriate. Secondly, a trip purpose limitation should be considered. For the purposes of tourism a restriction to pleasure travel with possibly duration and distance factors would be practical. The concept that the World Tourism Organization is attempting to introduce into the definition of tourism as being outside the usual environment should be considered within any description of travel incidence. In any event, an international agreement on the limiting factors would be required in order to make data from a variety of countries comparable. Without international comparability the use of incidence data as a part of a greater understanding of the consumer in tourism will be severely restricted.

The first four questions posed above deal with the proportion of people who travel. Data on this aspect of travel are scattered and inconsistent. This situation is unfortunate in that travel incidence is one of the most important measures of the consumption of travel and of the basic characteristics of the consumer. It is, first of all, a measure of the overall size of the travel market and a base for determining whether that market is growing, declining or remaining constant and of how fast changes are taking place over time. It is also the best measure of who is actually in the travel market and of who is entering and leaving it. When coupled with frequency of trip data it is also the basis for determining who are the heavy users of travel, and who are the light users.

Data sources

For illustrative purposes data are drawn from two studies that consistently measure travel intensity. The first of these is the Travel Analysis from West Germany. It is an annual study, conducted since 1970, based on 6000 interviews representative of the population of the former West Germany over the age of fourteen. The survey was extended in 1990 to cover all of unified Germany. The second study is the Canadian Travel Survey which is conducted biennially and covers the Canadian population aged fifteen years and older. The sample size is approximately 6000 households done quarterly in the years the survey is conducted.

Analysis

The critical incidence question in the German survey asks if, in the past year, the respondent has taken one or more holiday trips of at least five days in duration. The Canadian survey asks the respondents if they have taken a non-business trip in the nine-month period preceding the three-month period covered by the quarterly survey. Recent development in Germany of The German Travel Monitor has permitted collection of incidence data on all trips of at least one night away from home. In the future the travel incidence of the German population for all pleasure trips of one night or more will be available for analysis.

The Travel Analysis study clearly shows a consistent growth in the proportion of the population who have taken at least one five-day holiday trip. In 1970 41.6 per cent had taken such a trip, by 1990 the figure stood at 68.2 per cent. In absolute terms the West German market had increased from 18.5 million travellers to 33.4 million. An analysis of German data done for *Stern* magazine came to the conclusion that: 'At all levels of income the consumers with a higher education are at an advantage' (*Stern*, 1983, p. 14). Thus education level becomes an essential aspect of travel incidence and one that is important in the development of products for this market.

In Canada the annual incidence of overnight non-business travel grew from 69.0 per cent in 1984 to 71.1 per cent in 1988. There is a wide range in travel market participation across the country, from a low in 1988 of 61.9 per cent in Newfoundland and Prince Edward Island in the east to a high of 80.7 per cent in Alberta and 82.9 per cent in Saskatchewan in the west. Travel incidence in Canada is very similar for both metropolitan and non-metropolitan places. There is, however, a difference between the two groups when the destination of travel is concerned. The non-metropolitan areas have a higher incidence of travel within Canada, 66.8 per cent to 62.4 per cent, while metropolitan areas have a higher incidence for foreign travel, 20.0 per cent to 17.8 per cent to the United States and 11.4 per cent to 4.8 per cent for all other foreign destinations.

Incidence of travel increased with levels of education and of household income. Overall, travel incidence is highest in the 35–44 age group, but travel to the United States peaks in the 45–54 age group, and that to all other foreign destinations in the 55–64 group.

Discussion

By not utilizing this type of data, a rich resource for understanding tourism in its broadest sense and in determining where tourism fits into the economic and social priorities of populations is being missed. The examples used should indicate the kind of analysis that can and should be done. The relationship between travel incidence and the standard of living by country may be an indicator of the future trends in travel around the world. On a practical basis the data define who is not in the market and hence, for the travel marketer, is not of real concern. From a social standpoint and for an understanding of how the travel market reacts to economic difficulties, the movement in and out of the travel market in times of economic recession may well be of significant interest.

Travel philosophy

Introduction

A concept of travel philosophy has been developed as part of research into market segmentation in a number of studies conducted by Tourism Canada. It is part of a three-fold segmentation process that is based on the following assumptions:

1   There are recognizable groups in the population based on how people organize and value travel, i.e., how they think about travel.
2   There are recognizable groups in the population based on the benefits sought from specific pleasure trips.
3   There are recognizable groups in the population based on the activities, interests, location and facilities required in order to realize the benefits sought from specific pleasure trips.

While all three of these segmentations are needed for an understanding of the tourist consumer, the first is the one most pertinent to the topic of styles of travel. This aspect is concerned with how people think about travel in terms of its value to them, how they go about organizing travel and how they actually travel. The data provide a source from which to answer the last three questions posed in the introduction to this chapter.

Data sources

Market research studies conducted by Tourism Canada in the 1980s and 1990s have provided the data for this section. Three major studies are involved:

1   Attitudes of (then) West Germans to Canada as a holiday destination, conducted by Basis Research Ltd, Dusseldorf, in December 1981 and January 1982.
2   Canadian Tourism Attitudes and Motivation Study (CTAMS), conducted by Statistics Canada for Tourism Canada as an adjunct to the Canadian Labour Force Survey in the fall of 1983. Segmentation analysis was done by Burak-Jacobson Research Partners Inc., of Toronto.
3   Pleasure Travel Markets to North America, sponsored jointly by the United States Travel and Tourism Administration and Tourism Canada, and conducted by Market Facts of Canada Ltd.

The following countries have been studied as part of the Pleasure Travel Market series: France (1986, 1989), Japan (1986, 1989), United Kingdom (1986, 1989), West Germany (1986, 1989), Hong Kong (1987), Singapore (1987), Switzerland (1987), Australia (1988), Brazil (1988), Italy (1988), Mexico (1988), South Korea (1990) and Venezuela (1990). These studies are based on personal in-home interviews averaging fifty minutes in duration, with respondents who had taken a long-haul vacation of four nights or longer in the three years preceding the survey or who intended to take such a trip in the next two years. Long-haul was defined geographically for each country; for Europe the criterion was beyond Europe and North Africa. Similar limits were established for the other geographic regions. The number of interviews ranged from 1200 to 2000 per country.

These studies permitted the development of three different segmentations of the travel market. The basis of the segmentation was outlined earlier. In this review of information the travel philosophy segments, i.e., those segments that divide the population on the way they think about travel, value travel and organize travel, have been used.

Analysis

Respondents in the 1981 West German study were asked to respond to a list of thirty-three items on a five-point scale of desirability. Four segments emerged from an analysis of these data:

1 The uninspired fellow-traveller, 33 per cent.
2 The busy-sightseeing tourist, 20 per cent.
3 The comfort-loving relaxation vacationer, 26 per cent.
4 The globe-trotter adventurer, 21 per cent.

The emergence of a group not very interested in travel as the largest segment of the West German overseas travel market was surprising and provided the impetus to see if this group was unique to Germany or not, There were indications that this segment accompanied travellers from Group 4 (the adventurers) on holidays. The critical point seemed to be that they were not individually motivated to travel and were essentially taken along by other people. They were not an independent market that could be targeted for travel.

The Canadian Tourism Attitudes and Motivation Study for 1983 examined the Canadian adult population of fifteen years of age and older utilizing an initial sample of 14,180. Those respondents who had not travelled for pleasure purposes in the twelve months preceding the survey were eliminated for questions that dealt with current travel. The travel philosophy segments were based on the entire sample. Four such segments emerged:

1 Planned adventurer, 31 per cent.
2 Casual traveller, 27 per cent.
3 Low-risk traveller, 24 per cent.
4 Stay-at-home, 18 per cent.

The latter group was composed of people who did not see travel as an integral part of their life style and who did not enjoy travel. While they were not completely non-travellers, they travelled but little. In the overseas studies that followed, this group would not have met the basic criteria for inclusion.

There is, then, on the basis of the Canadian study, a group in the population that contributes little, if anything, to the travel market. No follow-up study has been done that would enable the dynamics of this group to be studied over time. It is likely that every population will contain a group that is for all intents and purposes outside of the travel market. Travel incidence studies if carried out on a regular basis will describe the broad parameters of the non-travellers, but they should be included in segmentation studies from time to time so that the underlying characteristics can be studied.

When the stay-at-home group is eliminated from the analysis, three groups are left that bear a good deal of resemblance to the groups that were developed for the overseas markets. These three groups can be described using the terminology that has been adopted for this chapter:

1 Planned travel, 37.5 per cent.
2 Independent travel, 33.5 per cent.
3 Reluctant travel, 29 per cent.

In order to establish a common terminology for the travel philosophy segments, the names that are used in this report differ from those used in the original reports. The term 'planned travel' has been developed to replace the term 'package travel'. Planned travel need not be package travel, although it is a major component of the segment.

Independent travel describes a group of people who prefer to make their own travel arrangements, often while they are on a trip. They tend to avoid guided tours and vacation packages. Reluctant travel categorizes a segment to whom travel is not part of their life style. To this group spending money on travel is not a priority; they are lukewarm to the whole idea of travel. When they do travel they tend to leave all arrangements to someone else.

Thirteen different countries were studied between 1986 and 1990, four of them on two occasions. There is, then, a broad and valuable data base available. Three philosophy segments have been recognized in all of the countries. While these three groups did not appear in the original reports for France, Switzerland, United Kingdom and West Germany, a review of the original data showed that the three-group solution was one of several offered for them. This three-group solution has been used in this analysis.

The statements that distinguish each of these groups in all countries are as follows:

1 Planned travel:
    — I usually buy vacation packages which include both accommodation and transportation.

— I prefer to go on guided tours when vacationing overseas.
— I usually use a travel agent to help me decide where to go on vacation.
— I usually travel on an all-inclusive package vacation.
— I like to have all my travel arrangements made before I start out on vacation.
2 Independent travel
   — I enjoy making my own arrangements for vacation trips.
   — I like to make my arrangements as I go along on a vacation.
   — I usually travel on reduced air fares.
3 Reluctant travel
   — Making arrangements for major trips can be such a bother that I end up not travelling.
   — I would just as soon spend my money on things other than vacation travel.
   — I usually choose travel places where I have been before.
   — Once I get to my destination, I like to stay put.

These statements clearly describe the main characteristics of the three groups. They are applicable in all of the countries where the three groups were identified (Table 13.1). Hence, the groups are transnational and transcultural. They do not, however, exist in all countries in the same proportions.

The countries can be divided into three groups on the basis of which group is the largest in each country. Germany and Switzerland each appear in two of the groupings as the two groups are of the same size.

1 High independent travel:
   — France (both studies);
   — United Kingdom (both studies);
   — Australia, South Korea, Switzerland.
2 High planned travel:
   — Brazil, Germany (1989), Hong Kong, Italy, Singapore, Venezuela.
3 High reluctant travel:
   — Germany (both studies), Japan, Switzerland.

In the three countries where data exist for both 1986 and 1989, some slight shifts in the proportions have been observed. In the United Kingdom there was an increase in planned travel, from 29 per cent to 33 per cent, at the expense of both independent and reluctant travel. In France there was a slight decrease in planned travel and an offsetting increase in reluctant travel. Germany showed an increase in independent travel at the expense of planned travel. With only two points in time these changes are interesting but cannot be considered a trend.

Table 13.1 Travel philosophy segments: proportional distribution by country

Country (year)	Planned travel (%)	Independent travel (%)	Reluctant travel (%)
United Kingdom (1986)	33	36	30
United Kingdom (1989)	29	39	32
France (1986)	27	38	35
France (1989)	30	38	32
Germany (1986)	33	28	39
Germany (1989)	39	22	39
Japan (1989)	34	27	38
Hong Kong (1987)	51	19	30
Singapore (1987)	44	24	32
Switzerland (1987)	23	38	38
Italy (1988)	41	35	25
Australia (1988)	33	35	32
Brazil (1988)	43	26	31
Mexico (1988)	53	24	23
Venezuela (1990)	51	23	26
South Korea (1990)	19	44	37

Discussion

These three philosophy segments occur in several countries and on the basis of the evidence available three of them would appear to be relatively stable. Further studies in the future are required to see whether significant shifts in the structure of travel markets are occurring. Careful thinking about the implications of these three groups is needed. Across all of the countries studied the groups each represent about one-third of the long-haul travel market, although exceptions appear in Hong Kong, Singapore, Brazil, Mexico, Venezuela and South Korea. In each of these countries one group tends to dominate the market. These countries are recent entries into the international travel market as origins. Further study is needed to see whether these markets develop towards the pattern of the older, more established markets.

In the older markets, one-third of the travellers prefer to travel on their own terms, another third wants as many of the unknowns removed before starting a trip, and a final third is not really keen on travel. Each of these three groups would need a separate style of marketing approach and the industry response to their travel needs would have to reflect the different ways they look at travel.

Further analysis utilizing the benefit and product segments for each country as they relate to these three groups would be needed to work out the full implications of this aspect of travel. That further analysis is beyond the scope of this chapter.

Conclusions

The fact that some universals in travel segments are starting to emerge should provide an impetus for more research. In order for this research to be most useful, there is a need for an international agreement on the type of survey to be done, the questionnaire content, and on the methodologies of administration and analysis. Such an international approach will not be easy as there is still great difficulty in agreeing on the definition of a tourist without getting into the complexities of different kinds of tourist based on a multi-segmentation approach.

If target marketing and the development of product lines relative to market segments is the future of tourism activity, then some international approach to the development and classification of multi-segments will be required. It will be necessary to be able to identify appropriate segments not only in the population of a country, but also in a visiting population. It would not be possible to administer the type of questions to visitors on an ongoing basis that can be used in an in-home interview. A fast means of identifying the groups will be a high priority.

The use of both travel incidence and travel style data opens the door to a greater understanding of tourism on an international basis. Comparable data can be developed world-wide. These data provide a means for monitoring changes in travel markets and are vital to the process of adapting tourism marketing to the changes.

A growth in independent travel, a decline in planned travel or the reverse clearly signal the need for the marketing and development of tourism aimed at such a country to be reviewed and, if necessary, revamped. In the same way a country where the travel incidence is rising will be of more interest to marketers than one where the incidence is falling.

When incidence and style are analysed at the same time, the fact of change will be accompanied by the direction of change. Tourism cannot afford to overlook the implications of these data as a means of improving knowledge of the markets and of increasing the opportunities for customer satisfaction.

References

Statistics Canada (1991) *Tourscope, 1990*, Domestic Travel, Canadians Travelling in Canada, Catalogue 87–504, Ottawa, October 1991. (Available biennially since 1980)

Stern (1983) The German holiday maker – projections to 1990. *Stern Magazine,* Hamburg

Study Group for Tourism (annual) *Reisenalyse,* Starnberg (available annually since 1970)

Taylor, G.D. (1986) 'Multi-dimensional segmentation of the Canadian Pleasure Travel market. *Tourism Management,* 7(3), 146–53

Unger, Klaus (1991) German Travel Monitor, 1990. *FVW International,* No. 7, 97–8

Pleasure Travel Markets to North America, published by Tourism Canada, Ottawa:
  (a) Full reports for individual countries:
       — France, Japan, United Kingdom, West Germany, 1986
       — Switzerland, Hong Kong, Singapore, 1987
       — Australia, Brazil, Italy, Mexico, 1988
       — France, Japan, United Kingdom, West Germany, 1989
       — South Korea, Venezuela, 1990
  (b) Highlights reports for all countries studied in a year.

14 Tourist behaviour and the new European life style typology

Josef A. Mazanec and Andreas H. Zins

Introduction

The construction of traveller and tourist typologies is not a new under-taking in travel and tourism marketing. Reports published in the pro-ceedings of the Travel and Tourism Research Association have covered this issue regularly (Darden and Darden, 1976). Social science approaches to tourism research repeatedly touched upon typological methodology (Cohen, 1988; Dann et al., 1988; Pearce, 1982). It is also common practice to consider traveller or tourist types as potential market segments for travel and tourism marketing (Smith, 1989). Marketing theory distin-guishes between a priori and a posteriori market segmentation depend-ing on the segment-defining variable(s) being either predetermined or assigned during the construction of previously unknown segments (Bagozzi, 1986; Vavrik and Mazanec, 1990).

During the 1970s life style criteria became popular in consumer segmentation studies (Wells, 1974, 1975). Tourism and leisure research followed suit (Bernard, 1987; Mayo and Jarvis, 1981; see Veal, 1989, for a critical comment). Recently, the life style concept experienced a revival in international marketing research for tourism. The Austrian National Tourist Office has used the life style data available from the Europanel group (Kreutzer, 1991), which is an association of fifteen European commercial market research institutes. This information, however, originates from consumer panels in the tourism-generating countries and conveys nothing about the life styles of the guests while staying in Austria. The Austrian National Guest Survey (Mazanec et al., 1991) adopted the Eurostyles methodology in order to examine the life style structure of travellers to Austria during the 1991–2 summer and winter seasons.

Given the data on actual tourist behaviour collected in the resorts there should be ample information on the interlace of life style and guest characteristics. Thus, marketing managers can expect conclusive findings about the strengths and weaknesses of the Eurostyles typology for tourist market segmentation. The main question pertains to the overall usefulness of the Eurostyles as 'prefabricated' market segments. What does it mean for a tourist to belong to a particular life style segment in terms of consumer choice behaviour, activities, spending habits etc.? Does a life style transfer its unique attributes into a (similar or contrasting) vacation style? Tourism marketers on the national level are primarily concerned with generating countries. Does the Eurostyles typology assist in the assessment of the tourism generators? Does Eurostyles stick to its promise of providing an analytical link between actual guests in Austria and potential visitors in their respective home countries?

It is not the purpose of this chapter to discuss the construction of the Eurostyles typology at length. As an obviously successful result of commercial market research it is taken for granted. However, the assumption has to be verified that individual styles or so-called 'socio-targets' (groups of styles) contribute to the advancement of tourist market research and render tourism marketing more efficient.

The Eurostyles concept

The Eurostyles system (Europanel, 1989; Kramer, 1991) is a multinational life style typology developed by the Centre de Communication Avancé (CCA) of the Havas-Eurocom group. Since 1989 the system has been in commercial use in fifteen European countries. The measurement instrument covers five principal dimensions of life style:

1 Objective personal criteria.
2 Behavioural attributes.
3 Attitudes.
4 Motivations and aspirations.
5 Sensitivities and emotions.

The database allows the monitoring of 'socio-waves' (Cathelat, 1985), or socio-cultural mainstreams.

The Eurostyles approach offers the analyst various indicators, such as a 'topography of socio-climatic zones' which serves as a basis for the socio-cultural segmentation of the population, a socio-cultural 'compass rose' which reveals the main cultural trends, or a number of scenarios describing hypotheses about the medium-term future. By linking so many

aspects of everyday life together the Eurostyles typology inspires product development thus serving as an instrument of innovation (Cathelat,
1985). The Eurostyles system consists of sixteen different life style types.
These types may be regarded as a portrait gallery resulting from a series
of multivariate analyses (factor, correspondence, cluster analysis). The
sixteen Eurostyles uniformly apply to each European country and to all
sectors of activity (e.g. politics, advertising, media habits, buying and
consumption of goods and services).

Figure 14.1 delineates the Eurostyles system by positioning the sixteen
European life style types on a two-dimensional map. The horizontal axis
links two opposing poles named 'settlement' on the right and 'movement'
on the left. The vertical axis is a bipolar dimension of 'valuables' (pleasure)
in the north and 'values' in the south. Percentages in parentheses are the
portions of the overall European population located in the right or left
and the upper or lower hemispheres respectively.

The settlement pole or region may be characterized by values such as:
priority to the individual's defence and survival at the current social
status, convergence on habits and traditions, group protection, obedience
to the cultural rules of life. In contrast, movement means dynamism,
freedom of criticism, priority to the individual, distance *vis-à-vis* social
norms, law and authorities.

On the second main axis the northern region may be characterized by
values of pleasure, sensuality and hedonism which altogether are strongly
associated with tangible values of money and material equipment in a
system of expenditure and even waste. Figure 14.1 exhibits the distribution of the cultural mainstreams in Europe by featuring the sixteen
Eurostyles in the two-dimensional grid. Each life style type bears a label
for easy reference.

In order to determine the potential of various social mentalities or
consumption patterns it is necessary to know the share of each of the
sixteen Eurostyles. For all fifteen European countries analysed, the diameters of the circles in Figure 14.1 indicate the shares of the sixteen
styles. The major types in Europe are the Rocky (13.5 per cent), the Defence
(8.5 per cent), and the Romantic (7.8 per cent). Of course, the size of each
style is not the same for each country. Figure 14.2 exhibits the distribution
of the Eurostyles for ten European countries: the type Rocky, for example,
dominates the socio-cultural landscape particularly in the Netherlands,
in Great Britain, France and Switzerland. The share of the Moralist and
the Romantic is very high in Germany, Austria, Belgium, and Switzerland. On the other hand, Denmark and Sweden show an above average
share for the Pioneer type.

Many intricate correlations may be derived from the database covering
a variety of life style facets. The analyst may combine existing consumption
patterns of a particular product category with attitudes towards several

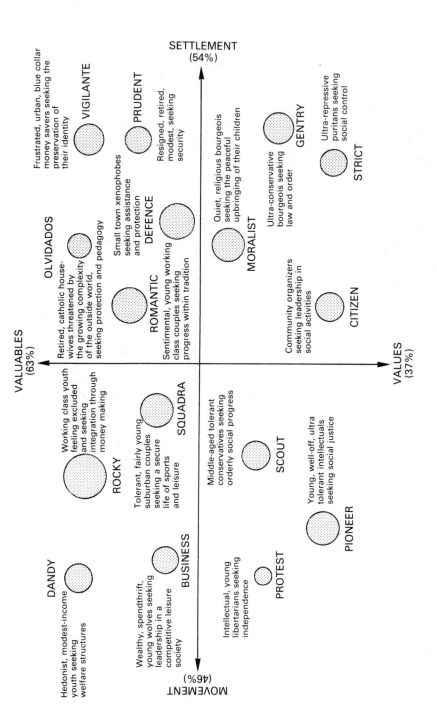

Figure 14.1 The sixteen Eurostyles in Europe. (Source: CCA/Europanel)

socio-cultural trends. Such cross-tabulations assist in revealing the market potential as well as the innovative power of a new product line. The marketing practitioner also diagnoses the spending propensities of the Eurostyles on the regional, national and international levels. Another strength of the Eurostyles system is the interlacement of the life style findings to the wealth of national consumer panel data. Once a target segment has been defined, the market researcher obtains supplementary information on media habits, communication styles and themes, images and preferences.

Usage of the Eurostyles typology in international tourism marketing

Before employing the Eurostyles typology management must distinguish two different cases:

1 Accepting the Styles as ready-made market segments.
2 Using the Styles as additional criteria (passive variables) to depict already defined segments more comprehensively.

Before choosing the first alternative one must check whether the styles prove to be homogeneous within and heterogeneous between types in terms of tourist behaviour. An affirmative result would justify selective market operation. If sufficient disparities are not detected amongst the styles there is a second option. Market segments are constructed by means of other more discriminative traveller characteristics. Then some of these segments may exhibit an over-proportional share of one or more particular Eurostyles. In this case the supplementary life styles descriptors lead to improving promotional messages directed to potential visitors in their home countries.

A Eurostyle qualifies as a ready-made market segment on condition that its members significantly differ from those of other styles in terms of at least one elementary traveller attribute such as:

- Main trip *vs* second/third or short trip.
- Number of visits, travel experience.
- Travel motives and expectations.
- Actual usage of tourist services.
- Preferred activities.
- Amount and composition of daily expenditure.
- Satisfaction, intention to repeat visit, loyalty.

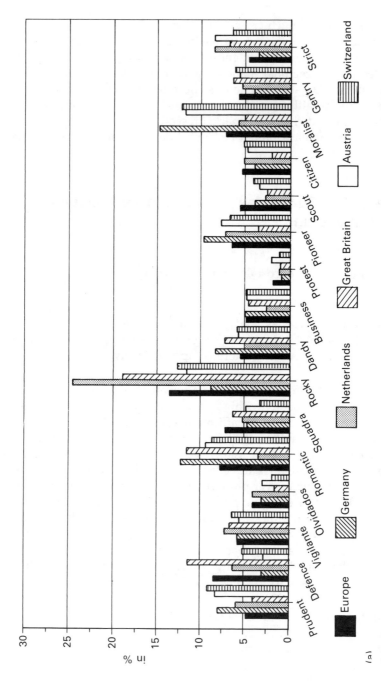

Figure 14.2 The distribution of Eurostyles within the population of ten European countries

(a)

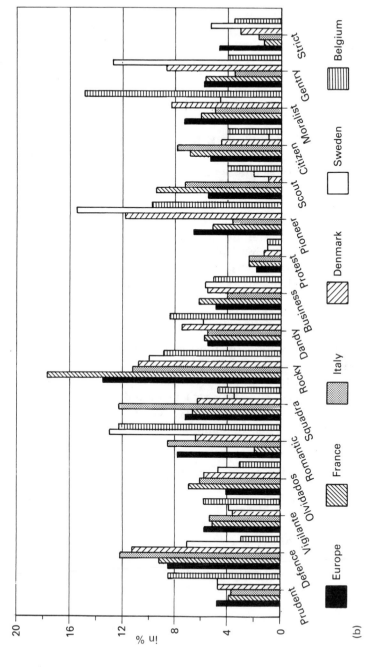

Figure 14.2 (continued)

Empirical findings on the direct usage of the Eurostyles for construct-
ing tourist market segments are reported first. The indirect usage for
evaluating tourism-generating countries will be addressed afterwards.

The Austrian case: empirical findings

Predicting guest behaviour with individual Eurostyles

To put it in brief, the sixteen original Eurostyles cannot be considered to
be ready-made segments for tourism marketing. The differences regarding behavioural criteria are not convincing. In other words, life style is
a poor predictor for the components of guest behaviour. These findings
need not be taken as a failure. It is evident that travellers' choice in
favour of a particular destination must have a 'smoothing' effect. Guests
surveyed solely within Austria are likely to have more homogeneous
psychographics and behaviours than travellers headed for a diversity of
destinations.

A number of attempts to group individual Eurostyles into socio-targets
(that is, combinations of styles) may be feasible. Styles may be merged
according to their location on the two-dimensional Eurostyles map.
Another solution emanates when the sixteen original styles are hierar-
chically clustered with a similarity measure based on, say, the benefits
sought by each style. This approach produced satisfactory contrasts
between seven socio-targets. The next section contains still another
combination of Eurostyles, exploiting their mutual similarity in terms of
travel motives and activities.

Grouping Eurostyles into socio-targets

The common approach of merging styles into socio-targets is based on
behavioural differentiation. A tourist's decision to spend his holidays in
Austria, however, exerts a filtering effect comparing the distribution of
life styles in the population of the generating countries and among
Austria's guests: tourists patronizing the same destination are expected
to be more similar to each other than those headed for different receiving
countries. Nevertheless, it may be argued that doing the same thing is
perceived and evaluated differently by different individuals, a phenomenon frequently encountered in the field of services and intangibles.

Therefore, the aggregation of the sixteen Eurostyles should not be based
primarily on attributes such as the choice of accommodation or the length
of stay but on a bundle of travel motives and activities. A hierarchical
cluster analysis was performed with eleven motives (e.g. recreation,

pleasure, new experiences, cultural interest etc.) and ten activities (e.g. playing tennis, golf, water sports, relaxing, shopping, visiting museums, concerts, theatres etc.) as active variables and the sixteen Styles as objects. After checking the degree of homogeneity, five clusters were retained for interpretation. Figure 14.3 again depicts the configuration of the sixteen Eurostyles on the two-dimensional map. The diameters of the circles show the relative share of each style in Austria's total guest population. In addition, the hatched fields in the map demonstrate the affiliation of each style with one of the five socio-targets which is homogeneous in terms of travel motives and activities.

The first socio-target comprises six styles on the eastern side of the map (with an aggregate share of 47 per cent). Its motive structure relates to recreation and health by doing nothing and/or hiking. The second segment combines the neighbouring Romantic and Squadra styles with an aggregate share of 16 per cent. This type likes to take its recreation in colourful surroundings and likes to indulge in activities such as cycling, swimming, horse riding or sun bathing offering variety and change. The third socio-target occupies the western region of the socio-cultural map and ties three styles together (resulting in a share of 21 per cent). Pleasure and sports (tennis, cycling, water sports, golf) in combination with mental training are the prevailing motives. The fourth cluster seeks cultural events but is uninterested in sports and physical strain. It can be found in the north-east and the far west on the movement–settlement axis, accounting for a share of 14 per cent. The remaining style represents outsiders of about 2 per cent of the guest mix. They are interested in sports, culture and shopping – just for fun.

Socio-demographics (e.g. age, profession, size of residential town, household income) as well as behavioural and travel-related variables (e.g. party size and composition, intention to repeat visit, length of stay, accommodation and boarding, purpose of travel, benefits sought, spending pattern) reveal significant differences between the five suggested socio-targets (see Tables 14.1 to 14.3). These results are a promising basis for segmenting the European travel market with an overt preference for Austria as a destination country. Drawing on the Eurostyles as a gateway to the plenitude of panel data collected in the individual home countries, both sources of information may be combined for segmentation purposes.

Incorporating the Eurostyles into strategic planning

Identifying the repeat visitors' potential is a crucial issue in the design of marketing strategy. The differentiation of life styles favourable and unfavourable with respect to repeat visitation may be helpful. The guests' intention to repeat their visit is commonly regarded as a valid indicator

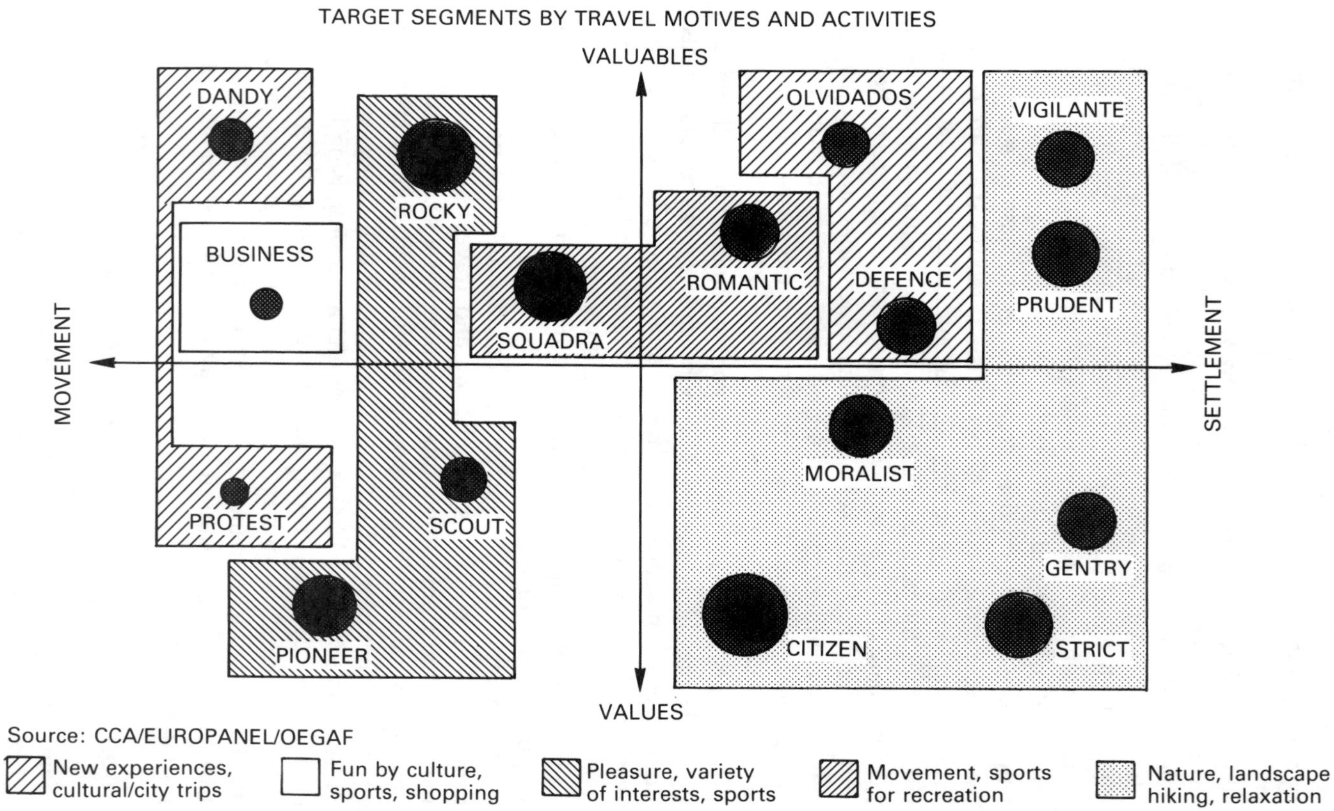

TARGET SEGMENTS BY TRAVEL MOTIVES AND ACTIVITIES

Source: CCA/EUROPANEL/OEGAF

Figure 14.2 Building five socio-targets

Table 14.1   Socio-demographics and socio-targets

Variable	Average	Socio-targets					F ratio	χ^2	Sig.
		1	2	3	4	5			
Share (%)		47	16	21	14	2			
Age of travel party (yr)	47	52	44	41	46	42	161.05		0.0000
Size of town of residence								50.09	0.0000
< 100,000	60	61	64	58	65	51			
> 100,000									
Profession of interviewee								237.42	0.0000
Self-employed	14	13	9	16	13	15			
Employed	59	51	72	68	59	60			
Retired	27	36	19	16	28	25			

Table 14.2   Trip characteristics and socio-targets

Variable	Average	Socio-targets					F ratio	χ^2	Sig.
		1	2	3	4	5			
Share (%)		47	16	21	14	2			
Share of repeat visitors (%)	74	77	74	72	70	67	7.72		0.0000
Main trip of the year (%)	60	63	62	56	54	46	11.15		0.0000
Party size	2.1	2.1	2.3	2.1	2.0	2.0	17.73		0.0000
Accompanied by children under 14 (%)	13	11	18	14	11	11	9.09		0.0000
Lodging in hotels and pensions (%)	65	66	56	68	69	83	14.21		0.0000
Share (%)		47	16	21	14	2			
Length of stay in Austria in days	12.3	13.6	11.6	11.4	10.8	9.9	25.41		0.0000
Expenditures per day and capita (US$)	64	61	57	67	71	85	13.19		0.0000
Shopping exp. for whole party and trip (US$)	227	231	217	190	270	222	2.58		0.0355

Table 14.3 Benefits sought and socio-targets

Variable	Average	Socio-targets 1	2	3	4	5	F ratio	χ^2 Sig.
Share (%)		47	16	21	14	2		
Benefits sought (%)								
Walking/hiking lanes	73	79	77	65	62	53	44.24	0.0000
Calmness of resort	72	80	71	65	63	54	41.58	0.0000
Variety of landscapes	62	66	65	55	57	40	21.07	0.0000
Value for money	63	67	65	57	55	53	18.37	0.0000
Service in accommodation	62	67	57	57	59	63	15.12	0.0000
Service in restaurant	63	67	61	55	61	61	13.26	0.0000
Reachability	52	55	56	45	48	45	12.98	0.0000
Environment	92	93	93	90	89	79	11.80	0.0000
Friendliness of population	78	82	77	75	75	63	11.66	0.0000

of guest satisfaction. Intention to repeat a visit, however, is an asymmetric indicator. A weak intention does not necessarily denote dissatisfaction. But a strong intention reveals good prospects to gain loyal tourists from the market segments structurally resembling the profile of the highly satisfied guests. In order to strengthen the contrasts between socio-targets, only two groups of Eurostyles are formed. Styles with an average share of repeat visitors are ignored and the ten Eurostyles with the strongest or the weakest intention remain in the analysis. 'Strong' means at least 4.5 percentage points above average (i.e. 39 per cent). This applies for the styles: Prudent, Vigilante, Olvidados, Citizen and Moralist (31 per cent of all guests). 'Weak' means at least 5.7 points below average, involving the styles: Rocky, Dandy, Protest, Pioneer and Scout (26 per cent of all guests).

The resulting dichotomy exhibits significant differences for a couple of relevant guest attributes, e.g.

- Age (fifty-two *vs* forty years on average).
- Share of retired persons (33 per cent *vs* 13 per cent).
- Share of city travellers (8 per cent *vs* 15 per cent).
- Preferred activities.
- Advance bookings and arrangements.
- Daily expenditure per capita ($74 *vs* $82).
- Average length of stay (thirteen *vs* ten nights).
- Benefits sought.

From the guest data it becomes apparent that there are tourists who might be transformed into loyal visitors more easily than others. The Eurostyles typology now provides a tool for assessing the loyalty potential in various generating countries where the frequency distribution of the styles is known.

Both the strong and the weak loyalty group may lead to condensing Eurostyles and generating countries into a single portfolio diagram. The preponderance of the intention to make a repeat visit as a symbol for appreciation of a country's tourist performance is not confined to market strategies aiming at customer loyalty. Weak loyalty in travel and tourism may be caused by many factors other than satisfaction. A tourist seeking diversity, preferring short trips, or going on a long-haul trip once in his life, need not be dissatisfied in order to vary his choice of destinations. Loyal as well as fluctuating travellers make a balanced guest mix. But the promotional approach ought to be tailored to each of the two extremes.

A generating country accommodates a typical mixture of Eurostyles each with a particular amount of affinity for, in this case, Austria as a tourist destination. Suppose that tourism managers are rather conservative in their segmentation policies and thus want to cater to the loyal visitors. In this case they are likely to focus on those Eurostyles that show a strong intention to repeat their visit when asked during their stay in an Austrian resort.

The Eurostyles called Prudent, Vigilante, Olvidados, Citizen and Moralist were already identified as the most sympathetic towards Austria. Comparing the share of all loyal styles in the respective country of origin X with the share among guests from X results in one of four possible outcomes. The share lies . . .

- Above average in the home country and above average in Austria.
- Below average in the home country and above average in Austria.
- Below average in the home country and below average in Austria.
- Above average in the home country and below average in Austria.

Adopting the pictorial representation common in portfolio models (Day, 1977; Day, 1986; McNamee, 1985; Wind et al., 1983), generating countries are portrayed in four quadrants (Figure 14.4). The size of the circles denotes each country's contribution to the total volume of guests recorded in Austria. The first quadrant (north-east) contains those markets where Austria already has exploited her opportunities ('success markets'): 'Austria-prone' life styles are over-represented within the origin population as well as amongst the visitors to Austria. A weak representation of Austria-prone styles in an origin country combined with high frequency of these styles among the guests implies a high degree of market saturation ('empty markets'). A less than proportional frequency of

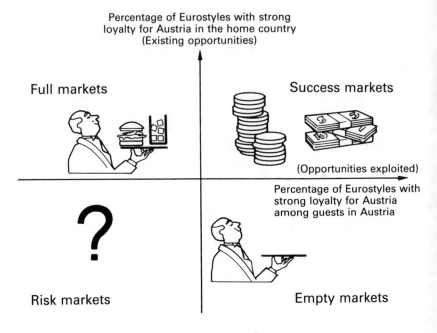

Figure 14.4   Portfolio of tourism markets

Austria-prone styles at home and among the guests in Austria is indicative of a market with doubtful opportunities ('risk markets'). A 'full
market' offers a large share of its population belonging to Austria-prone
styles combined with a small share of these styles among the tourists
actually travelling to Austria.

Merging the Europanel results with the guest survey findings produces
a portfolio chart of generating countries for Austria (Figure 14.5). It depicts
Austria's market opportunities in terms of Eurostyles. Germany, Switzerland and Austria herself offer the most promising chances which are
already utilized. The marketing climate is somewhat less favourable in
France, Belgium and Denmark, in the Netherlands, and in Italy. From
France, however, Austria could extract more than her fair share. Great
Britain and Sweden are rather brittle in terms of Austria-prone life styles,
with the UK showing a markedly better transformation rate of potential
visitors into actual guests.

What about the Eurostyles with a low propensity to repeat their visit?
The styles called Rocky, Dandy, Protest, Pioneer and Scout are relevant
here. The occasional or even once-and-never-again travellers to Austria
may have other attractive features (e.g. a high expenditure level). It will
pay to look at a second portfolio for the non-loyal styles (Figure 14.6).

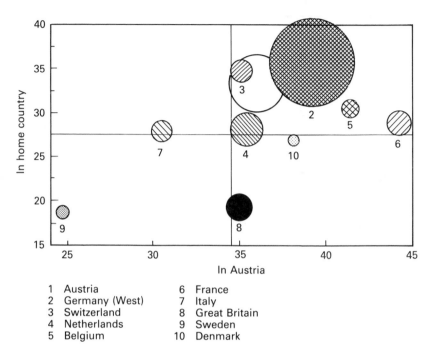

Figure 14.5 The high loyalty potential for Austria in Europe

Half the number of origin countries gather in the third quadrant (south-west). Austria, Germany, Switzerland, Britain and Denmark have a small share of Eurostyles with less affinity for Austria if one compares them to the Netherlands, Belgium or France. These countries also account for a below-average share of non-loyal styles among the visitors to Austria during summer 1991.

Italy and Sweden do not line up. Austria was quite successful in at-tracting occasional guests from these two countries. If a province (region, resort) were prepared to deviate from the typical Austrian cliche of restful summer vacations and, therefore, were to tackle the non-loyal (but affluent) segments (i.e. Rocky, Dandy, Protest, Pioneer and Scout), Italy and Sweden ought to be given priority.

Conclusion

The Eurostyles typology was shown to be of practical value for destina-tion marketing provided that certain amendments are applied. The original

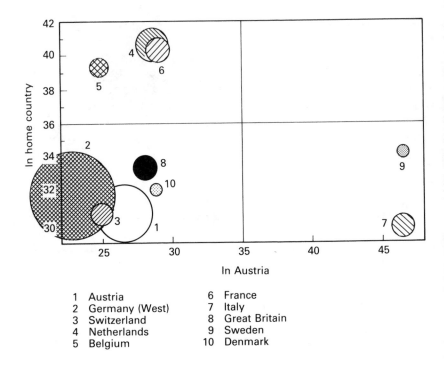

Figure 14.6 The low loyalty potential for Austria in Europe

consumer life style types have to be merged into groups of types (i.e. socio-targets). The grouping process must employ a travel-related and behaviourally relevant set of criteria (such as travel motives or activities). Once a grouping of styles has been found, it lends itself to segmentation purposes on international (i.e. European) levels. Beside the opportunity to define segments across borders, management will benefit from a multitude of data accumulated during normal panel operation. Socio-targets are not new entities but consist of well-known components. Thus, they are easily portrayed in terms of consumption patterns, shopping habits or media usage for increased marketing efficiency.

The evaluation of tourism generating countries is a routine task in any National Tourist Office where strategic thinking guides the marketing planning process. The Eurostyles have been proved to contribute in this effort, with visitors' loyalty taken as an example. The reader may have wondered why an assessment of generating countries with respect to repeat visitors takes a detour via Eurostyles. There are two arguments: unlike the life style data, the information on travellers' loyalty to a destination is rarely available for all major countries, and, Eurostyles help in transferring strategy into action. Once the manager has become familiar with the typology he treats the styles just like 'old friends', whatever country he may look at. Depending on the database of media habits, Eurostyles lend themselves for selective mass communication in a particular country. Where media usage is rather uniform across life style types, a better understanding of consumer mentalities and value systems at least provides inspiration for more effective advertising messages and artwork.

References

Bagozzi, R.P. (1986) *Principles of Marketing Management*, Science Research Associates, Chicago

Bernard, M. (1987) Leisure-rich and leisure-poor: Leisure lifestyles among young adults. *Leisure Sciences*, **10**, 131–49

Cathelat, B. (1985) *Styles de vie*, Vols 1 and 2, Editions d'organisation, Paris

Cohen, E. (1988) Traditions in qualitative sociology of tourism. *Annals of Tourism Research*, **15**(1), 29–46

Dann, G., Nash, D. and Pearce, P. (1988) Methodology in tourism research. *Annals of Tourism Research*, **15**(1), 1–28

Darden, W. and Darden, D. (1976) A study of vacation life styles. In *Proceedings of the 7th Annual Conference of the Travel and Tourism Research Association*, Boca Raton, Florida, pp. 231–6

Day, G.S. (1977) Diagnosing the product portfolio. *Journal of Marketing*, **41**(2), 29–38

Day, G.S. (1986) *Analysis for Strategic Market Decisions*, West Publishing Co, St Paul

Europanel (1989) Euro-styles, Eine europaweite Landkarte mit 16 sozio-kulturellen Typen. *Marketing Journal*, **22**, 106–111

Kramer, S. (1991) *Europäische Life-Style-Analysen zur Verhaltensprognose von Konsumenten*, Dr. Kovac, Hamburg

Kreutzer, R. (1991) Länderübergreifende Segmentierungskonzepte – Antwort auf die Globalisierung der Märkte. *Jahrbuch der Absatz – und Verbrauchsforshung*, **37**(1), 4–27

Mayo, E.J. and Jarvis, L.P. (1981) *The Psychology of Leisure Travel*, CBI, Boston

Mazanec, J., Mikulicz, H. and Zins, A. (1991) *Gastebefragung Osterreich – Osterrich-Bericht*, Osterreichische Gesellschaft fur angewandte fremdenu erkehrs wissenschaft, Vienna

McNamee, P. (1985) *Tools and Techniques for Strategic Management*, Pergamon Press, Oxford

Pearce, P.L. (1982) *The Social Psychology of Tourist Behaviour*, Pergamon Press, Oxford

Smith, St L.J. (1989) *Tourism Analysis. A Handbook*, John Wiley and Son, New York

Vavrik, U. and Mazanec, J. (1990) A-priori and a-posteriori travel market segmentation: tailoring automatic interaction detection and cluster analysis for tourism marketing. *Cahiers du Tourisme*, Série C, No. 62

Veal, A.J. (1989) Leisure, lifestyles and status. *Leisure Studies*, **8**, 141–53
Wells, W.D. (ed.) (1974) *Life Style and Psychographics*, AMA, Chicago
Wells, W.D. (1975) Psychographics: a critical review. *Journal of Marketing Research*, **XII** (May), 196–213
Wind, Y., Mahajan, V. and Swire, D. (1983) An empirical comparison of standardized portfolio models. *Journal of Marketing*, **47** (Spring), 89–99

15 Opening of the Eastern bloc countries

Stephen F. Witt

Introduction

The political changes which resulted in the death of communism in Eastern Europe had their origins in the establishment of the independent workers' union Solidarity in Poland in 1980. This was followed by the adoption of the policies of *perestroika* (restructuring) and *glasnost* (openness) by the Soviet Union in the second half of the 1980s. As a result there was a demand for radical political change, and over the period 1989–91 the communist system collapsed in all the Eastern bloc countries.

The political events which have occurred in Eastern Europe since 1989 have opened up this area for international tourism. Prior to these events, a mass of restrictions made travel to Eastern Europe a bureaucratic obstacle course, thus restraining demand. Similarly, the travel and currency restrictions placed on residents of the Eastern bloc countries resulted in very low levels of outbound tourism to the West. The political and economic upheavals which have taken place in Eastern Europe since 1989 have led to substantial changes in these previously established patterns of travel to and from the Eastern bloc countries.

In this chapter attention focuses on inbound tourism to what were previously the Soviet bloc countries of Eastern Europe – Bulgaria, Czechoslovakia, the former German Democratic Republic (GDR), Hungary, Poland, Romania and the former Soviet Union (USSR). These countries should not be thought of as a monolithic bloc; they are at different levels of development, possess different cultures and display widely varying attitudes towards international tourism. For example, Hungary is the most Westernized country in the group, and also the one which attracts the highest number of tourists. The union of East and West Germany, however, means that in terms of administrative formalities, visiting the eastern part of Germany is now no different from visiting other Western countries, and the 'Westernization' of the former GDR is proceeding rapidly. On the other hand, the disintegration of the former USSR has resulted in political instability, which is not conducive to the development of international tourism.

In spite of the differences among the Eastern bloc countries, however, there is now a general increase in interest from the West in travelling to the various countries of Eastern Europe. The mass of restrictions facing most Western tourists wanting to travel to Eastern Europe, such as minimum daily exchange requirements and unrealistic official tourist exchange rates, has been substantially reduced.

The following section examines the Eastern bloc countries as tourist destinations, and traces their development over the period of political changes. This is followed by a discussion of the opportunities for and constraints on tourism development in the Eastern bloc. Finally, conclusions are drawn.

Eastern bloc countries as tourist destinations

In comparison with similar Western countries, it appears that Eastern European destinations have been underperforming in terms of attracting international tourists and international tourism receipts.

Tourist/visitor arrivals

Table 15.1 shows tourist/visitor arrivals for the seven Eastern European countries, together with several Western European comparator countries, over the period 1986–90. Thus 'sun and sea' destinations Bulgaria and Romania are compared with Greece and Spain, while 'lakes/mountains/historical buildings' destinations Czechoslovakia, the GDR, Hungary, Poland and the USSR are compared with Austria and the Federal Republic of Germany (FRG). It should be borne in mind that arrivals data definitions vary considerably among countries, as the notes to the table show, and hence caution should be exercised in interpretation.

It can be seen from Table 15.1(a) that tourism in Bulgaria has grown steadily over the period (29 per cent). Tourism in Romania showed initial increases, declined in 1989 as a result of political instability, but recovered strongly in 1990, giving an overall increase of 44 per cent. These growth rates compare well with those of Greece (27 per cent) and Spain (15 per cent). The growth of the popularity of lakes/mountains/historical buildings destinations in Eastern Europe is depicted in Table 15.1(b). The following increases in arrivals were recorded between 1986 and 1990:

Table 15.1 Arrivals of tourists/visitors from abroad (millions)

Countries	1986	1987	1988	1989	1990
(a) 'Sun and sea' destinations					
Bulgaria (T)	3.5	3.6	4.0	4.3	4.5
Romania (V)	4.5	5.1	5.5	4.9	6.5
Greece (T)	7.0	7.6	7.9	8.1	8.9
Spain (T)	29.9	32.9	35.0	35.4	34.3
(b) Lakes/mountains/historical buildings destinations					
Czechoslovakia (T)	5.3	6.1	6.9	8.0	8.1
GDR (T)	2.0	2.1	2.2	3.1	n.a.
Hungary (T)	10.6	11.8	10.6	14.5	20.5
Poland (T)	2.5	2.5	2.5	3.3	3.4
USSR (V)	4.3	5.2	6.0	7.8	7.2
Austria (A)	15.1	15.8	16.6	18.2	19.0
FRG (A)	12.2	12.8	13.1	16.1	17.0

T, tourist arrivals at frontiers; V, visitor arrivals at frontiers; A, arrivals in registered tourist accommodation.
n.a., not available.
Source: World Tourism Organization (1992).

Czechoslovakia – 53 per cent; Hungary – 93 per cent; Poland – 36 per cent; and the USSR – 67 per cent. Data for the GDR for 1990 are unavailable – economic and monetary union with the FRG took place on 1 July 1990 – but a 55 per cent increase in arrivals was recorded between 1986 and 1989. Within these totals, considerable variation in the pattern of development took place. Czechoslovakia, the GDR and Poland experienced steady growth, whereas arrivals in the USSR declined in 1990 in the presence of political uncertainty. However, although arrivals in Hungary declined in 1988, they rose strongly in 1989 and massively in 1990 as a result of the opening of Hungary to the West accompanied by a stable political situation. The growth figures for the Eastern bloc countries again compare well with the corresponding figures for Western Europe: Austria 26 per cent and the FRG 39 per cent. However, the *scale* of arrivals in Eastern Europe is generally much lower than in Western Europe; for example, Spain attracts eight times as many tourists as Bulgaria, and Austria probably considerably more than even Hungary (bearing in mind that arrivals in registered tourist accommodation are likely to be substantially lower than tourist arrivals at frontiers for a given country). The much smaller international tourism base in Eastern Europe allows high growth rates to be achieved relatively easily.

International tourism receipts

International tourism receipts for the various countries under consideration are shown in Table 15.2 (with the exception of East Germany for which these data are unavailable). As the receipts are denoted in US dollars, they may increase or decrease partly as a result of a change in the strength of the dollar compared with other currencies. Nevertheless, movements in tourism receipts in Eastern European countries *relative* to those in Western Europe are indicative of strengthening or worsening positions in Eastern Europe compared with the West. Thus Table 15.2(a) indicates that the 'sun and sea' destinations of the Eastern bloc fared badly compared with the Western comparators over the period 1986–90; international tourism receipts in Bulgaria increased by 11 per cent and in Romania *decreased* by 40 per cent, whereas Greece and Spain recorded increases of 40 per cent and 54 per cent respectively. By contrast, the growth of international tourism receipts over the period 1986–90 in the 'lakes/mountains/historical buildings' destinations of the Eastern bloc was of a similar order of magnitude to the corresponding Western destinations. Table 15.2(b) shows that international tourism receipts increased by 40 per cent in Czechoslovakia, 64 per cent in Hungary, 96 per cent in Poland and 66 per cent in the USSR, whereas Austria and the FRG recorded increases of 87 per cent and 70 per cent respectively.

Table 15.2 International tourism receipts (US$ millions)

Countries	1986	1987	1988	1989	1990
(a) 'Sun and sea' destinations					
Bulgaria	356	357	359	362	394
Romania	178	165	176	167	106
Greece	1,834	2,268	2,396	1,976	2,575
Spain	12,058	14,760	16,686	16,174	18,593
(b) Lakes/mountains/historical buildings destinations					
Czechoslovakia	336	386	436	581	470
GDR	n.a.	n.a.	n.a.	n.a.	n.a.
Hungary	611	827	759	798	1,000
Poland	136	184	206	202	266
USSR	163	198	216	250	270
Austria	6,954	8,863	10,090	10,717	13,017
FRG	6,294	7,678	8,449	8,658	10,683

n.a., not available.
Source: World Tourism Organization (1992).

It is clear that while receipts increased substantially between 1986 and 1990 in the 'lakes/mountains/historical buildings' destinations of Eastern Europe, the rate of growth of receipts in the 'sun and sea' destinations was much lower or even negative. The unique appeal of each of the 'lakes/mountains/historical buildings' destinations resulted in the ability to command a reasonably high price, whereas the homogeneity of the 'sun and sea' product resulted in competition on the basis of price only.

Table 15.2 gives a very clear indication of the sheer difference in scale of international tourism receipts in Eastern and Western Europe; in 1990 total tourism receipts for six of the seven former Soviet bloc countries (excluding the GDR) amounted to US$ 2.5 billion, whereas tourism receipts for Spain alone were US$ 18.6 billion – more than seven times this figure.

It should be borne in mind that international tourism generates balance of payments effects that are far more complex than those of the initial tourism receipts (the *primary* effect). In particular, the extent to which tourism expenditures in a destination country generate import demand in that country can have a major impact on the foreign exchange generating ability of tourism. The *secondary* effects on the balance of payments include imports of supplies by the providers of tourism services (such as hotel operators and restaurant operators), expenditures on marketing abroad, and payments to overseas investors in the form of interest and dividends. For many Eastern European countries, these secondary effects are quite large in the case of Western tourists.

Tourism receipts as percentage of exports

Table 15.3 demonstrates the importance of tourism in terms of international trade for the various Eastern European countries (again excluding East Germany) compared with the West. There is considerable variation in the ratio of tourism receipts to exports, ranging from 0.3 per cent for the USSR to 10 per cent for Hungary in 1990. The latter country is exceptional, however, with the second highest ratio recorded being 4 per cent. Compared with its closest equivalent in Western Europe (Austria), even Hungary does not fare well; for Austria international tourism receipts represented 31 per cent of exports compared with 10 per cent for Hungary in 1990. West Germany is a highly industrialized country with a huge volume of exports, and hence even though international tourism receipts are high, the ratio of receipts to exports is low. As a result, Hungary, Czechoslovakia and Bulgaria were ranked ahead of West Germany in 1990. Table 15.3(a) indicates the completely different scale of importance of tourism in terms of international trade to the 'sun and sea' destinations of Eastern Europe compared with Western Europe – for the Eastern bloc countries international tourism receipts are below 3 per cent

Table 15.3 International tourism receipts as percentage of exports

Countries	1986	1987	1988	1989	1990
(a) 'Sun and sea' destinations					
Bulgaria	2.5	2.2	2.1	2.1	2.9
Romania	1.4	1.5	1.4	1.4	1.7
Greece	32.5	34.8	40.4	35.9	32.1
Spain	44.4	43.2	41.7	36.4	33.4
(b) Lakes/mountains/historical buildings destinations					
Czechoslovakia	1.6	1.6	1.8	4.0	4.0
GDR	n.a.	n.a.	n.a.	n.a.	n.a.
Hungary	6.6	8.6	7.6	8.3	10.3
Poland	1.1	1.5	1.4	1.5	2.0
USSR	0.17	0.18	0.20	0.23	0.26
Austria	30.8	32.6	27.4	33.0	31.1
FRG	2.6	2.6	2.6	2.5	2.6

n.a., not available.
Source: World Tourism Organization (1992); and personal communication.

of exports, whereas for the Western countries the ratio of international tourism receipts to exports exceeds 30 per cent.

For each of the Eastern European countries the importance of international tourism receipts in exports increased over the period 1986–90. In particular, the percentage rose sharply in 1989 (Czechoslovakia), or 1990 (Bulgaria, Romania, Hungary, Poland), or both (USSR).

Development of Eastern bloc tourism: opportunities and constraints

Eastern Europe has many attractions, including natural resources (such as unspoiled countryside, forests, lakes, mountains and beaches), beautiful cities, historical sites and cultural resources (museums, art galleries, etc.). Western tourists are also likely to be attracted by the relatively low prices in most of Eastern Europe, the appeal of Eastern Europe as being somewhere different and exciting which was hitherto rather inaccessible, and the fact that Eastern Europe is generally far less crowded than the West. The proximity to the major tourist generating countries of Western Europe makes travel to Eastern Europe quite straightforward.

The large migrant communities in the West, most notably in the United States, are an important potential source of tourists to Eastern Europe. As well as visits to relatives in Eastern Europe, migrants and their descendants may wish to explore their family roots; many have retained linguistic, cultural and historical links with Eastern Europe.

There are various problems which are likely to constrain the growth of tourism to Eastern Europe. In several of the countries political unrest is still evident and/or travel restrictions are still in force. More generally, the infrastructure is completely inadequate by Western standards and the quality of provisions for tourists tends to be poor. Furthermore, there is a lack of education and training for staff working in tourism. Poor marketing is another major constraint.

Hundreds of new hotels are needed throughout Eastern Europe in order to bring its tourism industry up to Western standards. As the political climate in Eastern Europe has changed, the countries in this region have become much more receptive to joint foreign-capital ventures, and this is seen as a major avenue for increasing and upgrading hotel provision in Eastern Europe. Although the process had already started prior to the events of 1989, it has accelerated considerably since then. Examples of such projects are the opening of the Savoy Hotel in Moscow in September 1989, which was renovated by a Soviet-Finnish joint enterprise; and the opening of the Marriott Hotel in Warsaw in October 1989, which was a joint venture together with Lot (the state airline) and an Austrian construction company. The opportunities afforded in Eastern Europe by the creation of joint ventures in tourism are discussed in Buckley and Witt (1990) and Franck (1990).

Tourism education

Improved education for those working in the tourism industry is essential if Eastern Europe is to compete successfully with the West. *Management* education, which so far has been largely absent in Eastern Europe, is likely to play a key role in this process. Furthermore, to the extent that certain management subjects, such as *economics,* were taught under the previous communist regimes, these courses have had to be changed to concentrate on market economies. Also it has been necessary to alter *foreign language* education in response to the anticipated substantial influx of Western tourists.

The implications of the political events of 1989 for tourism education are enormous – from the tour guide who now does not have to adhere to the Party line on information provision (a propaganda exercise), to the manager of a tourism enterprise who now needs to know how to function in a market economy; and from a lack of knowledge on the part of the tourism industry as to how to deal with foreign partners (travel agents, tour operators, etc.) to a lack of management teaching staff.

The general practice of teaching Russian as the first foreign language in the former Soviet 'satellite' countries is changing as closer economic ties with the West are developed. The replacement of Russian by English/ German/French as the first foreign language is likely to benefit tourism from the West to Eastern Europe, as the removal of language barriers decreases resistance by Westerners considering travelling to Eastern Europe.

Golembski (1991) discusses the needs of tourism education in the former Soviet bloc countries, with special reference to Poland. He stresses the necessity for profound changes in the systems of education resulting from the recent political and economic changes, and identifies the major problem in tourism education as being that of lack of knowledge and experience of the teaching staff with regard to market economics, marketing, Western languages etc. Golembski suggests that cooperation in the following areas with Western higher education institutions involved in tourism is the best approach to instigating the required changes quickly and effectively:

1 The West should be asked to provide access to modern teaching materials and advice with regard to the appropriate contents of courses.
2 Experienced staff from Western higher education institutions should do some teaching on the new courses set up in Eastern Europe, particularly during the initial phases.
3 Staff (particularly younger members) from universities, polytechnics etc. in Eastern Europe should be sent to corresponding institutions in the West in order to receive appropriate training which would enable them to carry out their new duties more effectively.

Conclusion

The attractiveness of Eastern Europe to Western tourists has increased markedly as a result of the major political changes which have taken place since 1989. This is reflected in the time series on international tourist/visitor arrivals in the Eastern bloc countries.

Eastern Europe is still largely unexplored by Westerners, and as such represents somewhere new and exciting. There are, however, major constraints on the growth of tourism to Eastern Europe, such as inadequate infrastructure, insufficient supply of good quality accommodation and the generally poor quality of tourist products/services. Better education and training, the injection of Western capital and expertise through joint ventures, and improved marketing of the undoubted attractions of Eastern Europe will go far in overcoming the problems faced by the region as a tourist destination area.

To end on a cautionary note, however, it must be recognized that tourism will only flourish in an atmosphere of stability and safety. The political and economic instability which has resulted from both the disintegration of the former USSR and ongoing changes elsewhere in Eastern Europe (for example in Czechoslovakia), together with the breakdown of law and order which is occurring in many of the Eastern bloc countries, could be disastrous for the future of tourism in these countries. Above all, tourists value their personal safety, and the ability to travel around within a destination without threat to this safety is paramount.

References

Buckley, P.J. and Witt, S.F. (1990) Tourism in the centrally-planned economies of Europe. *Annals of Tourism Research*, **17**(1), 7–18

Franck, C. (1990) Tourism investment in Central and Eastern Europe: preconditions and opportunities. *Tourism Management*, **11**(4), 333–8

Golembski, G. (1991) The needs of higher level education in tourism in post-communist Countries of Middle-Eastern Europe (as illustrated by Poland). *Tourist Review*, **46**(1), 3–5

World Tourism Organization (1992) *Yearbook of Tourism Statistics*, WTO, Madrid

Part Four

Changing Directions: Planning and Development Issues

Introduction

The emergence and maintenance of tourism as a dynamic rather than a static industry depends in large measure upon the adoption of a strategic approach to planning and development. The success of such an approach is largely dependent upon a systematic and structured analysis of the broad environmental factors affecting tourism demand as an essential part of the planning process.

Faulkner suggests in Chapter 16 that since tourism demand is highly discretionary, a strategic approach to tourism marketing is essential for long-term effectiveness. The current international preoccupation with advertising among tourism promotion agencies may well be counter-productive to sustained visitor growth and can progressively undermine any competitive tourism advantage currently enjoyed by a destination area.

Historically, in Latin America, tourism began as a tool for economic development following the Second World War when the economies of Brazil and most of the Spanish speaking countries south of the United States had been devastated. Tourism was seen as one 'quick and painless' method of improving the region's economy. Since tourism in Spain was prospering, and Latin America had the physical resources most North Americans wanted (sun, sand and sea – the three Ss), investment in tourism seemed a natural method for economic growth and regional development.

Schlüter traces the history of tourism within the region in Chapter 17 and suggests that in addition to the three Ss, the culture of the region and its historic resources began to be sold to potential visitors. Because of the ancient and mysterious pre-Columban civilizations, tourists could also be attracted to the area's rich cultural heritage. It was believed that tourists would have little negative cultural impact since the region had been exposed to foreign influence for well over four centuries.

Since every country in Latin America had certain species of flora and fauna that could not be found in industrialized countries, and since there was a growing world-wide concern for protecting the environment, ecotourism was adopted as a viable alternative method of tourism development. The author points out however that although there are abundant natural and cultural resources available, 'real' growth in tourism will occur, not when the large international lobbies deem it appropriate, but rather when the region's residents have a greater voice and more important role in national decision-making.

Hawkins compares the growth of ecotourism with the overall growth of international tourism (Chapter 18). He relates further that owing to increasing concern for the environment, the primary markets for ecotourism are special interest, nature-orientated travellers. There has been significant growth in the number of visitors to developing countries for nature tourism related experiences. However, a number of authorities have expressed concern that in order to maximize the economic benefits of tourism, some developing countries may wish to concentrate their development efforts on mass tourism projects rather than on low impact, environment-sensitive forms of tourism.

Ecotourism strategies must be implemented in developing countries in order to promote sustainable development. A four pronged strategy is proposed consisting of: consumer awareness and education; tourism industry actions; destination planning and development; and an expanded concept of marketing ecotourism to developing countries. Each strategy is then further explained, enlarged upon and illustrated with specific development guidelines.

Although tourism is generally regarded as less destructive to the environment than most other industries, nevertheless, its sheer size and widespread presence has already created negative physical, social and environmental damage. Furthering the concept of sustainable development, Murphy (Chapter 19) relates the notion that an inexorable relationship exists between the economy and the environment. Some national governments such as Canada have changed their views on economic development and environmental protection, viewing them as mutually supporting rather than mutually exclusive. Such a perspective suggests that sustainable development can indeed be compatible with business objectives, and given the appropriate safeguards, the tourism industry can continue to grow and prosper as a private business within these new parameters.

Two case studies are provided which show the relationship between, and the different strategies that can be used to successfully integrate both environmental and business considerations. An ecological model for tourism development is proposed which includes the seven dimensions of sustainable tourism development reported by Tourism Canada. These are interrelated with a number of other components, that when taken together, form the requisite guidelines for sustainable tourism development.

The final chapter in this section deals with the planning and development issue, the role of government incentives in tourism. In Chapter 20 Wanhill suggests that, historically, governments have intervened in order both to assist and to regulate private sector tourism development. Owing to the complex nature of tourism, it is improbable that the private sector can satisfy completely government policy objectives fostering a balance between host and guest benefits. Incentives are viewed as policy instruments that can help ensure cooperative development between the private and public sectors. The rationale for sustainable development is the alleviation of absolute poverty and the replacement of renewable natural and cultural resources.

A classification system of government incentives is presented, including financial incentives and investment security. Rationales for each incentive are offered as well as a series of graphic information intended to illustrate the impacts of such incentives on the total amount of investment provided. Finally, in order to assess the effectiveness of the tourism project (from government's perspective), benefit analyses are discussed and illustrated examples are provided.

16 Towards a strategic approach to tourism development: the Australian experience

H.W. Faulkner

Introduction

In any country, the emergence and continuation of tourism as a dynamic and viable industry is dependent upon the adoption of a strategic approach to planning and marketing. The hallmark of such an approach is the inclusion of a systematic and structured analysis of broader environmental factors affecting tourism demand as an integral part of the planning process.

This approach is necessitated by the highly discretionary nature of tourism demand, and its consequent sensitivity to both transitory shocks and long-term trends in the broader environment. A full appreciation of these factors is essential if public sector tourism organizations and private sector tourism enterprises are to exploit new opportunities as they arise and adapt to potentially threatening changes.

While the above may appear to be a mere statement of the obvious to many readers, the approach advocated is either not generally applied, or it is only applied in a partial sense. This point is developed by referring to the case of public sector tourism marketing in Australia, where there has been a focus on advertising at the expense of a more balanced strategic approach. It would appear that, while the Australian experience may not necessarily be typical in this regard, it is at least widespread.

Essential ingredients of the strategic approach

For the purposes of this analysis, the strategic approach is regarded as involving the following essential ingredients:

- A comprehensive and integrated plan of action for an enterprise organization.
- A clearly enunciated set of goals and objectives which provide the focus for the plan of action. These will reflect the corporate view of what is essential for the long-term effectiveness and survival of the organization and its product.
- The establishment of systems for monitoring and evaluating progress towards goals and objectives.
- An approach to planning which explicitly reconciles the inherent competitive advantages and limitations of the organization (or its product) with the challenges (opportunities and threats) of the environment.

The development of the latter aspect of the strategic approach usually involves what is referred to as SWOT analysis – i.e., Strengths, Weaknesses, Opportunities, Threats (Johnson and Scholes, 1984). SWOT analysis includes an assessment of existing, and anticipated opportunities and threats within the environment. Its main purpose is to determine whether or not, in the light of emerging opportunities and threats in the environment, the weaknesses of an enterprise (or product) have the potential to undermine its long-term survival. If this is so, then those weaknesses will need to be remedied. Alternatively, the enterprise may have certain strengths which may put it into an advantageous position for exploiting new opportunities.

In the Australian context there are several symptoms of a general lack of strategic thinking in tourism. First, there is a prevailing 'boom and gloom' mentality, with dramatic shifts between the extremes of optimism and pessimism reflecting a tendency to over-react to short-term events and developments. Secondly, there is an inclination to rely on gut-feelings and anecdotal evidence as a basis for making decisions, rather than drawing upon readily available objective research. It is human nature to assess a situation in a way that reinforces our preconceptions and prejudices. The first impression is thus often reinforced by selectively drawing on anecdotal evidence which tells only part of the story. Then, when more soundly based research contradicts what has become the conventional wisdom, it is the research which is questioned rather than the conventional wisdom. Finally, following on from the previous point, there is a parsimonious attitude to investment in research.

The first two symptoms, in particular, reflect the incomplete picture of the environment affecting tourism held by many decision-makers. That is, the assessments they make are not balanced by an appreciation of the full range of factors influencing events. This point is considered in more detail subsequently when public sector tourism marketing in Australia is examined more closely. Aspects of the third symptom, relating to the lack of commitment to research, are also considered in this context.

The Australian experience   233

Tourism marketing in perspective

Most analyses of tourism marketing (see, for example, Greenley and Matcham, 1971) highlight distinguishing features of the tourism product by referring to such characteristics as:

- Intangibility (product cannot be seen, touched, tasted or sampled prior to purchase).
- Perishability (production is fixed in time and space and the product cannot be stored for future use).
- Heterogeneity (it is difficult to achieve standardization to the extent that is possible in mass produced goods).
- Inseparability (the act of production and consumption is simultaneous).

While this approach may have been useful for pin-pointing characteristics of the tourism product which have a bearing on the marketing process, in these respects tourism is in fact no different from services in general. Furthermore, Middleton (1983) and others (for example, Wyckham et al., 1975) have argued that services are not really distinguishable from goods in terms of these dimensions in any case.

Whatever one's position on the issues in this debate, there are two features of tourism that have a fundamental bearing on the subject of this paper, but which are neither emphasized nor generally recognized in the literature.

First, tourism is an amalgam of complementary services which are destination-specific. While Medlik and Middleton (1974: 29) and Jeffries (1971), for instance, recognize the 'amalgam' characteristic, they do not specifically emphasize, or spell out the implications of tourism being destination-specific.

The implications of this from a marketing point of view are that some emphasis has to be placed on promoting the destination, rather than individual elements of the amalgam *per se*. Also, because the organization of the services at a particular destination is fragmented, a considerable amount of coordination is required in this process. The need for this coordination has resulted in government intervention (Gilbert, 1990), and in fact the main role of the public sector in tourism development (in Australia if in all countries) has focused on generic marketing of regions, states and the country as a whole.

To appreciate the second prominent feature of tourism marketing which is most relevant to the point of this paper, it is necessary to go back to the classical 'four Ps' framework (i.e. Product, Price, Promotion and Place) attributed to McCarthy (1981). Using this framework, tourism marketing could be described as being:

- The process of identifying the needs and propensities of consumers (or, more specifically, different segments of the consuming public).
- Developing or modifying the product in accordance with the needs of identified target markets.
- Devising mechanisms for facilitating awareness of, interest in, and access to the product.
- Translating the above into sales through distribution networks, pricing mechanisms etc.

However, given that the attractions or attributes of a destination are relatively fixed, there is a considerable element (at least in the short term) of adjusting consumer wants to the product. We thus have a typical chicken and egg situation in the marketing process, which was explicitly recognized by Kottler (1961) over thirty years ago:

> Marketing's short-term task is to adjust consumers' wants to existing goods, but its long-term task is to adjust the goods to the customers' wants.

Of course, when considering tourism we should substitute 'products' for 'goods', as this statement clearly applies across the board to both goods and services.

The problem with public sector tourism agencies in Australia, and probably the world over, is that they have become fixated on the short term aspect of tourism marketing by putting all their efforts into packaging regional icons into images designed to appeal to consumers in advertising programmes. This process usually involves some marketing research (group sessions, sample surveys, market segmentation analyses etc.), which is used to identify those features of the product that have an affinity with the attitudes and preferences of consumers. However, as a consequence of the emphasis on advertising programmes, agencies have lost sight of the fact that consumer decisions occur within the context of a range of broader environmental factors. These factors impact on the propensity of specific market segments to make discretionary expenditures, and they influence the trade-off between tourism and other outlets for leisure activity which must also be taken into account.

A strategic approach to marketing therefore requires a more rigourous analysis of these contextual factors than has been the case to date. To elaborate on this point, an outline of what constitutes the environmental (or contextual) factors is provided in Figure 16.1. This provides the background required for the analysis of recent developments in public sector tourism agencies in Australia which leads to the conclusion that they are losing sight of the plot.

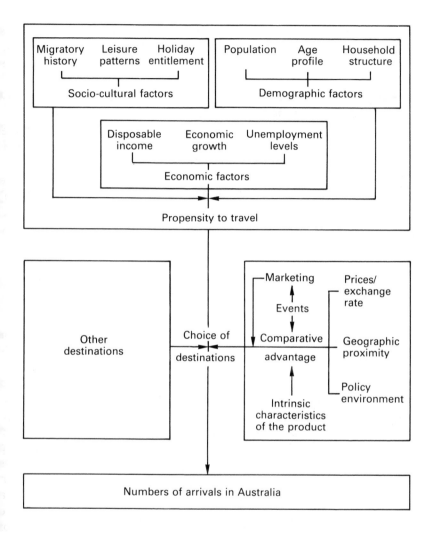

Figure 16.1   Factors affecting visitor arrivals in Australia

The dynamics of the inbound market

For the purposes of elaborating on the strategic considerations which need to be taken into account in tourism marketing, we will examine the dynamics of the inbound market. The range of factors influencing the market is described in Figure 16.1, where a distinction is made between:

- Factors that affect the propensity of populations to travel; and
- Factors that affect the comparative advantage of the destination in question and, therefore, the potential for it to be the chosen one.

At this point it is important to note that the model has been developed for illustrative purposes only. It is not intended to provide a comprehensive or exhaustive coverage of all factors at this stage, although it could be construed as having the potential to provide a heuristic framework for doing so in the longer term. Again, examples from the Australian situation will be used for clarification purposes.

Considering the factors that affect the propensity to travel first, one of the main sets of variables relates to *economic factors*. The general health of the economy, as reflected for instance in gross domestic product (GDP), has a bearing on:

- Disposable incomes, and therefore the ability and preparedness to spend on discretionary items such as travel. The significance of this variable is reflected in the fact that, according to Middleton (1983), three-quarters of world travel is generated by the twenty countries with the highest per capita disposable incomes. The distribution of incomes within the population is also important as this will influence the proportion of the population who have sufficient income to travel.
- The general health of the economy also affects unemployment levels, which in turn have a fundamental influence not only on the size of the population with the required disposable incomes, but also on the overall confidence of the market to spend on travel. High unemployment generates uncertainty within individuals about their future income earning capacity, and thus reduces their preparedness to spend on discretionary items such as travel.

The significance of economic growth, and its bearing on tourism through its effect on disposable incomes, unemployment levels and general consumer confidence is highlighted in Figure 16.2. The trend in visitor arrivals to Australia over the past twenty years reveals only three periods when arrivals actually declined – 1975, 1983 and 1989. All these reversals coincided with periods of general world-wide economic downturns. The more pronounced reversal in 1989 reflects the additional effects of other contributing factors, such as:

- Time-switching effects associated with the 1988 World Expo in Brisbane.
- The appreciation of the Australian dollar.
- An Australia-wide domestic airlines pilots dispute.

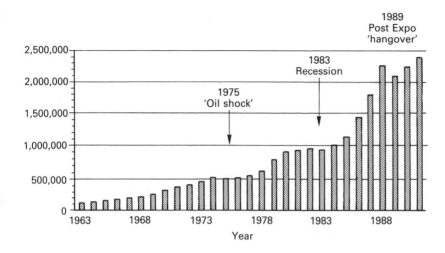

Figure 16.2 Short-term arrivals in Australia, 1963–1991

- An increasing proportion of holiday visitors in the Australian inbound market, which has the effect of making the market more volatile because of its increasingly discretionary nature (Faulkner, 1990).

The second set of factors affecting propensity to travel relate to *demographic factors* such as the size, age profile and family structure of the population:

- After taking into account disposable incomes and the distribution of incomes, the actual size of the population is obviously critical in determining the number of travellers that can be generated by a particular market.
- Ageing populations often generate more travel owing to the higher proportion of retirees who not only have more free time at their disposal for travel, but also have relatively high disposable incomes despite being income-poor.
- Household structure has a bearing on the nature of demand through its influence on household disposable incomes through, for example, the incidence of double income households with no kids (or DINKS) and the free time available for holidays (e.g. DINKS have an inclination for short breaks because of difficulty of arranging concurrent leave).

The third set of factors affecting propensity to travel relate to the *sociocultural background* of the population. Relevant factors include:

- The migratory history of the population, which will have a bearing on travel to the extent that it generates visits to friends and relatives (VFR) traffic.
- Institutional factors such as holiday entitlements affect the amount of free time a population has at its disposal for travel *vis-à-vis* other leisure pursuits. For instance, travel for Japanese is constrained by them having only two weeks annual leave.

As population and wealth are two of the more easily measurable and potent factors affecting the potential of individual markets, various markets are classified in terms of these two factors in Figure 16.3. Here each country has been plotted according to its population (on the vertical axis) and GDP per capita (on the horizontal axis). If it is assumed that wealth takes precedence over the size of the population (China is a low generator of overseas travellers despite its huge 1.1 billion population because few of its people can afford to travel), then each group's potential to generate visitors can be ranked in accordance with the numbering system adopted in the graph.

If we look at how each market has performed in terms of the number of arrivals in Australia in Table 16.1, however, we can see that there are a number of anomalies:

- Japan has almost double the number of arrivals compared with the USA, despite these two countries being in the same group.
- The UK stands out as having up to ten times the number of arrivals of other countries in its group.
- Singapore, New Zealand and Hong Kong registered more arrivals than most of the wealthier and larger countries in the previous group.
- New Zealand is the second largest inbound market despite its being one of the smallest countries.

To address these apparent anomalies, we need to look at the second set of factors in the model – i.e. factors affecting the *competitive advantage* of Australia *vis-à-vis* other destinations. These include such factors as:

- Geographical proximity, which in turn affects costs of getting to Australia in terms of both time and money, the level of inconvenience associated with time zone adjustments, and what the geographers refer to as intervening opportunities.
- Comparative prices of various aspects of the product which, in turn, can be influenced by relativities between countries in price inflation and exchange rates.
- The political stability of a country will affect its attractiveness as a destination to the extent that this influences safety considerations (note the impact of political events on visitor numbers to Thailand

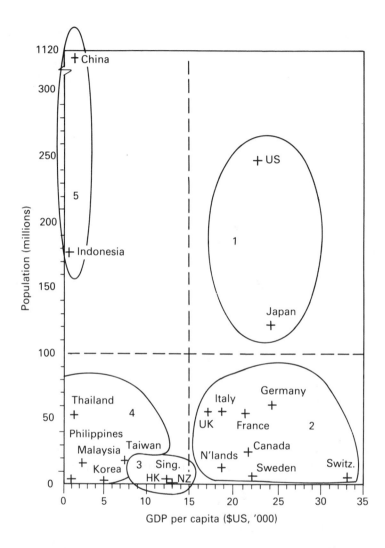

Figure 16.3 Population and wealth of major markets

and Fiji in recent years). Meanwhile, the policy environment in the destination can have a profound effect on its competitiveness. The micro-economic reform agenda in Australia has enhanced its competitiveness as a destination through the impact of deregulation on the price and quality of domestic airline services.
- As we have seen in the recent history of inbound travel to Australia, events such as the 88 Expo can have a profound short-term effect on visitor numbers. They can also have a longer-term promotional effect.

Table 16.1   Visitor arrivals from major market groups

Group	Country	Arrivals in 1991 (000's)
1	USA	271.8
	Japan	528.5
2	Germany	77.7
	France	22.7
	Canada	53.4
	Switzerland	29.6
	Netherlands	21.4
	Italy	24.3
	Sweden	19.1
	United Kingdom	263.8
3	Singapore	87.5
	New Zealand	480.6
	Hong Kong	62.8
4	Taiwan	34.7
	Korea	23.6
	Malaysia	48
	Thailand	24.7
	Philippines	15.7
5	China	16.7
	Indonesia	37

Given that Australia is a long-haul destination for most countries, international airfares make up a substantial proportion of the total cost of visiting this destination. The effect international airfare fluctuations can have on visitor numbers is highlighted in Figure 16.4, which shows a peak in arrivals to Australia from the USA coinciding with the heightened competition on the US–Australian route that accompanied the entry of Northwest Airlines. This figure also highlights the response of the US market to the 1989 World Expo in Brisbane.

The two remaining factors that affect the competitive position of a destination are the natural and man-made attributes (or intrinsic characteristics) that affect its appeal as a place to visit, and the effectiveness of the marketing of the destination. Advertising and promotional activities are fundamental catalysts by virtue of the role they play in stimulating the overseas markets' awareness of, and interest in, travelling to the destination.

In the analysis of inbound markets in terms of wealth and population we noted several anomalies. These anomalies become somewhat more understandable if we take into account just one of the more readily

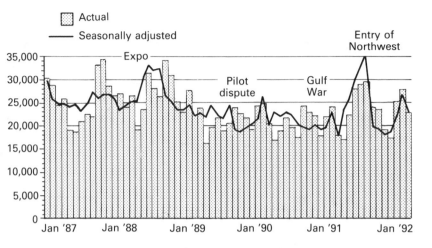

Figure 16.4 Short-term arrivals from the USA

quantifiable factors referred to above as contributing to comparative advantage – i.e. geographical propensity. When we superimpose the geographical proximity factor on this classification, as in Figure 16.5, it can be seen that most of the anomalies exceed expectations because of their greater geographical proximity to Australia.

What stands out from this sort of analysis is the impression of transience in the factors affecting demand. It seems that the combination of variables which is most influential varies in time, with each variable (or set of variables) coming into play periodically as some threshold is reached, which represents the point at which the market becomes sensitive to the variable in question. If this is the case, then it is little wonder that empirical studies fail to agree on a common set of dominant variables (Crouch and Shaw, 1990). This suggests that constant surveillance and analysis of all these factors are necessary if the dynamics of the market is to be properly understood.

Public sector tourism marketing in Australia

The above model highlights the need to analyse macro-level factors affecting tourism demand in order to provide a context for other aspects of marketing research. Indeed, the analysis of these factors is essential for the establishment of a truly strategic approach for two specific reasons:

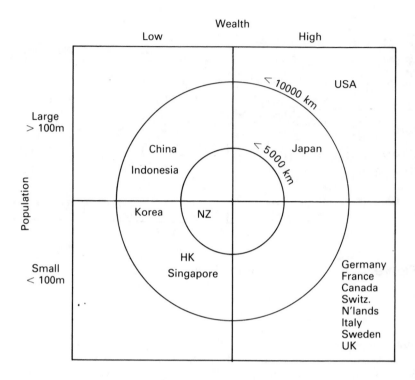

Figure 16.5   Geographical proximity of major markets

- Such analyses provide the basis for identifying, and therefore target-ing, those markets that exhibit the greatest potential to travel.
- In evaluating the effectiveness of promotion programmes, variables which affect the response of markets, but which are less susceptible to manipulation through the advertising process, must be taken into account.

In reviewing the progress of public sector marketing in Australia to-wards the satisfaction of these requirements one would have to conclude that, at best, we have had mixed success. There have been some positive developments, which represent a tentative step in the right direction, but progress beyond this point has faltered owing to a shift in priorities towards an all-consuming concentration of resources on advertising.

On the positive side, the establishment of the Australian Bureau of Tourism Research (BTR) in 1987 resulted in the concentration of state and Commonwealth resources to create the critical mass required for an effective research programme. Also, through this initiative, a more co-ordinated approach to tourism research at the national level has been established. Systems for monitoring the levels and characteristics of tourist activity have been upgraded and progress has been made in the analysis of factors affecting demand, especially through work carried out on the development of forecasting models. In line with the BTR's designated role of promoting the more effective use of research in tourism development, it has been instrumental in fostering the adoption of a strategic approach by making government and industry more aware of these factors.

In general, marketing research carried out by government tourism bodies has consisted mainly of market segmentation studies aimed at calibrating advertising activities and, incidentally, to provide input to product development. Tracking studies have also been carried out for the purposes of gauging the immediate effect of individual advertising campaigns on changing the awareness of, and interest in, the product. Meanwhile, some satisfaction surveys have been conducted from time to time. These surveys have not always involved the degree of methodological rigour that would justify the conclusions drawn from them.

The recognition of the influence of contextual factors has been to some extent forced upon the Commonwealth and state tourism agencies by their respective Departments of Finance and Treasuries. The simplistic attribution of growth in tourism numbers directly to advertising campaigns, without reference to other factors, is no longer accepted as a credible justification for continued public funding of tourism promotion (Faulkner and Shaw, 1992). Such pressure was instrumental in the conduct of a more rigourous evaluation of the Australian Tourist Commission's (ATC) programme (see ATC 1991), which featured a detailed analysis of contextual factors (Crouch and Shaw, 1990).

Despite the impetus that the ATC initiative could have provided, there remains a general insensitivity to the level of commitment to research which is essential to the development of a truly strategic posture. Indeed, as mentioned previously, the prevailing trend among public sector tourism agencies in Australia is towards the concentration of resources on advertising programmes at the expense of research.

This phenomenon has been referred to as 'advertising fundamentalism' (Faulkner, 1991), the rationale of which appears to hinge on the following proposition.

> The key to gaining the competitive edge in the quest for maximizing market share resides in the manipulation of consumer awareness and choice through advertising programmes. In the context of limited funding and the high cost of maintaining electronic media exposure, therefore, the diversion of funds from research and other areas is justified.

While it is plausible that an increased commitment to advertising will increase market share, this will only occur if these programmes are integrated with a broader strategy encompassing product development and the effective identification and targeting of potential market segments. Also, the impacts of advertising and the marketing programme as a whole need to be continuously monitored and evaluated so that deficiencies can be remedied and adjustments made in response to changing circumstances. Without a sound research basis for these aspects of the marketing process, the overall marketing programme is flying blind.

In the Australian context, the advertising fundamentalists will appear to be vindicated in the short term, as inbound and domestic tourism demand is likely to pick up in response to improving international and domestic economic conditions over the next year or so. The extent to which increased visitation levels are actually attributable to the new emphasis on advertising will therefore be open to question, and will certainly not be verifiable if research functions are downgraded. More importantly, however, problems will be encountered in the future as the effectiveness of longer term (i.e. strategic) planning is jeopardized by the downgrading of research input.

Conclusion

The basic proposition of this chapter has been that the analysis of the contextual or environmental factors affecting tourism demand is an integral part of the more strategic approach to tourism marketing, which is so essential for long-term effectiveness. The trend towards advertising fundamentalism (at the expense of the commitment to research) among tourism agencies in Australia is therefore inconsistent with the development of the strategic marketing approach and will be counter-productive in the longer term.

From an Australian point of view, this trend will progressively undermine any competitive advantage its tourism product either currently possesses or has the potential to develop in the future. Of course, this will occur only to the extent that other countries, which provide alternative destinations, are not also falling into the 'advertising fundamentalism' trap.

It seems highly likely, however, that the failure to adopt a truly strategic approach is not unique to Australia. On an international scale, therefore, the implications of this phenomenon go beyond simply the effect it may have on the competitive advantage of individual countries *vis-à-vis* others. The real problem is that the prevailing approach to tourism development and marketing is likely to stifle the emergence of tourism as a dynamic and sustainable force in many economies.

References

Australian Tourist Commission (1991) *Evaluation of the Australian Tourist Commission's Marketing Impact*, Australian Tourist Commission, Sydney

Crouch, G.I. and Shaw, R.N. (1990) Determinants of international tourist flows: findings from 30 years of empirical research, *Proceedings of 21st Annual Conference of the Travel and Tourism Research Association*, 10–14 June, New Orleans, Louisiana, pp. 45–60

Faulkner, H.W. (1990) Swings and roundabouts in Australian tourism. *Tourism Management*, **11**(1), 29–37

Faulkner, H.W. (1991) The role of research in tourism development. *Tourism Update* (Bureau of Tourism Research), September qtr, pp. 2–3

Faulkner, H.W. and Shaw, R.N. (eds) (1992) The evaluation of tourism marketing campaigns, Occasional Paper No. 13, Bureau of Tourism Research, Canberra

Gilbert, D. (1990) Tourism marketing: its emergence and establishment. In *Progress in Tourism, Recreation and Hospitality Management* (ed. C. Cooper), University of Surrey, vol. 3, pp. 77–90

Greenley, G.E. and Matcham, A.S. (1971) Problems in marketing services. *European Journal of Marketing*, **17**(6), 57–64

Jeffries, D. (1971) Defining the tourism product: its significance in tourism marketing. *Tourist Review*, **26**, No. 1, pp. 2–5

Johnson, G. and Scholes, K. (1984) *Exploring Corporate Strategy*, Prentice-Hall, Englewood Cliffs, NJ

Kottler, F.H. (1961) *Marketing Management Analysis, Planning Control*, Prentice-Hall, Englewood Cliffs, NJ

McCarthy, E.J. (1981) *Basic Marketing: a Management Approach*, 7th edn, Irwin, Homewood, Ill.

Medlik, S. and Middleton, V.T.C. (1974) The tourism product and its marketing implications. *International Tourism Quarterly*, pp. 28–35

Middleton, V.T.C. (1983) Product marketing – goods and services compared. *Quarterly Review of Marketing*, Summer, pp. 1–10

Middleton, V.T.C. (1990) *Marketing in Travel and Tourism*, Butterworth-Heinemann, Oxford

Wychkam, R.G., Fitzroy, T. and Mandry, G.D. (1975) *European Journal of Marketing*, **9**(1), pp. 59–67

17 Tourism development: a Latin American perspective

Regina G. Schlüter

Introduction

One of the favourite subjects of tourism researchers from developed countries is the development of tourism in non-industrialized countries. Such countries are generally taken as a shapeless unit by those researchers, who have a tendency to forget that every continent and every country has specific characteristics which differentiate it from the others, and that these differences and unique situations can sometimes be found within the borders of a single country.

In Latin America, the label attached to the group of countries comprising Brazil and all the Spanish speaking countries south of the United States, sharp differences can be found within the national borders of each individual country. This is due to the fact that on the one hand borders were arbitrarily set, and on the other hand, geographical differences influenced the cultural occupation of the territory.

There are also historic elements that differentiate this region from other developing areas such as Africa or Asia. First, it has been exposed to European contact for 500 years and, except for Brazil, the whole region was colonized by Spain, whose cultural supremacy had very specific characteristics. Secondly, the independence movements arose as early as the end of the eighteenth century and the beginning of the nineteenth century. This is why the relationship with Great Britain and eventually with the United States was not one of overt domination but was framed within a context of influence on social, political and economic decisions.

These distinctive differences can also be seen in the development of tourism. The activity was first used by a Latin American government as a tool for development in the 1930s. The Argentine government tried to turn the small village of San Carlos de Bariloche into a tourism resort in order to reaffirm Argentina's sovereignty in the area through the settlement of a permanent resident population.

In the 1950s, however, when Latin America tried to achieve development through tourism, it applied the same policies followed by all the developing nations. Without critically assessing whether that was really the best for them, the countries in the region shaped their tourism policies as was the practice in other Central American countries.

Tourism development in Latin America from 1950

After the Second World War, Latin America realized the extent to which tourism was contributing to the fast recovery of the devastated economies. It also witnessed the expansion of the large American hotel chains and the growth and progress brought about by the tourism 'boom' in Spain. Consequently, many Latin American countries (as well as other developing nations) decided to incorporate tourism either as an economic alternative to achieve growth or as a supplementary aspect of the main economic activity.

In 1955, the economic model fostered by the Economic Commission for Latin America (CEPAL) was implemented. Lizama (1991) stresses that Latin American countries had to strive to go from the stage of primary goods production to that of industrialization. This required a rapid and intense development of industry which, in turn, called for investments and major state participation.

Governments tried to encourage large private corporations to invest in the country. When this was not achieved, the governments made the investments themselves. They also resorted to foreign financing from international agencies such as the World Bank, the Organization of American States (OAS), the United Nations Development Programme (UNDP), the Interamerican Development Bank (BID) etc.

In the case of Bariloche (Argentina), tourism was introduced as the response to a strictly domestic political problem. Those developments implemented after the 1950s, however, were orientated to create leisure resorts for residents of industrialized countries. Therefore, the characteristics of these developments were decided by the industrialized countries themselves and were accepted without hesitation by the countries on the periphery, who thought tourism was the magic solution to all their problems.

Thus, during the second half of the twentieth century, Latin America had to adapt its attractions to the requirements of the extra-regional market, and eventually these attractions became the three most required products (Schlüter, 1991a):

- the three Ss (Sun, Sand and Sea).
- exotic culture.
- ecotourism.

The first recipe applied in Latin America involved 'integrated tourism centres', whose favoured resource was the 'Sun, Sand, Sea' triad. 'Integrated' meant that even the unexpected was foreseen, taking into account the region's environmental, economic, social and cultural factors. The tourism centres of Cancun (Mexico) and Puerto Plata (Dominican Republic) are the clearest examples of such resorts in Latin America.

The 'three Ss' product

At the beginning of the 1950s, this was the product preferred by industrialized countries. Consequently, the Caribbean became the ideal destination, especially for Anglo-Saxon America. Owing to its proximity to the continental territory of the United States and the easy terms it offered to foreign investors, Cuba became the region's favourite destination. The city of La Habana and the beach of Varadero attracted the largest number of tourists.

Between 1950 and 1959, Cuba was visited by 1.7 million American tourists, who represented 85 per cent of the total number of arrivals. The most outstanding year was 1957, with 272,200 tourists, 87 per cent of whom came from the United States.

Following the successful Cuban Revolution led by Fidel Castro in 1959, problems arose between the United States and Cuba: there was a total rupture of relations between both countries as Cuba strayed towards the socialist bloc and the number of international arrivals dropped to very low levels.

The tourist flow from the United States turned massively to Puerto Rico. This country had an incipient tourism industry but was in no condition to make it grow at a rapid pace and provide good services. Instead of exploiting tourism the citizens exploited tourists. In this way, the country earned a negative image (Soto Cordero, 1991).

International tourism to Cuba increased again after 1973, when, owing to a change in the international situation, Cuba was able to attract once more the tourism flow coming from the most important generating countries. Currently, Cuba's main market is still North America, though it is not the United States but Canada. In 1990, Cuba had 113,500 beds and was visited by 341,329 tourists. By 1995, the country expects to have 50,000 rooms for international tourism and to receive 1.5 million tourists.

In order to reach this figure Cuba will have to attract 19 per cent of the non-American visitors who are expected to travel to the insular Caribbean this year (Alvarez Valdés, 1991).

Puerto Rico missed the opportunity of becoming the leading tourist attraction in the Caribbean between 1977 and 1984 due to a series of wrong tourism policies. The situation changed in 1985, however, when important hotel chains carried out large investments. These investments, together with a number of governmental policies, have made it possible for the tourism industry to dream of a future when Puerto Rico will be the main destination in the region (Soto Cordero, 1991).

For political reasons tourism development was a late event in the Dominican Republic, only starting in the 1970s. In 1971, INFRATUR was created. This was an agency similar to its Mexican counterpart of the same name (the current FONATUR), whose aim was the development of tourism in the country. With the advice of the United Nations Development Programme (UNDP) and funds from the World Bank, the building of an integrated tourist centre was started in Puerto Plata, a region that comprised two areas: Playa Dorada and Playa Grande. As the expected private investments did not materialize it was also necessary to ask for loans from various foreign banks (World Tourism Organization, 1991.)

Thanks to the political stability that was achieved in the Dominican Republic during the 1970s, it was possible to carry out a study of new tourism developments in the country. Five areas were identified: four at the seaside and one in a mountain area. Furthermore, the government also passed a number of laws regulating the tourism industry.

Towards the late 1980s, tourism was already becoming the triggering factor for economic development in the Dominican economy. Owing to the prevailing political stability, large investments were carried out in the hotel sector, which grew very fast, from 8560 hotel rooms in 1985, to 10,185 in 1987, and 16,288 in 1988. According to some estimates, 25,000 rooms were available in 1992. In 1989, the Dominican Republic received 1.4 million visitors, 384,939 of which were Dominicans living abroad.

At present the main generating markets for the Dominican Republic are: United States, 44 per cent, Canada, 38 per cent and Germany, 5 per cent. While more than 75 per cent of visitors travel for leisure, 36 per cent are repeat visitors. What tourists enjoy most are the hospitality, the beaches and the climate. What they dislike most is the bad service they encounter at airports, hotels and restaurants. They also dislike the water quality, the lack of electricity and the poverty (Aquino, 1991).

Surprisingly enough, tourism growth in Mexico is not based on its rich cultural heritage but on the development of a product based on the three Ss. Owing to its privileged geographical situation, the Mexican government has considered tourism the best alternative to achieve economic growth, regional development and population resettlement in isolated areas as well as a way of solving social problems such as the high unemployment rate among the illiterate population group.

In the 1970s, in order to achieve these aims, Mexico was forced to consolidate its traditional beach resorts, Acapulco, Mazatlan and Puerto Vallarta, and to create new integrated tourism resorts. Cancun, Ixtapa and Bahias de Huatulco are under the supervision and control of FONATUR (the National Tourism Fund). These tourism developments were supplemented with a series of specific policies related to transportation, service quality standards, advertising and the like. In this way, Mexico, with 6,392,700 arrivals in 1990, reached ninth place among the major destinations in the world (Guadarrama Munoz, 1991).

As far as the remaining Latin American countries are concerned, only Brazil was able to compete in the extra-regional market with its 'sun, sand and sea' product. In 1972–3, a project called 'TURIS' was launched. Its aim was to develop a chain of seaside resorts on the Atlantic coast, from Rio de Janeiro to Santos, for both domestic and international tourism. These resorts attracted mainly tourists from Argentina, who also visited the beaches that stretched from Santos to Porto Alegre. Later on, additional developments were carried out in north-east Brazil, where Dutch, Portuguese and Afro cultural remains combine with hedonism at vacation resorts such as Itaparica's Club Méditerranée. These developments succeeded in making the country more attractive for tourists from the United States and Europe. However, Rio de Janeiro, with 51.1 per cent of the total arrivals to Brazil, has remained the most visited city.

One of the characteristics of South American tourism is that over 70 per cent of the international arrivals originate in the sub-regions. The 'sun, sand and sea' product is ranked first among Latin American consumers, who imitate the vacation patterns of the large European markets.

This is why Uruguay, whose main market is Argentina, has become such an important destination (1,267,000 arrivals in 1990). Tourism growth in Uruguay was a spontaneous event brought about merely by the market law of supply and demand. However, some intergovernmental agencies such as the Organization of American States (OAS) and the European Economic Community (EEC), have sent experts to carry out studies which were never put into practice.

In the 1970s, Chile and Argentina also tried to offer a three Ss product in the international market, but in the face of their latitude, the three Ss became 'sun, snow and skiing'. On both sides of the Andes Chain, local entrepreneurs have built many winter resorts, whose main market is the South American countries. Extra-regional tourists mostly visit the resorts when world ski championships are held there, but they also travel to the region, to a lesser extent, for snobbery. It is nice to be seen walking about Miami airport carrying a pair of skis in July.

Culture as a tourism resource

Latin America has extraordinary archaeological remains of the three major pre-Columbian cultures: the Aztecs in Mexico, the Mayas in Mexico, Belize, Guatemala, Honduras and El Salvador, and the Incas in Peru and Bolivia.

The region also offers a wealth of sociocultural expressions in which pre-Columbian rituals are mixed with elements introduced by the colonial domination. It is worth mentioning the marked African influence, a result of the slavery system established in Brazil by Portugal. There are also some interesting religious events in which catholic and native rites have been fused, such as 'La Tirana' in Chile, 'Tinkunaco' in Argentina, 'La Diablada de Oruro' in Bolivia, 'La Mama Negra de Latacunga' in Ecuador, or the procession to 'Our Lord of Esquipulas' in Guatemala. The Rio Carnival, however, is the only cultural product highly competitive in the international market.

Peru and Guatemala, whose beaches are not good enough for these countries to offer the characteristic three Ss triad, have important archaeological remains, such as the Inca site Machu Pichu in Peru and the Mayan Tikal in Guatemala. Furthermore, the survival of ancient customs and the interbreeding between the native Indian population and the Spaniards have made it possible for both countries to have a share of the market by means of a cultural product.

In the early 1970s, however, Latin America realized that this tourism product had some drawbacks: when a certain culture becomes a tourism resource, it has to be kept unchanged. In other words, it is necessary to freeze a society in time. In practice, this is an impossible task for governments because it means that a social group will have to be deprived of the latest technological advances for the recreation of the inhabitants from developed countries and for the benefit of some transnational tourism corporations. This is why, at the end of the 1960s, the countries resorted to so-called 'staged authenticity', even in remote areas.

Despite this reasoning, Peru tried to develop tourism within the framework of the UNESCO–Peru Cultural and Tourism Plan, known as the COPESCO project, which is now undergoing its second stage. Its aim is expanding agriculture, the base economy of the Cuzco–Puno region, and protecting the Inca archaeological sites with the assistance of experts from the United Nations Educational, Scientific and Cultural Organization (UNESCO). Protection was focused on the Machu Pichu ruins, discovered by Hiram Bingham in 1911. A five-star hotel with a capacity of 200 beds was built there. In order to cater to the demands of extra-regional tourism a series of facilities were built at Cuzco, the access to the ruins and the main tourism destination in the area. During the period

1985–90 the hotel sector grew by 113 per cent, which meant 80,000 new hotel rooms for international tourism. The latest tourism policies involve the development of seaside resorts in the north of Peru and the fostering of ecotourism, especially in the Manu Natural Reserve and the Huascaran National Park. According to the World Tourism Organization (1992), 317,000 tourists visited Peru in 1991, which meant a US\$53 million income (excluding transportation) for the country.

Guatemala, on the other hand, is seeking to get some benefit out of the World of the Mayas Project, which at last, after twenty-five years, is being implemented with the EC's technical support. This project, formerly called La Ruta Maya (the Mayan Route), aims at achieving a sustained tourism development in the countries involved. It comprises a 1,500 miles long circuit which connects the different Mayan sites in Mexico, Guatemala, Honduras, Belize and El Salvador (Acerenza, 1991). However, there is still a long way to go before this project is fulfilled.

At present, with 508,000 international arrivals, Guatemala together with Mexico are the two countries that benefit most from this project, primarily because of their proximity to Cancun (Mexico), the seaside resort that serves as a starting point for excursions to the ruins.

Ecotourism

The concern about the deterioration of the environment grew deeper at the beginning of the 1970s. Ten years later this concern was reflected in the tourism activity in developing countries. Terms such as 'soft', 'sustained', 'green', 'responsible' or 'appropriate' came into fashion, while the share of the market that looked for 'undisturbed nature' as its vacation destination increased in the major generating countries. Gradually, a new international movement for sustainable development emerged, ecotourism.

Consequently, all Latin American countries lacking 'sun, sand and sea' decided to develop ecotourism in order to benefit from this 'ecological wave'.

Every country in the region has certain species of flora and fauna that cannot be found in industrialized countries. Costa Rica, however, had the largest number of them in its small territory and has eventually become *the* ecotourism destination in Latin America.

In the face of the fluctuating prices of their staple products, coffee and bananas, the Costa Rican government successfully devoted all its efforts to the development of a non-aggressive ecotourism product. According to Chacón (1991), 435,030 tourists arrived in Costa Rica in 1990, which meant a 15.7 per cent increase over the previous year, and a foreign currency income of $266 million. Assuming that the imported component of the tourism sector is 50 per cent, there was a net income of $133 million. Costa Rica has 6000 beds to meet the needs of international tourism. The Costa Rican government has entered into agreements with several important international and Spanish corporations in order to incorporate to the country's present infrastructure 2000 first class rooms (five stars) and 2000 rooms in other categories. Besides, 5000 direct jobs and 15,000 indirect jobs will be created, and $140 million in foreign currency income will be generated in 1994.

The Amazonas region is becoming the most important ecotourism product in South America. In this context, Brazil is the country making the greatest efforts to hold its position as the main extra-regional destination, in spite of the constant sensationalist press coverage it receives from the mass media of industrialized countries. The OAS has funded some feasibility studies related to the Amazon ecotourism project.

The Galapagos National Park (Ecuador), created in 1959, was already an important ecotourism destination before the term 'ecotourism' was coined. The islands, whose name derives from the giant turtles called Galapagos, began to be massively visited in 1970 when the first cruise ships arrived. The first plan for the management of the park was prepared between 1973 and 1974, and established the carrying capacity of the park at 12,000 visitors a year. As this figure was soon exceeded, the master plan was revised in 1985 and the new limit was set at 25,000 visitors per year. In 1990 the islands were visited by 45,000 people (Machlis and Costa, 1991).

A kind of tourism which fell within the category of what is currently called ecotourism was already a common practice in Bariloche, Argentina, at the turn of the century. The activity started when a national park was created and certain guidelines had to be followed in order to avoid deterioration of the environment.

The works carried out following the directions of the National Parks Administration to meet the tourism requirements created a high demand for outside labor. Two hundred workers were employed just during the pre-operational stage of the Llao Llao hotel. Eventually these workers stayed in Bariloche and began to work in tourism-related activities. The slow transformation from an agricultural and stockbreeding economy into an economy orientated to the service sector had already begun.

During the 1937–8 season, 2560 people arrived in the city while in the 1942–3 season, the figure increased to 10,900 (Eriksen, 1970). The number of foreign visitors, who came mainly from neighboring countries and from the United States, began to grow in the 1960s. The total number of tourist arrivals increased from 45,400 in 1960 to 151,000 in 1967. In 1970, Bariloche was visited by 234,259 tourists, and in 1985, by 422,757 tourists. The city's population also showed a steep increase. In 1915, there were

1000 inhabitants and by 1939, that figure had doubled. During the second half of this century, Bariloche was the city with the highest population growth between two censuses in the Patagonia region. In 1960 there were 21,960 inhabitants; in 1988 the city had 81,130 inhabitants (Landoni, 1988).

Latin American tourism planning: successes and failures

Notwithstanding the large number of tourism developments that were planned for Latin America, only a few have been carried out. The integrated seaside resorts in Mexico are the best example. The countries in the region look up to Mexico as an example to be followed, and many of them, such as the Dominican Republic and Costa Rica, are considering the creation of an agency similar to FONATUR in order to succeed with their own tourism undertakings.

Mexico's National Tourism Fund, FONATUR, was established in 1974 and had two priorities: to consolidate already popular tourism centres, and to create new integrated tourism resorts (Schlüter, 1991b). The new agency oversaw the granting of land reservations, established guidelines for the use of loans, prepared the master plans for the development of the integrally planned tourism resorts, and supervised, controlled and assessed their operation.

The following are some of the reasons that explain why so many development plans failed in the other Latin American countries:

1   They are the result of foreign initiatives and of large amounts of money available in the industrialized countries to be given as assistance to developing nations.

Ever since John F. Kennedy's presidency, when the Peace Corps was born, it has been considered best to send 'experts' and not money to developing nations, as the funds might otherwise not be used as allocated. Besides, this system offered an additional advantage: the money never left the developed country where the expert had his permanent address.

Regardless of the experts' technical knowledge, they generally know little more about the country than what can be read in a travel guide. Furthermore, there are so many countries requiring this sort of assistance that the phenomenon of 'if it's Tuesday this must be Panama and if it's Wednesday it must be Zimbabwe' is often encountered. The recipes to be applied do not offer many alternatives; if the country has beaches and a good climate, the option will be an integrated seaside resort; in all other cases it will be ecotourism.

2   With very few exceptions, the highest executives in the tourism area are appointed for political reasons and their term in office is subject to the will of the person who appointed them. They are expected to provide political responses and not technical ones; thus, they consider it more important to sign an agreement than to carry out a project. Very often, technical assistance agreements are signed by the Ministers of Foreign Affairs of the countries involved, and the heads of the tourism areas learn of them once they have been signed.

3   The technical experts in the public administration are subordinated to the political authority and, despite a certain job stability, the technicians run the risk of being 'frozen' if they disagree with the official guidelines. For this reason, even constructive criticism is avoided.

Consequences of the tourism developments

The economic consequences of international tourism are generally assessed in terms of the foreign currency income to a given country. In most cases, the countries state the gross income and avoid mentioning the public investment which has not been recovered with real income and which has become part of the country's foreign debt. To establish the exact amount of the economic benefits brought about by tourism in Latin America is not only a complex task, but the results may be misleading as well.

The countries that developed three Ss tourism resorts consider that they have been successful because the aims they wanted to achieve with such resorts have been reached: there was a population resettlement in non-productive areas, new jobs were created, and there was a process of economic growth which was of benefit to marginal areas. This can clearly be seen in Cancun (Mexico), a formerly small village with few inhabitants which in 1991 became an urban centre with 300,000 inhabitants (World Tourism Organization, 1991). Something similar happened in Puerto Plata (Dominican Republic), which concentrates 42 per cent of the total number of beds in the country and where 8000 new jobs have been created (World Tourism Organization, 1991) in a previously underdeveloped area.

In a paper on employment in Mexico, Rodriguez Woog and Hiernaux Nicolas (1992) concluded that the four- and five-star hotels generated 73 per cent of the jobs in the hotel industry, or 10 per cent of the direct jobs in tourism. They also found that those services related to the hotel sector such as restaurants, cafes and canteens, generated the highest relative number of jobs.

The job-creating power of tourism is assessed from the social and economic points of view in Latin America. In the economic field it has a multiplying effect on the economy of a country and prevents the income produced by international tourism from leaving the country.

However, the tourism activity very often attracts labour from other productive sectors, such as agriculture and fishing; in such cases these specific activities are abandoned in order to provide services. Bacal (1991) studied this phenomenon in Maceio, Brazil, where the fishermen rowed the tourists to the reefs during the high season. During the low season they spent long hours and even days trying to 'catch' a tourist wishing to do the trip. They did not return to their fishing activities because there was not enough demand to grant them a fair price for their catch.

Bariloche's population growth is explained by the fact that it became an attraction pole for individual workers who had previously worked in the farms on the Patagonia plateau, and very often, for their families too. Although the workers usually moved to the city for the tourism season only, most of them eventually settled there, and they either stayed with relatives or friends, or lived in small wooden houses in the city's southern suburbs (Landoni, 1988).

As regards the social aspect, tourism enables people to satisfy their basic and intellectual needs without depending on government subsidies or charity organizations. However, tourism brings native workers and tourists, who are also workers themselves, into close contact. As a consequence, the former find out that by doing the same job in an industrialized country they would have a better living standard. According to Esteve Secal (1983), the desire to imitate such a living standard leads the worker to consider the possibility of emigrating to the country where the tourists come from.

The task of assessing the socio-cultural impact of tourism is a very complex one because such an assessment is based on qualitative, not quantitative factors. It is also nearly impossible to study this impact in isolation, without considering the influence of the mass media (especially TV) which, together with missionaries, adventurers and government bureaucracy, always precede tourists (Schlüter, 1991b). Besides, the socio-cultural impact also depends on the degree of foreign influence to which the cultural group being studied has been exposed. Several surveys carried out in Argentina (Ferrari, 1992; Monedero Gálvez and Schlüter, 1986; Schlüter, 1984; Winter, 1991) have shown that closed communities, i.e., communities that adhere to their traditions and refuse to accept any changes, generally reject the idea of being visited by tourists. On the other hand, open communities, i.e., communities that foster all sorts of exchanges and want to get hold of new technologies, and those communities that benefit directly from the tourism activity, want to increase the tourist flow as much as possible, even at the expense of social, cultural or environmental damage.

In some integrated tourism resorts, a certain degree of resentment has been detected concerning the deep changes affecting the way of living. In Bahias de Huatulco, Mexico, Long (1991) found that some of the families who had been relocated in order to build vacation clubs and hotel complexes were filled with anger. He also stated that the local population was facing some problems owing to the increases in the price of the basic commodities and to the lack of job opportunities. Most jobs required the workers to have at least a good command of English, a language which they could not speak and which they would never have a chance to learn.

The kind of tourism which emphasizes the preservation of the cultural and natural environment also brings about major changes. In Bariloche, Argentina, the farms in the surrounding area began to produce food supplies such as milk, cheese, butter, eggs and fruit. These supplies were then sold directly to the tourists, especially to campers. The small landowners frequently turned their facilities into restaurants and lodging houses. In other cases, however, they subdivided and sold part of their land in order to build housing facilities and camping sites for tourists.

The unrestrained and speculative subdivision of land influenced the expansion of the city of Bariloche. This expansion, together with the mountain topography (30 per cent of the city is built on a mild slope of 25–27°) created an irregular settlement belt along the Nahuel Huapi Lake. For this reason, there are small neighbourhoods, sometimes made up of a few houses, that are scattered at long distances from the urban centre and that are not reached by the services rendered by the municipality. Consequently, the basic services are unequally rendered, the aesthetic appearance has been damaged and there has been a marked deterioration of the soil and the forests.

The National Parks Administration is not the only agency that monitors the development of the area; several non-governmental agencies concerned with environmental protection have also been active in Bariloche since the 1960s. Nevertheless, the sewage is disposed of in the Nahuel Huapi Lake, the drinking water is polluted, the forests are becoming smaller, and there is noise and air pollution (Mazzuchelli, 1991)

In 1985, Costa Rica became the ecotourism destination *per se*. Its approach was very successful as regards both the conservation aims and the tourism activity. Nevertheless, some problems soon arose due to the continuous arrival of tourists who, after visiting the virgin nature sites, requested the services usually provided to 'resort' tourists. To satisfy their requirements, a number of facilities were built. Eventually, these facilities gave rise to serious problems between the population and the chief national authorities, causing a lot of controversy because of the environmental pollution they produced.

In Costa Rica, contrary to what is usual in other Latin American countries, the local population is very environment-conscious. They fear that the lack of control regarding sewage treatment, lack of noise level limits for the engines of cruise ships and motor boats, and the large numbers of tourists who will visit the resorts, among other reasons, might cause such a deterioration in the environment that the tourism activity itself might be killed.

All this has given rise to heated arguments and has caused the local population to reject the projects that were being carried out. For the time being, the local population is expressing its opinion through the media and through decorated T-shirts. In Latin America, these are the most usual means of expression, unless the country is going through a pre-election period during which the candidates can express the people's opinions. After that period, there is only oblivion, for even after 150 years of independent life, the democracies in the region are not mature enough to ensure the fulfilment of the promises that have been made.

Conclusions

With few expectations, tourism in Latin America, as well as in the other developing countries, began to be used as a tool for development after the Second World War.

The process started with the application of a basic recipe, the three Ss, that met the requirements of the extra-regional market. This recipe, however, was only applied some years later owing to the lack of political stability in the region or to the fact that the governments did not consider tourism the only alternative to achieve their aims.

At the same time, a cultural product was being sold in the major markets. However, as it was not in great demand, it had to be supplemented with 'sun, sand and sea' or with ecotourism. In general terms, Latin America has not become a relevant destination for major tourism-generating markets, but it has been successful in smaller scale projects in the regional market.

Contrary to what might be expected, the cultural product is the one that has been less affected by tourism. This is because the pre-Columban civilizations have been exposed to foreign influence for over four centuries and have found their own methods to survive the various forms of domination.

The three Ss product has a positive aspect for the local population, the improvement of quality of life, but it has also given rise to some resentment on the part of that sector of the population that has been excluded from the benefits of development.

On the other hand, ecotourism, which must combine both perpetuation and use of natural resources, has generated some very negative reactions, as the local population knows that protecting a certain species (whether animal or vegetables) is not enough. It is also necessary to take other general measures to protect the environment. Such measures should include some less romantic factors as sewage treatment and noise and air pollution control.

The future for tourism in Latin America will probably be brighter once the voters, and not the large national or international lobbies, have a more important role in national decision-making.

References

Acerenza, Miguel Angel (1991) La integracion de itinerarios para visitas a atractivos turisticos situados en paises limitrofes, islas y subregiones, y mejoramiento de atractivos turisticos especificos. Paper presented at the XVI Interamerican Congress of Tourism, Panama

Alvarez Valdés, Jesus (1991) Desarrollo turistico de Cuba. In *Desarrollo Turistico de América Latina*, (ed. CESTUR), CESTUR, Mexico, pp. 67–80

Aquino, Luis Felipe (1991) Desarrollo turistico de la República Dominicana. In *Desarrollo Turistico de América Latina* (ed. CESTUR), CESTUR, Mexico, pp. 87–102

Bacal, Sarah (1991) El impacto del tourismo en núcleos receptores de paises en desarrollo: Efectos socioculturales. *Revista Latinoamericana de Turismo*, **1**(2), 97–109

Chacón, Luis Manuel (1991) Desarrollo turistico de Costa Rica. In *Desarrollo Turistico de América Latina* (ed. CESTUR), CESTUR, Mexico, pp. 31–41

Eriksen, Wolfgang (1970) *Kolonisation und Tourismus in Ostapatagonien*, Bonn, Ferd. Dumlers Verlag

Esteve Secal, Rafael (1983) *Turismo, Democratización o Imperialismo?* University of Malaga

Ferrari, Olegario (1992) lsla Martin Garcia y el turismo: Opiniones de los residentes, *Estudios y Perspectivas en Turismo*, **1**(1), 15–20

Guadarrama Muñoz, Gerardo (1991) Desarrollo turistico de México. In *Desarrollo Turistico en América Latina* (ed. CESTUR), CESTUR, Mexico, pp. 7–29

Landoni, Marcela (1988) *Patagonia y . . . una forma especial de turismo*, CIET. Buenos Aires

Lizama Hernández, Carlos (1991) Desarrollo turistico de Costa Rica. In *Desarrollo Turistico en América Latina* (ed. CESTUR), CESTUR, Mexico, pp. 43–9

Long, Verónica H. (1991) Government–industry–community interaction in tourism development in Mexico. In *The Tourism Industry: An International Analysis* (ed. Sinclair, M.T. and Stabler, M.J.), CAB, London

Machlis, Gary E. and Costa, Diana A. (1991) Little Darwins: a profile of visitors to the Galapagos Islands. Proceedings of the 22nd Annual Conference of the Travel and Tourism Research Association, Long Beach, California

Mazzuchelli, Sergio (1991) San Carlos de Bariloche: La problemática ambiental urbana. *Medio Ambiente y Urbanizacion*, **37**(9), 75–92

Monedero Gálvaz, Fernando and Schlüter, Regina G. (1986) *Receptividad de los residentes del Valle de Punilla frente al turismo*, CIET, Buenos Aires

Rodriguez Woog, Manuel and Hiernaux Nicolás, Daniel (1992) Turismo y abscorción de la fuerza de trabajo: el caso Mexico, *Estudios y Perspectivas en Turismo*, **1**(1), 21–43

Schlüter, Regina G. (1984) *Percepción del residente frente al turismo en Puerto Madryn*, CIET, Buenos Aires

Schlüter, Regina G. (1991a) Latin America tourism supply: facing the extra-regional market, *Tourism Management*, **12**(3), 221–8

Schlüter, Regina G. (1991b) Social and cultural impacts of tourism plans and programs in Latin America. *Cahiers du Tourisme*, Série CN 53, Centre des Hautes Etudes Touristiques, Aix-en-Provence, France

Soto Cordero, Salvador (1991) Desarrollo turistico de Puerto Rico. In *Desarrollo Turistico de América Latina* (ed. CESTUR), CESTUR, Mexico, pp. 81–6

Winter, Gabriel (1991) Receptividad de los residentes frente al turismo. *Revista Latinoamericana de Turismo*, **1**(2), 110–19

World Tourism Organization (1991) *Centros Turisticos Integrados (Resumen)*, WTO, Madrid

World Tourism Organization (1992) *Compendio de Estadisticas del Turismo 1986– 1990*, 12th edn, WTO, Madrid

18 Ecotourism: opportunities for developing countries

Donald E. Hawkins

Ecotourism is one of the fastest growing trends in the world-wide tourism industry. The term 'ecotourism' has been defined in many ways, and is generally used to describe tourism activities which are conducted in harmony with nature, as opposed to more traditional 'mass' tourism activities. Comprehensively, ecotourism has been defined by the Ecotourism Society as

> purposeful travel to natural areas to understand the cultural and natural history of the environment, taking care not to alter the integrity of the ecosystem, while producing economic opportunities that make the conservation of natural resources financially beneficial to local citizens (Ecotourism Society, 1992).

The role of the tourist is stressed by Hector Ceballos-Lascurain, who states that the main point of ecotourism 'is that the person that practices ecotourism has the opportunity of immersing him or herself in nature in a way most people cannot enjoy in their routine, urban existences. This person will eventually acquire a consciousness . . . that will convert him/ her into somebody keenly involved in conservation issues' (Ceballos-Lascurain, 1987).

The resource conservation role is emphasized by Karen Ziffer, who describes ecotourism as 'a managed approach by the host country or region which commits itself to establishing and maintaining the sites with the participation of local residents, marketing them appropriately, enforcing regulations, and using the proceeds of the enterprise to fund the area's land management as well as community development' (Ziffer, 1989).

There seems to be general agreement that ecotourism involves minimum density, low impact activities which can take place where there are natural sites of sufficient biological, cultural and geographical interest to attract tourists. The major factors contributing to the boom in ecotourism are an international awareness of global ecological realities, the desire among a rapidly growing and relatively affluent segment of the industrialized world's tourists to have nature-based experiences, and the developing world's conviction that natural resources are finite and must be conserved for future generations.

Ecotourism as a sector of the tourism industry is still in its infancy, but an analysis of the markets where it has made strong inroads indicates that developing countries, with their abundant variety of physical attractions, have most of the natural qualities necessary to position ecotourism as a prime offering of their tourism industry.

Influence of ecotourism

Ecotourism is interrelated with the overall growth of tourism in the world today. In spite of recessions, civil disturbances and natural catastrophes, international tourism continues to grow. Indeed, travellers in the 1990s consider vacations as a basic necessity. Tourism is making a major contribution to the economic viability of many countries of the world today.

According to the World Travel and Tourism Council (WTTC) tourism is now the world's largest industry, expected in 1993 to generate more than US$3.5 trillion of world output, which is 6 per cent of the world GNP and a bigger industry than the auto, steel, electronics or agricultural industries. The travel and tourism industry employs 127 million workers (one in fifteen workers world-wide). Overall, the tourism industry is expected to double by the year 2005 (World Travel and Tourism Council, 1992).

Within this perspective, the World Tourism Organization has conducted forecasts of international tourism, which grew by more than 57 per cent in the past decade and is expected to grow by 50 per cent in this decade. Although the growth rate is slowing, a 3.7 per cent average annual growth is expected throughout the 1990s, with an expected 650 million international tourism arrivals by the year 2000. Nature tourism, in 1989, generated approximately 7 per cent of all international travel expenditures, according to World Tourism Organization estimates (1991). Developing countries, in particular, represent major untapped destinations featuring unique cultural and natural attractions.

Supporting general tourism growth is the projected growth of air travel. With increases in income and a decline in travel costs, air travel will increase again 100 per cent over the next fifteen years. Boeing, the world's largest aircraft maker, predicts a three-fold increase in revenue passenger miles by the year 2010 (Boeing, 1991).

Ecotourism is growing rapidly and is influencing the overall tourism industry both as (a) a special interest form of travel and (b) a 'greening' influence on the tourism field in general, stressing environmentally friendly approaches to tourism product development, operations and consumption. These two dimensions of ecotourism are described in the following sections.

Ecotourism as a specialty travel market

The primary market for ecotourism is special interest nature-orientated travel which reflects the increasing concern for the environment in the world's major tourism-generating countries. For example, data on the US ecotourism market substantiate this growth.

Ecotourism is a rapidly growing segment, but clear-cut statistics do not exist. Studies indicate, however, that the most popular special interest tours are related to nature orientated outdoor activities. US tour operators report that between 4 and 6 million Americans travel overseas for nature-related travel each year. Several selected special interest travel market segments follow:

- Bird watchers – 80 million Americans interested and account for $14 billion on equipment, travel and related expenses.
- Skin and scuba diving – 3 million divers in the US, increasing 16 per cent annually – 500 thousand new divers certified annually: 98.5 per cent of divers have a valid passport and 66.2 per cent of divers travel outside of the US on diving trips.

Nature travel is estimated to grow by 20–25 per cent between 1990 and 1995 and related culture and adventure travel will grow from 10 to 15 per cent (Mudge, 1991).

The US Travel Data Center determined that nearly 7 per cent of US travellers, or 8 million Americans, report having taken an ecotrip. One-third of those interviewed said they would take such a trip again, which equals 35 million adults. A recent study conducted by McKinsey & Co. indicates that 7 million tourists are willing to pay US$2,000–3,000 for a nature-related tour. The McKinsey study estimated that there are 275 guided nature tour operators in the United States who provided tours for 108,000 travellers during 1991, producing gross revenues of $95 million and profits of $4 million. Interestingly, these tour operators reported that 63 per cent of the travellers would pay $50 and 27 per cent would pay $200 towards conservation of the area visited (Ecotourism Society, 1992).

The Ecotourism Society also reports extensive growth in the number of visitors to developing countries for nature tourism-related experiences. For example, 47,000 people visited the Galapagos Islands in 1990, a 44 per cent increase since 1987. Tourism to the national parks and protected areas in Costa Rica grew by 80 per cent from 1987 to 1990 (Ecotourism Society, 1992).

Four basic types of tourists have been identified as favouring tourism destinations which feature natural attractions (Lindberg, 1991):

• Hard core – scientific researchers or members of tours specifically designed for education, removal of litter, or similar purposes.
• Dedicated – people who take trips specifically to see protected areas and who want to understand local natural and cultural history.
• Mainstream – people who visit the Amazon, the Rwandan gorilla park, or other destinations primarily to take an unusual trip.
• Casual – people who partake of nature incidentally as part of a broader trip.

A single individual may fit into different categories at different times. The typology, however, provides a simple description of market segments for planning purposes. For example, hard core and dedicated nature tourists are more likely to be tolerant of limited amenities than casual tourists.

The greening of the tourism industry

The environment has taken the centre stage in tourism planning and development world-wide. In 1990 the George Washington University conducted an international assembly on global tourism policy issues. The participants listed the environment as one of the top tourism agenda issues for the 1990s. Global climate change, ozone loss, deforestation, disappearing species and toxic waste were all considered crucial issues related to a sustainable tourism environment. Conservation and preservation policies have reached considerable momentum in many developing and industrialized countries of the world. Referred to as 'greening', the objective is for tourism to become both a tool for economic development while simultaneously preserving and conserving physical and cultural resources.

Policy-makers and planners must work with the knowledge that tourism can have negative impacts on personal security, transportation, urbanization and cultural integrity. Good tourism management means assessing the physical and social carrying costs of tourism development (Tourism Policy Forum, 1991).

Recognizing the environment and development issue as paramount, the World Travel and Tourism Council formed an environment research centre at Oxford Polytechnic in 1991 to create a world-wide database and information network concerned with environmentally compatible growth of the tourism industry world-wide. The centre will identify the types of impacts related to tourism development and promote environmental practices which would minimize costs and optimize benefits (World Travel and Tourism Council, 1992).

Many observers question whether developing countries can expect to capitalize successfully on their enormous tourism potential by concentrating development efforts almost exclusively on mass tourism projects such as traditional resorts and hotels of 500-plus rooms on the beach. The experience of some developing countries suggests that the existing infrastructure cannot sustain intensive development without breaking down altogether. Although both the public and private sector fully recognize the need to plan carefully for growth, concern has often been voiced that development will come first, and that the necessary human requirements and public works infrastructure will come a late second.

If the experience of other countries can serve as a useful guide to policy-makers, developing countries can learn a great deal from countries such as Costa Rica, Indonesia, Kenya, Nepal and Ecuador. These countries are blessed with beautiful natural scenery and unique flora and fauna. Unlike most developing countries, they have all concentrated their efforts on developing a low impact, environment-sensitive form of tourism, described today as 'ecotourism'. Their experiences – the mistakes as well as the successes – can have a profound bearing on a developing country's tourism industry, whose many promoters may discover that it can prosper more equitably if it strikes a balance between different development philosophies.

In order to fully grasp ecotourism's implications, it is essential to understand a relatively new concept which is becoming central to public discourse in this decade of 'sustainable development' which is now on public policy agendas. Governments and private interests alike agree that the principle of sustainable development must be the guiding force behind public policy and private initiative as mankind enters the twenty-first century. Our global community no longer has the luxury of spawning growth that deteriorates our already fragile balance of nature. The principles of sustainable development, if applied wisely, will do much to establish sound patterns of growth and well-being in many areas of human endeavour, including the tourism industry.

Ecotourism has extraordinary potential as a tool for sustainable development; conversely, the principles of sustainable development are central to ecotourism. These two forces are already having a strong impact on the industry.

A succinct exposition of the implications of tourism growth on our environment was presented at Globe '90, a conference on Global Opportunities for Business and the Environment, sponsored by the Canadian government in Vancouver in March, 1990. The conference report defined sustainable tourism development as:

leading to the management of all resources in such a way that we can fulfill economic, social and aesthetic needs while maintaining cultural integrity, essential ecological processes, biological diversity and life support systems. (Globe '90, 1991)

The report then elaborated on the need to make sustainable development an essential tenet of tourism policy world-wide:

Tourism and its role in sustainable development are currently the subject of much concern. A number of studies and conferences have examined the scope and implications of 'green' approaches to tourism. It seems clear that sustainability holds considerable promise as a vehicle for addressing the problems of mass tourism, as well as supporting 'alternative tourism' and 'ecotourism'.

The environment is tourism's base. Tourism shapes and affects the environment. A widely acknowledged problem is the extent to which ill-conceived and poorly planned tourism developments can erode the very qualities of the natural environment that attract visitors. Recognition of this problem is required at the national regional levels. Particular attention must be paid at the local level where impacts and concerns are most apparent.

The concept of sustainable development explicitly recognizes interdependencies that exist among environmental and economic issues and policies.

Sustainable development is aimed at protecting and enhancing the environment, meeting basic human needs, promoting current and intergenerational equity, improving the quality of life of all peoples.

The real challenge for the tourism industry and sustainable development must be met now. Nationally and internationally we require a vision of balanced development [which] establishes a working partnership between tourism and other sectors. (Globe '90, 1991)

The report's introduction closes with a call for action that establishes the tourism industry as a vehicle for sustainable economic development:

New mechanisms for coexistence must be developed through an integrated planning process that gives equal weight to tourism and other economic development activities. Tourism development requires the active exercise of ecological and social responsibility at the international, national and local levels. (Globe '90, 1991)

Ecotourism strategies for developing countries

It should be clear that the concept of sustainable tourism development spans a very broad spectrum of issues, all of which have a bearing on the decisions developing countries' tourism policy-makers must address in the very near future. At stake are not either–or, growth-versus-development issues, but something far more basic: how to provide opportunities for employment, income and improved local well-being, while ensuring that all development decisions reflect the full value of our natural and cultural environment.

A policy that promotes sustainable tourism development will be created when the efforts and active participation of three groups are co-ordinated in one joint enterprise. A new political paradigm of developing countries requires that each sector play a well-defined role in the planning and policy development process and that the combined efforts of all sectors be integrated into policy. If tourism leaders from all sectors work together they will eventually mobilize the human resources necessary to design and implement a series of tourism development policies and plans which truly address the enormous tourism potential of developing countries.

A four-pronged strategy approach is needed which includes:

1   Consumer awareness and education.
2   Tourism industry actions.
3   Destination planning and development.
4   An expanded concept of marketing ecotourism to developing countries.

Consumer awareness and education

Ecotourism is one of the major manifestations of environmental concern by the general public, particularly in developed countries. Although the average consumer has been sensitized to environmental issues, such as global warming, depletion of the ozone layer, air pollution, health and sanitation problems, more needs to be done to develop an awareness of the tourist's responsibility to preserve and enhance environmental quality of destinations. It is essential to promote ethical standards concerning the use of natural and cultural resources and to assist consumers in choosing tour operators who follow conservation guidelines. Interpretation programmes need to focus on pre-trip preparation, on-site educational programmes at destinations, and follow-through activities supportive of ecotourism principles.

The tourism industry

The private sector is responsible for delivering products and services to the tourist. It must take responsibility for the protection of biosphere by minimizing pollution which causes environmental damage (e.g., herbicides on golf courses, use of craft that damage reef structures and vehicles that damage sensitive ground cover) and sustaining the use of resources such as land, water and forests; reducing and disposing of waste via recycling; effective sewage treatment and waste disposal; adopting energy efficient practices; minimizing environmental and health risks; undertaking 'green marketing' by promoting 'soft' tourism that minimizes adverse environmental impacts; providing complete and credible information for tourists; incorporating environmental values in operation management; and conducting environmental audits.

Strong alliances with inbound and outbound tour operators need to be developed, particularly in terms of harmonizing the efforts of adventure and nature operators. The industry needs to develop standard codes of conduct and disseminate accurate and reliable information to all parties involved in tourism. Possibly, each country should develop an ecotourism association to serve as an information clearinghouse and as an organizer for cooperative efforts.

The industry should also work together to develop guidelines for resort developments and concession operations which utilize low-impact design criteria and the latest technologies for recycling and conserving resources. Recently, the United States National Park Service held a low-impact resort design workshop, in November 1991 in St John, USVI National Park, in cooperation with Maho Bay Camps, Inc. and the American Institute of Architects Committee on the Environment. The objective was to formulate a handbook on ecotourism resort development principles and practices in cooperation with destination planning and development authorities. This is a good example of industry working with government and non-governmental organizations in developing tourism products that are consistent with sustainable development principles.

Destination planning and development

Governments and non-governmental organizations need to share responsibility for ecotourism development. Governments would be well advised to assume the following roles recommended in the Globe '90 Conference Report:

- Undertake research into the environmental, economic and cultural effects of tourism.
- Support the development of tourism economic models to help define appropriate levels and types of economic activities for natural and urban areas.
- Assist and support lower levels of government to develop their own tourism development strategies.

- Develop standards and regulations for environmental and cultural impacts assessments, monitoring and auditing of existing and proposed tourism developments.
- Apply a sectoral and/or regional environmental accounting system for the tourism industry.
- Design and implement consultation processes (such as tourism advisory boards) that involve all interested entities in tourism-related decisions.
- Develop new economic indicators which define well-being in the context of sustainable development, which incorporate environmental and resource services and resource depletion.
- Educate the public on the issues of sustainable tourism development.
- Set design and construction standards that ensure that projects are in harmony with local culture and natural environments.
- Ensure that resource carrying capacities are not over stretched – a basic tenet of sustainable development.
- Regulate and control tourism in environmentally and culturally sensitive areas.
- Include tourism in land-use planning.
- Ensure that all ministries involved in tourism underwrite the concept of sustainable development and collaborate in this regard.

Non-governmental organizations also play a major role, since they essentially represent and protect the interests of the public, and have access to local information, expertise and labour. According to Globe '90 Conference Report, they should:

- Be part of sustainable tourism advisory boards at all levels of government and industry, and offer input into planning and development.
- Seek local support for appropriate sustainable tourism development as well as focusing opposition to inappropriate development.
- Offer to other agencies information on locally innovated sustainable tourism products and proposals, including the use of locally appropriate technologies.
- Promote education of the public on the economic importance of sustainable tourism development, the need for a secure resource base (e.g., natural landscape), appropriate behaviour related to sustainable tourism on the part of government, industry and tourists.
- Be encouraged to identify and communicate to the appropriate agencies those issues related to sustainable development as well as solutions to those problems, such as monitoring the impact of sustainable tourism on the local culture and environment, impacts of other sectors of the economy on sustainable tourism, and government and industry commitments to sustainable tourism (Globe '90, 1991).

Expanded concept of marketing

Traditional marketing has been described as the four Ps: Product, Promotion, Place, Pricing. These are briefly reviewed in terms of ecotourism in the following section.

Product

From the customer's viewpoint, the ecotourism product is a mixture of benefits. For example: white water rafting is not boating, but rather, is an activity which satisfies a desire for adventure and excitement in an outdoor natural setting.

Promotion

A range of communication and sales activities are needed to stimulate actual and potential customers to become aware of the ecotourism product and to buy it. Communications are important: new travel magazines – *European Travel Guide, Travel Today, Traveler, Trips* – join established ones – e.g., *Travel and Leisure* – specialty periodicals – *Adventure Travel* and *Specialty Travel Index* – and others – *Adventure Vacation Catalog* and the *Adventure Book*.

Research by the Forestry Private Enterprise Initiative, US AID and the Southeastern Center for Forest Economics Research identified promotion response problems relevant to ecotourism. They requested information on nature-orientated tourism from 230 tourism offices representing 116 developing countries, including 116 US-based embassies, fifty-nine US-based tourism boards and fifty-five promotion offices located in host countries (Ingram and Durst, 1989). The results were startling:

- Only 52 per cent of the requests elicited responses (surprisingly, 40 per cent of the US-based tourism promotion offices did not respond).
- US-based offices took an average of twenty-four days to respond. Overseas offices took over three times longer.
- Frequency of nature-specific activities promoted was: wildlife viewing, hiking/ trekking, bird watching, hunting/fishing, botanical study, mountain climbing, rafting/canoeing.
- Most of the respondents provided visually appealing literature (75 per cent) but only 58 per cent respondents included a full colour brochure.

Place

The distribution system in which the customers buy ecotourism products was covered earlier and includes both profit and non-profit organizational efforts. Electronic media/telecommunications linkage for reservations and information retrieval/dissemination are important. New databases are being created – for example, the Adventure Society, Adventure Atlas, the Official Recreation Guide, and Ultran.

Tour operators play an essential role. A recent study of US-based-nature orienated tour operators provided the following results (Ingram and Durst, 1989). The operators considered the following elements limiting the growth of nature-orientated tourism: image 58 per cent, poor marketing 26 per cent, and, followed by: US political relations with the host country government, economic changes and competition.

The major problems tour operators have with organizing nature/adventure tours to developing countries are:

- International air travel, 50 per cent.
- Local transportation, 47 per cent.
- Political stability, 44 per cent.
- Health and safety, 38 per cent.
- Food services 34 per cent.
- Currency fluctuations 34 per cent.
- Followed by: lodging, local service suppliers, customs/visa regulations, local tour operators, local taxes or duties.

Most frequent positions held by host country nationals were guides and interpreters, 20 per cent; drivers, 8 per cent; porters 8 per cent; cooks 6 per cent and 8 per cent commonly hired locals as managers/tour operators. Overall, 78 per cent stated the demand for nature-orientated travel will increase and 13 per cent indicated it will stay the same; 9 per cent did not respond. No one indicated it would decrease.

Pricing

Value is more important than price. In the case of ecotourism, multi-tiered pricing can improve both equity and efficiency. Two-tiered pricing policies in the form of user levies (usually entrance fees) have increased revenues. In countries like Costa Rica and Kenya, where tourists visit more than one park, system-wide fees could be paid at one point and would be valid for all parks. Fees need to be constantly adjusted for changes in inflation and demand for the attraction within the tourism market.

The complexity of ecotourism marketing also requires an expanded concept of marketing, which includes five other Ps – Positioning, Partnership, Programming, Packaging and People.

Positioning

The market niche that a destination selects and puts priority focus on developing for ecotourism needs to be carefully defined. In order to differentiate your ecotourism product from your competitors, accuracy and authenticity are essential. Too often destinations are promising access to flora and fauna in their promotional offer which cannot be experienced directly, thus leading to visitor dissatisfaction.

Partnership
Ecotourism requires integrated marketing involving the public and private sector. Cooperative advertising is essential.

Programming
Special events, seasonal activities, festivals and other hallmark activities which expand, enhance or augment the ecotourism product can motivate people to select a particular destination, extend length of stay, increase spending and help cope with seasonality problems.

Packaging
Providing combinations of transport facilities and services to individuals or groups for a single price, purchased in a single transaction provides predictable capacity, reduces cost of sales, hence lower prices, and most importantly, it saves the consumer time.

People
Usually, travel consumers are actively involved in ecotourism – most nature types of tourism involve extensive 'do it yourself' activities. Highly trained ecotourism personnel are in short supply world-wide. More extensive training efforts are needed, particularly those involving local guides and interpretive personnel.

The future

The future for ecotourism world-wide is bright. The viability of developing countries as quality tourist destinations may be largely dependent upon the extent to which their destinations are able to implement sustainable development practices and attract a share of the international ecotourism market. If all of the players understand and accept their responsibilities and are environmentally motivated, policies should eventually emerge that reflect the needs and interests of all concerned.

Policy-makers and industry have the challenge, responsibility and mandate in the 1990s to bring market forces into harmony with the need for environmental protection and social equity. If accomplished, ecotourism may well become an example of how economic, social and environmental development can be achieved on a sustainable basis to the benefit of visitor, host and industry alike.

References

Boeing Commercial Airplane Group (1991) *Annual Marketing Report*, Seattle, WA
Ceballos-Lascurain, Hector (1987) The future of ecotourism. *Mexico Journal*, 27 January
Globe '90 (1991) Tourism Stream Conference, Action Strategy for Sustainable Tourism Development. Tourism Canada, (1989) Ottawa
Ingram, C. Denise and Durst, Patrick B. (1989) Nature-oriented tour operators: travel to developing countries. *Journal of Travel Research*, Fall, pp. 11–15
Lindberg, Kreg (1991) *Economic Policies for Maximizing Nature Tourism's Contribution to Sustainable Development*, World Resources Institute, Washington, DC
Mudge, Susie (1991) *Notes on Ecotourism*, Ernst & Young, Washington, DC
Ecotourism Society (1992) *Definition and Ecotourism Statistical Fact Sheet*, Ecotourism Society, Alexandria, VA
Tourism Policy Forum (1991) *Global Assessment of Tourism Policy*, George Washington University International Institute of Tourism Studies, Washington, DC
World Tourism Organization (1991) *Yearbook of Tourism Statistics*, WTO, Madrid
World Travel and Tourism Council (1992) *The WTTC Report: Travel and Tourism in the World Economy*, WTTC, Brussels
Ziffer, Karen A. (1989) *Ecotourism the Uneasy Alliance*, Conservation International and Ernst & Young, Washington, DC

19 Tourism and sustainable development

Peter E. Murphy

Introduction

The world is changing and experiencing shifts in social values that effect the way we act as individuals, businesses and governments. Part of this change is due to the longest recession, or period of economic stagnation, that many parts of the developed world have experienced in recent memory. It has caused all of the above to reassess their priorities and led to the slogan 'do more with less'. Part of the change is a growing recognition that past growth and development have led to some serious impacts on the environment. Some have been highly visible, such as shrinking water supplies or homeless garbage barges; but others have crept up on us insidiously and still remain something of a mystery, like global warming.

Such economic and environmental forces led many nations, companies and individuals to the June 1992 United Nations Conference on the Environment and Development (UNCED) in Rio de Janeiro. There they attempted to address a controversial agenda designed to protect the earth's environment and to foster less destructive industrialization and development. A binding theme of the conference was to find ways to replace the old emphasis on economic growth with a push for sustainable development (*Business Week*, 1992). It was not a great success, for changing fundamental societal beliefs and expectations will not be easy; but it was part of an ongoing process of reassessment and one in which tourism has become involved.

Tourism's interest in sustainable development is logical given this is one industry that sells the environment, both physical and human, as its product. The integrity and continuity of these products has become a major concern of the industry, as can be seen in its participation in the two Global Opportunities for Business and the Environment conferences (Globe '90 and '92) in Vancouver, BC. In the first conference, designed to generate awareness of the environmental issue, the tourism stream made several recommendations regarding the industry, tourist and organizational roles in promoting sustainable tourism development (Tourism Canada, 1990). At the Globe '92 conference in Vancouver the focus shifted to finding practical solutions to environmental challenges, including those of the tourism industry. But more articulation of the issues and options needs to be undertaken, before the concept of sustainable development can move from a mental state to a physical and economic reality.

Growth and definition of sustainable development

The need for a renewed relationship with the environment and the recent interest in sustainable development has been building over the past twenty years. In 1972 Danella and Dennis Meadows shook the world's complacency with their book *Limits to Growth* (1972). They argued the earth's resources and ability to absorb pollution are finite. Using computer simulations, they predicted the earth's population and development progress would experience physical constraints within a century. After this first warning came more research and deliberation into the long-term consequences of continued industry and population expansion. This led to the publication of the *World Conservation Strategy* by the International Union for the Conservation of Nature and Natural Resources (IUCN, 1980), which was one of the first reports to introduce the concept of sustainable development. This was followed by the World Commission on Environment and Development report in 1987, entitled *Our Common Future* (WCED, 1987), which placed the concept of sustainable development centre stage and promoted it as a vehicle for deliverance.

The sustainable development concept is not new, but increasing pressures on the world's finite resources and environmental capacity have led to a more deliberate restatement of the philosophy, along with evolving guidelines to put it into practice. *Our Common Future* described sustainable development as 'development that meets the needs of the present without compromising the ability of future generations to meet their own needs' (WCED, 1987). This is not very different from the view that we do not inherit the earth from our forefathers but borrow it from our children, and the old philosophy that something should be left for future generations. As such, sustainable development builds on the old principles of conservation and stewardship, but it offers a more proactive stance, that incorporates continued economic growth in a more ecological and equitable manner. In this regard the opening definition above is supplemented with more specific implications and guidelines throughout the WCED report.

Table 19.1 illustrates some of the guidelines that emerged from *Our Common Future*, which in turn have stimulated further discussion at various government levels and within business. The first nine components were extracted from the WCED report and formed the basis of Canada's early attempts to integrate this type of philosophy into its national policy (Canadian Environment Advisory Council, 1987). Following the WCED report other writers and agencies have added to the list of components in Table 19.1. This list is not designed to be exhaustive but to illustrate the ongoing refinement of the concept and the increasing emphasis on its application.

It has been noted, for example, that the priority on maintaining ecological diversity and distributing more productivity to developing regions implies increased community control (Component no. 10), which in turn fosters increased regional self-reliance (Rees and Roseland, 1988). Likewise, these two authors and Stanley (1992) maintain there is a need for more international agreements and business–government partnerships (no. 11) to direct national and individual actions. To the ecological limitations and social equity of the sustainable development philosophy must be added the concept of economic viability (no. 12) according to the British Columbia Round Table on the Environment and the Economy (1991).

The business community and literature have been responding to the environmental – economic opportunities that exist within the 'greening' process. Howatson (1990) reports that an evolution is taking place. A minority of corporations are still in the early phase of responding to environmental problems as they arise. The majority of corporations have established systems and programmes to comply with the new regulations, but a further minority has moved 'beyond compliance' into a proactive mode of management. This evolutionary process is slowly leading to the complete integration of the environmental dimension into corporate strategic planning (no. 13). To bring environmental considerations and sustainable development into the mainstream of corporate planning requires increased accountability and the environmental audit has been gaining credibility in this area. Hunt and Auster (1990) contend a 'strong auditing programme' is essential to successful proactive environmental management (no. 14).

The growing interest and support for sustainable development is not without its critics and sceptics. Some maintain that it is such a fuzzy concept that it may prove to be of little practical use in tackling the environmental issues that are emerging. However, as Table 19.1 illustrates, the short definition of sustainable development should only be viewed

Table 19.1 Sustainable development components

1	Establishing ecological limits and more equitable standards	'requires the promotion of values that encourage consumption standards that are within the bounds of the ecological possible and to which all can reasonably aspire.'
2	Redistribution of economic activity and reallocation of resources	'Meeting essential needs depends in part on achieving full growth potential and sustainable development clearly requires economic growth in places where such needs are not being met.'
3	Population control	'Though the issue is not merely one of population size but of the distribution of resources, sustainable development can only be pursued if demographic developments are in harmony with the changing productive potential of the ecosystem.'
4	Conservation of basic resources	'sustainable development must not endanger the natural systems that support life on Earth: the atmosphere, the waters, the soils, and the living beings.'
5	More equitable access to resources and increased technological effort to use them more effectively	'Growth has no set limits in terms of population or resource use beyond which lies ecological disaster . . . But ultimate limits there are, and sustainability requires that long before these are reached the world must ensure equitable access to the constrained resource and reorient technological efforts to relieve the pressure.'
6	Carrying capacity and sustainable yield	'most renewable resources are part of a complex and interlinked ecosystem, and maximum sustainable yield must be defined after taking into account system-wide effects of exploitation.'
7	Retention of resources	'Sustainable development requires that the rate of depletion of non-renewable resources foreclose as few future options as possible.'
8	Diversification of the species	'sustainable development requires the conservation of plant and animal species.'
9	Minimize adverse impacts	'Sustainable development requires that the adverse impacts on the quality of air, water, and other natural elements are minimized so as to sustain the ecosystem's overall integrity.'
10	Community control	'community control over development decisions affecting local ecosystems.'
11	Broad national/ international policy framework	'the biosphere is the common home of all human-kind and joint management of the biosphere is prerequisite for global political security.'
12	Economic viability	'communities must pursue economic well-being while recognizing that [government] policies may set limits to material growth.'
13	Environmental quality	'Corporate environmental policy is an extension of total quality management.'
14	Environmental audit	'An effective environmental audit system is at the heart of good environmental management.'

as a summary goal, and that from this have evolved a series of more specific objectives and methodologies. Others consider that it is a passing fad, akin to the energy crises of the past. But this perception fails to acknowledge that evidence of environmental stress started over twenty years ago, and instead of disappearing it has gradually increased to the point where admitted non-environmentalists are beginning to take notice. One author who has addressed such scepticism and doubts is George Winter (1988), who developed a listing of pros and cons for forty issues regarding the introduction of an integrated system of environmental business management.

Relevance to tourism

Tourism is reputed to be the world's largest industry with estimated revenues of US $3.1 trillion and 130 million employees in 1992 (World Travel and Tourism Council, 1991). It is one industry which should be involved in sustainable development, because it 'is a resource industry, one which is dependent on nature's endowment and society's heritage' (Murphy, 1985). It sells these resources as part of its experiential product, but it also has to share the same resources with other users, including local residents. Consequently, it is in tourism's own interest to be active in the quest for sustainable development and to work in cooperation with other groups, industries and government to ensure that the integrity of its resource base survives.

Although the industry is regarded as being kinder to the environment in general than most other industries, its very size and widespread presence has created negative environmental impacts, both of a physical and social nature, in certain locations. Consequently, there has arisen a demand for more management of this activity, which has encouraged greater government involvement and more private–public sector partnerships. 'Sustainable development (in tourism) is premised on the notion that the economy and the environment are but two sides of the same coin; in other words, the two are intimately linked' (Slater, 1992). In Canada this has led to the creation of a federal *Green Plan* that 'represents a fundamental shift in the way the government of Canada looks at economic development and environmental protection . . . [in that it tries] to make them mutually supporting rather than mutually exclusive' (Slater, 1992).

The Canadian experience and evidence from around the world demonstrates that sustainable development can be compatible with business objectives, and that with appropriate legislative safeguards and inducements the tourism industry can continue to prosper as a private business within these new parameters. Porter, who is the champion of competitive advantage, considers 'the conflict between environmental protection and economic competitiveness is a false dichotomy . . . [but] turning environmental concern into competitive advantage demands we establish the right kind of regulations' (Porter, 1991). Others have made similar observations, that industry can profit from 'greening' its product in the consumers' eyes and can lower operational costs through the development of environmental practices. One example of this in tourism can be seen in the Canadian Pacific Hotels and Resorts environmental programme. This programme has set as its target to reduce landfill waste by 50 per cent and paper use by 20 per cent over a two-year period. It will save energy and water by retrofitting lightbulbs, showerheads and taps with 'Environmental Choice' equipment, and will purchase more environmentally friendly products for cleaning and running the hotels (Checkley, 1992).

The move to a more sustainable development approach in tourism is taking hold and it is time to examine the themes and implications of this process so the industry is better able to adjust and prosper with this new reality.

Dimensions of sustainable tourism development

It is apparent from the proceeding discussion that sustainable development is a complex and multi-dimensional concept and that tourism, as a component of this process, will reflect this diversity. This chapter will take as its working definition that offered by the combined efforts of the Globe '90 tourism stream. For this group, Tourism Canada (1990) reports that *sustainable tourism development* was envisaged as:

> leading to management of all resources in such a way that we can fulfil economic, social, and aesthetic needs while maintaining cultural integrity, essential ecological processes, biological diversity and life support systems.

The seven dimensions incorporated within this definition provide an excellent example of the general multi-dimensionality and interdisciplinary concerns.

The first dimension noted is the need for *resource management,* for in this crowded world with diminishing resources little can be left to chance. Such management needs to reaffirm that tourism is an *economic* activity, which must be capable of making a profit in order to survive and benefit the community. This is the point Porter (1991) and others have made when they say environmental legislation must leave room for individual employment and economic well-being to operate within the ecological parameters. The third dimension points out the need to fulfil *social* obligations. This means more than intergenerational equity, it means respect for other livelihoods and customs. Such variety and heritage is a major resource for tourism in a world that is fast becoming homogenized into a global economy. A major component of environment and culture is their *aesthetic* appeal. While the focus has often been on international markers, such as world renown heritage sites, the aesthetic qualities of regular townscapes and general landscapes should not be overlooked.

All of the above needs should be addressed within *ecological parameters* to sustain both the physical and human environments. In addition to the very real concerns about the natural environment, conservation of cultural legacies should not be ignored. The ecological process needs to be understood so that tourism intrusions will have the minimal impact, especially in sensitive areas like shorelines, mountains and wetlands. The concern over maintaining our *biological diversity* is particularly germane to tourism, which thrives on the appeal of different flora and fauna along with a distinctive sense of place. Finally, the need to sustain our basic *life support systems* is paramount. If these basic needs are not met, then our higher level and discretionary needs like travel will fail to materialize.

Research priorities

As in the real world, all of the above dimensions are interrelated. This means any sustainable tourism development will involve a holistic management approach that requires integrated ecological, economic and institutional research. Since this is a major research undertaking, some thought has been given already to categorizing the scope of the problem and prioritizing the research questions. In 1985 Murphy proposed an ecological model for tourism research and development. This model demonstrated the need to consider tourism as an ecological function that involved different community scales of emphasis and a balance between resident (individuals and business) and visitor (tourist and tourist industry) needs. Taylor and Stanley (1992) have recommended a matrix of research priorities based on scale and time considerations (Table 19.2). All scales are relevant and interrelated in an ecological sense, but the pressures and issues will vary at each level. Some research questions are considered to be more pressing and have been placed under the 'now' category, whereas others are either less urgent or are logical secondary steps. As Taylor and Stanley observe, all research should have a monitoring function to observe changes over time and be able to identify adjustment strategies where needed.

Table 19.2 Suggested research areas and priorities for sustainable development in tourism

Scope	Now	Medium term	Long term
Site	Case studies on a variety of topics Operations Employee involvement Benefit-cost Corporate culture Environmental audit	Value of protected areas (economic, aesthetic) Willingness to pay Means of enhancing experiences Monitoring change in case studies	
Locality	Destination studies Carrying capacities: economic, social, physical Image studies	Longitudinal studies Nature of change studies	Social indicators Economic indicators Physical indicators
Region	Inventory of resources Studies of market needs and attitudes	Longitudinal studies of market needs and attitudes Measurement of benefits, costs	
Nation	Coordination Dissemination Standards	Networking Clearing house Methodologies Models, paradigms	
International	Cooperation Adaptation	Clearing house Definition of terms	

Source: Taylor and Stanley, 1992: 67.

Measurement issues

While it is relatively easy to conceptualize and to proselytize about the needs for sustainable tourism development it is far more challenging to develop an effective, yet practical, measurement process. An important issue in the Taylor–Stanley matrix is establishing the carrying capacity levels for tourism in a variety of locales and circumstances. This essential

building block to sustainable development suffers from the same operational difficulties as its parent concept. Barkham (1979) noted that:

> Carrying capacity is a phrase delightful in its simplicity, complex in its
> meaning and difficult to define, as in different situations and to different
> people it is understood in different ways.

The literature on this subject shows carrying capacity techniques have
been applied in a variety of circumstances, often clarifying and confirm-
ing levels of suspected environmental or social stress, but they leave
open to discussion what it all signifies and what policy should be undertaken. A major difficulty is that carrying capacity implies the existence of
fixed and determinable limits to development and that if one stays below
those threshold levels no changes or deterioration will occur. We now
appreciate that all changes and modifications to the environment have
an incremental effect, so some degree of change must be acknowledged
and accounted for at all developmental stages.

  This is the philosophy behind the 'limits to acceptable change' (LAC)
process of measurement proposed by Stankey et al. (1985). The LAC
system is a framework for establishing acceptable and appropriate resource use 'with the primary emphasis now on the conditions desired in
the area rather than on how much use an area can tolerate' (Stankey et
al., 1985: Summary). The process is a combined measurement and planning
system, but as its authors point out, it is a process – not a policy. It still
requires political decisions regarding what is acceptable and of course
personal perceptions will be an interpretive factor at all stages of the
process.

  Both the carrying capacity and LAC processes examine the sustainable
tourism issue from the supply side of the host community, but if tourism
is to be a sustainable economic proposition it cannot ignore its customers. Hence, more thought is now being applied to the demand implications
of sustainable tourism development, specifically the benefits visitors are
seeking and the marketing strategies that can be applied to service both
the customer and the host. The modern interpretation of marketing has
moved beyond simply promoting and selling to take into account the
long-term management goals of companies and organizations. In some
cases this now includes marketing to reduce consumption, as with utility
companies, or to recycle, as with beverage companies. In a tourism context we see more evidence of attractions explaining to customers why
certain areas are temporarily closed or out of bounds.

  The broader view is provided by Mill and Morrison (1985), who noted
that tourism marketing is:

> a management philosophy, which in light of tourist demand, makes it
> possible through research, forecasting and selection to place tourism

products on the market most in line with an organization's purpose for the greatest benefit.

Such a definition has particular relevance to a sustainable development strategy. It makes marketing part of a more general management strategy. It supports the notion that marketing should balance the tourists' needs with those of the host organization. Market research will help to identify which tourism niche is most appropriate from a business and environmental viewpoint. It can indicate a destination's or business' position on the product life cycle which could guide future marketing and development strategies.

This type of marketing analysis and strategy is being practised in certain Canadian national parks. Parks Canada has introduced a Visitor Activity Management Process (VAMP) into three parks, moving away from the traditional promotional and operational focus to one which attempts to manage visitor opportunities and encourage public understanding of the parks' twin mandate of conservation and recreation (Graham et al., 1988). The process uses market research to select target markets, specify the most appropriate public and private mix of recreation opportunities, and to guide the design of programmes, services and facilities. The authors maintain it is a 'shift of emphasis away from a reactive controlled development-orientated mode to a pro-active recreation resource management mode' (Graham et al., 1988: 62).

An essential element in market research designed to assist in sustainable development initiatives is the need to monitor visitor patterns and satisfaction. Monitors are needed on an annual and seasonal basis, since the volume and type of visitor activity can vary significantly over these periods. A demonstration project on Vancouver Island, British Columbia revealed that a basic monitoring of visitors could be achieved efficiently and at low cost through industry–destination partnerships (Murphy, 1992). This demonstration project has since been adopted by Tourism Victoria, the destination association for the provincial capital of Victoria, on Vancouver Island. It has conducted three exit surveys since 1988 over a variety of seasons to provide a visitor profile and strategy guide to the destination and individual business members.

Various tourism markets

There is a wide variety of tourist types within the tourism market today, so much so that the term 'average tourist' has become irrelevant (Murphy, 1985). One type of tourist which has generated a lot of interest among those supporting sustainable development is the 'alternative tourist', described by Krippendorf (1987) as those who 'try to establish more contact with the local population, try to do without the tourist infrastructure and use the same accommodation and transport facilities as the natives'. Such travellers are considered desirable market niches for those communities which are unable or unwilling to accommodate mass tourism, and they are perceived as being worthy targets because they are small in number yet often well-educated and wealthy. This would appear to be a perfect match for those areas where carrying capacity could become an issue and where the host community wished to control the size of the industry.

However, alternative tourism has been criticized as being elitist and spreading tourism to areas that are not yet spoiled by tourism. One who has issued such a warning is Butler (1990). He notes that in a free society and highly fragmented industry it is in fact difficult to control the numbers and types of tourist admitted to an area. If it can be achieved, a focus on the alternative market may not bring about the perceived desirable effects over the long run. Butler suggests:

> In the short-term there is little doubt that alternative tourism appears, and almost certainly is, much less conducive to causing change in destination areas than mass tourism, in part because of its dimensions and in part because of the need for fewer and smaller facilities. However, as time goes by, some factors can assume much greater significance under alternative tourism and result in greater and more serious long-term change. (1990: 41)

Butler illustrates this by noting the intimate contact described by Krippendorf can become a social burden over time, as privacy is lost and there is nowhere to retreat from the tourist gaze. Similarly the 'back-woods' penetration by such visitors can do more environmental harm over time to these areas than the controlled mass tourism which permits distant viewing only. What host communities need to focus on is the type or types of tourism they wish to attract and can accommodate over the long term. As Jones observes, 'some of the clues and solutions from alternative tourism can be used to inform and advise policy and practice in the development and management of mass tourism' (1992: 103).

Many of the observations relating to alternative tourism apply to one subset that is particularly germane to the sustainable development movement – ecotourism. Ecotourism occurs where the visitor is an active contributor to the well-being and development of the host ecology. As such, ecotourists are champions of the environment and sustainable development. In Costa Rica several ecotourism principles have been developed which support the sustainable development philosophy, according to Fennell and Eagles (1990: 23). These include a mutual agreement between tour operators and visitors to limit the levels of crowding, to permit tour operator control of site visits, government agreements with tour operators on park entrance permits, and agreements on the appropriate marketing image. Such partnerships are relatively easy to initiate when both parties have the same goals and the numbers involved are small, but they also provide hope and direction to the application of similar strategies to a broader cross-section of the tourism industry.

In the final analysis, however, 'the most crucial contribution that applied research can make toward sustainable tourism is to show rather than say what this involves' (Sadler, 1992: 127). As we have seen there are a growing number of advocates, sufficient paradigms and some basic measurement techniques that should now be put into practice in order to demonstrate the feasibility of all this rhetoric. This too will be a slow process given the variety and complexity of the topic, but to illustrate what can be achieved, two case studies will be offered.

Case studies

The two cases proffered are from opposite sides of the North American continent and involve different approaches to sustainable tourism. One is the experience of a private company that took marginal Central Florida land and converted it into a local environmental triumph along with an internationally renowned tourist attraction. The other is a group of small communities in Western Canada which in the face of a declining forest economy turned to the ecomuseum concept to help restore their sense of place and confidence in the future.

Walt Disney World

Disney World has built upon the success and lessons of Disneyland to produce a sustainable tourism attraction that is able to combine 25 million visitors a year with restful resorts and golf courses, all next to a conservation area where native plants and animals have been attracted to a reclaimed area of Central Florida wetlands. To achieve these remarkable feats the Disney Corporation has emphasized excellence in the four basic business areas of resources, capital, labour and markets.

The initial land base was 27,400 acres of marginal ranch land and swamp which required an investment of $600 million before it was ready for the public (Zehnder, 1975). A major portion of this funding was needed to prepare the site through a process of water management. To do this the company built self-adjusting barrages (dams) to control the flow of water onto the property. The goal was to protect approximately 18,000 acres for development, build canals and reservoirs to control the flooding, and recreate the original wetland landscape in the conservation area. The whole process was designed to work with nature and top up the 'kidney function' of the subsoil. The topping up process was enhanced by treatment of human waste in a tertiary sewage treatment plant that returns near pure water to the ecosystem, via the irrigation of golf courses and an ornamental tree farm. Due to this pre-planning and investment the Disney area has not experienced the same drops in water table levels as other parts of Florida, and has developed a green and aesthetic setting for its tourism activities (Murphy, 1987).

Before the Disney organization could undertake such investment, it needed to secure complete development authority over its property and requested a new jurisdiction be established to achieve this. The neighbouring counties and the State agreed, after some deliberation, to create the Reedy Creek Improvement District. This political move gave the Disney Company via its District authority the right to establish by-laws, to levy taxes and issue bonds, which enabled the company to establish higher building codes and development standards than neighbouring jurisdictions and assisted in the raising of capital.

One area where the Disney Company built upon the success of its Disneyland experience was in the area of human resources. Peters and Waterman (1982) have reported on the excellence of the Disney training, which has now evolved into a separate business function offering business seminars and various training sessions. Walt Disney World celebrated its twenty-first anniversary in October 1992, and in order to sustain its business levels it had predicted and responded to changing market demographics. The project was built upon the attraction of the theme park, but it has developed as a resort destination. To ensure the area appeals to a broad cross-section of tourists, Disney World now offers a variety of activities (including golf courses, water parks and a lakeside village) along with a variety of accommodation (ranging from deluxe resort hotels to campsites and private holiday chalets). This means the destination can appeal to more visitors outside of school vacation periods, and keep them longer by offering a wider range of on-site activities, including a balance of hectic and relaxing experiences.

Over the past twenty-one years the Disney Company has demonstrated the benefits of careful environmental and business planning. The site is now capable of maintaining major visitor volumes year round with minimal disturbance to the environment thanks to the water management and land use planning. These have focused human activity into raised, and in some cases hardened, environments while leading visitors swiftly through the surrounding open space and woodland. Where tourist activity had been located in the flood plain areas it has been restricted to compatible land uses like golf or been modified to minimize loss, such as chalets on pedestal bases. Such attention to detail not only assures a quality environment for the visitor, it ensures fewer long-term costs for the company.

The Cowichan–Chemainus Valleys Ecomuseum

An ecomuseum is a museum without walls that is designed to involve local people with their past, present and future. In the Cowichan and Chemainus Valleys of Vancouver Island it has been supplemented with a regional natural park focus that incorporates tourism as part of the sustainable economic development strategy for the area. The ecomuseum started in 1988, encompassing an area of 400 square miles and a population of 53,000, including nineteen native bands. It was a partial response to the need to diversify a sagging local economy and to restore pride and confidence in the natural and cultural history of the area (Murphy, 1990).

The ecomuseum's primary theme is the 'forest legacy' (Wood, 1990), which is used to demonstrate the past, explain the present and assist with the future. The forest legacy is shown through the British Columbia Forest Museum, which is one of the region's twelve museums and its biggest. The present forestry practices are revealed in a 'demonstration forest', where the different stages of cutting, replanting and regrowth are explained, along with tours of active mills. The future is described through the efforts of the Tree Nursery and Research Station, along with the growing interest in a community forest venture, that is attempting to develop sustainable timber practice on municipally owned land areas.

In addition to the forestry emphasis the region recognizes it must diversify into other economic activities. In this regard the ecomuseum has worked with other agencies to conserve the recreation and scenic resources of the area, to build on its cultural heritage and diversity and to make the area more attractive to tourists and retirees from nearby metropolitan areas. The Cowichan native band has opened a Native Heritage Center to represent a broad range of Northwest native cultures and various local museums reflect the cultural backgrounds of the early pioneers. To ensure local employment is bolstered by these strategies the ecomuseum has organized local artists, artisans and small manufacturers into using a generic local label for their products, and has trained local curators and support personnel for the various museums, festivals and events.

All of the above measures have been initiated for the benefit of local residents, to provide more diversified employment opportunities within a more sustainable resource base, to ensure the physical beauty and cultural heritage of this region is not lost, and to restore a sense of pride and confidence in the future. A calculated part of this strategy has been an effort to make the region more attractive to retirees and tourists. This element has been successful in that several retirement communities and subdivisions have been developed, and the number of visits to the regional museums and galleries has grown from 68,583 in 1988 to 394,746 in 1991. In 1991 the tourism economic impact was estimated to be $17 million which makes it a major player in the broader economic base of the area.

Summary

Sustainable development is becoming a more recognized term as concern for our environmental future spreads and the topic receives more attention via the media. What is not so clear is what this concept involves and how it can be applied to tackle the perceived problems. However, with the growing sense of urgency and recognition that something must be done to balance our growth and conservation objectives, more effort is being put into identifying the different dimensions of the concept and ways in which they can be operationalized. Part of this process has been the important link between the ecology and the economy. It is in this regard that tourism and tourism research can play a significant role, for this industry's future prosperity depends on a healthy and continuous physical and human environment.

As part of the growing refinement of the sustainability concept, tourism research and development should explore ways in which to combine environmental and business considerations so that synergistic relationships can emerge. Two case studies have been presented which show such relationships are possible and that different strategies can be expected in different circumstances. However, both demonstrate some constant characteristics and these, along with the present research priorities, could guide future tourism endeavours.

The combination of business *and* environmental objectives in a company's or destination's development strategy can bring out the comparative and competitive advantages of the local area. It is instructive to see that the business researchers are coming to similar conclusions and concepts as the environmentalists. Moore (1992) has shown how Porter's 'value chain' concept can provide a good illustration of how to integrate environmental inputs and outputs into a business, overall strategic planning and positioning. It shows that companies can be held responsible for the impacts of their raw material collection and their product's final disposal, and, given the appropriate legislative guidelines, still operate in a profitable manner. This is certainly the case in Disney World, which established the Reedy Creek Improvement District, in part, to be able to set its own high technical standards.

The sustainable approach also brings to the fore the importance of the customer. The expectations and perceptions of the visitor and the resident are important elements for a sustainable business or destination development. Consumers are going 'green' and supporting companies that act accordingly. The concern for the future (recycling) has been added to those of the present (value) and a growing desire to retain the best of the past (quality). Such temporal concerns and the growing sense of pride and commitment they engender are evident in the Cowichan–Chemainus Valleys case.

Overall, the momentum for sustainable tourism development is growing and this reflects the more general concern for the environment. Sustainable development is intended to be a pro-active strategy and for an industry that is associated with change to the natural and human environments it is necessary to examine such events from a broad sustainability perspective. Tourism has been called the leisure industry, but it has the opportunity now to broaden its contribution to society and become a prime economic agent for the sustainable development of our natural environments and cultural heritage.

References

Barkham, J.P. (1979) Recreational carrying capacity: a problem of perception. *Area*, **5**, 218–22

British Columbia Round Table on the Environment and the Economy (1991) *Sustainable Communities*, British Columbia Round Table on the Environment and the Economy, Victoria, BC

Business Week (1992) Growth vs. environment. *Business Week*, 11 May, 66–75

Butler, R.W. (1990) Alternative tourism: pious hope or Trojan Horse? *Journal of Travel Research*, **28**(3), 40–5

Canadian Environment Advisory Council (1987) *Canada and Sustainable Development*, CEAC, Ottawa

Checkley, A. (1992) Canadian Pacific hotels and resorts update: environmental program. In *Tourism–Environment–Sustainable Development: an Agenda for Research* (ed. L.J. Reid), Conference Proceedings of the Travel and Tourism Research Association (Canada), Ottawa, 1991, pp. 34–7

Fennell, D.A. and Eagles, P.F.J. (1990) Ecotourism in Costa Rica: a conceptual framework. *Journal of Park and Recreation Administration*, **8**(1), 23–34

Graham, R., Nilsen, P. and Payne, R.J. (1988) Visitor management in Canadian national parks. *Tourism Management*, **9**(1), 44–62

Howatson, A.C. (1990) *Toward Proactive Environmental Management*, Conference Board of Canada, Ottawa

Hunt, C.B. and Auster, E.R. (1990) Proactive environmental management: avoiding the toxic trap. *Sloan Management Review*, **31**(2), 7–18

IUCN (1980) *World Conservation Strategy*, IUCN, Gland, Switzerland

Jones, A. (1992) Is there a real alternative tourism? *Tourism Management*, **13**(1), 102–3

Krippendorf, J. (1987) *The Holiday Makers*, Heinemann, London, p. 37

Meadows, D. and Meadows, D. (1972) *Limits to Growth*, Universe Books, New York

Mill, R.C. and Morrison, A.M. (1985) *The Tourism System*, Prentice Hall, Englewood Cliffs, NJ, p. 358

Moore, K. (1992) Greening corporate strategy – extending the firm's value chain, Paper presented at the Administrative Sciences Association of Canada, Quebec City, June

Murphy, P.E. (1985) *Tourism: a Community Approach*, Methuen, London, p. 12

Murphy, P.E. (1987) Conservation and tourism: a business partnership, *Tourism and the Environment: Conflict or Harmony*, Symposium Proceedings of the Canadian Society of Environmental Biologists (Alberta Chapter), pp. 117–27

Murphy, P.E. (1990) British Columbia's cultural tourism: selected experiences, *Cultural Geography*, **11**(1), 109–23

Murphy, P.E. (1992) Data gathering of community-oriented tourism planning: a case study of Vancouver Island, British Columbia, *Leisure Studies*, **11**(1), 65–79

Peters, T.J. and Waterman, R.H. (1982) *In Search of Excellence*, Warner Books, New York

Porter, M.E. (1991) Essay-America's green strategy, *Scientific American*, **264**(4), April, p. 168

Rees, W.E. and Roseland, M. (1988) *Planning for Sustainable Development*, School of Community and Regional Planning, University of British Columbia

Sadler, B. (1992) Sustainable tourism and tomorrow's heritage: toward policy and research that make a difference, *Tourism–Environment–Sustainable Development: an Agenda for Research* (ed. L.J. Reid), Conference Proceedings of the Travel and Tourism Research Association (Canada), Ottawa, 1991, pp. 122–7

Slater, R.W. (1992) 'Keynote address – understanding the relationship between tourism environment and sustainable development', *Tourism–Environment–Sustainable Development: an Agenda for Research* (ed. L.J. Reid), Conference Proceedings of the Travel and Tourism Research Association (Canada), Ottawa, 1991, pp. 10–13

Stankey, G.H., Cole, D.N., Lucas, R.C. et al. (1985) *The Limits of Acceptable Change (LAC) System for Wilderness Planning*, US Forest Service, Washington, DC

Stanley, D. (1992) Synthesis of workshop sessions, *Tourism–Environment–Sustainable Development: an Agenda for Research* (ed. L.J. Reid), Conference Proceedings of the Travel and Tourism Research Association (Canada), Ottawa, 1991, pp. 116–18

Taylor, G.D. and Stanley, D. (1992) Tourism, sustainable development and the environment: an agenda for research, *Journal of Travel Research*, **31**(1), 66–7

Tourism Canada (1990) *An Action Strategy for Sustainable Tourism Development: Globe '90* Tourism Canada, Ottawa, p. 3

WCED (1987) *Our Common Future*, Oxford University Press, Oxford, p. 43

Winter, G. (1988) *Business and the Environment*, McGraw-Hill, Hamburg/New York.

Wood, W.A. (1990) *Maintaining and Enhancing the Sense of Place for Small Communities and Regions*, University of Calgary Symposium, Calgary, pp. 80–9

World Travel and Tourism Council (1991) Travel and tourism, *The Economist*, 12 October, p. 14

Zehnder, L.E. (1975) *Florida's Disney World: Promises and Problems*, Peninsula Publishing, Tallahassee, Fla

20 Role of government incentives

Stephen Wanhill

Introduction

The importance of tourism world-wide has made it an investment opportunity that few governments can afford to ignore. In most countries the development of tourism is a partnership between the private and public sectors. Where the line is drawn in this partnership depends on the prevailing economic, political and social policies of the country. The private sector may have many reasons for investing in tourism, but in the end must be concerned with the viability of the investment in terms of generating adequate returns to the capital employed.

The case for public sector involvement in tourism rests on concepts of market failure, namely that those who argue for the market mechanism as the sole arbiter in the allocation of resources for tourism are ignoring the lessons of history and are grossly over-simplifying the nature of the product. In the United Kingdom, for example, the growth of the seaside resorts during the nineteenth century was a result of a partnership between the public and private sectors. The local authorities invested in the promenades, piers, gardens and so on, while the private sector developed the revenue-earning activities which enhanced the income of the area and in turn increased property tax receipts for the authorities.

Tourism is a multi-faceted product: it includes accommodation, transport, restaurants, shopping facilities, attractions, entertainment, public infrastructure support and the general way of life of the host community. Embodied in the tourist product are goods and services which are unlikely to be provided in sufficient quantity by the market mechanism. These are known as public goods: items which everyone can enjoy in common and are equally available to all. Their principal feature is that they are non-excludable. If the good or service is to be provided at all, it may be consumed by everybody without exception, and usually without charge at the point of use. The single-minded pursuit of profit may be self-defeating, as several Mediterranean resorts have found to their cost. The outcome may not be the integrated tourism development which distils the essence of the country in its design, but a rather crowded, over-built and placeless environment with polluted beaches.

The major hotel developments that took place in the resorts of southern Spain during the 1960s and early 1970s were completed under *laissez-faire* expansionism with little consideration given to planning or control. In general, the public infrastructure was overloaded and this has only been put right in the second half of the 1980s. New moves are now taking place to refurbish the resort centres to give more 'green' space in the form of parks and gardens. What is clear is that the complex structure of the product lends itself to the fact that in any tourism development programme there is often a marked difference between private and social benefits and cost.

The precise nature of a country's stance on tourism investment is determined by the kind of development the government is looking for and what role it envisages for the private entrepreneur. In the past, most of the emphasis of Eastern European countries was on social tourism which allowed the population to benefit from subsidized holidays through workers' organizations and central government provision. Currency movements were arranged on a country-to-country basis through the form of bilateral swaps. The success criteria were based on visitor numbers and most tourist facilities were heavily subsidized. This is now changing, and the influx of Western visitors, as for example in Hungary, has tended to price Eastern European tourists out of the market. African countries have recognized the importance of tourism for conservation. By giving wildlife an economic value, funds are generated to support game reserves, preserve endangered species and help eradicate poaching. Many Caribbean countries have strong views about the wisdom of developing casinos for tourists, because of the possibility of criminal involvement and also on moral grounds.

Tourism objectives

Incentives given by governments for tourist developments are the instruments used to realize the objectives set by the country's tourism policy. A list of strategic objectives which are commonly found in tourism plans is shown in Table 20.1. It is important from the outset to ensure that strategic objectives do not conflict with each other and that incentives offered to investors are compatible with those same objectives. For example, maximizing foreign exchange earnings may be seriously at variance with conserving tourism resources, dispersing the economic benefits of tourism and aiding peripheral regions. Unfortunately, for political reasons, governments often want the tourist industry to meet multiple and various

Table 20.1   Strategic tourism policy objectives

- Develop a tourism sector which, in all aspects and at all levels, is of high quality, though not necessarily of high cost
- Encourage the use of tourism for both cultural and economic exchange
- Distribute the economic benefits of tourism, both direct and indirect, as widely and to as many of the host community as feasible
- Preserve cultural and natural resources as part of tourism development. Facilitate this through architectural and landscape designs which reflect local traditions
- Appeal to a broad cross-section of international and domestic tourists through policies and programmes of site and facility development
- Maximize foreign exchange earnings to ensure a sound balance of payments
- Attract high spending, 'up-market' tourists
- Increase employment
- Aid peripheral regions by raising incomes and employment, thus slowing down or halting emigration

---

objectives, and so tourism policy as exercised by the national tourist authority is not usually one of maximizing but rather one of optimizing subject to constraints, the most common being the balance between foreign exchange, employment and regional development.

Classification of incentives

Bodlender (1982) and Jenkins (1982) have considered the variety of incentives that are available in tourism, and these may be broadly classified as follows:

- Financial incentives
    Reduction in capital costs
    Reduction in operating costs
- Investment security

Financial incentives

The objective of financial incentives is to improve returns to capital so as to attract developers and investors. Where there is obvious market potential the government may only have to demonstrate its commitment to tourism by providing the necessary climate for investment security. Such a situation occurred in Bermuda during the early 1970s, and so, in order

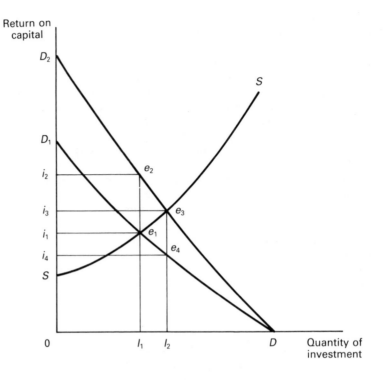

Figure 20.1   Financial incentives on capital

to prevent over-exploitation of the tourism resources, the Bermuda
government imposed a moratorium on large hotel building.

The impact of financial incentives on the amount of investment is
illustrated in Figure 20.1. The schedule SS represents the supply of investible funds while D_1D is the schedule of returns to capital employed. D_1D
slopes downwards from left to right as more and more investment opportunities are taken up – the declining marginal efficiency of investment.
In the initial situation, equilibrium is at e_1 with the amount of investment
being I_1 and the internal rate of return i_1.

The government now implements a range of financial incentives, which
has the effect of raising the internal rate of return per unit of capital to
i_2, moving the marginal efficiency of investment schedule to D_2D. The new
return i_2 equals $(1 + s)i_1$, where s is the effective rate of subsidy. If the
amount of investible funds available for tourism is limited at I_1, then the
impact of incentives serves merely to raise the return to investors by
raising the equilibrium point to e_2. The loss to the government treasury
is the area $i_1 \, e_1 \, e_2 \, i_2$, which equals the gain to private investors.

There is no doubt that many countries have been forced by competitive pressures for foreign investment into situations that are similar to those above. Countries can become trapped in a bidding process to secure clients and as a result the variety of financial incentives multiplies together with an escalation of the rates of benefit, without evaluating their necessity or their true cost to the economy.

Given that the supply of investment funds is responsive or elastic, the net effect of an incentives policy is to expand the amount of tourism projects to I_2 and the rate of return settles at i_3, the equilibrium point being e_3. In this situation the net gain in returns to tourism developers is $i_3 I_2 - i_1 I_1$ which is equal to the sum of the areas $i_3 e_3 e_1 i_1$ plus $I_1 e_1 e_3 I_2$. The cost to the treasury is $si_4 I_2$ which, in turn, is equal to the area $i_3 e_3 e_4 i_4$.

The area under the D_1D curve represents the total output of the tourist sector for different levels of investment. For the initial situation, the amount going to other factors of production, labour in particular, is the area $D_1 e_1 i_1$. With a level of investment of I_2, income to other factors is now $D_1 e_4 i_4$, giving a net gain of $i_i e_1 e_4 i_4$. Thus the total income gain to the private sector is $i_3 e_3 e_1 i_1$ plus $I_1 e_1 e_3 I_2$ plus $i_i e_1 e_4 I_4$. The net income effect is therefore the area $I_1 e_1 e_4 I_2$. The private opportunity cost of the investment funds is the area under the supply curve, $I_1 e_1 e_3 I_2$. The latter is greater than the income effect. This is not surprising, as the justification for government intervention in tourism development is that the social rate of return is higher than the private rate. By stimulating investment the government is attempting to capture the spillover benefits of tourism which may be represented by the area $e_1 e_2 e_3 e_4$. Moreover, the cost of public funds is often lower than rates in the private sector and so the public offer curve lies below the SS curve shown in Figure 20.1. This further raises the social return to the economy. A related issue is the matter of displacement: there is concern that government initiatives should not 'crowd out' other private investments which could do equally as well. In practical terms, all these matters are usually resolved by translating net income into employment creation and calculating the investment cost per job from which comparisons across projects may be made.

It is important to note that there are frequent instances where it is gross uncertainty, as in times of recession, rather than limited potential that prevents the private sector investing. In such situations the principal role of government intervention is to act as a catalyst to give confidence to investors. Thus public funds are able to lever in private money by nature of the government's commitment to tourism and enable the market potential of an area to be realized.

Reduction in capital costs

Incentives to reduce capital costs may include: capital grants, 'soft' loans, equity participation, provision of infrastructure, provision of land on concessional terms and tariff exemption on construction materials.

Capital grants are cash payments which have an immediate impact on the funding of the project, as do matching benefits in kind such as the provision of land or facilities. They are usually preferred by investors because they are one-off transactions involving no further commitment and therefore risk-free. From the standpoint of the authorities they are relatively easy to administer.

'Soft' loans are funds which are provided on preferential terms. At their most simple they may be the granting of interest rate relief on commercial loans. Beyond this the government will normally have to put aside loan funds and create a development agency to administer them. The extreme case is where governments themselves set up a Tourist Development Corporation and invest directly in revenue-earning activities such as hotels, which are traditionally regarded as the preserve of the private sector. Examples around the world include New Zealand, Malaysia, India, Egypt and many African countries, but the rising trend towards market economics during the 1980s has led states increasingly to divest themselves of trading operations which could be undertaken by the commercial sector.

World wide, the common features of most 'soft' loans relate to generous interest rate terms, extended repayment periods, creative patterns of repayment and usually some restriction of the debt/equity mix so as to ensure that the project is not too highly geared in terms of loan finance, which makes it vulnerable to downturns in the market. In some instances loans may be tied to specific sources of supply; this is very common in country-to-country (bilateral) aid programmes. Creative repayment patterns are methods designed to counter the risk profile of the project or the nature of the cash flow over the project's life. Thus a tourist project, such as an attraction, which may be particularly vulnerable in its early stages may be given a moratorium on all repayments for several years. Alternatively a hotel in which the greater part of the cash flow accrues in the second half of the loan term may be granted 'balloon' financing in which the principal is paid back towards the end of the term so as to ensure greater freedom of operation during the initial years of the investment.

Bodlender and Ward (1987) point out that providing loan funds for tourism is more acceptable politically than the provision of grants. The argument in favour of loans rests on the fact that the funds will be recycled and the cost to the treasury will only be the preference element. This is not a rational argument as all incentives have a grant element. Consider the 'soft' loan plan shown in Table 20.2. The development company is being offered $40 million with a three-year moratorium or 'grace' period followed by a five-year repayment plan on a straight-forward mortgage basis at a nominal interest rate of 5 per cent. The latter implies an annual repayment of $9.24 million in the manner presented

Table 20.2 'Soft' loan plan ($ millions)

Year	Loan amount	Repayment plan
0	40	–
1		–
2		–
3		–
4		9.24
5		9.24
6		9.24
7		9.24
8		9.24

in Table 20.2. This is calculated by multiplying $40 million by a capital recovery factor of 0.2310. Suppose the commercial cost of capital is 12 per cent, then discounting the repayment plan in Table 20.2 by this value to obtain the present worth of the cash outlays, yields a value of $23.71 million. The grant element of the loan is therefore the difference of the two sums, namely $16.29 million. Thus in a world of reasonable certainty the development company is indifferent between a grant of $16.29 million or a concessional loan of $40. In a world of uncertainty the grant is riskless, while the loan plan becomes part of the risk environment of the project. Any risk premium attached to this environment will differ from project to project, so that the equivalence of the preferential element of the loan and the capital grant can no longer be assured. The instance under which the loan is chosen in preference to the grant would correspond to the situation where the investor is unable to raise the capital funds over and above the grant from elsewhere. This begs the question as to the cause of the inability to raise funds: it may be due to matters of investment security and then it is up to the government to give the necessary guarantees.

Reduction in operating costs

To improve operating viability governments may offer: direct and indirect tax exemptions, a labour or training subsidy, subsidized tariffs on key inputs such as energy, special depreciation allowances, and double taxation or unilateral relief. Indirect tax exemptions cover such items as waivers on import duties for materials and supplies, exemption from property taxes, licences and so on. Exemption from direct (income) taxes through tax 'holidays' of five to ten years and special depreciation allowances only have meaning when the project is profitable (hence viable

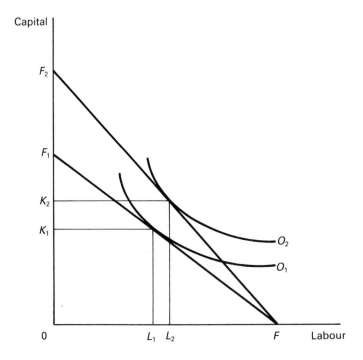

Figure 20.2   Positive impact of capital subsidies on employment

since debt charges are normally deducible), and therefore unlikely to require support. Such exemptions do however raise the returns to equity and may therefore be instrumental in attracting the project to the area in the first place.

The matter of a labour subsidy is indicative of the employment creation objective in tourism development. Factor subsidies can alter the choice of technology in the supply process. One criticism of capital subsidies is that they will tend to promote a capital-intensive structure whereas the emphasis is on generating jobs. A labour subsidy will always improve employment opportunities whereas the effects of a capital subsidy are indeterminable. This aspect is illustrated in Figures 20.2 and 20.3.

In Figure 20.2 the effect of a capital subsidy is to move the relative factor price line from FF_1 to FF_2. This moves the business on to a higher level of output as given by the shift from isoquant O_1 to isoquant O_2. In this instance both the amount of capital and labour employed increases from OK_1 to OK_2 and OL_1 to OL_2 respectively. But for Figure 20.3 the impact of the subsidy is greatly to increase the utilization of capital at the expense of labour. It was with this in mind that the Trade and Industry

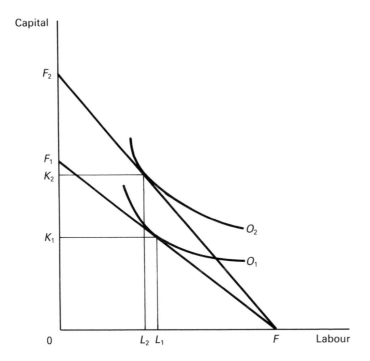

Figure 20.3 Negative impact of capital subsidies on employment

Committee of the UK House of Commons (1985) recommended that, on an experimental basis, the UK government should pay a grant of 30 per cent of the employment costs of tourist facilities remaining open for one month longer than the previous year.

As a rule, tourist authorities counter the contrasting effects of subsidizing capital by giving priority in funding to employment-creating projects. A ready method of doing this is to tie the amount of grant to the number of full-time equivalent (FTE) jobs. The latter allows for the fact that a good number of tourism jobs are often part-time or seasonal. This presumes an element of discretion in the awarding of incentives, which is not always possible when they have been laid down by legislation and are therefore automatic.

Double taxation and unilateral relief are country-to-country or single-country agreements to ensure that multi-national investors are not taxed on the same profits in different locations. Suppose a company controlled in Country A trades in Country B through a permanent establishment in the latter country, it will pay tax on its trading profits both in Country A and Country B, but if there is a double taxation agreement between these countries, then a tax credit in respect of Country B's tax will be allowed against Country A's tax. If there is only unilateral relief, the company will be entitled to offset its tax liability elsewhere against tax payable in Country B.

Investment security

The objective of providing investment security is to win investors' confidence in an industry which is very sensitive to the political environment and the economic climate. Action here would include: guarantees against nationalization, ensuring the availability of trained staff, free availability of foreign exchange, repatriation of invested capital, profits dividends and interest, loan guarantees, provision of work permits for 'key' personnel, and availability of technical advice. To support these actions, there is the broader issue of the government's support for tourism. This may be demonstrated by marketing and promoting the region, particularly abroad, reducing administrative delays, simplifying the planning process, easing frontier formalities, initiating liberal transport policies and so forth. Clearly, without the confidence in the government to set the right economic climate for the tourist industry to prosper, investment incentives on their own may be of limited value in attracting outside funds. It is for this reason that a good deal of World Bank lending, particularly in Africa, goes towards structural adjustment policies to set the economic framework within which market-orientated projects may function.

Implementation

In implementing a tourism investment policy the government has to decide to what extent incentives should be legislated as automatic entitlements, as against being discretionary awards. It has already been noted that automatic incentives may give too much money away, when what is required to ensure that the treasury receives maximum benefit from its funds is the application of the concept of additionality. The latter seeks to provide financial support or the equivalent benefits in kind to the point where the developer will just proceed with the project.

The implication of additionality is an ideal situation where all incentives are discretionary and therefore offered selectively. The legislation would be fairly general, empowering the ministry responsible for tourism to offer loans, grants, tax exemptions and equity investment as it sees fit. Such legislation is embodied in the UK 1969 Development of

Tourism Act. The granting of incentives to prospective developers would be in accordance with ministerial guidelines. The latter should be regularly reviewed in response to the level of tourism activity. An example of such guidelines can be found in the conditions governing the award of financial assistance by the Wales Tourist Board (1991):

> The schemes administered by the Board are all discretionary and in general terms consideration can only be given to viable projects which involve capital expenditure and for which a need for Board assistance can be demonstrated. All projects must, in addition, be available to the general public when completed and be likely to attract visitors to Wales.
>
> Each application for assistance is assessed on its merits, the Board's decision being final. The Board seeks to maximize the benefits accruing to Wales with the limited resources available under these schemes and takes careful account of a number of factors in assessing applications. Priority is given to projects which:
> - provide full-time employment opportunities;
> - help extend the effective length of the season;
> - enhance the range and quality of the facilities and amenities provided by the industry;
> - have potential for attracting both domestic and overseas visitors;
> - provide significant benefit to the community in terms of:
>   — income and employment creation
>   — improving local infrastructure
>   — preserving local landscape;
> - are of good standards of design;
> - exhibit sound marketing potential;
> - are potential viable projects in their own right.

To have only discretionary incentives, however, is a counsel of perfection. Competition for tourism investment frequently requires countries to legislate for automatic financial help in order to attract investors in the first instance. Some countries may legislate for all the incentives discussed here; others for a subset of them. Many countries have been guilty of copying the incentive legislation of their neighbours without any real grasp of the meaning of this legislation.

The appropriateness of the various financial incentives available depends on understanding the nature of the business risk and the likely returns of the tourist industry, as well as the ability of the country to afford them. Thus developing countries may find themselves in no position to offer grants or cheap loans. It is well known that part of the business risk in tourism projects lies in the fact that services are non-storable (a hotel bed unsold is lost forever) and in demand being generally seasonal. This implies that peak demand determines capacity so that the industry is always facing excess capacity at other times.

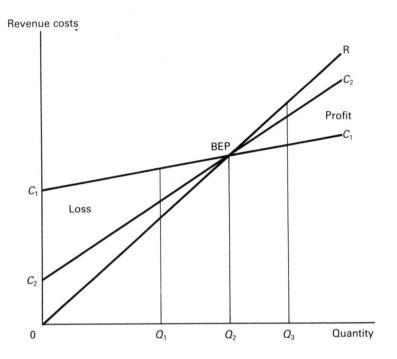

Figure 20.4   Effects of operating leverage

Cost structures

Not always apparent is the dominant cost structure in the industry. Typically, tourist projects have a high operating leverage, that is a high level of fixed costs arising out of the initial capital investment and low operating costs. This makes pricing difficult, because operating costs are no longer a reliable guide as to what to charge, and also results in businesses which are very sensitive to variations in demand. The problem is illustrated in Figure 20.4. Two projects are assumed to have exactly the same revenue line R and break even point BEP. One project, however, has a high operating leverage, as shown by the cost line C_1, and the other a low operating leverage represented by C_2. The possible outcomes of these two projects are shown by Q_1, Q_2 and Q_3. Suppose Q_3 sales are achieved, then it is clear that the project with the high operating leverage makes substantially more profit (represented by the difference between the revenue and cost schedules) than the other. On the other hand, if the outcome is Q_1 sales then the project with the cost structure C_1 will make large losses. Thus a 1 per cent variation in load factors on aircraft may be critical to the profitability of tour operators, and when things do go wrong the consequences are often spectacular: the nightmare scenario for governments is where a major tour operator collapses either depriving its millions of customers of previously arranged holidays or leaving them stranded abroad.

In addition to the above, tourism at the destination end deals, perhaps more than any other industry, with the development of real estate. But the non-transferability of assets such as hotels hinders their worth as a property investment. The upshot of this is that tourism projects are known to be risky investments and if the objective is to improve viability, the preferred form of financial incentives are those which reduce capital costs (Wanhill, 1986).

Evaluation

It is well known that tourism is a demand-led industry whose influence pervades many different sectors of the economy. There is no single industrial classification called tourism, so the starting point for evaluating tourism projects, from the government's perspective, is to measure the economic impact of tourist spending and derive appropriate multipliers, in particular income and employment multipliers. Tourists come to a destination for many reasons, so if the requirement is to establish the worth of a project which has been assisted through public funds, the first step is to establish the criteria for assessment.

Benefit analysis

Suppose that there exists a tourist destination with two attractions and a seaside. Visitors are surveyed at both attractions and on the beach to ascertain what motivated them to come to the destination. Total spending at the destination (T) amounts to expenditure at Attraction X (T_x) plus expenditure at Attraction Y (T_y) plus all remaining expenditure (R). The pull factor (reason for visit) for Attraction X is a. Attraction Y is b, leaving $1 - a - b$ as the significance of the beach. It follows therefore that attributable tourist expenditure by drawing power is:

$$\text{Attraction X} = aT_x + aT_y + aR$$
$$\text{Attraction Y} = bT_x + bT_y + bR$$
$$\text{Seaside} = (1 - a - b)\,(T_x + T_y + R)$$
$$T = T_x + T_y + R$$

The local tourist board has put public money into Attraction X and so wishes to evaluate its worth in terms of its contribution to tourist spending and employment in the area. The benefits of Attraction X (*B*) are the difference between with and without the project. The without situation is:

$$
\begin{aligned}
\text{Attraction X} &= 0 \\
\text{Attraction Y} &= bT_y + bR \\
\text{Seaside} &= (1 - a - b)\,(T_y + R) \\
T_w &= (1 - a)\,(T_y + R)
\end{aligned}
$$

Hence

$$
\begin{aligned}
B &= T - T_w \\
&= T_x + a\,(T_y + R)
\end{aligned}
\tag{1}
$$

If the visitors to Attraction X would have come to the area anyway, then the benefits would simply be T_x.

Employment effects

The benefits shown in equation (1) are in two parts. The first term on the right hand side is on-site expenditure and the second, off-site expenditure. The amount of off-site expenditure attributable to the attraction depends on its ability to generate additional visitors. Hence, this may be termed the visitor additionality factor. The application of employment multipliers per unit of tourist spending to equation (1), either on an FTE or employment headcount basis, will give the gross employment (*E*) generated by the project. These multipliers are calculated so as to measure the direct employment effects of the project, the indirect effects arising out of intermediate purchases made by the project and the induced effects on the local economy as a result of the re-spending of local incomes derived from the project, and similarly for off-site expenditure. Thus:

$$
E = T_x e_x + a\,Oe_o
\tag{2}
$$

Where e_x is the employment multiplier appropriate to the attraction, O is the sum of off-site expenditure ($T_y + R$) and e_o the required employment multiplier. However, equation (2) ignores any demand diversion from elsewhere in the area: this is termed displacement and in this respect it is important to define the boundary of the project. As observed by Johnson and Thomas (1990):

> In the case of the economy as a whole it is sometimes argued that all expenditure, and consequently employment, is diverted and there is in effect a zero-sum game. This point is of some importance from the point of view of public bodies providing funds. Local authorities and the

Treasury for example might have very different views on what is the net impact because they are concerned with different reference areas.

At a national level this argument assumes that market forces are moving the economy towards full employment equilibrium so that public investment expenditure is simply displacing private funds in the capital market. Similarly, the operation of the project is displacing demand in the same or related product markets and likewise in the labour and property markets. In reality economies do get stuck at a level of Keynesian unemployment disequilibrium and one of the major objectives of regional policy is to 'kick-start' a demand-deficient economy so as to raise the level of output through the multiplier process. This discussion does not imply that displacement should be neglected so that policy decisions are made in terms of the gross effect only, but merely raises the issue that the logic of the crowding out effect ends up with a 'do nothing' policy.

If d is the proportion of locally diverted demand (or demand diverted from other assisted projects) in equation (1), then, from equation (2), net employment is:

$$N = E - dE$$
$$= (1 - d)\,(T_x e_x + a\,Oe_o) \tag{3}$$

Equation (3) forms the core of the basic evaluation model which can be used to judge in employment terms the return to public funds given to the project by way of the whole range of incentives discussed earlier. As an example, consider the data presented in Table 20.3. The total on-site and off-site expenditure arising from the project is $25,050,000. Visitor surveys have shown that only about 12 per cent of staying visitors came to the destination because of the existence of the attraction. As is to be expected, this percentage is much greater for day visitors and local residents. From equation (1):

$$B = \$8,500,000 + 0.12 \times \$12,920,000 + 0.9 \times \$2,200,000$$
$$+ 1.0 \times \$1,430,000$$
$$= \$13,460,400$$

It is known that the attraction creates 87.5 FTEs directly on-site and so the relevant addition to this number is the employment generated by the indirect and induced effects of on-site expenditure. Using the appropriate FTE multipliers in Table 20.3, the number of jobs is $(0.0412 + 0.0059) \times \$8,500,000 = 40.0$. Off-site jobs created amount to $0.1078 \times \$4,960,400 = 53.5$. Thus the value of equation (2) is:

$$E = 87.5 + 40.0 + 53.5$$
$$= 181.0 \text{ FTEs}$$

Table 20.3 Calculating the employment impact of an attraction

	On-site expenditure	Off-site expenditure
Market segments		
Stay visitors	$2,210,000	$12,920,000
Day visitors	$2,465,000	$2,200,000
Local residents	$3,825,000	$1,430,000
Total	$8,500,000	$16,550,000
Visitor additionality		
Stay visitors	n/a	12%
Day visitors	n/a	90%
Local residents	n/a	100%
Displacement		
Stay visitors	0%	0%
Day visitors	30%	30%
Local residents	70%	70%
FTE multipliers per $10,000 of visitor spend		
Direct	0.0765	0.0628
Indirect	0.0412	0.0391
Induced	0.0059	0.0059
Total	0.1236	0.1078

n/a, not applicable.

So far the analysis has only measured gross FTEs generated by the attraction. The net figure has to account for the displacement factors given in Table 20.3. Suppose that the evidence indicates that there will be no displacement of staying visitors since the attraction is providing them with more 'things to do' but there will be a 30 per cent diversion of day visitor spend and 70 per cent for local residents. It could be argued that there should be a 100 per cent displacement of local resident demand, but, while this may be a good working assumption in that residents have many opportunities to spend in the local area, it does imply that there is no flexibility in residents' leisure spending budgets. Using the information on expenditure in Table 20.3, the weighted overall displacement factor is 0.3724, hence the solution to equation (3) is

$$N = 181.0 - 0.3724 \times 181.0$$
$$= 113.6 \text{ FTEs}$$

It is this number of FTEs that is traded against the estimated grant element of the incentives offered, in order to give the cost to public funds of job creation.

The core model given by equation (3) is capable of further adjustment to take into account factors such as: project additionality, business displacement, differential impacts on the local labour market and externalities.

Incentive legislation used in the UK is hedged about with the concept of additionality. As stated before, this lays down the criterion that a grant (or loan) would only be forthcoming if the project would not proceed without it. Assessment of this position by project officers involves considerable subjective judgement about the likely future behaviour of the investor and in practice requires the investor to sign a document to the effect that the funds are a necessary condition for the project to go ahead. In reality there are degrees of project additionality, for the investment could have gone ahead at a later date, on a smaller scale or at a lower quality. If a numerical value can be placed upon such assessments then they can be included in the model. Similarly business displacement may arise in several ways: the funded project crowds out a competing investment opportunity; the investment replaces an existing business on the same site; or the project may result in a property move to a new site, leaving the old site vacant.

Replacement of an existing business may have a beneficial effect if there is a quality and cost improvement that raises long-term viability. Many assisted tourist projects have been built on derelict sites and have therefore resulted in a net improvement. Differential impacts on the labour market relate to the use of unemployed as opposed to people already in jobs, improving the skills of the workforce, full-time, part-time and seasonal jobs, the male/female ratio, local people versus outsiders and so on. Externalities would account for the agglomeration benefits arising by virtue of the synergy of one project with another and its linkages with the rest of the economy to ensure a balanced growth of facilities at the destination, in order to meet the many and changing needs of visitors. However, as the model moves through increasing levels of sophistication so data requirements spiral upwards. Given that data sources are imperfect and there is always pressure on time, the practical effect of this is to increase the level of economic assumptions made, which in turn downgrades the robustness of the core model presented in equation (3).

Conclusions

Around the globe governments have intervened to assist and regulate the private sector in the development of tourism. This is because the complex nature of the tourist product makes it unlikely that private markets will satisfy a country's tourism policy objectives to produce a balance of facilities that meet the needs of the visitor, benefit the host community and are compatible with the wishes of that same community. Incentives are policy instruments that can be used to correct for market failure and ensure a development partnership between the public and private sectors. The extent of public involvement depends on the economic philosophy of the government. The trend towards pure market-led economics in recent years has led to a clawback of state involvement and the questioning of incentives as mechanisms more likely to lead to market distortions. This is in total contrast to the concept of sustainable development which challenges the ability of private markets to improve the distribution of income and protect the environment.

The baseline scenario for sustainable development is the alleviation of absolute poverty and the replenishment of the resource stock so that at a minimum no one generation is worse off than any other. The spillover benefits of tourism are well known, and, more than any other industry, tourism deals with the use of natural and cultural resources. The lessons of the past indicate that it is unwise for the state to abandon its ability to influence the direction of tourism development either through the provision of finance or through legislation. The short-term gains sought by capital markets are often at odds with the long-term sustainability of tourism environments.

References

Bodlender, J.A. (1982) The financing of tourism projects. *Tourism Management*, 3(4), 277

Bodlender, J.A. and Ward, T.J. (1987) *An Examination of Tourism Incentives*, Howarth and Howarth, London, p. 20

Jenkins, C.L. (1982) The use of investment incentives for tourism projects in developing countries. *Tourism Management*, 3(2), 91–7

Johnson, P.S. and Thomas, R.B. (1990) The economic impact of museums: a study of the North of England Open Air Museum at Beamish. Proceedings of a conference on Tourism Research into the 1990s, University of Durham, December 1990, pp. 388–402

Trade and Industry Committee (1985) *Tourism in the UK*, vol. 1, session 1985–1986, London, HMSO, p. xxxvii

Wales Tourist Board (1991) *Schemes of Financial Assistance*, Factsheet No. 9, Cardiff

Wanhill, S.R.C. (1986) Which investment incentives for tourism? *Tourism Management*, 7(1), 2–7

Part Five

Facilities, Programmes and Services: Resource Issues

Introduction

The provision of high-quality, creative, relevant and meaningful experiences are the most critical challenge facing the visitor industry today. Consumer perceptions concerning the quality of their own individual tourism experiences are central issues in tourism management. All tourism organizations are in the service business, but only those organizations that focus on service excellence as the cornerstone of their operations will be sustained.

When special events are purposely developed and promoted as tourist attractions, there is always the risk that they may become too commercialized. If this potential risk is allowed to occur, it may detract and eventually destroy authenticity, a scarce commodity, and the very thing visitors may have been seeking.

Getz (Chapter 21) provides a graphic description of special events held in different parts of the world. Examples include events that are indigenous to certain areas as well as others that have been 'invented' in order to attract tourists and generate greater income. In each of these examples, authenticity plays a pivotal role as a 'pull' factor in attracting tourists.

A typology of special events is proposed, based upon the range of events and their interpretive roles, from the most authentic (and usually most site-specific) to the most general community event. A planning, programming and evaluation framework for special events is proffered, and specific guidelines for ensuring authenticity are also suggested in order to help ensure visitor satisfaction.

Industrialized countries are changing from the traditional production economy to an information-based economy. Tourism-related activities have been classified as convenience services. At the national level, tourism's future success may well depend on the ability of each country to educate not only tourism employees, but also tourists and destination area residents about each other's culture in order better to understand and appreciate one another. According to Go (Chapter 22), continued prosperity in tourism will depend largely on well-educated people who are able to think, weigh and judge crucial issues in addition to providing quality tourist services.

The evolution of tourism education is presented, and the suggestion is made that tourism thinking has passed through two distinct stages: (1) the early 1940s-1970s characterized by pragmatic concerns of educators for such things as career preparation and placement; and (2) beginning in the early 1980s, a shift from the pragmatic to the academic, emphasizing research and methods of enquiry. However, the 1990s are seen as a period of transformation brought about by social change, concern for the environment, a global economy and rapid advancements in technology.

The dual forces of technology and globalization will raise the competency demanded for all positions in the tourism industry and turn effective education into a competitive necessity. Industry, government and academic institutions must recognize that productivity and quality gains are derived from increased employee skills and knowledge. These value-added skills must continue to be developed if the tourism industry is to survive.

One of the important issues in strategic planning of facilities and amenities is understanding the activities of tourists during their visit to a particular destination. For many tourists, an integral part, or to others the entire purpose, of the visit according to Jansen-Verbeke (Chapter 23) is shopping. In fact, shopping is a major time-use for many tourists, regardless of their primary travel motivation.

The results of a recent survey of Japanese tourist's shopping behaviour in Amsterdam indicated that Japanese tourists clearly behave differently from other target market groups, and that even within this segment of the market, there are clear distinctions between age, travel motivation, length of stay and, above all, travel organization. To the Japanese tourist, the system of tax-free shops in Amsterdam offers special advantages not commonly found elsewhere.

Especially in urban areas, the spatial relationship of tourist activities such as shopping and sightseeing must be directly related to hotels and transportation as a precondition for synergism. Therefore, taking into account the actual time budgets of tourists, the creation of intervening shopping opportunities along predictable sightseeing routes is one of the most effective planning instruments in developing an urban area's tourism potential.

The majority of Western societies are beginning to experience the impact of one of the twentieth century's most important socio-political and economic movements, the 'greying' of the population. Therefore, one of the most important targets for leisure travel is the mature market. The number of individuals over age sixty-five is increasing, and many of them have the time and are willing to spend a significant portion of their incomes for travel. Older people hold a large share of a nation's discretionary income since their children are usually grown and their homes are paid for. In addition, due to healthier life styles and advances in medicine, they are in better health and can expect to live longer than ever before.

Knowledge about older people's travel behaviour is still developing. Although it is recognized that older markets clearly have the desire to travel, little empirical evidence is available that helps explain why they travel, how they travel and the benefits they seek through travel. van Harssell conducted a study of retired persons for a large, travel and entertainment company in order to help design programmes and promotions geared to meet the needs of the older travel market.

His findings (Chapter 24) indicate that today's older traveller can best be characterized as being different, diverse and demanding.

Finally, in Chapter 25 Morgan looks at the future of established seaside tourist resorts, especially those along the Mediterranean coast. He argues that most such resorts are homogeneous, and as such have begun to lose some of their appeal to the public, resulting in a loss of market share. As the decline stage in the product life cycle concept nears, since they are no longer in favour with the travelling public, established resorts face the decision either to let their facilities die gradually, or somehow to rejuvenate these ageing resources.

The author provides a brief history of seaside resorts and describes the conditions that have led them first to be established, then to become homogeneous. Changing economic and demographic factors as well as product maturity have influenced tourists' holiday decisions. The adoption curve is used to illustrate how such facilities have also fallen out of fashion since, as they no longer attract either innovators or allocentrics, the general public begin to look for other destination options.

Market dependence, distribution channel control, maintenance and enhancement of facility quality are guidelines presented for developing resorts. In addition, several strategies for resort survival are presented, including: developing of new markets and new products; changing from a static destination area to a touring centre; upgrading product quality; and promoting a new image. Ultimately, the challenge for established resorts is to provide facilities and resources of a standard demanded by the international tourist market while developing and retaining its unique character.

21 Event tourism and the authenticity dilemma

Donald Getz

Introduction

When festivals and other special events are consciously developed and promoted as tourist attractions, there is the risk that commercialization will detract from celebration; that entertainment or spectacle will replace the inherent meanings of the celebrations. In other words, tourism might destroy cultural authenticity, the very thing contemporary travellers appear to be seeking.

The dilemma, however, is that the benefits to be realized from tourism offer the means to create or expand festivals, restore and cultivate traditions and foster community spirit and sharing. Can there be a balance, therefore, between marketing and social/cultural goals in the field of event tourism? Can authenticity be preserved in the face of ever-increasing tourist pressure?

This is not a debate solely for academics and traditionalists, as just about every community seems to have a festival or special event that it wishes to see grow and prosper, while at the same time not being overwhelmed by visitors or commercialism. And in more traditional societies, where customs and quaintness are easily converted into cash through eager tourism entrepreneurs, there is the risk of loss of innocence and purity, if not outright assimilation. Is the price too high?

Definitions and concepts

Festival

Festivals are simply defined as themed, public celebrations. Yet the term is rich in tradition and meaning, with many anthropological and socio-logical studies documenting the close links between festivity, religion and community (e.g., Falassi, 1987; MacAloon, 1984; Manning, 1983). True festivals are produced explicitly for public, not private consumption, and are celebrations of something which has value in the community. Many festivals celebrate community itself, and have been created specifically to give people something to share, to unify them, to foster community pride. Others are invented with the goal to foster a particular form of arts or sports.

To the anthropologist, festivals have a multitude of potential meanings and encompass a number of paradoxes (Lavenda, 1991): as 'texts' which are stories told by members of a culture about themselves; as performances, or social dramas full of conflict and power statements; as communications about social ties in the society; as art forms; as deliberate inversions or role reversals, mocking but simultaneously reinforcing social norms.

According to Lavenda, three paradoxes emerged from his study of festivals in small Minnesota towns. The events simultaneously reduced and increased uncertainty in the social life, contributed to both order and disorder, and conveyed the image of a stable community while at the same time changing the community through the festival's evolving membership. Accordingly, a researcher could look for expressions of power (who runs the events?), conformity to established ways of doing things (no new ideas in twenty years?), licence to commit revelry versus tight controls on drinking, take-overs by new arrivals in town, and so on.

Special event

From the point of view of the consumer, or audience, a special event is an opportunity for a leisure, social or cultural experience outside the normal range of choices or beyond everyday experience. From the organizer's point of view a special event is any one-time or infrequently occurring event outside their normal programme of activities. What is 'special' to the organizer might not be of any interest to potential consumers, so from a marketing perspective the product must be matched to carefully defined target segments. Some segments exist which can be described as 'event tourists' – those who seek out events of particular types.

All festivals should be special events, both to organizers and consumers. Many special events, however, are not festivals: they lie in the domain of sport competitions, commercial promotions, or meetings and shows. Increasingly, however, we are seeing a blending, with sports events in particular adding festival-like programming to make them more attractive.

Event tourism

Many businesses, communities and destination marketing organizations are now engaged in the systematic planning, development and marketing of festivals and events as tourist attractions, image-makers, catalysts for other developments or as animators of built attractions. This is 'event tourism' at work, and so significant is the business that more and more event development corporations are being established, with the success of Indianapolis often held up as a prime example of what can be accomplished (Macnow, 1989).

To the extent that events are often inexpensive to develop, and if properly organized will generate little negative impact, they can be viewed as being more sustainable than other forms of tourism development. And because they are essentially cultural in nature and lead to host–guest contacts, increasingly event tourism is being looked upon as a clear alternative to mass tourism.

In addition to their tourism potential, festivals and special events are being created by more and more organizations and agencies, both private and public. Events can help raise money, foster community development or the arts, provide leisure opportunities and make excellent communications tools (indeed, much of the growth of events in the past decade is attributable to sponsorship). As argued in Getz (1991), the popularity and specialness of festivals and events are closely related to their ability to achieve multiple goals.

Authenticity

Authenticity means genuine, unadulterated or 'the real thing'. With respect to tourism, use of the term generally carries one of two connotations: tourists seldom get access to authentic cultural experiences, owing to the commercialization of culture in destinations; tourism demand tends to destroy genuine cultural traditions by turning them into commodities. These notions are much debated in the literature, including the related question of whether or not contemporary tourists actually seek out authentic experiences, or can even recognize them.

Vallee (1987) maintained that 'Authenticity is a desired and actively pursued experience by tourists which is perceived to reflect or give access to the true and unadulterated nature of everyday life in the destination.' Redfoot (1984), however, noted that some scholars believe the modern tourist is generally uninterested in the authentic (e.g., Boorstin, 1961), while others have suggested that tourists are engaged in a quest for the authentic (e.g., MacCannell, 1976).

MacCannell, in his much-quoted book *The Tourist* (1976), suggested that modern tourists seek authenticity precisely because it has become so scarce. The tourist wants a spontaneous experience that reveals, or better yet allows the sharing of some aspect of the daily life of a different culture or community. He used the term 'backstage' to describe the physical setting in which a visitor could observe, meet or share something authentic. The term 'staged authenticity' was coined to describe events created with the intention of fooling observers.

Cohen (1979) and Pearce (1982) have added to the debate by arguing that visitor satisfaction will depend not only on the nature of the event (whether or not it is authentic) but also on the visitor's perception of whether or not authenticity exists and their need for authentic experiences. For example, one visitor will want a festival to be an authentic cultural expression of the host community and will be disappointed if he or she finds a highly commercialized, tourist-orientated event. Another visitor will not care, and still others will not know the difference. Authenticity can be considered as a part of the event product, because it is something that can motivate certain tourists, and it is a benefit that can at least partially be controlled by organizers.

There are interesting cases documented in the literature which tangibly illustrate the issues surrounding authenticity, and which offer possible answers to the dilemma. A few personal experiences of the author are also illustrated below.

A Basque festival

An often-cited example of the negative impacts of tourism was Greenwood's study of a Basque festival in Spain. In his first report on the festival the researcher was critical of tourism as a force which attacked an authentic tradition by commercializing it for presentation to tourists. Greenwood (1989) lamented: 'local culture . . . is altered and often destroyed by the treatment of it as a tourist attraction. It is made meaningless to the people who once believed in it.'

But in his second analysis of the festival, written as an epilogue, Greenwood questioned whether tourism has any unique effects in transforming culture – as opposed to, say, mass communications and economic globalization. He concluded: 'Some of what we see as destruction is construction; some is the result of a lack of any other viable options; and some the result of choices that could be made differently.' Regarding authenticity, Greenwood dismissed the notion that an anthropologist could compare 'traditional models' with 'what is presented to the tourist' and then make a pronouncement. Rather, all cultures continuously change, within cultures there is great diversity, and what is 'authentic' might become a highly political issue. Finally, Greenwood conceded that under some conditions, tourism might be a positive cultural force.

The Pentecost Land Jump

For a positive example, there is the case of the Pentecost Land Jump in the South Pacific island nation of Vanuatu, as reported by Sofield (1991).

The ritual – called the 'naghol' – is steeped in Melanesian legend, and appears to be the precursor to bungee-jumping. Men of the tribes leap from high platforms, their fall broken by a flexible vine tied to ankles. Fearing commercialization of the ritual, the chiefs formed a tourism council to manage the events and the tourists, generating significant local income in the process. The national tourism office works with the industry, including Air Vanuatu, agents and wholesalers, to bring up to fifty tourists to the site at one time, and no more than eight times a year.

Sofield concluded: 'The unique selling proposition of the naghol is the authenticity of the event which can only be guaranteed by control remaining in the hands of the eight villages of south Pentecost. It is an example where the objectives of viable tourism, traditional culture and social values on the one hand and commercial gain on the other are not mutually exclusive.'

In addition to local ownership and control of the event, Sofield concluded that a supportive government was also required – both to promote the event and to protect it from outside influences. Other criteria for maintaining cultural authenticity were derived from this case study, along with directly related objectives and business and marketing implications. For example, 'broad community support with appropriate organizational structure' is a key criterion; it requires an 'acceptable decision-making process'. 'Priority accorded to cultural integrity over commercial consideration' is another crucial criterion, requiring 'commercial imperatives made to fit around, not debase, the ceremony'.

The Amish

Buck (1977, 1978) found that staged, tourist-orientated events helped to prevent direct contact with privacy-loving Amish people in Lancaster County, Pennsylvania. In this way, unauthentic events can be used to maintain a social boundary between curious tourists and reluctant host communities. As long as the tourists are satisfied, even if they know they are witnessing an event put on for their entertainment or education, then it hardly seems to matter whether the event is culturally genuine or not – it serves a very useful function. Indeed, in this age of mass travel and a better informed traveller, it is probably the rare, naive tourist who actually expects to discover unadulterated cultural festivals!

Creating a theme

Consultants have recommended that a winter carnival in Newfoundland, Canada, should make greater use of its mascot – Leif the Lucky, in Viking costume – in developing and marketing their event as a tourist attraction. More ambitiously, a set of Viking Games could be invented to package sports tournaments and participatory recreational events all year round. Already existing in the region is a Viking Trail with its own destination marketing association.

While there is some historical association with Vikings in their part of the world, it is clearly a marketing tool rather than a reflection of contemporary culture. Indeed, the Viking motif, attractive and full of merchandizing promise, is as novel a theme to residents as it is to tourists. On the one hand, creation of themed events and promotional devices might awaken interest in the area's history, but it might also reduce historical facts to trivial slogans and characters. To combat that possibility, another recommendation was to create a 'Discovery Days' festival with the goal of celebrating and interpreting the early western Newfoundland explorers, including the Vikings and Captain James Cook.

Appropriateness

In Costa Rica, the Central American country noted for ecotourism, but not cultural attractions, the idea was raised by a coffee company to develop a festival with a coffee theme. It is a major export, and a special event themed on that product would promote the crop, reflect an important aspect of Costa Rican life, and act as a cultural attraction. The idea raises the questions of whether the event is appropriate to the country, and whether explicit commercialism will negate cultural value.

Festivals with higher levels of authenticity, including the religious celebrations found in Costa Rican communities, might not be appropriately promoted as tourist attractions. Their sacred and intensely personal nature might preclude them from ever being considered a fun attraction, while their host communities might be totally unable or unwilling to organize and market them for tourists. In this context, the invented, commercial event might be more appropriate.

Becoming a tradition

An example of a successful 'invented' festival is Dickens on the Strand, founded by the Galveston Historical Society (in Galveston, Texas) to attract attention to, and raise money for, heritage restoration (cited in Getz, 1991). Held annually in December, the event is a major tourist attraction as well as being very popular with residents – many of whom are volunteers, while others dress in Victorian costume in order to gain free admission. This event successfully meets its heritage objectives while providing a valued social experience for residents.

Many such 'instant traditions' have been created in the world of special events. They fulfil a real need for community sharing, leisure outlets and pride in accomplishments. Indeed, many people seem to think that community events are not significant unless tourists are attracted.

In North America and other new nations, traditional festivals and events are in short supply, while the mobility of the population is high. Given the absence of 'authentic' celebrations, communities have invented their own. Who is to say that these events are less authentic than centuries-old festivals?

Conceptualizing the authenticity dilemma

Three perspectives on authenticity must be reconciled. From a social anthropology point of view, authenticity is a measure of the inherent cultural meanings of festivity and celebration; that is, people come together to share valued elements of their culture. To the planner of festivals and events in the contemporary world, where multiple goals are pursued – including tourism – authenticity can be viewed as a measure of community control and success in mobilizing residents to support and participate in the event. This perspective will also encompass, explicitly or implicitly, the notion of self-image. In other words, if the community or large components of it reject the theme or the image being portrayed of the community, they will stay away or make their objections known. Authenticity in this sense means acceptance.

The third essential perspective is that of the visitor. By definition, the tourist or visitor is an outsider who is not necessarily sharing culture with residents, but nevertheless enjoys being able to participate in an event with local significance. More pragmatically, the tourist is most likely to be attracted to, and enjoy events which are popular with the host community. Here, authenticity is a measure of the tourist's perceptions. Unthinking tourists may view a commercial event as being authentic, or may perceive it correctly but still enjoy the production. Other tourists seek out authenticity and are disappointed when they (correctly or incorrectly) do not find it. To the tourism planner and marketer, this is a problem of tourist satisfaction and can be countered through better product–market matching.

Figure 21.1 is an illustration of the three perspectives of event authenticity (i.e., community control and acceptance; cultural meanings; tourist perspective). At the pyramid's apex a very traditional, uncommercialized festival or ritual is almost certainly one which is based on high community control and acceptance – even if witnessed by tourists. The Pentecost Land Jump is a prime example.

At the mid level, 'invented' and tourist-orientated events might initially have low cultural meaning, but this can change over time. The result should be a convergence of meaning and community acceptance, until – hypothetically – new traditions are created. On this topic, Cohen

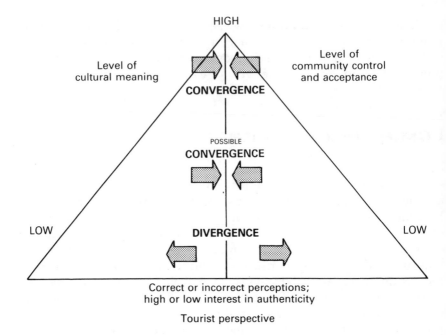

HIGH

Level of
cultural meaning

Level of
community control
and acceptance

CONVERGENCE

POSSIBLE
CONVERGENCE

LOW

DIVERGENCE

LOW

Correct or incorrect perceptions;
high or low interest in authenticity

Tourist perspective

Figure 21.1   Three perspectives of event authenticity

(1988) suggested that 'emergent authenticity' is a process by which a contrived cultural product comes to be perceived as authentic, over time. Planners of events will hope that this happens, and the evidence of festivals like Dickens on the Strand is positive.

Other rituals or events might be valued only by small minorities within society and will have to engage in public relations to attract wider community support or acceptance. Ethnic and multicultural festivals often have this planned convergence as an explicit goal – that is, they create the event to bring diverse groups together and attract the attention and understanding of unrelated cultural groups.

However, events with low community control and acceptance are unlikely to achieve any cultural authenticity, while events low in inherent cultural meaning are likely to be perceived as alien and undesirable – resulting in divergence. There is no particular type of event which necessarily fits this category, but they are most likely to be highly commercialized or imposed on an unresponsive community.

At the pyramid's base lies the variable perspective of the visitor or tourist, whose perceptions and reactions are, at the level of individuals, unpredictable. Those seeking high levels of authenticity will presumably be attracted to events at the apex and repelled by events at the base. But purely commercial entertainment events can be low on authenticity and community acceptance while still attracting tourists. Accordingly, the tourist perspective is the subject for market research, with the aim of matching the right event to the desires of target segments.

Heritage events

Of contemporary interest is a class of events which have historical themes or which celebrate some dimension of a community's or cultural group's heritage. By definition, these events should embody high levels of authenticity – but that cannot be taken for granted.

Heritage events are public, themed festivals and other special events which celebrate a nation's or community's traditions, values and sense of place. They may have an explicit heritage theme, such as a commemoration or a folk festival, or they may be broadly programmed community celebrations. They may be site-specific or community-wide. They may be produced by an ethnic or special interest group, or by a public or private agency. There is no single style of heritage event, nor any correct way of producing them. Indeed, one of the hallmarks of heritage events is their unlimited diversity.

Events and interpretation

Heritage events can also be viewed as tools for interpreting the community by bringing people into direct contact with historical facts, objects and re-created events or ways of life, thereby increasing their knowledge and appreciation of traditions. Interpretation, according to Tilden, one of its early advocates (1977), is an 'educational activity which aims to reveal meanings and relationships through the use of original objects, by first hand experience, and by illustrative media'. More specifically, Cherem (1988) said that heritage interpretation 'can make the heritage identity of an area come to life for residents and visiting guests'. To do so requires 'real and authenticated, first-hand sensory interaction with the resources of that area'. Moscardo and Pearce (1986) have argued that historical re-creations, as in heritage sites and events, can be considered authentic if they faithfully simulate past conditions.

Also relevant is Cherem's definition of community interpretation, which 'tells the stories of – and facilitates – heritage expression in a community'. In a related vein, Binks (1989) said: 'The common ground where interpretation and community development meet is in a concern to create or enhance a sense of place, to establish what is significant and valued in the environment or heritage . . . and to provoke action for its wider appreciation and conservation.'

Little attention has been paid to the potential of festivals and other special events as interpretation tools. One obvious connection is the folklife festival, which McDaniel (1986) describes as being 'inherently grassroots in nature'. Its combination of entertainment and education makes such a festival a 'classroom for the teaching of history to the general public'. The historian, according to McDaniel, has the task of weaving history into the programme: indeed, 'programming is the historian's interpretive statement'.

From these basic definitions and ideas several essential ingredients (or evaluative criteria) can be derived for planning heritage events as interpretive tools:

1   Heritage events reveal meanings (e.g., the values, traditions and sense of place of the community).
2   They reveal interrelationships (e.g., between people and the environment, between social and cultural groups).
3   They provide direct contact with important heritage objects, sites, places or recreated historical events and ways of life.
4   They must be 'alive', or truly 'special' events, which require a programme and ambience capable of stimulating not only intellectual curiosity but also emotions.
5   They allow residents and visitors (i.e. tourists) to participate in the living community.
6   They are authentic in reflecting community values and accurately portraying historic events or objects.

Although authenticity is an essential ingredient of heritage and community interpretation, there are limits which apply to such events. As noted by Rumble (1989), entertainment is a major component of festivals and special events, and this attraction has to be balanced against authenticity. Rumble said 'almost any interpretation has to be selective and incomplete' and this is particularly true of events. Uzzell (1989) provides a related insight, advocating events as 'hot interpretation'. Noting that living history groups abound in Great Britain, often putting on battle re-enactments, he argued that interpretation sometimes 'has to be shocking, moving and provide a cathartic experience'. No matter how authentic are the costumes and activities, 'visitors' perceptions will always be influenced by their present-day attitudes and values'.

'Hot interpretation' is not without its critics. Millar (1989) asked: 'Does the future for heritage interpretation lie in the gloss of superficial entertainment in the form of the special event?' Instead of bland living history or war re-enactments, Millar advocates 'community interpretation' which will avoid bogus history and pandering to nostalgia. Community interpretation would involve multi-purpose heritage sites which function as tourist attractions, become a focus of community identity, provide opportunities for formal and informal education and act as economic catalysts.

A typology of heritage events

Table 21.1 shows a range of events and their interpretive roles, from the most authentic, and usually site-specific, to the most general community festival. Some generic examples are given for each type, and their interpretive roles are noted. This chart could be easily expanded to also note the marketing value of events, but that is a different topic.

Table 21.1 Types of heritage events and their roles in interpreting the community

Types of event	Examples	Roles
Authentic re-creations at heritage sites	Battles Holiday celebrations Demonstrations of seasonal work (e.g., harvests)	Integral part of 'living history' Authentic in theme and relationship to the site Showcases the community's past
Unrelated events at heritage sites (the heritage site as an event backdrop)	Antique shows Themed parties Exhibitions, ethnic and multi-cultural festivals	Fosters site–community links Identifies the site as part of the living, changing community
Off-site events produced by heritage agencies	Travelling 'living history' Events produced on request	Takes specific interpretation events to the community Demonstrates relevance of the site or agency
Community festivals and celebrations	Specific elements of community-wide heritage or non-heritage events	Links fostered between heritage agencies/sites Skills of interpreters applied to event programming Involves the entire community in interpretation Stresses the living community

From the figure, interpreters and other event planners can determine common interests and appropriate roles. For example, the interpreter might desire the participation of certain community groups in producing an on-site, living history event. Community leaders might call for the participation of heritage agencies and interpreters in producing a very general community celebration. The heritage site is seen as one part of the community, with important roles to play in bringing the community's heritage alive. Interpretation expertise, and the assets of heritage sites, should be made available to external events. In this way, interpreting the community is a partnership between specific heritage resources and the community as a whole.

Each of the four types of heritage events present unique issues and challenges. At many heritage sites the visitor is entertained and simultaneously educated about history and the site's restoration through authentic re-creations. Standard living history techniques, including special events which go beyond the daily interpretive programme, add colour and excitement. Colonial Williamsburg, Virginia, is one of the best-known sites in which living history is both instructive and fun. However, these events do not interpret the living community within which the site operates; they are often disconnected from contemporary reality.

Sometimes unrelated events are held at heritage sites, tangibly connecting the site to the community. An example is the holding of an antique car rally at a pioneer village. There is perhaps a dubious link with the period or theme of the site, but in the public's perception the two may be quite compatible.

Any number of examples can be given of good heritage events, but it is not easy to find examples of community-wide heritage events produced by heritage agencies – this is an area deserving increased attention. Modest examples might include a travelling 'living history' show or exhibition, while more ambitious agencies could create major themed festivals. The potential roles of heritage agencies and interpreters in community festivals must be better defined through practice and evaluation.

Turning to general community festivals and celebrations, a fascinating example is that of Chemainus, British Columbia where the community interprets its heritage through wall murals. This amazingly successful innovation is being copied in many other communities, sometimes in conjunction with an annual festival. Murals, and other forms of art or artefacts, do require some interpretation, if only in the form of signs or guidebooks. A festival shaped around such conspicuous objects is an interpretive tool, drawing attention to the objects and the living community, bringing hosts and guests into contact, facilitating residents' involvement and pride, and also generating revenue.

A planning framework for heritage events

Table 21.2 presents a framework that can be used to help plan, programme and evaluate authentic heritage events which interpret the host community. While planning methods are beyond the scope of this chapter, the recommended process should be considered in light of the issues and challenges described above. Other pertinent sources to use in planning heritage events include: Peart (1979) on goals and styles of interpretation; Getz (1991) on theming; Christensen (1990) on learning modalities; Field and Wagar (1984) on evaluation.

Conclusions

One of the great themes in the tourism literature is that tourists tend to destroy the very things that attract them. This applies to natural and cultural landscapes, both of which are sensitive to commercialization and 'erosion'. Traditional festivals and special events are particularly susceptible to commercialization as tourists will pay highly for all forms of entertainment. Nevertheless, the weight of evidence found in the literature suggests that tourism need not destroy traditional meanings, and that cultural preservation or reinvigoration can actually derive from the incentives offered by modern tourism. Furthermore, tourists can hardly be blamed for the underlying forces that have changed the earth, bringing traditional cultures to abrupt contact with destructive social and economic forces. Tourism, in most cases, is a side product of those powerful factors: population growth; economic development; mass global communications and travel technology.

Events produced for the explicit purpose of being 'consumed', either by residents or tourists, are more common. They are created and sustained for multiple goals – of the organizers, the grant-givers, sponsors, volunteers and increasingly, tourist organizations. Authenticity means something different for traditional and created events. It has been argued that the degree of community participation and support is a measure of authenticity for most special events.

The pyramidal model presented in this chapter attempts to inter-relate three key perspectives on festival and event authenticity. All festivals and special events contain cultural meaning, ranging from traditional, uncontaminated rituals and celebrations to mass sporting events like the Superbowl. Using the broad category of 'heritage events' to illustrate concepts, it was shown that they can be used to interpret living, changing communities, as well as the relics of the past.

Table 21.2 Framework for planning, programming and evaluating authentic heritage events

Goals
   Interpreting the community; education
   Managing heritage sites and resources
   Economic development; tourism
   Community development
   Marketing of heritage sites
   Revenue generation
   Fostering site–community links
   Fostering links among heritage sites/agencies
Heritage resource evaluation
   History of the community
   Heritage sites and objects
   Possible themes
Determine theme and type of event
   Historical re-enactment
   Commemoration
   Ethnic or multi-cultural; folkways
   Arts and entertainment (contemporary)
   Recreational or competitive sport and play
   Shows and exhibitions; sales
   Parades
Organization
   Type of organizing body (new or existing)
   Roles of heritage agencies and interpreters
   Planning the event
   Marketing the event
   Raising funds (e.g., grants; sponsors; sales; events)
The programme and production
   Essential services (access; communications; safety; health; information;
      special visitor services; food and beverages)
   Elements of style: spectacle; games; belonging and sharing; entertainment;
      ritual and ceremony
   Designing and managing the setting(s)
   Manifestation of the theme (through name, logo, mascots, design, activities,
      attractions, food, beverages, souvenirs etc.)
   Learning modalities and interpretive mechanisms
Evaluation
   On-site evaluation and problem-solving
   Attainment of goals
   Efficient use of resources
   Unanticipated and external impacts
   Conflict resolution
   Re-statement of goals and programme, if appropriate

Guidelines for ensuring authenticity

Given that the essence of authenticity is its cultural meaning, the bottom line must be that host communities determine what is meaningful to them. In this sense, authenticity is not so much the ritual, games, spectacle or celebration itself as it is the degree to which these components have been manufactured, modified or exploited just for tourists, the media or financial success. In other words, has the event any cultural meaning for the host community and the participants, or is it merely a commodity to be sold? Do the hosts and performers think of the event as having importance in their lives, or are they cynically involved in a tourist rip-off? Will people come to accept, over time, that the invented festival is an important part of their cultural life?

Guidelines have been established for successful community-based tourism (e.g., Cooke, 1982), and Sofield (1991) has proposed criteria for ensuring authenticity in cultural events. To these we should add the criteria discussed earlier for planning heritage events. The conclusion is that authenticity of festivals and events will be maximized when they:

1 Reflect indigenous themes; reveal meanings about values, traditions and sense of place.
2 Reveal interrelationships between people, and people and the environment.
3 Are controlled by the host community and protected against potentially damaging external influences; appropriate organizations and decision-making processes are in place.
4 Are valued and well attended by residents.
5 Stimulate both emotional and intellectual curiosity.
6 Offer culturally genuine goods and performances, such as local foods, costumes, dances, crafts; provide direct contact with important heritage objects, sites, events or ways of life.
7 Do not exploit tourists through profit maximization at the expense of quality; commercial goals are made to fit cultural goals.
8 Allow hosts and guests to mingle and to participate in the living community.
9 Accurately portray historical events or objects.

From the tourism perspective, the real issue is maximizing visitor satisfaction, with the realization that events popular with the host community are likely to be more pleasing, and that authentic cultural performances, settings, food and merchandise will be enduring attractions.

One important lesson stated by Lavenda (1991) is that 'When festivals are effective, it is because they offer multiple meanings to individuals and to the figurations that those individuals form'. So when debating what is or is not 'authentic', no consensus is likely. Rather, one's perspective and ways of evaluating 'meanings' come into play.

Tourist organizations should be sensitive to the desires of cultural groups who do not want to be exploited as tourist attractions, or do not want pseudo-events put on for tourists. Not all festivals and events should be viewed as tourism resources – the real event tourism resource is people, and the community must be given the right to decide for itself.

References

Binks, G. (1989) Interpreters in the community: a discussion paper. In *Heritage Interpretation*, Vol. 1 (ed. D. Uzzell), Belhaven Press, London Ch. 21, p. 191

Boorstin, D. (1961) *The Image: a Guide to Pseudo Events in America*, Harper and Row, New York

Buck, R. (1977) Making good business better: a second look at staged tourist attractions. *Journal of Travel Research*, **15**(3), 30–2

Buck, R. (1978) Boundary maintenance revisited: tourist experience in an old order Amish community. *Rural Sociology*, **43**(2), 221–34

Cherem, G. (1988) Interpretation as the vortex: tourism based on heritage experiences. In *Interpretation and Tourism, Ottawa/88*, Proceedings of a Conference on Heritage Interpretation, pp. 5, 37

Christensen, J. (1990) Interpretation can target everyone. *Legacy*, **1**(1), 11–15

Cohen, E. (1979) Rethinking the sociology of tourism. *Annals of Tourism Research*, **6**(1), 18–35

Cohen, E. (1988) Authenticity and commoditization in tourism. *Annals of Tourism Research*, **15**(1), 371–86

Cooke, K. (1982) Guidelines for socially appropriate tourism development in British Columbia. *Journal of Travel Research*, **21**(1), 22–8

Falassi, A. (ed.) (1987) *Time Out of Time: Essays on the Festival*, University of New Mexico Press, Albuquerque

Field, D. and Wagar, J. (1984) Visitor groups and interpretation in parks and other outdoor leisure settings. In *On Interpretation: Sociology for Interpreters of Natural and Cultural History* (G. Machlis and D. Field, eds), Oregon State University Press, Corvallis

Getz, D. (1991) *Festivals, Special Events, and Tourism*, Van Nostrand Reinhold, New York

Greenwood, D. (1989) Culture by the pound: an anthropological perspective on tourism as cultural commoditization. In *Hosts and Quests: the Anthropology of Tourism*, 2nd edn (V. Smith, ed.), University of Pennsylvania Press, Philadelphia, pp. 171–85

Lavenda, R. (1991) Community festivals, paradox, and the manipulation of uncertainty. *Play and Culture*, **4**, 153–68

MacAloon, J. (1984) *Rite, Drama, Festival, Spectacle: Rehearsals Towards a Theory of Cultural Performances*, Institute for the Study of Human Issues, Philadelphia

MacCannell, D. (1976) *The Tourist: a New Theory of the Leisure Class*, Schocken Books, New York

McDaniel, G. (1986) Folklife festivals: history as entertainment and education. In *Public History: an Introduction* (B. Howe and E. Kemp, eds), R. Kreuger Publishing Co, Malabar, Fla, p. 279

Macnow, G. (1989) Cities get into the game, *Nation's Business*, November, p. 48

Manning, F. (ed.) (1983) *The Celebration of Society: Perspectives on Contemporary Cultural Performance*, Bowling Green Popular Press; Bowling Green, Ky

Millar, S. (1989) Heritage management for heritage tourism. *Tourism Management*, 10(1), 9–14

Moscardo, G. and Pearce, P. (1986) Historic theme parks, an Australian experience in authenticity. *Annals of Tourism Research*, **13**(3), 467–79

Pearce, P. (1982) *The Social Psychology of Tourist Behaviour*, Pergamon Press, Oxford

Peart, B. (1979) An application of the Foley–Keith objectives framework to interpretation activities, other than in national parks or related federal reserves. In *Papers of the Seventh National Conference of Interpretation Canada*

Redfoot, D. (1984) Touristic authenticity, touristic angst, and modern reality. *Qualitative Sociology*, **7**(4), 291–309

Rumble, P. (1989) Interpreting the built and historic environment. In *Heritage Interpretation*, Vol. 1 (D. Uzzell, ed.), Belhaven Press, London, ch. 3, p. 30

Sofield, T. (1991) Sustainable ethnic tourism in the south Pacific: some principles, *Journal of Tourism Studies*, **2**(1), 56–71

Tilden, F. (1977) *Interpreting Our Heritage*, 3rd edn, University of North Carolina Press, Chapel Hill, p. 8

Uzzell, D. (1989) The hot interpretation of war and conflict. In *Heritage Interpretation*, Vol. 1 (D. Uzzell, ed.), Belhaven Press, London, ch. 4, p. 46

Vallee, P. (1987) Authenticity as a Factor in Segmenting the Canadian Travel Market; Master's thesis, Department of Recreation and Leisure Studies, University of Waterloo, p. 27

22 Emerging issues in tourism education

Frank M. Go

We are entering an Age of Unreason, when the future, in so many areas, is there to be shaped, by us and for us; a time when the only prediction that will hold true is that no predictions will hold true; a time, therefore, for bold imaginings in private life as well as public, for thinking the unlikely and doing the unreasonable.

Charles Handy (1989), *The Age of Unreason*

The present shift, especially in the industrialized countries, from a resource-based and labour-intensive economy to one that is knowledge-intensive rigorously challenges the present acting and thinking in the tourism field. Traditionally, tourism-related services have been classified as convenience services, as opposed to knowledge services (Tettero and Viehoff, 1990). But as organizations prepare for the global economy and resources are being shifted out of low-wage activities into higher value-added activities where advanced technology, knowledge and service provide a competitive edge, the continued prosperity of tourism will depend largely on well-educated human talent – people who are able to think, weigh and judge critical issues in addition to providing quality service know-how on the strategic and operational level respectively (Gronroos, 1989).

The future success of tourism on the national level may depend largely on whether or not each country is 'prepared to educate not only tourism employees, but also tourists and the population of tourist receiving areas so as to impart an adequate level of general culture and etiquette which is essential for all concerned in this wide-ranging and rapidly growing sector' (World Tourism Organization, 1987). However, it seems that most countries and the educational institutions within these countries are not up to the challenge because they face persistent problems in tourism education (Lavery, 1989).

The problems within the educational system are complicated because tourism businesses in general have failed to make the necessary skill investments (EIESP, 1991) and pay the higher wages required to get the necessary human talent to employ new technologies. On a geographical level, tourist destinations have largely lacked the leadership to shape tourism as an integral element of an economic and sustainable development strategy. Optimal tourism development and positive relationships between the travel industry interests, visitors and host communities are essential, but are not often accomplished. There is a critical need to encourage communities to learn the leadership skills necessary to develop and manage special places, including natural, historic, cultural and folkloric settings. The long-term aim of educational efforts should be to shape growth in host communities through sustainable tourism that not only raises the standard of living but also improves the quality of life for local residents in destination areas.

Tourism may be defined as the moving of individuals and groups from one geographic location to another for pleasure and/or business purposes on a temporary basis, the catering to the needs of travellers while en route and at the destination, and the economic, socio-cultural and ecological impacts both travellers and the industry have on the destination area. This definition implies that tourism should be viewed as (a) an industry comprised of attractions, transportation, facilities/ services, and information and promotion (Gunn, 1988); (b) a social act in that it allows people to express themselves while travelling for business and leisure; and (c) a reflection of local cultural expression, identity and social composition. In this regard tourism can play an important part in the broader environmental planning and concern for environmental quality, especially on the local level (Ashworth, 1991).

In this chapter tourism education is viewed from a management perspective due to the author's background and is regarded as the intellectual development of a person through, for example, literacy, foreign languages, computational skills, knowledge of countries and cultures without particular concern for specific jobs or responsibilities. In contrast, training is the process of bringing a person to an agreed standard of skills proficiency through instruction.

As tourism is still a largely unrecognized industry, whose economic importance is difficult to measure (and therefore frequently underestimated), it is a significant challenge to obtain priority for tourism education on the national level. A small cadre primarily representing academia and government have been attempting to find a place for tourism education on the public agenda. Though in certain jurisdictions these individuals have been extremely successful, the overall picture shows a lack of significant support and leadership for tourism education. In a constantly changing environment, however, two vital members of this environment, educational institutions and the business sector, will have to alter this picture by cooperating to prepare learners for imaginative leadership roles in business and society both domestically and globally.

There is a growing realization in both industry and government circles that education holds the key to unlocking potential economic growth opportunities to achieve a competitive advantage in the tourism sector. In addition, there is an emerging recognition that competitive advantage begins in the classroom. Hence the present argument is that the practice and theory of tourism are to a great extent interrelated, and that tourism education offers great potential to make a significant contribution towards the creation of value-added activities in the tourism sector and the sustenance of its competitive advantage.

The evolution of tourism education

What abilities and concepts should a programme of tourism education impart? Educators have to be able to answer that perennial question in new ways as the tourism field and the study of tourism evolve.

Shifting markets and world-class competition require destination organizations and tourism businesses to change. As adapting to change requires more flexible decision-making and the search for solutions beyond what organizations already know through learning, educators have to question whether the present framework they have developed will ensure the success of tourism education in the 1990s and into the third millenium.

Review and preview

The scanning of issues is an exercise that requires a forward orientation. But before we focus on the future, it is useful to look back to gain a perspective on the evolution of tourism education.

Historically, tourism thinking has gone through two phases and has recently entered into a third (D'Amore, 1985). In contemporary times tourism research has been conducted by scholars such as Hunziker and Krapf from Switzerland in the 1940s. Among Swiss social scientists there seemed to have been an awareness of the need to extend the tourism research horizon (Kaspar, 1989).

Among the early British writers on tourism were Ogilvie, Norval and Lickorish and Kershaw. But it took until the 1970s before Anglo-American academics began to map the uncharted waters of tourism studies in earnest. For instance, Medlik and Burkart, who were affiliated with the University of Surrey, took the lead in Britain while Clare Gunn of Texas A&M University and Robert McIntosh of Michigan State University were among the early pioneers of tourism education in the United States of America.

Like the great explorers of centuries gone by, the early tourism educators had to cope with significant challenges, largely because: (1) 'in nearly all cases [programmes were] developed as a result of academic enterprise rather than industrial demand', and (2) 'certain segments of the tourism industry seemed to accept specific academic qualifications' (Christie-Mill, 1979: 58). These findings, which are based on an analysis of Lawson's comparative study *Teaching Tourism: Education and Training in Western Europe* (1974), serve as an important reminder that tourism education in the 1970s and 1980s was primarily educator-driven. Furthermore, Lawson's comparative analysis of newly introduced tourism courses in Western Europe paid considerable attention to the ongoing concern expressed by tourism educators for highly pragmatic matters, particularly the career placement of students and tourism career path development.

The second phase of tourism education began in the early 1980s when a review of the state-of-the-art of the rapidly expanding field of tourism education co-edited by Jafari and Ritchie (1981) shifted the focus of tourism education from the pragmatic to the academic level. By expanding the scope of tourism education, Jafari and Ritchie set the stage for further enquiry into the field of tourism education and, increasingly, research. With their review Jafari and Ritchie attempted in particular to reach the following objectives:

1 To place tourism in a broader context and identify major concerns prior to defining tourism education and curriculum content.
2 To examine alternative disciplinary approaches to the study of tourism.
3 To focus on a number of critical issues in tourism education.

Among the key observations Jafari and Ritchie made regarding the gaps in tourism research which they perceived to be both weaknesses and opportunities were:

- The lack of empirical research on which to base the design of tourism curricula.
- The conceptualization and design of tourism courses and programmes by individual educators in relative isolation as opposed to groups of educators representing various educational institutions.
- The highly vocational nature of the manuscripts submitted for publication (Jafari and Ritchie, 1981) received from North American sources, compared to other geographical regions such as Europe where tourism 'is being conceptualized in much broader terms'.
- The emergence of tourism as an interdisciplinary field of studies.

The emerging emphasis on tourism research in the 1980s was particularly appropriate in that it was a decade of significant change, especially in terms of technological advancement and industrial restructuring.

In the early 1990s we reached a new watershed in the evolution of tourism education. It has been brought about by the changes in both exogenous variables and those endogenous to the profession. Current geo-political events in combination with advancing technology and altering demographics are producing a period of discontinuous change (Handy, 1989). Though there is uncertainty as to what the implications may be for the development of human resources within organizations, in general it seems certain that the changes that are taking place will radically affect the workplace and therefore tourism education. Perhaps tourism educators have come to a crossroads. They can choose to continue the path along which they have come and teach what they have taught in the past or they can explore the second path leading them into a new direction.

It is the mandate of educators to serve, particularly to conduct research, to teach students new ideas and to be visionaries of the tourism phenomenon. Are tourism educators making a genuine contribution by drawing the attention of their students and tourism industry practitioners away from tools and techniques and towards discussion, debate and reflection on the critical issues? Or do they emphasize the same techniques and tools today as fifteen years ago? Are students sufficiently challenged to broaden their horizons? Or do they get a rather ethnocentric education which will be of little use in the global village wherein their career will unfold?

In the current dynamic environment and based on the discussion thus far an important question arises, namely: what might be the role of tourism education and specifically of individual tourism educators not only in responding to emerging critical tourism issues but in helping to shape them? The foundation for determining what knowledge learners need is to understand the society and in particular the industry educators are preparing them for.

External factors

The tourism phenomenon is being transformed by a variety of global issues. These global issues were identified in the Policy Forum Report based on a three-day First International Assembly of Tourism Policy Experts which attracted eighty tourism officials from around the world and was held at the George Washington University in November, 1990 (Ritchie, 1991). The critical issues are concerned with the relationship of tourism's industry-wide prosperity and survival to the broader well-being of society. This approach stands in contrast to the concern of tourism

as a self-sustaining industry with a tendency to react to market forces
and trends for profit and survival.

Social change

The physical environment is taking centre stage in tourism development
and management. As our natural resources comprise the basic tourism
product, the tourism industry must be pro-active in ensuring the international preservation and restoration of quality environments. Within
this context, financially burdened countries such as Brazil are trading
their international debt for land to be held as natural preserves.

From the perspective of the student of tourism the change to a greater
concern for the physical environment requires a fundamental shift in
thinking from the stimulation of volume in terms of tourist arrivals to
value-creating processes that include a greater concern for the preservation
of nature and the promotion of cultural diversity.

A broad range of social and economic policies have to be implemented
to accommodate the tourism education needs of developing countries
(Theuns and Go, 1992). Education programmes can play a crucial role in
the harmonization of environmental protection and help to bring about
greater social equality in the developing countries.

Globalization

The shift from economic dominance by the United States to a world in
which economic power is more widely spread has significant implications for students of tourism, in that 'we can more easily hope to recognize
truth coming from many sources' (Hofstede, 1983). In particular, it should
further the realization that the management of tourism facilities is deeply
embedded in culture. Or, to quote Drucker (1989): 'What managers do in
[West] Germany, in the United Kingdom, in the United States, in Japan,
or in Brazil is exactly the same. How they do it is different.'

The growing significance of the multi-cultural market and workplace
contributes to the emerging need for the effective education of cross-
cultural communication. At present, most tourism courses and programmes have an ethnocentric character, that is, they take the study of
domestic tourism and give it an international dimension with the least
possible change. If today's student is to become the effective tourism
industry practitioner of tomorrow, educators cannot be blind to the idea
that the management and organizing of tourism 'are culturally dependent'
(Hofstede, 1983). It is therefore essential that students are exposed to the
subject of intercultural communication in order to understand and motivate both individuals and groups, from another culture than their own.

Technology

The advancement of technology, especially the application of new information and decision technologies, has changed the nature of competition
in all industries. As a result of new information technologies, work is
becoming increasingly detached from place, operations from their central
headquarters. Telecommunication networks, spanning the globe with
bursts of data speeding thousands of kilometres, mean the break-up of
old geographic habits and locations. Bell (1988) observes 'a change of
extraordinary historical and sociological importance – the change in the
nature of markets from places to networks'. The perspective of tourism
as a 'vast, complex network of businesses engaged in lodging, transportation, feeding and entertainment of the traveller' (EIESP, 1991) and the
opportunities it offers to gain competitive advantage through social innovation will require tourism students and industry practitioners to extend
their horizons well beyond the traditional trade channels of distribution.

Students and programmes

The number of students enrolling in tourism courses – on the university
level, on the college level within, for example, business schools, and on
the vocational training level, focused on a narrow definition of tourism
and hospitality – continues to expand internationally. In Britain, for example, the growth in the tourism education and training sector has been
particularly impressive – there were twenty-five tourism degree courses
and programmes in Britain in 1990; there were none in 1985. Though it
must be gratifying to educators that tourism studies are in demand, with
a growing number of students in many countries, the growth of tourism
programmes raises serious concern, especially when one considers that
there is a lack of a clear career path for new entrants and an urgent need
to relate the annual output of students seeking careers to tourism industry
manpower requirements (Lavery, 1989).

The recent introduction and promotion of tourism competence-based
qualifications in Britain (Guerrier, 1991) and accreditation and certification in North America is a logical development in education in capitalistic
societies. But regardless of their possible validity in addressing quality of
service problems in industry, these schemes should be viewed as the
'acting' part that supplements the 'thinking' component of a solid tourism
curriculum. Specifically, the conventional tourism curriculum tends to
emphasize 'acting' as opposed to 'thinking'. Though the acting versus
thinking debate among educators continues, it is reasonable to expect
that credible tourism curricula should find an appropriate balance between
practice and theory.

Research and scholarship

A reading of the literature, and conversations with other tourism educators, suggest that the study of tourism has achieved a certain amount of intellectual maturity, and, even become 'legitimate' (Ritchie, 1988). One sign of this is that graduate tourism and hospitality programmes are producing a new generation of PhD holders who in many cases have been exposed in their studies to an interdisciplinary approach of examining tourism, as opposed to a unidisciplinary approach. Another is that the subject of tourism has begun to attract the attention of scholars whose traditional research did not include tourism as a research subject. A third is that the quantity and (in many instances) the quality of scholarly publications in tourism and hospitality journals has both increased and been improved. There is at present an impressive list of scholarly journals in tourism and hospitality studies that are published, almost exclusively, in the United States of America and Britain.

Faculty and staff development

The shortage of experienced tourism educators makes it an imperative to pay significant attention to the continuous development of faculty and staff. In instances where the staff development concerns faculty members who have a background in an area or discipline other than tourism, there may be a need to provide individuals with insights of industry sectors or the tourism industry at large. Opportunities for staff development of this sort are offered by the regular (co)sponsorship of seminars and conferences that focus on tourism, or sectors of the industry, by trade associations and non-governmental organizations, including the International Hotel Association, Pacific Asia Travel Association, World Travel and Tourism Council, and World Tourism Organization.

Several forums provide tourism educators with the opportunity to keep abreast of developments in education and research in relation to the tourism and hospitality fields, including the Council of Hotel, Restaurant, and Institutional Educators, International Association of Scientific Experts of Tourism, and the World Association for Tourism Training.

On the tertiary level a number of institutions have begun to focus on the teaching of tourism both by conducting research and (co)sponsoring courses and conferences on the subject. For example, the University of Surrey in cooperation with the University of Calgary offered a unique international forum specifically designed and organized by tourism educators for tourism educators, researchers, trainers and other professionals both from the private and public sectors to debate education and human resource issues in the broadest sense of the word. The first tourism education conference, entitled 'Tourism Teaching in the 1990s', was international in scope and hosted by the University of Surrey, Guildford, UK in July, 1988. This conference attracted more than 100 delegates from twenty-seven different countries and was acclaimed as a milestone in the maturing of tourism education (Ritchie, 1988). The aim of the New Horizons Conference, held at the University of Calgary, Alberta, Canada in 1991, was to explore and prioritize issues, ideas and initiatives in tourism education. Though the New Horizons Conference built on the findings that emerged from the University of Surrey forum in 1988, its focus was somewhat different in that it paid special attention to examining the cascading effects of the 'issues-chain', that is how global issues affect national strategies and in turn how public policy in particular sets the stage for the development (or the lack thereof) of tourism education and training (Go, 1991).

Education as a value-creating process

The relationship between the study and practice of tourism is considerable, in that as Blank (1989) has observed: 'all tourism resources are the result of human development'. At the same time it should be observed that in the pursuit of excellence in tourism education there is no sure-fire recipe for success. But in a business environment characterized by more aggressive global competition and technological change, this is no less true for tourism industry practitioners. Rarely in seeking to identify the reasons for excellence in the tourism industry is one able to find a single common denominator. Excellence is sometimes based on proprietary electronic tools such as SABRE, American Airline's reservation system, which 'eventually became a computerized reservation system (CRS)', (Hopper, 1990) and eventually with other such leading systems transformed marketing and distribution in the tourism industry. Sometimes excellence is based on the ability to render superb service on a consistent basis, as is the case in the Disney theme parks; sometimes on the economies of scale derived from mergers and takeovers, as for example in the hotel industry.

During the 1980s the tourism industry exploited mergers and acquisitions, corporate diversification and other sources to the fullest. In the 1990s, however, conditions have changed significantly because with across-the-board deregulations, a boom in new technologies and global competition, a company's technological or financial edge can be lost overnight.

The dual forces of technology and globalization will raise the competency demanded by jobs on all levels in the tourism industry and turn effective learning into a competitive necessity. Within this context a heightened focus on human resources and education in particular will emerge as a source of competitiveness. In the 1990s and into the twenty-first century every organization involved in tourism, including corporations, government, educational institutions and non-government agencies, has to make substantial efforts to apply the concept of continuous improvement to the learning process to ensure the competitiveness of tourism, both as an economic sector and a field of employment. Though the tourism industry has been considered a 'low-tech' as opposed to a 'high-tech' sector of the economy, it is more and more likely that making its product through the application of a high-tech process will lead to competitiveness. For example, the application of computerized reservation systems and yield management capabilities allow certain tourism corporations to apply sophisticated price discrimination. The tourism corporations that are able to apply the new technology are effectively creating the expertise that enables them to force corporations that may be better tourism operators out of business.

Within the competitive tourism industry the weakest link within the service delivery system, comprised of customers, employees and the (business) organization, has been the quality of workers which tourism businesses are able to recruit, train and retain. As the acquisition of value-added skills commences in the classroom, the attempt to satisfy buyers should be perceived as much a problem for educators as for practitioners. Within this context it is the responsibility of educators and managers respectively to allow students and workers 'to grow and develop as needs and opportunities change' (Drucker, 1989). This is especially the case if one recognizes the notion that shortcomings in education can result in a regression of a nation's international competitiveness (Hayes and Abernathy, 1980). Therefore, educators have an obligation to ensure that tourism education research and training will contribute to the competitiveness of tourism corporations and the standard of living of the host society.

How can tourism educators respond to their mandate? By providing and disseminating an interdisciplinary knowledge base that leads to a better understanding of tourism and by making two assumptions as a basis for the unfolding of their initiatives, namely that: (1) the conventional ways of education may possibly limit individual growth and initiative and hence the overall effectiveness of the educational system; and (2) educators may have to substantially re-think the way in which they organize the learning process and the way in which students learn.

Emerging tourism education issues

So much for the argument that the practice and theory of tourism are interrelated and that tourism education holds the potential to contribute in a significant manner to the development of value-added activities in the tourism industry. If the developments that have been discussed in this chapter to some extent resemble reality, both in terms of tourism practice and tourism thinking, then there should be both opportunities and challenges for individual tourism educators and tourism education as a field of study.

Opportunities

The opportunities for the expansion of tourism education stem in particular from the scale of tourism growth, which will place substantial pressure on the private and public sectors to provide the appropriate infrastructure, facilities and human resources to deliver the quality service required by visitors. By extension, and because tourism is an industry requiring talent with knowledge, technical and attitudinal strengths, there is likely to be considerable pressure on tourism curricula and their output – from the secondary school to the PhD level, in all categories, and in every host country. Furthermore, tourism has to be and should remain, competitive with other industries and be perceived as a responsible sector which provides for sustainable industry development and a balanced approach to economic and environmental issues. To enhance competitiveness and responsible development in tourism simultaneously requires solutions. The existing and evolving body of knowledge offers educators great opportunities to contribute substantially – for example: to (a) improve the quality of service; (b) eliminate the many travel barriers still found in international tourism; and develop the ability to (c) strike a balance between the expansion of tourism and respect for the environment.

Challenges

In order to determine the major challenges currently facing tourism educators the author surveyed the delegates of the New Horizons Conference held in Calgary in 1991. The survey was designed to solicit views from educators, as well as from senior managers in tourism organizations. The respondents were asked to prioritize the issues they identified in a broad way. A sample of seventy-two New Horizons Conference delegates completed the questionnaire. They identified key issues that were highly likely to influence changes in the workforce, in the industrialized countries in the next fifteen years, that in turn would be highly likely to affect tourism education. The responses were prioritized as shown in Table 22.1.

Perhaps not surprisingly the survey findings reveal the significant importance of the development of workers and managers in relation to

Table 22.1 The relative significance of selected trends on the future workforce in industrialized countries

• A strong and competitive national economy depends on the appropriate development of worker and managerial talents through education and training	93.5%
• The ability to manage complexity will require the re-design of many jobs to include computer-based tasks and new requirements for education	93.4%
• Over the next two decades a growing number of women will be counted among the 15–25 people in each of the largest organizations who 'run the show'	93.4%
• Corporate mergers and acquisitions will continue with more international actors involved	85.5%
• The workforce in the industrialized nations faces wrenching changes in its structure and composition that will radically alter how employers recruit, hire, manage and hold on to their staff	82.9%
• Pedagogical methods are likely to change to reflect the growing understanding among educators/trainers of the learning process	82.9%
• Sweeping political and economic changes will alter market basics	78.9%
• Training and education will increasingly be perceived as the key to growth of the travel and tourism industry and therefore become a major public agenda item	77.7%
• Corporations are likely to reach deeper into the educational system to influence the quality of its supply of workers	72.4%
• There is a growing mismatch between the literacy and other skills workers possess and the requirements of tomorrow's jobs.	51.3%

Percentages indicate the extent to which respondents 'Fully agree' or 'Agree somewhat' with the identified trends.

education and training. Furthermore, it is interesting to note that a technology issue (computers in the workplace) and a social issue (the ascending power of women in organizations) were perceived to be equally important. The corporate restructuring and subsequent changes in the workforce structure and composition were seen to have implications with regard to the further internationalization of tourism and human resource management respectively.

Though specific educational issues were not perceived to be among the top five most important issues, the findings of the survey demonstrate the belief of respondents that tourism education will become more important both as a political agenda item and in commercial terms in that corporations may be expected to intervene in education to boost the quality of its supply of workers. There seems to be a consensus among respondents that the global nature of tourism has made it mandatory to provide the tourism student with an international perspective.

Considering the limited amount of resources, how can educators make tourism education programmes more global while simultaneously sensitizing students to national differences?

Defining value-added skills

The theme of 'doing more with less' in education seems to be recurring in the literature and raises the question, what emphasis should be given to the development of the various personal characteristics and the value-added skills of students enrolled in tourism courses and programmes? The feedback from the respondents (Table 22.2) of the New Horizons Conference survey suggests that tourism curricula should focus on the following learning clusters:

1 *Management skills.* Developing creative problem skills in conjunction with the development of analytical, decision-making, planning and organizational, team play abilities, leadership skills and willingness to change were perceived by the respondents as important attributes within the curriculum. This cluster of management skills within the tourism curriculum may offer the potential to link tourism education with corporate strategy practice. This may be achieved for example by writing and using case studies to learn in particular how to build organizational capability through people in order to improve the quality of service delivery.

2 *Emphasizing ethics.* The study of ethics is relevant in the tourism curriculum because there are many potential conflicts between the economic performance of organizations that have an involvement in the tourism sector and their social performance in relation to, for example, the host community's quality of life, employees' working conditions, and consumer advertising. Students enrolled in tourism courses should be aware of all the possible consequences of their future decisions from an ethical perspective. Almanza (1991) reported that students showed extreme interest 'in ethical issues and would like to take a class in ethics'. Hence tourism educators should consider incorporating ethics across all functional areas of the curriculum, if they have not already done so.

3 *Providing experiential learning opportunities.* The respondents also seem to recognize that effective tourism education means providing learning opportunities and developing the commitment to ongoing learning in students.

> Learning is about providing the framework for further learning. The various methods of learning (full-time, part-time and distance learning) all have a role to play; as do the various means of learning – between

Table 22.2   The emphasis that should be given to the development of various skills and personal characteristics in tourism curricula

• Effective communications	97.4%
• International perspective (including sensitivity to national differences)	94.7%
• Creative problem-solving skills	94.5%
• Analytical	93.9%
• Decision-making	93.3%
• Planning/organizing	88.8%
• Team play	88.7%
• Leadership skills	87.5%
• Willingness to change	87.1%
• Initiative	85.1%
• Ethics	84.9%
• Socio-cultural aspects of tourism	83.7%
• Commitment to ongoing learning	77.1%
• Computer skills	74.3%
• Experiential learning skills	73.7%
• Entrepreneurship (risk-taking)	71.2%
• Foreign language skills	69.4%
• World and tourism geography	63.0%

This table identifies the percentage of respondents who are of the opinion that 'Much' or 'Very much' emphasis should be placed on the development of specific student skills and personal characteristics.

> students themselves, from staff, from books and other distance material, as well as reflective self-learning. (Lloyd, 1990)

Experience is an invaluable learning tool and this may in part explain the inclusion of 'experiential learning skills' which respondents ranked fifteenth. In North America, there is an increasing interest in cooperative education on the part of academic institutions, employers and the government. Three-way partnerships, between business, education and government in Britain assist students enrolled in higher education to learn about industrial practices through project-orientated courses that require effective interaction between students and business clients in the local community. Furthermore, educators can bring the 'real world' to the tourism classroom through computer applications that enable students to gain hands-on experience by using similar or the same data and analytical tools that are being used by industry practitioners.

Space does not permit that all the challenges facing tourism education can be dealt with here, but let me offer one suggestion before concluding.

If the next generation of leaders is to solve tomorrow's complex tourism problems effectively, they will have to be exposed to more than today's commonly required professional and technical skills courses. Owing to rapidly changing global conditions in particular, in conjunction with the present shortage of 'tourism talent' or human resources, Hawkins and Hunt (1988) emphasized the need for developing professional tourism education programmes in post-secondary institutions. They also stressed, however, that these professional programmes be based on basic principles, be placed in a valid conceptual context, and be interdisciplinary in nature.

Given that educators are facing critical obstacles to improve the quality of tourism education in the future, including the lack of funding, the recruitment of quality faculty members and the appropriate administration both within the programme and on campus, how can they overcome the odds? The challenges of tomorrow will require tourism educators to rethink their premises by turning conventional logic upside down, to realize that they might have to be more innovative than they presently are. Among the available options cited by Dunn (1983) are educational innovations that:

- recognize and certify experiential learning;
- consider more flexible programming;
- build more links between education and industry;
- offer in-house professional development programmes for organizations and businesses;
- make increasing use of businesses for internships, research and consultancy;
- draw on corporate human resources development specialists;
- pool resources with other educational institutions;
- use, where appropriate, mass media such as television to deliver course content.

Innovation in tourism education is most likely to be stimulated by the cross-fertilization of ideas between different academic disciplines with colleagues on and off campus and between education, industry and government. Tourism educators should start bridge building to capitalize on the opportunities for individual and collective learning and to become true partners in progress.

Conclusion

The tourism field is ill-prepared to be the world's number one industry because it has relatively few innovative thinkers, leaders and high quality education and training courses and programmes to cultivate the talent required to deal with critical issues and thereby to ensure the long-term prosperity of tourism as a part of the broader society. Educators should take trends such as the globalization of the economy, the rising importance of the physical environment, and the advancement of technology, into account to avoid aimless drift, or worse, potential irrelevance. Though there may be uncertainty about what the implications of the impending changes will be, there is a growing realization in both industry and government that better education is the key to unlocking the human resource potential to achieve and sustain a competitive advantage in tourism. To become competitive, the global tourism industry has to develop productivity and quality gains that flow from value-added work, that is, work that employs a higher degree of investment in employees' skills and knowledge. There is an emerging recognition that the development of value-added skills and knowledge required by the tourism industry begins in the classroom. It is critical that educators provide the leadership to foster the extensive collaboration between business, the government and education, because neither 'cash starved' educational institutions nor companies will be able to deliver educational and training needs effectively in isolation in the 1990s and beyond.

References

Almanza, Barbara A. (1991) Student opinions of ethics in the hospitality industry. In *New Horizons in Tourism and Hospitality Education, Training and Research* (Conference Proceedings) (ed., Robert D. Bratton, Frank M. Go, and J.R. Brent Ritchie), University of Calgary, Calgary

Ashworth, G.J. (1991) *Heritage Planning: Conservation on the Management of Urban Change*, Geo Pers, Groningen

Bell, Daniel (1988) The World in 2013. *Dialogue*, **81**(3), 3–9

Blank, Uel (1989) *The Community Tourism Industry Imperative: The Necessity, The Opportunities, Its Potential*, Venture, State College, PA, p. 101

Christie-Mill, Robert (1979) Tourism education: its development and current status, *Journal of Hospitality Education*, **3**(2), 49–62

D'Amore, Louis J. (1985) A third generation of tourism thinking towards a creative conspiracy. *Business Quarterly*, Summer, p. 6

Drucker, Peter F. (1989) *The New Realities; In Government and Politics/In Economics and Business/In Society and World View*, Harper and Row, New York, pp. 229–30

Dunn, Samuel L. (1983) The changing university, survival in the information society. *The Futurist* (August), pp. 55–60

EIESP (1991) *Education for Careers in European Travel and Tourism*, European Institute of Education and Social Policy, Paris, pp. 29, 58

Go, Frank M. (1991) Introduction to new horizons proceedings. In *New Horizons in Tourism and Hospitality Education, Training and Research* (Conference

Proceedings) (ed. Robert D. Bratton, Frank M. Go, and J.R. Brent Ritchie), University of Calgary, Calgary

Gronroos, Christian (1989) Service Management Principles. Working Paper 90: 1, Service Research Centre, University of Karlstad, Sweden

Guerrier, Yvonne (1991) Developing and assessing management competencies on undergraduate hotel and tourism degrees. In *New Horizons in Tourism and Hospitality Education, Training and Research* (Conference Proceedings) (ed. Robert D. Bratton, Frank M. Go and J.R. Brent Ritchie), University of Calgary, Calgary, pp. 171–80

Gunn, Clare A. (1988) *Tourism Planning*, 2nd edn, Taylor and Francis, New York

Handy, Charles (1989) *The Age of Unreason*, Harvard Business School Press, Boston, Mass.

Hawkins, Donald E. and Hunt, John D. (1988) Travel and tourism professional education. *Hospitality and Tourism Educator*, **1**(1), 8–14

Hayes, Robert H. and Abernathy, William J. (1980) Managing our way to economic decline. *Harvard Business Review*, **58**(4), 67–76

Hofstede, Geert (1983) The cultural relativity of organizational theories. *Journal of International Business Studies*, **XIV**(2), 75–90

Hopper, Max D. (1990) Rattling sabre – new ways to compete on information. *Harvard Business Review*, May–June, pp. 118–25

Jafari, Jafar and Ritchie J.R. Brent (1981) Toward a framework for tourism education. *Annals of Tourism Research*, **8**(1), 13–34

Kaspar, Claude (1989) Recent developments in tourism research and education at the university level. In *Tourism Marketing and Management Handbook* (ed. Stephen F. Witt and Luiz Moutinho), Prentice Hall, New York, pp. 361–3

Lavery, Patrick (1989) Education and training in tourism. In *Tourism Marketing and Management Handbook* (ed. Stephen F. Witt and Luiz Moutinho), Prentice Hall, New York, pp. 119–22

Lawson, Malcolm (1974) *Teaching Tourism: Education and Training in Western Europe: A Comparative Study*, Tourism International Press, London

Lloyd, Bruce (1990) A learning society: the real challenge for the 1990s. In *The Association of MBAs Guide to Business Schools*, 8th edn (ed. Stanley J. Paliwoda), Pitman, London, pp. 58–9

Ritchie, J.R. Brent (1988) Alternative approaches to teaching tourism. Paper presented at the Tourism Teaching into the 1990s Conference (July), University of Surrey, Guildford

Ritchie, J.R. Brent (1991) Global tourism policy issues: an agenda for the 1990s. *World Travel and Tourism Review Indicators: Trends and Forecasts*, Vol. l (ed. D.E. Hawkins, J.R. Brent Ritchie, Frank Go and Douglas Frechtling), CAB International, Wallingford

Tettero, J.H.J.P. and Viehoff, J.H.R.M. (1990) *Marketing dienstverlenende organisaties – Beleid en uitvoering*, Kluwer, Deventer, p. 36

Theuns, H. Leo and Go, Frank (1992) Need led priorities in hospitality education for the Third World. In *World Travel and Tourism Review Indicators: Trends and Issues*, Vol. 2 (ed. J.R.B. Ritchie, D.E. Hawkins, Frank Go, and D. Frechtling), CAB International, Wallingford

World Tourism Organization (1987) *Education and Training for Tourism*, WTO, Madrid

23 The synergy between shopping and tourism: the Japanese experience

Myriam Jansen-Verbeke

Introduction

Understanding the activities of tourists during their visit to a particular destination is a key issue in the strategic planning of facilities and amenities. So far, the role of shopping as a tourist activity has tended to be underestimated, despite the fact that a considerable percentage of the time and money budget of tourists is spent on shopping.

Recently more marketing-inspired views have led to new approaches in developing urban tourism potentials which take into account the wide range of activities tourists actually engage in. Therefore the process of developing a sustainable and profitable tourist product implies spatial planning and management based on an understanding of the tourist system in general and of the functional associations between the different product elements in particular. Spatial zoning of tourist attractions in combination with the relevant supporting amenities such as shopping, hotels and transport is considered to be the precondition for synergism.

This view is illustrated by some results of a recent survey carried out amongst Japanese tourists in Amsterdam. From their behaviour pattern in time and space while staying in this city, some conclusions can be drawn concerning the role of shopping as a tourist activity. The objective is to identify the preconditions for developing and promoting shopping as part of the cultural tourist programme. Although the results of this survey are specific to the group of Japanese tourists in a European historical city (Amsterdam), the issue of 'Shopping Tourism' is relevant within a wider perspective.

The Japanese travel boom gives many tourist destination areas considerable opportunities, so that understanding the characteristics of this market segment in international travel and especially their attitude towards shopping in combination with their programme of visits can be a key to a targeted tourism development strategy (Nozawa, 1992).

The results of this case study can contribute to the understanding of the role of shopping as a tourist activity and especially to strategic policies in terms of spatial planning.

Conceptual framework

The urban tourist product

The urban tourist product consists of a mixture of elements which interact with one another. This interaction is the result of spatial connectivity and a functional association from the users' point of view, between the different product elements (Jansen-Verbeke and Ashworth, 1990). As a consequence, spatial zoning of these tourist product elements can create the optimal conditions for synergism (Leiper, 1990). Looking at the benefits of spatial clustering also makes sense from the point of view of tourism development and especially of entrepreneurs working in the tourism supporting industry.

Tourist zoning through spatial clustering and by anticipating potential functional associations is considered to be the logical outcome of tourist time–space budgets (Pearce, 1988). Both the spatial structure of the urban tourist product and tourist time–space behaviour are key issues in marketing an urban tourist product (Law, 1992). The identification of tourism clusters implies a series of analytical steps. The first step is a spatial analysis of the dispersal pattern of the distinct tourist product elements (Jansen-Verbeke, 1988). The elements which constitute the tourist product can be defined as being:

- **Core elements** of the tourist product which are in their own right, or the main motive for a tourist visit and therefore unique to each destination area.
- **Secondary elements** which, by definition, play a supporting role. These facilities and amenities are not exclusive to tourists only, and in most cases, are not the main motive for a tourist visit. However, their attraction can be such that they can encourage prolonging the stay or planning a repeat visit. In fact they function as additional attractions to the core elements of the tourist product.

- **Additional elements** of the tourist product also include a number of preconditions for functioning as a tourism magnet, such as accessibility and information.

The second step implies an interpretation of the spatial clustering from the tourists' point of view, taking into consideration the profile of visitor groups. Motives for the visit and length of stay are useful parameters in categorizing tourists (Hsieh et al., 1992). This exercise leads us to an understanding of the functional coherence of tourism clusters.

Shopping as a tourist activity

The travel motives of tourists can be very different. The intention to go shopping is seldom mentioned as a prime motive, despite the fact that this activity is apparently a very common element in the behaviour pattern of the average tourist (Kent et al., 1983). In some exceptional cases shopping facilities have developed into such a core element of the tourist product that they have become the main motive for the visit. This has happened for instance in several cities in national border areas in Europe which have greatly benefited from the differences in prices and taxes in neighbouring countries.

There are as of now several arguments for looking at leisure shopping as a tourist activity (Jansen, 1989). So far little research has been carried out concerning the preconditions in terms of environmental setting and shopping mix (Jansen-Verbeke, 1990, 1991). That an attractive and inviting environment can create the incentives and opportunities for impulse shopping is as yet unproven. However, the tourism industry fully realizes the importance of this resource in developing an attractive tourist product. In fact shopping tends to be a predominant time-use for many tourists, irrespective of their primary travel motive (Hsieh et al., 1992). Being able to search for, discover and anticipate the pleasures of purchasing certain merchandise is enjoyable to millions of people and is for them, a minor, if not a major reason for travelling. This being so, the development of attractive shopping facilities is an important instrument in the promotion of tourism. An inviting shopping environment is characterized by:

1 A wide variation on the supply side, with a flavour (or an illusion) of uniqueness.
2 Diversity in the types of shops, with the predominant image being that of high quality.
3 The spatial proximity of supporting amenities such as restaurants, pubs and entertainment facilities.

4   Pedestrian areas, good accessibility and parking facilities.
5   Multi-functionality of the environment which guarantees that the place feels 'alive'.

In fact, the potential for shopping to develop into a tourism resource largely depends on the quality and attractiveness of the environment involved rather than on the supply of goods. A strategic issue is the way in which shopping facilities are linked with the major tourist attractions. Creating intervening opportunities for shopping along connecting routes suggests an understanding of the actual spatial behaviour pattern.

Methodological issues

Visitors time–space and expenditure budgets hold the key information about the role of shopping as a tourist activity. So far little research has considered the issue of the spatial behaviour patterns of tourists. The number of visitors to particular attractions are registered but empirical information about how these activities fit into the time–space budget during their stay is usually lacking. The time–space budget approach allows for a systematic analysis of activities and a mapping of the activity space during the period of stay in a particular destination. From the results of such an analysis, the actual impact of tourism becomes more clear. In urban areas in particular it is most interesting to investigate the activity pattern which characterizes the profile of different visitor groups. This opens new perspectives on people/place combinations and the opportunity sets which fit in best. This approach also deals with routes which the individual regards as acceptable and attractive for the pursuit of specific activities. As a rule tourist action space is structured in close proximity to the core elements of the tourist product which, by definition, form the main motive of tourists' visits. Creating as many intervening opportunities as possible in the core area or along the access routes is a planning strategy which can prove to be efficient in many ways.

A survey is needed to identify the behaviour pattern of tourists during their stay. The main objective of the survey in Amsterdam was to assess the relevance of the spatial proximity between core elements of the tourist product and the supporting facilities. More specifically the question was as to whether Japanese tourists would combine the visit to major tourist attractions with (impulse) shopping. By mapping the location of hotels, tax free shops and the major tourist attractions, the clusters of special interest for this target group became apparent. In addition, the information about their tax free shopping (when, where and what) gives an indication of the relative importance of shopping to them as a tourist activity.

Characteristics of the Japanese tourist market

Organizational aspects

The Japanese travel market has expanded rapidly and, according to several forecasts, this growth will continue in the near future. Japanese tourists have the reputation for being big spenders, sophisticated consumers and enthusiastic but clever shoppers (Keown, 1989; Nozawa, 1992). For these reasons a case study on shopping amongst Japanese tourists can be an eye-opener in the strategic planning and marketing of tourist areas.

Some characteristics of the Japanese tourist are very relevant to the context of shopping. In the first place there is a clear preference for travelling in a group and choosing package tours. The travel programme is prearranged in detail. Most travel arrangements and package tours are arranged by JATA (the Japanese Association of Travel Agents). There is a clear distinction between the major travel agencies and the sub-agencies. The first is specialized as a wholesaler and has by far the largest market share in international and domestic travel. The organized trips carry 'brand names' and are targeted towards major groups of consumers (primary or national brands). Secondary brands would include more specific tailored packages. According to the experts in Japanese outbound travel, their market share is expected to increase considerably in the near future.

The most important characteristic of Japanese tourism is the degree of organization. Individual travel arrangements are rather exceptional. In general a complete programme, which includes the places to visit, to eat, to shop and to entertain, is offered. As a consequence, the behaviour pattern of these tourists during their stay in a particular destination is highly predictable.

Another relevant characteristic of the Japanese tourist is their preference for short stops in one place. The average travel time for a 'Europe trip' is two weeks, the stay in one country (usually one city) being limited to about two nights. As a consequence the time-use is very intensive, leaving hardly any free time for non-scheduled activities. Prior to the trip the available information is studied in detail in order to optimalize the benefits and not to miss any opportunities.

The culture of 'brand name' shopping

'Shopping in Europe' seems to be an important selling slogan and is, in many cases, a motive for the choice of a particular destination. Obviously Paris and London still are on the top of the list. Gradually the image of Europe as a travel destination has become more diversified and other cities have come into focus as well. This trend can be explained on the one hand by the more competitive promotion of other European countries and cities and, on the other hand, by an increasing number of return visits to Europe. 'Hearsay' information is by far the most important promotion channel.

As a rule the trip is well prepared in advance, to the extent that all information available is studied carefully and this includes a shopping guide. It is very customary to draw up a shopping list before departure. The question of where to buy which item of a particular brand name seems very important. This attitude leaves little or no opportunity for impulse shopping.

Interest is keen in so-called 'ethnic' products such as fashion products and perfumes (e.g. in France), chinaware, crystal, jewellery, artwork, handicrafts etc. In addition, the shopping list includes numerous gifts which are a 'must' to take back home. In social networking as well as in the Japanese economy in general, the tradition of exchanging gifts plays an important role (Moeran, 1983). This tradition is even accentuated in the case of travel leading to a 'souvenir culture' (Keown, 1989). They are more interested in brand names and high quality products which have been promoted through the Japanese media than are other tourists. Buying an 'authentic' brand product in the country of origin is 'the' thing to do. Obviously, this propensity for buying on the part of Japanese tourists can be seen to be of interest to many tourist destination areas.

The outbound Japanese travel market has three particular market segments. We will look at these in turn.

The younger market

This covers the age group twenty to twenty-nine, which is 16.5 million people or about 13 per cent of the Japanese population. The desire to travel overseas is high and still increasing. Twenty-eight per cent of them now travel abroad, which accounts for about 32 per cent of the total number of Japanese travelling to Europe. Some relevant subsegments in this market are, firstly, the students, who are developing the tradition of finishing their studies with a trip to Europe. The trend for choosing a group arrangement seems to be losing attraction and the number of individual travellers in this age group is growing. In terms of activity patterns, choice of accommodation and spending budget they tend to differ from the average Japanese tourist in Europe.

A second subgroup are the so called 'office ladies', single career business women, usually in well-paid jobs, still living with their parents and with a relatively high spending budget. They tend to travel in groups, are very much attracted to shopping facilities as such, adopt a specific life style and fully enjoy the escape from routine when travelling to Europe.

They have a clear preference for four- or five-star hotels and tend to include only a limited number of visiting places in their programme in order to have more free time (i.e. time for shopping).

A third market of interest is the group of honeymooners. Every year 750,000 marriages are registered and many couples have been saving to achieve their ambition of a honeymoon outside Japan, preferably in a top-class hotel.

The 'silver' market

As in most countries, the generation of fifty years and older has become an important market segment, also from the international perspective. Some 35.7 million Japanese are in this age group, forming 29 per cent of the total Japanese population. This percentage is increasing rapidly. The tradition of travelling outbound is relatively new but already accounts for 2.1 million overseas trips (25 per cent of the total of overseas trips). European destinations account for 210,000 trips per year, this being one-quarter of the total number of overseas trips. This market includes many retired people, many experienced travellers and, above all, a high-income group. The preference for travelling in a group appears to be consistent.

Business travellers

Taking into account the wide international interests of Japanese business, the number of business travellers is very important. The age group of thirty and forty-nine is strongly represented and is predominantly male. In fact there is a tendency to combine business trips with more educational and cultural activities. Changing attitudes of the Japanese concerning the value of work and leisure are gradually affecting their attitude towards travel. Many visits to the Netherlands, referred to as 'technical visits', include a training programme, a visit to a congress or trade fair and, as a rule, some tourist sightseeing. In contrast to the previous market segments these visitors travel individually or with a small party and the programme of visits is usually organized by a local contact person.

Forecasts

According to Polunin (1989) the travel boom in Japan will continue. His arguments are:

- There is a continuous growth of the number of overseas travellers (12.2 million in 1992).
- The Japanese market has 120 million consumers (1992).

- Economic progress in Japan can support an increasing spending budget for leisure and travel.
- The percentage of house owners is increasing rapidly and this creates new opportunities for other personal investments.
- There is a changing life style and attitude towards work and leisure.
- There is an ageing population, with the increased desire of retired people to travel outbound.
- Travelling overseas is increasingly becoming a status symbol and part of a desirable life style.

Position of the Netherlands in the Japanese tourist market

Despite the fact that the prime destinations of Japanese outbound travel are still the USA, Korea and Taiwan, the attraction of other regions is becoming more important. A general characteristic is the relatively high spending budget of the average Japanese tourist (US$3,146 per trip). Taking into account the total volume of 10.6 million trips per year, this is an enormous potential amount, however, an important share remains in Japanese hands (travel agencies, hotel chains, tour operators, Japanese-run shops etc.).

Nevertheless the European tourist market is hoping to acquire a growing share of this market. The problem is that Europe, as a selling point, does not exist, 'interesting destinations' being limited to a few traditional tourist sites or, as happens now, a combination of short visits to the most important European, top league cities. The increasing percentage of repeat visits might change this pattern in the near future and open new perspectives for other interesting places. The Netherlands are not at the top of the list, although the number of Japanese visitors has increased (Netherlands Tourist Board, 1990). More than half of this group stay in Amsterdam. However, there are recent signs of a declining interest in Amsterdam amongst Japanese visitors. This trend is seen as an indication that Amsterdam is still relatively well positioned with respect to the Japanese tourist market but is losing its attraction in favour of other Dutch cities and locations.

The forecasts for Japanese tourism to the Netherlands need to take into consideration:

- The general decrease in Japanese travel to Europe and the changing preferences of the tourism market due to newly promoted destinations having an increasing impact.
- The decline in the Netherlands share of Japanese travel to Europe. This is probably linked to the current tendency to make shorter trips to Europe and also to the fact that the Netherlands is not a prime destination.

Despite these weak points and possible threats, the Netherlands Tourist Board nevertheless anticipates an increase in Japanese tourists. Promotion campaigns are especially targeted to increasing the length of stay. Promotion policy needs to deal strategically with the demographic changes in Japan which surely affect the tourism market and the specific market segmentation (Polunin, 1989). The segment of young and single women will continue to grow, as will the 'silver' market segment.

In most cases, Japanese visitors to the Netherlands prefer a group arrangement guided by a Japanese tourist guide. The current image of the Netherlands is still limited to traditional items such as flowers, clogs, windmills and its historical heritage. Changing the image of a country as a tourist destination is a long-term objective and a major challenge.

Urban tourism in Amsterdam

Characteristics of the Japanese tourist

The profile of the Japanese tourist can be drawn up from the following characteristics: age, travel motive, length of stay and organization of the trip. It was assumed that each of these characteristics is relevant in explaining the activity patterns and actual shopping behaviour. In terms of travel motives a clear distinction can be made between visitors with mainly tourism motives, those with business motives and those with a combination of different motives. The latter group can include visits to family or friends. It was assumed that the travel motive would be reflected in the length of stay. In fact business visits were the shortest (with 61 per cent staying only one night), tourist visits usually include two nights and visits to friends and relatives tend to be somewhat longer (with 26 per cent staying three or more nights).

The pattern of combining a visit to Amsterdam with other European cities predominates. An overnight stay in Amsterdam does not necessarily mean a day visit to Amsterdam. The city is often used as a basis for excursions to other places of interest in the country. When combining the information on age and travel motives, it shows that 'real' tourists are mostly to be found amongst the older group of tourists.

Furthermore there is a significant relationship with the organizational characteristics of the trip. Apparently, the impact of Japanese tour operators on the organization of the trip is very strong. The percentage of individual arrangements is said to be increasing but, right now, it only accounts for one-fifth of the visits, which are mostly to relatives or friends. This pattern may be different in the case of a repeat visit.

Table 23.1 The tourist product of Amsterdam

Core elements (major attractions)

1 **Historical heritage**

Built environment	Urban history
Urban morphology and architecture	Historical associations
Water and canals	Folklore
Historical buildings and monuments	Cultural identity
Churches – convents – beguinage – palace	Urban scenery

2 **Cultural amenities**

Museums	Cultural programmes
Exhibitions	Cultural ambiance
Theatre – concert halls	Typical life style
Libraries	Ethnic diversity
Events and festivals	

3 **Outdoor recreation facilities**
Canals and boat trips
Urban parks and zoo
Botanical garden

Secondary elements

Shopping facilities and streetmarkets,
Catering sector – pavement cafes, bars, coffee shops, restaurants
Hotels, congress and convention facilities
Entertainment and the red light district

Tourist attractions in Amsterdam (Table 23.1)

In many ways Amsterdam functions as the gateway for international tourism to the Netherlands. The historical image and the compactness of the urban morphology are its main strong points. Most tourist attractions and the secondary elements of the tourist product are therefore within walking distance. Contrary to other products, the tourist product is not defined by the suppliers of product elements, but rather results from the actual activity pattern of the tourists themselves.

Each individual visitor makes his or her own selection, according to personal preference and within the constraints of a specific time–space budget. In this perspective it makes no sense to offer a complete inventory of what a city has to offer to tourists. The most interesting issue lies in understanding why a particular combination of activities occurs and why, as a consequence, particular product elements seem to be less in the focus of specific target groups.

In the case of Japanese tourists in Amsterdam, a selection takes place in the number and type of tourist attractions which they visit. Within the limited time spent in this city, the programme tends mainly to include the traditional core elements of the urban tourist product. The list of core elements relevant to the Japanese tourist in Amsterdam is, in fact, limited to some well-defined targets. The number one tourist attraction is a sight-seeing tour on the canals which offers a general impression of the historical heritage of the city. In second place come visits to the Van Gogh and Rembrandt Museums which are part of the traditional pattern.

These major tourist attractions also figure in the programme of business tourists. In fact, there is no significant difference according to sex in the type of tourist attractions visited. It is the difference in behaviour pattern according to age group which seems to be more relevant. The older group of Japanese tourists clearly sticks to the top tourist attractions, whereas the younger tourists especially (under the age of thirty) tend to engage in a more varied pattern of sightseeing within the city and include smaller and special interest museums, streetmarkets, etc. This fits within the earlier statement that younger tourists are less inclined to join organized parties.

The aspect of repeat visits is equally relevant in explaining the variation in sightseeing patterns. Repeat visitors are more strongly represented amongst the older tourists and this, in turn, is reflected in their preference for excursions to other places in the Netherlands. Variation in the sightseeing pattern is closely related to the length of stay. From the results of the survey it can be concluded that shopping, as a time use, increases considerably amongst those tourists who stay longer than two nights.

On average there is little variation in the sightseeing pattern of Japanese tourists and this is clearly the result of a pre-arranged and programmed tour. In this context there is little time left for non-planned or impulse activities such as shopping or window-shopping.

Shopping in Amsterdam

Taking into account the image of the Japanese tourists as big spenders and keen shoppers its makes sense to look more closely at their actual shopping behaviour. For non-European visitors the system of tax free shopping offers special additional advantages. The total expenditure in tax free shops in Amsterdam accounts for an income of US$9 million in 1991, of which 7 per cent is brought in by Japanese customers. The largest investment comes from US visitors (15.5 per cent). There are clear indications of a growing interest in tax free shopping. The most important branches are gift shops, closely followed by chinaware. The latter includes the Dutch favourite brand product 'Delfts Blue'. The attraction of tax free shopping for Japanese tourists seems far less important for ladies fashion, department stores and jewellery. Obviously Amsterdam does not hold a leading position for these articles. Nevertheless 58.4 per cent of the tax free shopping of Japanese tourists takes place in Amsterdam (US$611,700).

In fact, there is a most interesting increase in tax free shopping expenditure in the Netherlands, despite the fact that Amsterdam is losing its position somewhat. Preferred shopping items for the Japanese tourists in the Netherlands are souvenirs, chinaware, food, flower seeds or bulbs, diamonds and jewellery.

There are clear differences according to sex, age and travel motives in the type of items bought. Men – especially older men – tend to be better customers for diamonds and jewellery, while women are the most important spenders on souvenirs. Younger people spend relatively more on food products. As could be predicted the longer the stay the higher the propensity to buy goods. During the short stay the emphasis lies on souvenirs, during a longer stay other articles such as flower seeds and bulbs, diamonds and jewellery and chinaware catch their attention. Amongst tourists who stay longer, the expenditure on food increases considerably.

Strong and weak points of the tourist product

According to the Netherlands Tourist Board (1990) there are some general features of the Netherlands and Amsterdam which are considered to be the strong points of the tourist product with respect to the Japanese target group:

- The hospitality and friendliness of the Dutch people.
- The international reputation of the Netherlands as a small and beautiful country.
- 'Nichiran' which refers to the historical links between the Netherlands and Japan.
- The acceptance of other cultures.
- The romanticized image of historical cities in the Netherlands.
- The international fame of painters such as Rembrandt, Van Gogh and others.

On the other hand the weak points of the tourist product for the Japanese market were also assessed:

- The absence of a unique selling point, such as for instance the Eiffel tower or the Statue of Liberty.
- The narrow image of the Netherlands, still strongly associated with tulips, which are in fact a seasonal support to the tourist product.

- No specific reputation as an interesting shopping place.
- Very few Japanese signs in shops, hotels or in public spaces.

The survey was used to identify in more detail the attitude of the Japanese tourist in Amsterdam concerning shopping opportunities, interesting aspects of shopping, the drawbacks concerning shopping in particular and concerning Amsterdam as a destination in general. The overall quality of shopping facilities in Amsterdam was estimated to be fairly good according to 73 per cent of the Japanese respondents. On average, the most positive attitude was expressed concerning the low prices, the friendly service, the use of English being fairly general (especially appreciated by female tourists), the spatial concentration of shops and the many exchange offices (especially appreciated by male visitors and business tourists).

Amongst the more negative respondents the percentage of female tourists was significantly higher. In addition, negative reactions tended to be stronger amongst tourists staying longer and amongst the older tourists. The main weakness of shopping in Amsterdam from the tourists' point of view was the strict regulation of opening times. In addition, the absence of a major shopping mall, the untidiness of public space, a certain feeling of insecurity and, to some extent, the language barrier, were the most frequently mentioned weak points.

From the perspective of strengthening synergetic interrelations between shopping and tourism, some clear indications became obvious and both were related to the quality and diversity of shops and to the quality of the public environment. The role of tax free shopping in the tourist attraction of Amsterdam is still far below its potential. Only 44 per cent of Japanese tourists use this facility. The main reasons for this were difficult to trace. For most Japanese tourists the lack of time to do window-shopping and to discover shopping facilities at leisure is the most likely relevant explanation. However, the lack of an attractive supply of goods and the limited supply have also been frequently mentioned. According to Moeran (1983), the Japanese tourist has a special interest in high quality products and brand name products, which apparently are not easily to be found in Amsterdam. In order to improve its attraction as a tourist destination for the Japanese more specific information concerning tax free shopping should be included in the general promotion material.

Locational patterns

The actual strength of the interrelationship between shopping and other tourist activities depends on several preconditions. The analysis of time–

space use of tourists was regarded as an effective instrument in understanding and explaining the behaviour patterns. As a rule, the action space of tourists is structured around a set of fixed components, being the location of the hotel, the location of the major tourist attractions and the location of the intervening opportunities such as shops. Each of these elements of the tourist product in Amsterdam was mapped in detail. The idea is to be able to identify the spatial zoning of tourism, the network of functionally interrelated facilities and, possibly, the missing links.

Japanese tourists have a distinct preference for specific hotels, mostly those in the top categories. These are concentrated in four distinct clusters in Amsterdam. In Amsterdam the location pattern of hotels that particularly attract the Japanese tourists is important in analysing the action space of this target group. The distance and the pedestrian route between the hotel and the tourist attractions are what to a large extent determined the use made of the intervening opportunities for shopping.

The location of 'tax free shops' in Amsterdam has also been analysed in this perspective. In fact, the present situation in Amsterdam allows for a close locational interaction between hotels, tourist attractions and clusters of shops, including tax free shops. The spatial proximity and the limited walking distances between the elements of the tourist product offer genuine opportunities for a synergetic interaction.

The conclusion is that, in terms of spatial clustering, the situation in Amsterdam can be considered as being favourable to supporting the combination of sightseeing and shopping. This statement is based on the outcome of a detailed spatial analysis and the interpretation of individual time–space budgets of Japanese tourists. The method of mapping individual time–space patterns is quite complex but, in the case of Japanese tourists to Amsterdam, its complexity could be reduced to some prototypes. The intervening opportunities for shopping in the traditional sightseeing pattern are certainly present. The fact that Japanese tourists in Amsterdam are only using these opportunities to a limited extent is directly related to the organizational characteristics of their travel programme on the one hand and, on the other, to the poor image of Amsterdam as a shopping place.

Conclusions

The spatial organization of shopping facilities in relation to tourist attractions in a destination area can be underpinned by empirical knowledge of time–space budgets of the most important target groups. Constraints in the synergetic relationship between shopping and other tourist activities can also be the result of organizational and promotional handicaps. The example of the Japanese target group, assumed to be a group of big spenders, clearly indicates the strategies for the future.

Strategies aiming at a synergism between shopping and tourism need to be based on a profile study of the specific target groups. For instance, Japanese tourists clearly behave differently from other target groups and, even within this market segment, there is a clear distinction according to age, travel motive, length of stay and, above all, travel organization.

The propensity of Japanese tourists for buying souvenirs, gifts and 'ethnic products' implies a specific marketing strategy. The hypothesis was that spatial structuring of the tourist product (core elements and supporting elements) would be an essential precondition.

The results of this survey clearly demonstrate the role of Japanese tour operators in the programme organization. This implies that promotion and especially the promotion of shopping and tax free shopping as additional tourism resources should be targeted at the intermediate level of organizations in Japan rather than at the level of the individual tourist.

This conclusion is relevant for the specific target group in the Japanese tourist market, the programmed group traveller, which at this time includes the majority of Japanese tourists. However, the trend towards more individual travelling, especially amongst younger people, holds new challenges for the future. Information about the shopping facilities in a tourist destination area and the promotion of its image as an attractive place to visit and to shop might be an effective marketing instrument. The creation of intervening shopping opportunities along the predictable sightseeing routes, taking into account the actual time–space budgets of specific target groups, is far more sophisticated and probably the most effective planning instrument.

References

Hsieh, S., O'Leary, J. and Morrison, A. (1992) Segmenting the international travel market by activity. *Tourism Management*, **13**(2), 209–23

Jansen, A. (1989) 'Funshopping' as a geographical notion. *Tijdschrift voor Economische en Sociale Geografie*, **80**, 171–83

Jansen-Verbeke, M. (1988) Leisure, recreation and tourism in inner cities: explorative case studies. *Netherlands Geographical Studies*, No. 58

Jansen-Verbeke, M. and Ashworth, G. (1990) Environmental integration of recreation and tourism. *Annals of Tourism Research*, **17**(4), 618–22

Jansen-Verbeke, M. (1990) Leisure + Shopping = Tourism Product Mix. In *Marketing Tourism Places* (ed. G. Ashworth and B. Goodall), Routledge, London, New York, pp. 128–35

Jansen-Verbeke, M. (1991) Leisure shopping: a magic concept for the tourism industry? *Tourism Management*, **12**(1), 9–14

Kent, W., Shock, P. and Snow, R. (1983) Shopping: tourism's unsung hero(ine). *Journal of Travel Research*, Spring, pp. 2–4

Keown, C. (1989) A model of tourists' propensity to buy: the case of Japanese visitors to Hawaii. *Journal of Travel Research*, Winter, pp. 31–4

Law, Ch. (1992) Urban tourism and its contribution to economic regeneration. *Urban Studies*, **29**(3/4), 599–618

Leiper, N. (1990) Tourist attraction systems. *Annals of Tourism Research*, **17**, 367–84

Moeran, B. (1983) The language of Japanese tourism. *Annals of Tourism Research*, **10**, 93–109

Netherlands Tourist Board (1990) *Medium Term Plan: Japan and Other Far East Countries, 1990–1992* Leischendam, Netherlands.

Nozawa, H. (1992) A marketing analysis of Japanese outbound travel. *Tourism Management*, **13**(2), 226–33

Pearce, D. (1988) Tourist time-budgets. *Annals of Tourism Research*, **15**, 106–21

Polunin, I. (1989) Japanese travel boom. *Tourism Management*, **10**, 4–8

24 The senior travel market: distinct, diverse, demanding

Jan van Harssel

Introduction

The continued growth of the tourism industry in many societies over the next ten years may well depend on how well companies understand social and demographic trends affecting consumer buying behaviour. One of the most promising targets for leisure travel is the mature market. Most Western societies are beginning to feel the impact of one of this century's most important socio-political and economic movements, the greying of the population. With large numbers of early baby boomers entering this life stage within the next ten years it becomes vital that the industry is well informed about current and anticipated travel trends. In the United States, seniors are major consumers in the estimated $181 billion leisure travel market. Given that by the year 2030 there will be about 65 million older adults in the United States, two-and-a-half times the number in 1980, the number of individuals having the capacity to travel as an active leisure pursuit is staggering. It does not come as a surprise that the increasing number of older individuals and the large amount of unassigned time available to them has captured the interest of those examining travel characteristics of this market (Anderson and Langmeyer, 1982).

Population statistics indicate that mature people represent a potentially large share of the leisure and travel market. The travel industry is discovering a new love: elderly travellers. However, tourism industry marketers who pride themselves on knowing consumers and giving them what they want are fumbling with this huge new consumer group. 'Few marketers have successfully reached these important consumers, many more have succeeded in insulting them,' according to a conference speaker quoting from *American Demographics* magazine.

The mature market

People aged over sixty-five constitute a perfect market for the travel industry because many senior citizens have the time to travel and are willing to spend an appreciable amount of their income for this purpose. The older market also holds a large share of the country's discretionary income because their children are usually grown and their house payments are complete. In addition, the over sixty-five market can fill the peaks and troughs for airlines and hotels because of the flexibility of their travel schedules. In the United States, seniors have become the fastest growing segment of the population and seniors have become one of the most viable segments of the tourism industry consumer market. Clearly, the leisure travel and tourism industry is one specific area where the senior market segment of the population has significant impact.

Americans' attitudes toward ageing have traditionally been quite negative and often misinformed. This 'gerontophobia' has generated a widely accepted set of myths about what it means to grow older. These myths include: people over sixty-five are (1) old, (2) in poor health, (3) not as bright as younger people, (4) unproductive, (5) unattractive and sexless and (6) generally all the same (Dychtwald and Flower, 1990).

Most myths about older Americans are unsubstantiated. Today, 60 per cent of those sixty-five years of age and older report no activity limitations. In addition, the prospect for even improved health status are good, reflecting the better diets and living habits prevalent today (US Travel Data Center, 1990).

Healthier life styles and advancements in medicine have helped people live longer and more productive lives. According to the US Social Security Administration, a baby born today has a good chance of living to be seventy-five years old; twenty-seven years longer than a newborn at the turn of the century.

Figures associated with the growth of the mature market are impressive. In the United States, people aged fifty and over now represent nearly one-quarter of the total adult US population. By the year 2000 the fifty-plus age group will make up 38 per cent of the population and hold 75 per cent of the nation's wealth (Wolfe, 1990). Travel by the US mature market will significantly increase in the future, as its population increases nearly 12 per cent between 1990 and the turn of the century, and another 27 per cent between 2000 and 2010 (US Travel Data Center, 1990).

Today's older Americans are significantly different from earlier generations of seniors. They are better educated, more active and more vocal than any previous senior generation. Advanced years are now seen as a time of challenge rather than a time of despair (Forbes, 1987). While the data suggest a society that is getting older, the elders themselves are getting younger.

According to the US National Center for Health Statistics, more than half the persons over the age of 65 indicate that they do not limit their physical activities due to health problems.

The senior traveller

In an effort to assess the implication of America's changing demographics on the US travel industry the United States Travel Data Center (1989) prepared a report, published by the Travel Industry Association of America. The report describes both qualitatively and statistically seven generational groups now living in America, and provides indications of how the changing size and demographic structure of the US population will impact the travel industry as it approaches the twenty-first century. The report concludes:

> With the 'aging' of the population, two age groups that today show the highest incidence of travel (35–44 and 45–54) will increase rapidly in size, providing a significant impetus to increased travel in the 1990s. The changing age structure should, in and of itself, produce a 16 per cent increase in travel volume by the turn of the century.
>
> As late (born: 1955–1964) and early (born: 1946–1954) baby boomers join these age groups, they will bring with them their backgrounds, values, and interests, influencing dramatically their travel preferences. Their higher levels of education and incomes (two factors positively correlated with travel) will provide an additional stimulus to travel.
>
> Early baby boomers will be running the country by the year 2000. Over the next ten years, this group will reach the peak of their earning potential, and many will have sent their children to college and acquired their long-term assets. Early baby boomers are likely to be the premier travel market in the 1990s. Middle-age moderation is likely to shift many of them into less strenuous activities, changing perhaps the nature of the trips they prefer to take. Psychologically a group that enjoyed its 'uniqueness' and that tended to emphasize experiences over material possessions, early baby boomers could help stimulate the market for less traditional and perhaps 'soft adventure' types of travel experiences.
>
> While little growth is projected for the 55–64 and 65–74 age groups through the turn of the century, the World War II (born: 1935–1945) and Depression (born: 1924–1934) babies will be a stable and profitable market for certain segments of the travel industry in the years ahead. More affluent, travel-sophisticated, and probably healthier and more active than the individuals who preceded them into retirement age, this group is likely to place a higher priority on travel experiences such as cruises, tours, recreational vehicles, and off-season trips.
>
> Healthy and affluent, many World War II babies will be easy to mainstream with existing products, and their upbringing could steer them to look particularly for opportunities for social interaction and personal development as part of their travel experiences.

Depression babies will be a more challenging group to interest and satisfy because of life experiences very different from younger Americans. Bargain hunting, aversion to credit, and strong family and community ties are traits that have been used to describe many in this group. Yet, unlike the stereotype of older Americans, many will have the health, wealth, and time necessary for travel. To reach this potentially lucrative market segment, companies will find it increasingly important to pay attention to 'cognitive age' rather than chronological age and to downplay the use of such terms as 'senior citizen' in favor of other terms that appeal to one's interests and activities.

Supernaw (1985) suggested that there are three distinct categories of elders which are of interest to tourism industry suppliers. One market is comprised of experienced travellers. These people have travelled, and will continue to travel. Supernaw suggests that the travel industry can do little to influence this traveller. A second category consists of new entrants to the travel market. These elders want to travel but probably have not travelled a lot. They are predisposed to travel and are going to seek information. These people represent a market share that is going to be increasing by the millions year after year as travel is becoming part of the life style of increasing numbers of seniors. The third category, the largest and two times bigger than anything else (according to Supernaw), is the frightened potential traveler. These people have to be educated, taught, convinced and almost cultured into travel. This market segment needs to be educated about the ease of travel and taught that travel can be a material part of their life style.

The challenge to the hospitality industry

The opportunities and challenges that older travellers present to the leisure and travel industries continue to grow as an increasing number of suppliers look at this age group to derive a share of their market.

Knowledge about the travel behaviour of seniors is still developing, with little definitive research published examining many facets of older people's travel behaviour. With baby boomers entering this age group in ten years, there is a great need for research on the identification and monitoring of travel characteristics, travel patterns and marketing strategies to cater to this growing market.

Today's elders are pioneers, as are the businesses that provide leisure and travel services to this changing segment of the population. The increasing number of older individuals and the increased leisure time available to them has created a new consumer group of life style pioneers.

In order to reach the senior market effectively, marketers must understand that older consumers think differently from younger ones. They have more money to spend but prefer buying 'experiences' over possessions.

They do not like direct references to age or its limitations. What they do like are products that help them be active and vibrant and advertisements that help them look it.

Seniors will be the demographic discovery of this decade for two reasons. First, there are more of them. Secondly, their life styles are remarkably different from those of previous generations. With no models to guide them, the independent elderly are making new choices about how they want to live during a prolonged retirement.

Many older adults have the time and money to travel. However, this segment of the population is still given little attention by business which continues to focus on younger individuals (Linden, 1986). Their growth in number and the relative affluence of this population segment imply a steadily expanding potential market for tourism products aimed at the elderly.

Although members of the senior market clearly have the desire to travel, little seems to be known about why they travel, how they travel and the benefits they seek (Shoemaker, 1989).

There are two characteristics of the changing demography of the senior market which will have a very significant impact on marketing travel services to seniors. They are the high proportion of singles in this population and the higher proportion of women than men within this age group. Census figures for 1991 in the United States show that 10.9 per cent of men aged 55–64 live alone, 13 per cent of men aged 65–74 reside by themselves, and of older men aged 75 and over, 21.9 per cent live alone. The numbers are very different for women. Of women aged 55–64, 16.9 per cent live alone, for the age group 65–74 the figure jumps to 33.2 per cent and over half (50.9 per cent) of all women aged 75 and over live alone (US Bureau of the Census, 1991).

Women comprise nearly 60 per cent of the aged sixty-five and over section of the population of the United States, or in other words, there are approximately 150 women for every 100 men among those aged sixty-five and older. Half of all women over the age of sixty-five are widows, and for women aged seventy-five and older that figure rises to 69 per cent (Allan, 1981). The reasons for the gender difference appear to be clear: women live longer than men, women marry men older than themselves, and more widowers remarry than do widows (MacNeil, 1991). There are other variables to consider as well. While most depression-era women were brought up to get married and be supported by their husband, baby-boom women will have worked most of their lives, may still be working after they are fifty, and will be relatively financially independent with some savings. They will be psychologically different from older women of today because dependence will not be a part of their make-up. Many may be single and will have been single longer than the older widows of today because of the baby boomer's high divorce rate. Older women are prime prospects for travel, especially group travel, and yet the travel industry has been slow to recognize their particular circumstances. The widowed older women of today resent being penalized by hefty single supplements for having to travel alone.

From a travel and tourism industry perspective, the expanding population of older single women raises many challenges for which few answers have been proposed.

The opportunity

In the spring of 1992, the author conducted a research study sponsored by the AARP (American Association of Retired Persons) Travel Experience from American Express. Results of the study allow for the design of programmes and promotions aimed at meeting the needs of the important senior travel market.

The overall purpose of the research was to gather information about the perception and preferences of older pleasure travelers in the United States. Primary attention was devoted to identifying the needs that explain why older people travel and to establishing a behavioural profile of this market segment.

Findings

A common problem associated with travel was related to the health of the individual study participants. The people considered their health as a problem with travel as it either prevented them from enjoying the trip or it prevented them from participating in some activities. A 'fear of falling ill' also surfaced. In some situations, the security of having a doctor or a nurse close-by somewhat alleviated these health concerns.

Another common problem associated with travel was the language differences that occurred primarily in overseas travel. Some people felt this was a serious problem, while others found that tour guides and other people helped them overcome this barrier to enjoying their experience.

Problems with getting information about events, trips or potential trips were also a concern. Sometimes the events that were of interest were not promoted enough or shared in advance for the people to participate. There is a greater need for the sponsors of events to promote them more aggressively. Study participants felt that this information problem could in some part be alleviated by the use of a trip coordinator.

There was also concern about the details listed on the itineraries. It was felt that sometimes all of the necessary information was not clear or easy to follow. At times, it was not clear as to what time of day tourists had to be ready to leave or return. Overall, the scheduling on some of the group tours presented a problem for some of the senior travellers. Many also indicated that they needed more time to get ready.

There was also apprehension with regard to tours that stay in a city for one day and then go on to the next destination the following day. Some participants did not find this enjoyable. A more leisurely trip was preferred, and one that spent more time in each destination. One study participant observed: 'Tours restrict adventure.'

There was some concern mentioned about the tour guides on trips that were 'guided' trips. Some felt that these guides really were not qualified or knowledgeable enough. Others felt that the tour guides talked 'down' to senior travellers . . . 'I don't like to be talked to like a child!' It was suggested that the credentials of the tour guides be checked carefully prior to the trip. (It is important to point out, however, that some study participants did not have these problems at all with tour guides.)

Accommodations presented a problem to some study participants. Concerns ranged from assigned room mates to the size/condition of the accommodations.

A serious concern also surfaced here relating to the added cost or 'single supplement' added on when a person occupies a room alone. The cost of a single person's room is often higher than that of half a double room. Many study participants said that they 'hated to pay this extra charge'. Finding a room mate could alleviate this extra charge, but that was not always easy to do. Sometimes the tour groups offered assistance. Sometimes incompatibilities resulted, which often upset the travellers. Also, sometimes, participants felt the rooms themselves were smaller and less well kept for the single traveller (reference was made to a 'broom closet with a bed').

Another problem related to accommodations concerned the lack of lounges or restaurants at the hotels themselves. This made it difficult to get a meal or a drink upon arrival (or when arriving late). It was also felt that non-smoking rooms should be available.

World conditions and specifically certain country's political and economic conditions affected some of the study participants. They would not travel to certain destinations because of these problems. Also, some study participants had problems with customs, in that it often takes a long time to go through the procedures and/or travellers have to stand in long lines.

Those study participants who travelled on buses felt that these were often uncomfortable. Either the seats were not comfortable, there were not enough foot rests, or they did not have proper step-up stools to get on and off the bus. Several seniors were surprised that rest rooms were not standard on many European buses. One participant commented that long bus rides caused her ankles to swell. There was also concern for 'smoke free' buses, and for a rotation system of seat allocation so everyone had a chance for the more comfortable and bigger seats in the back or near the aisles.

For those study participants who were involved with longer trips, there was a concern regarding the one-night stops. Packing and unpacking was difficult. Often they were not told to pack one small bag for those one night stops.

One continuing concern of many of the study participants dealt with the method of travel. While many people enjoyed a variety of methods from car to bus to plane to boat, others complained that especially airplanes were overcrowded, overbooked, uncomfortable and overpriced. Those people tended not to take those commercial transportation methods that they did not like and preferred to go by themselves by car when travelling.

Lack of variety in meals served on tour emerged as a problem. One person observed: 'Most of the trips have chicken dinners at every place we go.' Several other respondents also pointed at the need for variety in meals, especially at breakfast. At times, restaurants did not honour special meal considerations requested in advance.

Often, tour participants are concerned about not being fully informed about the day's itinerary. Effective communications can remove many anxieties. One person commented: 'I remember hearing an announcement on the bus. I did not understand what was being said. That can really throw you into a panic.'

The overwhelming response to the question 'Why do you travel?' was to see new sights and scenery. Most of the people showed enthusiasm and excitement regarding travelling. Historic sights, museums, landscapes and any places they had not seen were mentioned as enjoyable and reasons for taking the trip. Participants saw these new experiences as adventures. There was also agreement that 'having educational experiences' was part of overall travel plans.

Some study participants expressed a strong desire to see and experience as much as they could about the culture and the people in the countries they travelled through. Some had experiences with actually living with people in that culture instead of staying at the usual tourist hotels. Others had people from other countries stay at their homes in the United States. All agreed that this exchange of ideas and attitudes was an important part of their travel experience. It could not always be obtained on the usual organized tour. Clearly, seniors view travel as a learning experience.

Another very common reason for travel was 'to visit family members'.

Many study participants travelled to see children or grandchildren who lived in different places.

Many of the study participants said that travelling was done 'to change their normal routine'. It gave them a chance to change their usual routine, and to get away from their everyday lives. This also included a change in climate, which many of the study participants wanted during the cold, winter months.

Other reasons for travel that were mentioned included 'to meet new people', 'to shop' and 'to share the travel experiences with friends at home'. One person commented: 'Travel increases the experience of living. I enjoy watching others have a good time.'

The overall reaction was that travelling is *not* relaxing, but most focus group participants agree that relaxation was not a major motivation for travel. Many assume a very active role in making sure they have an enjoyable experience. 'I only look at good things out there, not the bad. There is a lot of world out there. I like variety.'

Besides brochures, the study participants also use books, magazines, movies and other literature to learn more about places they might want to visit. Some look at the travel sections of the newspaper and some belong to different travel clubs from which they receive newsletters. Many study participants go to a travel agent to get information.

Many of the study participants talk to other people (word of mouth) when deciding what trips to take. They often find people (friends, neighbours) who have taken a trip and ask them for their reactions before deciding on a programme. Some take a trip because they were enticed to do so by a friend . . . 'I got hooked-up'.

There was discussion about what else would be of help in planning a trip. Since some study participants decide where they want to go and then get the information, there is a need for as much information as possible. It was suggested that a room could be set aside at an area college that offered programmes in travel, where information could be obtained about various places of interest. Different travel companies could put the information there. Also, videos could be found about the various places and these could be viewed by the interested people. Several participants mentioned that movies and slide-shows are very informative sources of information about a destination.

Weather conditions and the time of the year are other important variables in trip planning.

Trip planning is done in a variety of ways. Some study participants spoke to their friends or family members when trying to decide where to go. Many chose a place to go because they had friends or family there (for some this was the only reason they travelled). Others do 'research' by reading newspapers, travel books and other related literature. Many mentioned the library as a frequent source of good information. In general, participants are avid readers of travel-related articles, brochures and magazines.

Travel agents were used frequently as sources of information about places to visit as well as for planning and booking transportation and accommodations. When planning a trip, some people look to events that are happening in that specific place as an enticement to go there.

Hobbies and interests influence and inspire an interest in travel. 'Elder hostels' were also suggested as being enjoyable experiences for the mature traveller. These offer a variety of accommodations, activities and schedules.

For many of the study participants a travel club coordinator made many of the plans for their trips. This helped them greatly. This coordinator would find the best prices, hotels, transportation method and everything else necessary for the trip. The trip coordinator often chooses the places to go based on input from club members. The members are periodically questioned as to what interests and preferences they have with regard to trips they would like to take.

Some interesting responses: 'I want to travel, but I want someone else to do all the planning' and, 'When going to Europe I want to be led by hand everywhere, but I want to go across by myself!'

Most of the study participants felt very strongly that the best reason to travel was 'to see new things'. There was also a strong feeling that the best reason to travel was to get out of the normal routine, to do different things and to experience a new environment. One study participant said: 'I like the way a trip changes my life forever.' Another commented: 'I see the places I read about and get to live the way the people in the books do.'

Some study participants also felt that seeing family (such as children and grandchildren) was the best thing about travelling. There was a feeling also about 'being able to do it' as the best thing about travelling now, while they could still go on their own.

The worst thing about travelling to most people was 'waiting'. This was in the form of waiting for airplanes, connections, people, customs, any delays in transportation and 'the day to leave'.

Another common thought in the 'worst' category was packing and unpacking, as was the 'dirty laundry' problem when the trip was over.

Another concern about travelling dealt with 'finding someone to go with and someone to go where I want to go'. This concern was somewhat alleviated by the use of group trips, sometimes coordinated by a travel club.

Some study participants felt that bad accommodations, bad restaurants and long bus rides were unfortunate experiences. This, coupled with exhaustion, getting up early and too hurried a schedule often prevented them from enjoying the trip. Some felt that on group trips there sometimes were too many people which could make all of these concerns more severe. Also, the regimented schedule of a tour, with no room for side trips, was a concern.

Illness and health problems, if they occur while travelling, were considered by some to be the 'worst'.

Time schedules and time differences (and jet lag) were mentioned. Also, what to do with left-over money from a country visited emerged as a problem on tours. Others felt that tour guides and tour organizers helped to prepare the study participants with these concerns.

Overall, one last item considered to be the 'worst' was that the trip involved 'doing the same things I do at home'. The reason for travelling is to change the routine and see new things, so it is important not to do the same things that are done at home.

Many of the study participants had taken group trips. It depended on where they were going as to whether they preferred to travel alone or with a group. For example, for travel to some countries, say in South America or the Middle East, a group was preferred for safety reasons and possibly better accommodations. A group trip may also help overcome language barriers. Also when the trip involved travelling from country to country, and currency differences occurred, a group trip may help plan for changing currencies.

Guided trips may be good for destinations where there is a lot to see . . . 'they help you sort it all out'. Also, if the study participants do not know much about the country, the guides can help with the interpretation. There is a concern here, though, that the guides will show only certain things that are typical places for tourists to see. The real country, as lived in by the hosts, may not be experienced through guided tours.

Some people do not like guided tours at all. They feel that they are too regimented and that they do not allow for any spontaneity. Some study participants prefer to travel alone or to organize their own trips with a friend or family member. Others rely very heavily on the trip coordinator of their travel club.

Although most of the study participants did prefer group trips of some kind, as mentioned above, the single supplement or extra charge for a person travelling alone was a concern. Some of the study participants were married and travelled with their spouse, so this was not a concern for them. Most, though, were single and had to either have a room mate or pay extra. Although it was often difficult to find someone compatible, most felt it was important to try. Sometimes the group offered the name of someone who might be willing to share the room. Other times the person had to make their own arrangements.

When asked about types of people they liked to travel with most study participants said they would like to travel with people their own age, or close to it. Others felt that travelling with other older adults would be good . . . most agreed that teenagers and grandchildren would be unacceptable. When the purpose of the trip is to see a certain event or activity then the people who are travelling in the group should share that common interest. In that case diverse age and/or background would be more acceptable. A few people hoped to travel with a diverse group of mixed ages and from different places, feeling that would make it more interesting.

All seemed to agree that 'anyone who's fun to be with' would be a good person to have in the group. Two interesting comments were: 'I don't want to travel with old people' and 'You don't need men when travelling.'

As for the time of year to travel, most study participants wanted to go somewhere where the climate was different from that at home. There was also a preference on the part of some for 'off season', say fall or winter (depending on destination), when it might be less expensive (or better value). This preference, however, did not seem very important for most participants.

Some of the study participants felt that travel needs to be planned and that there are things they normally do at home that cannot be done when they travel. Others really just 'go with the flow' and look forward to changing their routine and picking up and going. Overall, the study participants all said they enjoyed travelling and therefore looked forward to any opportunity to do so. Mention was made of the need to create opportunities for travel. Examples included Senior Center clubs, church groups etc. One person made a very interesting comment: 'We go to the YMCA and exercise in preparation for our trips.'

Another study group member commented: 'When you travel you learn to adapt.' This statement seems to suggest that, while certain life styles are conducive to travel, the reverse is also true – frequent travel is conducive to a healthy life style.

Conclusions

Perhaps the most revealing finding of the research was a renewed appreciation of the diversity this age group represents. The popular perception suggests that seniors are all pretty much alike. Nothing could be further from the truth. Seniors, based on a lifetime of distinct experiences, differ greatly in their needs and wants.

It is also important to call attention to several characteristics related to the personality of the seniors we met which appeared to be universal. The seniors who participated in the study groups demonstrated a charm and warmth that seemed to result from a combination of experience, integrity and personal reflection. One study group participant captured the essence of this 'wisdom' when he said: 'You know that you are getting older when you have all the answers but nobody is asking the questions anymore.'

Participants in the focus groups appeared passionately committed to travel as a leisure time activity. These travellers view travel as an opportunity to change (escape from) daily routines, as an opportunity to stimulate their senses, and as providing a chance for social interaction. The senior traveller is a sophisticated and experienced user of the travel industry's products and services. An important finding is that apparently many senior travellers have encountered few problems with past travel experiences; they give the industry high marks for value, quality and responsiveness to their needs. Some concerns, however, were mentioned several times. They included:

1 The single supplement penalty.
2 Health/mobility constraints.
3 The fear of falling ill.
4 Uncertainty about political conditions.
5 Quality and quantity of information.
6 The pace of itineraries.
7 Language.
8 Packing and unpacking.
9 Meals.
10 Concerns related to transportation.

Primary travel motivators include:

1 The need to change routines.
2 Seeing new things.
3 Visiting friends and relatives.
4 Meeting new people and experiencing new cultures.
5 Expanding knowledge.
6 'Creating' memories.

When planning their vacations, seniors rely on the advice of travel professionals (travel agents and trip coordinators). They are avid readers of promotional and informational literature. Word of mouth (past experiences of others) also influences their travel purchasing behaviour.

When asked about the greatest benefits derived from travel the response is unanimous – meeting new people, experiencing new cultures, seeing new things. Seeing the things they read and know about creates powerful memories and adds to the degree of satisfaction with the travel experience.

Seniors dislike the single supplement fee, packing, the regimented schedule of tours and 'waiting'. Concerns about safety (security, mode of transportation), are real and are often cause for anxieties.

Seniors overwhelmingly prefer to travel in groups. Preferences about the make-up of the group relate less to age and gender than to shared pursuits. They like to travel with people who are fun to be with and have shared interests.

This summary of findings suggests that today's senior travel market can be characterized as being different, diverse and demanding. Today's senior traveller is different from other age groups and different from earlier generations of seniors. As an age group they are also diverse and made up of sub-groups worthy of further analysis. Too often, traditional marketing suggests that the senior market is still considered as a mass market, suitable for targeting tours with a generalized appeal. Such perceptions ignore the possibility that this large group has many segments, overlooking the emergence of special interest segments that might prefer specialized products and services. Perhaps the biggest challenge for the travel industry, as for society in general, is to develop an awareness of the diversity of the older traveller.

Mature travellers are also demanding consumers. They are experienced travellers who expect that the concept of value extends well beyond price.

References

Allan, C. (1981) Measuring mature markets. *American Demographics*, March, pp. 13–17

Anderson, B.B. and Langmeyer, L. (1982) The under 50 and over 50 travellers: a profile of similarities and differences. *Journal of Travel Research*, **20**(4), Spring

Dychtwald, K. and Flower, J. (1990) *Age Wave: How the Most Important Trends of Our Time Will Change Your Future*. Bantam Books, New York

Forbes, R.J. (1987) The US mature travel market. *Travel and Tourism Analyst*, November, pp. 17–21

Linden, F. (1986) The $800 billion market. *American Demographics*, February, pp. 4–6

MacNeil, R.D. (1991) The Times They Are A'Changing: the forthcoming age revolution. Presentation at Niagara University's Symposium on Reaching Out to the Senior Market, October

Shoemaker, S. (1989) Segmentation of the senior pleasure travel market. *Journal of Travel Research*, Winter, p. 14

Supernaw, S. (1985) Battle for the gray market. *The Battle for Market Share. Strategies in Research and Marketing*. Sixteenth Annual Conference Proceedings, Travel and Tourism Research Association

US Bureau of the Census (1991) *Marital Status and Living Arrangements*. US Bureau of the Census, March

US Travel Data Center (1990) *Discover America 2000: The Mature Market. A report on the impact of the changing mature market on the US travel industry.* Travel Industry Association of America, Washington, DC

US Travel Data Center (1989) *Discover America 2000. The Implications of America's Changing Demographics and Attitudes on the US Travel Industry.* Travel Industry Association of America, Washington, DC

Wolfe, D.B. (1987) The ageless market. *American Demographics*, July, pp. 68–77

25 Homogeneous products: the future of established resorts

Michael Morgan

Introduction

That tourist resorts tend to be homogeneous is not surprising. They all seek to offer the same core benefits. Nor is the homogeneity necessarily a problem. It can be argued that at certain stages of its development it is a positive advantage for a new resort to resemble established ones. Tourists may be reassured by the familiarity of their surroundings in a strange land. The problem comes not when the products are all perceived to be the same but when they are all perceived to be characterless, unfashionable and low in quality. This is how increasing numbers of potential customers are coming to regard the Mediterranean-style beach resort. The period of growth is over, new competitors are challenging their market share, and product differentiation and product quality are becoming the marketing priorities:

> We can guarantee a daily average of five hours throughout the year – but so can other destinations.

said an editorial in the Malta National Tourist Office newsletter July 1990. The traditional sun, sand and sea product is no longer enough to assure the future of established resorts.

In the manufacturing industry, products that reach the decline stage of their life cycle can be discontinued or completely redesigned and relaunched. Neither option is available to an established resort. You cannot 'close' Magaluf or Salou. Too many jobs and too much capital are at risk. Nor can any one organization 'redesign' a resort which is the result of years of interaction between private and public sector tourist undertakings and the local community.

This chapter will examine the strategies open to the established resorts. First the factors which have led to the current homogeneity will be outlined, with the implied lessons for newly developing resorts. Next, the issue will be placed in the context of the overall situation, or perhaps crisis, facing mass tourism in the early 1990s. The strategies adopted by a number of established resorts will then be assessed as possible models for others to follow.

Many of the examples given are from the author's study of the British market for Spanish resorts, but the process which has reached a highly developed stage there can be seen at work in beach resorts everywhere.

Why tourist resorts tend to become homogeneous products

Core benefits

One of the first principles of marketing is that people buy benefits and not product features (Kotler, 1988). The physical features and facilities of the resort, its transport links and the multinational network of tour operators and travel agents through which it is sold are all simply the means of 'delivering the desired satisfaction' (Kotler, 1988). In the case of beach tourism this is commonly described as 'sun, sand and sea' – which in terms of benefits means warmth, recreation, relaxation and an escape from the routines of working life. Some versions add other Ss to the list, such as sangria (or spirits) and sex, reminding us that holidays also satisfy social needs, and that one of the functions of the resort is to provide an environment where normal social inhibitions are suspended for the duration of the holiday. For many beach tourists the precise destination where they obtain these benefits is of secondary importance.

Tangible features

The tangible features of the resort develop from its core attractions of a beach, safe bathing and a warm climate. Hotels within walking distance of the sea, preferably with a sea view, are essential. Cafes for refreshment in the heat of the day, bars and nightspots for socializing in the warm nights soon follow. Shops develop to serve the needs of the tourists for souvenirs, beach wear, games equipment, cosmetics and gifts. It is inevitable that the land use of resorts follows predictable patterns distinct from normal residential and commercial developments (Lavery, 1971), with a Recreational Business District – 'a seasonally oriented grouping of restaurants, novelty and souvenir shops' (Stansfield and Rickert, 1970).

Packaging and distribution

These Mediterranean resorts are packaged by Northern European tour operators with very little emphasis on their geographical location. As Goodall and Bergsma (1990) say, 'The mass tour operator is marketing a holiday brand image emphasizing the quality of service of that operator and in which the image of a holiday in a given destination is unlikely to figure prominently'. Instead they are sold as a composite destination known as Summersun, or as tribal enclaves inhabited by like-minded tourists, normally segmented by age – Club 18–30, Twenties, Young at Heart, Golden Days etc. These very successful products sell by delivering the core benefits more effectively or more cheaply than their competitors. The local culture, scenery, history and architecture are optional excursions or a once-a-week folkloric floor show in the hotel. As the operators control the marketing channels, the individual hotels and the destination tourist board have little influence on how the resort is presented in brochures and advertising.

International markets, global products

The hotels and other facilities may be managed by local companies but the style of their services is deliberately international. A hotel in Spain with British, German, Scandinavian, Italian and Spanish guests tries to cater for all tastes with buffet meals and multi-lingual entertainment. The success of the Palma-based Grupo Sol, with 140 hotels from Bali to Venezuala, run on this multi-national formula, seems to support Levitt's famous assertion on the globalization of markets:

> The world is becoming a common marketplace in which people – no matter where they come from – desire the same products and life styles – (Levitt, 1983)

If the price is right, says Levitt, 'they will take highly standardized world products', including, one might add, purpose-built high-rise resorts with a standardized nightlife based on Coca-Cola, Budweiser and disco music.

Economies of scale

The successful growth of tourism in the period following the Second World War has indeed been price-led, based on the tour operators' ability to deliver hitherto inaccessible warm-climate destinations at prices affordable by the vast majority of people in Northern Europe (and North America). To do this the operators have needed to achieve economies of scale on charter flights and large allocations at resort hotels.

These low prices depended on the operators negotiating low rates from the hoteliers, which in turn were made possible by low wage levels and favourable exchange rates. As a result tourists were given three-star quality at prices that would hardly pay for a guest house in their own countries. This further encouraged the growth in the overseas market at the expense of the domestic market, especially in Britain.

Standardized building methods

To benefit from the rising demand for large numbers of beds at low prices, local hoteliers have had to employ standardized building methods and plot ratios more reminiscent of London or Manhattan than of their own vernacular architecture.

It is too easy to condemn architectural styles in the resorts when buildings in the same styles were being built with the same disregard for the historical and cultural environment in most towns and cities of the world at the time. The growth of mass tourism coincided with an era of architecture advanced in technology but limited in aesthetics. Functional simplicity was preferred to ornamentation and disguise, straight lines and rectangles to curves and ovals – admirably honest in theory, cheap to implement but monotonous in result. The spa resorts of the eighteenth century and the seaside towns of the nineteenth were equally mass produced and homogeneous in architecture but the crescents of Bath have to modern eyes an elegant charm we have not yet learnt to discern in the towers of Benidorm.

The reaction against such resorts can be seen as part of a wider post-modernist revolt against functionalism and internationalism in style. When the heir to the British throne described a modernist design for an extension to London's National Gallery as 'a monstrous carbuncle on the face of a well-loved friend', he could have been articulating many a tourist's reaction to the over-development of his favourite holiday area. Yet when they were developed the high-rise resort hotels symbolized to the local business community not only profit but prestige, modernization and an alluring Americanized life style.

Quality assurance

This symbolism also worked for the tourist. Standardized products promoted globally with a strong brand identity do not succeed only on price advantage. Their instantly recognized style and logos promise a standard quality, reassuring amid the the unfamiliar imagery of locally produced goods and services. To quote two current advertising slogans, 'You're never far from a Hilton, or 'If Thomsons do it, do it. If Thomsons don't do it, don't do it.'

For a tourist making his first visit to a country, the modern architecture and the multi-national logos of the hotels promise an enclave of familiarity and security in a strange and threatening world. Around the hotels, smaller businesses, often run by expatriates, offer a similar reassurance in the form of British, American or German style bars, cafes and supermarkets.

In some resorts, this sense of the tourist district as a safe enclave is only too accurate. Tourists in some African resorts and European and American cities are warned not to venture away from the hotel on their own. In others, such as beach resorts on the North African coast, there is literally nowhere to go – the nearest 'real' indigenous settlements being an hour or more's drive away. The resort, or even the individual hotel with its pool replacing the crowded and polluted beach, is self-contained, like a permanently moored cruise liner from which the 'passengers' disembark only for organized excursions.

New resorts in the Caribbean and Far East are designed specifically as Integrated Resort Developments (Stiles and See-Tho, 1991), with a range of sporting and social facilities such that the guest need not leave the site for the duration the holiday – a concept pioneered by holiday centres such as Butlins in the UK and the French Club Mediterranée. These take the concept of the brand image replacing the destination image to the logical extreme, but the same characteristics of self-contained uniformity are shared by many more conventional resorts.

Why has this formula succeeded in the past?

This formula works very successfully as long as the tourist's prime concern is for relaxation and recreation in a warmer climate among people with whom they feel comfortable. The very artificiality of the resort enhances the sense of the holiday as a break from the real world. The familiar symbols in a warmer climate create a relaxed mood in which the normal social inhibitions are suspended. The 'British pub' stays open all night, plays loud music, shows non-stop action videos, and garlands you with paper streamers. You are neither in Britain nor Spain, but Never-Never Land.

The function of the destination in this holiday experience is primarily to provide the warm climate and the low prices based on lower wage costs and favourable exchange rates. It also gives the holiday an exotic background, often experienced as superficially as that of a themed bar or restaurant at home. It is made tangible in souvenirs of the local national stereotypical symbols – famous buildings, wildlife or local customs – which bear little relation to the content of the holiday. Often they are not

relevant to the particular region, as with the ubiquitous flamenco dancing dolls in regions of Spain far from Andalucia. These souvenirs and
gifts help to give the tourist status on his return home from the exotic
destination.

Growth of the tourism market in the 1980s

In the growth market of the 1980s, tourist resorts proliferated. New
markets of first generation tourists took advantage of the short jet flights
and low prices to escape the uncertainties of the North West European
climate for their annual holiday. As can be seen from Table 25.1, the boom
was experienced not only in Spain but throughout the Mediterranean.

Newer destinations were added to operators' programmes and new
resorts built to cater for the demand. This led to the rapid development
of previously untouched coastline in places like the Turkish coast into
'high density, low grade holiday townships, lacking not only visual
attraction but also basic services' (Economist Intelligence Unit, 1989).
The Algarve in Portugal is another area often cited as a recent victim of
overdevelopment, having failed to learn the lessons from the development
of the Spanish Costas (Barrett, 1989).

In the meantime, the established areas of Spain went on increasing the
accommodation stock, 70,000 beds being added, for example, in Majorca
between 1986 and 1990 (Morgan, 1991).

This growth, primarily from the UK was fuelled by the low prices
commented on earlier. In 1986 the leading UK tour operator Thomson
reacted to the first signs of market saturation and potential loss of market
share with a dramatic series of discounts, sparking off a long price war
with its main competitors. The result was volume growth at the expense
of profit margins, which led to mergers and bankruptcies wiping out
several leading tour operators, including, in 1991, Thomson's main rivals,
the International Leisure Group.

Table 25.1 Tourist arrivals from abroad in selected
Mediterranean countries (millions)

	1985	1986	1987	1988	1989
Spain	27.4	29.9	32.9	35.0	35.3
Greece	6.5	7.0	7.5	7.9	8.1
Portugal	4.9	5.4	6.1	6.6	7.1
Turkey	2.2	2.0	2.5	3.7	3.9
Cyprus	0.7	0.8	0.9	1.2	1.4
Tunisia	2.0	1.5	1.9	3.5	3.2

Source: World Tourism Organisation (1990).

In the short term the price war benefited the tourists and the resorts, but the reduction in profitability affected the hoteliers as well as the tour operators. In Spain, particularly, the tourist industry was at the same time experiencing rising wage and other costs as the nation's standard of living rose in the era of democracy and European Community membership. Compared to its emerging competitors, it was no longer a cheap destination. There was therefore a lack of capital for refurbishment and renewal of the accommodation stock. As Fayos Sola (1992) writes of the Valencia region:

> the huge expansion of hotels at the beginning of the 1970s has not enjoyed adequate continuity or renovation. The approximately 900,000 hotel beds on offer are still concentrated in hotels with three star rating or less, and suffer from a high rate of obsolescence.

As long as the tourists kept coming, there was no perceived problem, except in the minds of a sensitive elite who were not the target market of resorts like Valencia's Benidorm. The complacency was well expressed by Farrell (1982), writing of another tourist enclave on the other side of the world:

> Outsiders and insiders alike point to Waikiki as a design disaster – yet the generally rising occupancy rates suggest that far from being repelled, tourists come back in greater numbers.

This attitude also helps to explain the lack of any product differentiation strategy in these resorts during the period of growth.

The changing scene in the 1990s

In recent years, however, tourism to the established Mediterranean resorts has been showing signs of decline. British visitor numbers to Spain fell in 1989 and were below 1986 levels in 1990. (British Tourist Authority, 1991). There are a number of factors at work in this downward trend.

Product maturity

To some extent it is an inevitable process. The Spanish resorts no longer offer unique benefits. New competitors have copied their formula for success. A wider choice of destinations in the eastern Mediterranean and further afield, most notably in Florida, offer the same sun, sand and sea resorts with an added novelty and status.

As the foreign holiday becomes commonplace, the consumer decision changes from what Engel, Blackwell and Miniard (1990) call an extended problem-solving exercise to a routine annual purchase. The success of the tour operator and the hotelier in taking the risk out of foreign travel has lowered the 'involvement' of the tourist in the decision. In these circumstances, consumer behaviour theory predicts, 'variety-seeking buyer behaviour' is likely to occur. If all the resorts are basically similar, the tourist is more likely to try a different one each time in a search for variety. If the new destination offers the status of a long-haul holiday at a competitive price, the appeal is even stronger.

Comparing 1986 and 1990, UK inclusive holidays to the USA more than quadrupled (111,000 to 472,000) while packages to Spain fell from 4.7 million to 2.8 million (British Tourist Authority, International Passenger Survey). The overall decline in UK–Spain visitor numbers was much less (5.9 to 5.1 million), offset by a rise in independent holiday visits and business travel. Nevertheless, the signs that the current Spanish product has reached the mature stage of its product life cycle (Kotler, 1988) are still clear.

Economic factors

This trend towards long-haul holidays has not been significantly affected by the world-wide economic recession. While consumer demand in general has been depressed, the effects on the tourist market have varied, with some categories suffering more than others. Rather than cutting out the annual holiday completely, commentators have observed customers switching categories to products offering greater perceived value for money (Mitchell, 1990). This has encouraged the switch from the homogeneous package to the motoring tour or the long-haul destinations. Couples may not take any holiday at all one year to save up for a trip with added exotic appeal and status value the next. Demographic factors are also at work as the effects of redundancy and high costs of home ownership are felt less severely by the older age groups.

Demographic factors

The generation now buying family holidays (25–45 years age group) have grown up taking the annual Mediterranean holiday for granted. They are therefore less apprehensive than their parents about foreign travel. They are likely to have stayed in education longer and are more likely to speak a foreign language. They have also grown up with the car and want the benefits of mobility on holiday.

Table 25.2 UK tourists' holiday visits to France and Spain (thousands)

	Independent		Inclusive		Total	
	1986	1990	1986	1990	1986	1990
Spain	1,481	1,821	4,076	2,816	5,557	4,637
France	2,548	3,123	1,234	1,871	3,782	4,994

Source: British Tourist Authority (1991).

The permanently moored cruise liner type of resort is therefore less attractive to them than a motoring tour based on a self-catering cottage or villa. They are also more vulnerable to economic recession and are looking for value for money.

For all these reasons, the fastest growth in the UK holiday market in recent years has been in holidays to France by car ferry. The number of accompanied cars crossing the English Channel grew by 20 per cent in 1989 and a further 6 per cent in 1990 (Transport Statistics GB 1991). Table 25.2 shows how the UK overseas holiday market has changed in the late 1980s with a growth in independent holidays to France and a decline in inclusive holidays to Spain, resulting in France replacing Spain as Britons' most popular holiday destination.

The over-55 age group is increasing in number, which can be of benefit to the established resorts as they are not tied to school holiday periods and so can help extend the season in resorts offering 'winter sun' products. But these 'empty nesters' with a higher disposable income than families or heavily mortgaged young couples are also the prime market for cruises and long-haul holidays, with which to celebrate their newly regained freedom!

Changing perceptions and expectations

With increased competition from rising destinations and the greater sophistication of the tourist, differentiation of the resort product is now at last being recognized to be essential (Fayos Sola, 1992). It is also being realized that the quality of the product, that is the fit between the tourist's expectations and experience (Parasuraman et al., 1985) has fallen. This is due to three main factors.

Lack of refurbishment

First there is the lack of refurbishment, both of the accommodation as previously mentioned, and also of the infrastructure of the resort itself.

When they were built in the 1970s the hotels, with their en-suite bath-rooms, balconies and extended meal times, seemed luxurious in com-parison with holiday accommodation in the domestic market. These facilities are now taken for granted and the general standard of furnish-ing, decor and fittings has not kept pace with the tourists' own standards at home, let alone with sophisticated new resorts. The attractions and entertainments available cannot compare with tourist complexes like Disney.

Environmental awareness

Secondly, there has been an increase in environmental awareness in Britain and most notably in Germany. That is not to say that the average beach tourist is a dedicated ecologist looking for sustainable tourism. What has happened is that stories in the popular media have made the average tourist aware of the threat of pollution and disease in Mediterranean resorts, of poor standards of hygiene and fire safety in holiday hotels, and so the names of the popular resorts have become associated with overcrowding and overdevelopment – half-finished hotels and noisy dusty construction sites (Astles, 1989).

Lager Louts

Thirdly, the price war years have produced a phenomenon known to the British press as the 'Lager Lout'. Encouraged by cheap discounted fares and holiday packages targeted at the teen and twenty market, large numbers of young British, Scandinavian and other North Europeans flocked to the big resorts with their all-night disco bars. The resorts gained a reputation for drunkeness, noise and fights, exaggerated, they would argue, by sensational coverage in the British media. The effect has been to deter the family market.

For all these reasons the established Spanish resorts, although retain-ing a price advantage, were no longer perceived as value for money compared to their newer competitors.

Out of fashion?

The concept of the adoption curve (Rogers, 1962) is relevant here. New products, such as destinations, are first bought by a relatively small group of 'innovators' who are attracted by the idea of trying something new and different. These people set the trend or fashion, which is copied first by 'early adopters', then by the majority and latterly by the 'laggards' who only adopt the most tried and commonplace products. Plog (1973) sees the diffusion in terms of psychological types; he considers that the allocentric or outward-looking type, who is interested in discovering the world and the people outside his previous experience, will be the first to seek out new and different destinations, while the psychocentric or self-focused type prefers the familiarity of established destinations where he feels 'at home'.

It is clear that the Mediterranean beach resorts have ceased to attract the innovators and allocentric tourists. What is worrying the tourist industry is that even the majority, mid- to psychocentric tourists are becoming dissatisfied and ready to move on. These fears were expressed in a trade press article by Charles Newbold, Managing Director of Thomson Holidays in the UK. After cataloguing the bad news stories and image problems described in the preceding paragraphs of this chapter, he wondered, no doubt provocatively, whether 'the package holiday as we know it is going out of fashion' (*Travel News*, 31 March 1989).

Moving on

The tourist and the tour operator can move on to newer, more distant destinations, switch to other types of holiday or revert to domestic tourism. The established resorts remain. As previously mentioned, in the boom years of the 1980s 70,000 extra hotel beds were added to Majorca's capacity. Now the local tourist authorities calculate that a similar number are surplus to capacity (Morgan, 1991). Tourism, which is responsible for 70 per cent of the island's employment, is as much a mono-culture as any Third World cash-crop, and communities which depend on it are just as vulnerable to fluctuations in world demand.

Lessons for developing resorts

It might seem easy in hindsight to prescribe lessons for newly developing resorts to avoid the mistakes of the past but the pressures that led to those mistakes still exist.

Avoid overdependence on particular markets, or on tourism at the expense of other industries and agriculture. Yet tourism has been a successful means of bringing prosperity to Spain and remains an attractive model for other countries in need of foreign currency for development.

Do not lose control of the distribution channel. But individual resorts cannot penetrate international markets effectively without the aid of intermediaries in the target countries. As East (1990) pointed out, the best way to sell a holiday hotel or resort in a foreign market is to make sure it is in a tour operator's brochure.

Maintain and enhance the quality of the resort facilities. This requires investment which in a price-led low-profit-margin industry can be difficult to generate on purely commercial grounds. It also requires development controls which in the early years of a resort's development could be politically difficult to impose.

It is nevertheless the public-sector tourism authorities with their concern for the economic and social benefits of tourism to the whole community who have been responsible for most of the initiatives to refurbish the established resorts. Often these schemes are attempting to rectify the consequences of a previous lack of investment in infrastructure and a lack of effective planning controls.

Newer resorts could save expense and problems in the long term by balancing the desire to grab the benefits of tourism with the need to control some of the most obvious environmental consequences from the start. An optimist would argue that the growing environmental awareness in the major tourism originating nations makes this task easier than it was for the resorts which developed in the 1970s and 1980s.

Strategies for survival

What, though, can be the already established resorts do? Marketing writers are generally agreed that the concept of a product having a life cycle is more helpful diagnostically than predictively (Haywood, 1986). Products that appear to be moving from growth to maturity and decline can be revived by the correct marketing strategy, starting, according to Kotler (1988) by 'modifying the customer mix, the brand's positioning and the marketing mix'.

In tourism these elements are interdependent. Resorts need to find new markets, both geographically and behaviourally segmented, to reduce their dependence on the British and German beach tourist. To attract these new markets changes will be needed to the marketing mix. For example, the product offered – in terms of accommodation attractions and access – may not suit the needs of the new markets, the price/quality offer may be wrong, and new distribution channels may have to be found. The resorts also need to find distinct positioning strategies to differentiate themselves from their competitors in the minds of both existing and potential customers. This again will require a review of the whole marketing mix, the product, price and place, and not just the promotion.

New markets, new needs

Promotion targeted at new markets is an obvious answer to overdependence on one declining market. The Balearic Islands, for example, have targeted the Netherlands, Switzerland and Scandinavia, and the growing Spanish domestic market, to compensate for a fall in British visitor numbers.

However, different nationalities have different needs, which means that a simple substitution is not possible. In recent winters the Spanish resorts have been busy with domestic tourists, many of them taking advantage of the subsidized holidays available to Spanish pensioners under a government scheme to prevent unemployment in the tourist industry. These new visitors do not have the same tastes or spending power as the North Europeans. As a result, though the hotels and promenades are crowded, many of the resort shops, bars and nightclubs, particularly those targeted at British or German tourists, remain shut.

Taking an example at the other end of the Mediterranean, when the number of US visitors to Israeli resorts fell as a result of terrorism fears in the mid 1980s, the shortfall in overall numbers was made up by a growth in European visitors. But within this overall picture there was in fact still surplus unsold capacity in the four- and five-star accommodation favoured by the Americans and a shortage of the lower-priced three-star hotels demanded by the European markets.

More often, new potential markets demand higher standards and are prepared to pay more for them. The upgrading and refurbishment programmes being undertaken in the Balearics and Valencia are in part aimed at attracting new and more discriminating European and North American visitors.

Investing in new products

The holiday product is more than just the destination. Tourists are more likely to be motivated by *what* they are going to do on their holiday than by *where* they are going to do it. Realizing this, Valencia's White Paper on Tourism targets specific 'product markets' with differentiated needs, e.g.:

sun and beach;
tourism for the retired;
congresses and conventions;
life style and cultural tourism;
sport and adventure tourism;
health and fitness tourism (Fayos Sola, 1992).

Each of these requires improvements and investment in special facilities and packages.

Taking the example of the conference market, several major British resorts have compensated for the fall in main holiday beach tourism by developing facilities for the business and conference markets. Bournemouth Council have invested £25 million in building a major international centre for conferences and entertainment. Conferences generate 278,000 bed nights per annum for the resort, bringing in £2.4 million per annum in tourist spending, and creating 3500 extra jobs by giving the hotels year-round business. The benefits have been felt largely though not entirely by the larger business-orientated hotels.

In Majorca the development of new product markets has tended not to benefit the established resort areas directly. Conference and incentive meetings visitors have used hotels in the main city of Palma. Marinas have developed in Palma and in new up-market resorts like Porto Portals. The outdoor activity market, for walking, riding and birdwatching, has focused on the northern resort of Porto Pollensa. The main southern resorts of the Bay of Palma, Magaluf/Palma Nova, Arenal/Playas de Palmas, which provide the majority of the beds and jobs, have not attracted these new tourists.

To extend the product range of these resorts, the emphasis is on watersports and on golf. Twenty new golf courses are planned for the island of Majorca by the end of the century. Golf in the sun is also one of the main themes in the Spanish National Tourist Office's (NTO) current advertising campaign.

To gain Magaluf a share of the yachting market, the local authority has approved in outline controversial plans for a large marina project which would counteract the Lager Lout image it has acquired. Its construction would require the demolition of some of the noisiest bars (which may not be coincidental). For the plan, the largest of several marina schemes for the island, to go ahead the council needs to find private developers and investors.

So to provide new products in old resorts requires considerable investment and may result in considerable changes in the customer mix and atmosphere of the area.

From resort to touring centre

The beach resort typically evolves to cater for tourists who arrive by mass transportation systems. This was true of British seaside resorts in the railway age and also of the Mediterranean resorts made accessible by charter flights in jet aircraft since the 1960s. Tourists arrived by plane and coach and were for the most part happy to spend their time between the hotel and the beach.

As demand for this type of holiday falls, the attraction of the hinterland of the resort becomes more important. British resorts have now to market themselves to tourists who are arriving by car and are prepared to drive up to forty miles from the resort for day excursions to attractions or scenic countryside. Bournemouth's product now effectively includes the National Motor Museum at Beaulieu (twenty miles to the east), the open landscape of the New Forest and the literary associations of Thomas Hardy's Wessex. So successfully have the inland cities and countryside of Yorkshire in Northern England sold themselves as tourist destinations that established resorts like Scarborough now market themselves as on the Yorkshire Coast, a reversal of the previous positioning.

Mediterranean resorts are also learning that the cultural, historical, scenic, wildlife and even industrial heritage of the region are now a means of creating a unique product position. The majority of visitors may not have a deep knowledge or interest in that heritage, but it still improves the image and status value of the resort for them. It also provides a motivation for a different market segment to use the resort as a touring base, particularly off-season.

The Spanish NTO advertising campaigns in the UK in recent years have used the historical and scenic attractions of Spain's interior to reposition the country as a destination offering much more than the three (or more) Ss. A romantic view of a hilltop castle is labelled 'One of our little bed-and-breakfast places'. Individual resorts and regions have followed the same strategy. Majorca, for example, promotes its associations with the composer Chopin who once spent a rather unhappy winter in the mountain village of Valdemossa.

Upgrading the product quality

While these attempts to find new markets and widen the product range offered are important elements in the resorts' strategies, their future still depends on retaining a viable share of the core beach tourism market. To do this they must seek to close the gap between the expectations of their customers and the quality of the experience they receive.

In Spain it is the governments of the autonomous regions (comparable to the individual states of the USA) who are taking the lead in this drive for quality. The Balearic Islands are approaching the challenge in two ways: direct investment in environmental and infrastructural improvements, and planning regulations to limit and zone new development. Spending on promenades, shopping precincts, parks, pedestrianization and general refurbishment totals £111 million. New hotels will have to be of at least four-star quality with 120 square metres of land for every bed provided, so preventing any more high-rise clusters. To limit the spread of low-rise development this restriction might otherwise encourage, a number of nature or scenic conservation areas have been designated, covering 30 per cent of Majorca and Ibiza and 45 per cent of Menorca. Laws controlling the noise from all-night bars and the exploitation of monkeys by photographers are among other measures designed to improve the quality and image of the resorts.

Tour operators and hoteliers are also responding to the crisis by improving the quality of their products. Thomson have invested £10 million in partnership with selected hotels to bring them up to the standard and style of service which their research shows the British clients of the 1990s expect. Significantly, these hotels, marketed as Sun Hotels in Thomson brochures, are moving away from the international style described earlier and instead provide decor, food and entertainment specifically for the British market – bacon and egg breakfasts, soft toilet paper and English comedians.

Promoting the new image

All these strategies require extensive promotion. Image-building advertising by the National Tourist Office has to be combined with trade promotion through brochures, trade exhibitions and workshops, and educational visits. The message must reach the agency staff at the point of sale with the public.

NTOs are increasingly relying on a strategy of what Middleton (1988) calls facilitation, bringing destination suppliers such as hoteliers and attraction operators into contact with the travel industry decision-makers in the target originating country. This is more cost-effective for the NTO than producing large amounts of consumer brochures for which it has no distribution network or consumer advertising which lacks a specific product proposition. Cooperative marketing between the NTO, the tour operators and the travel agencies is needed to create a desirable image and then convert the desire into action to purchase a specific holiday. The drawback of this approach is that the tour operators and agents will only be able to give individual resorts limited coverage in their brochures and promotions.

Press publicity is therefore a very important tool in communicating the changes in the resorts to potential holiday-makers. A journalist writing a feature on a resort is more likely to be believed than an advertisement. Running a press trip can obtain more press coverage at lower cost than an advertising campaign.

Refurbishment investment brings initial success

Over the period from 1988 onwards the author has studied the efforts of the Balearic Islands to tackle the challenges facing the established tourist resorts in the 1990s. Just as they were among the earliest to experience the tourism boom of the jet era, so they now are among the first to face the problems of the mature market. Their investment in improvements to the quality of the resorts and their environment appears to be producing results. After declining by 6 per cent in 1989 and 5 per cent in 1990, figures for 1991 suggested a 3 per cent rise in overall visitor numbers, with strong growth in visitors from mainland Europe and a levelling off of the fall in the British market (Balearic Islands Tourism Council press release, November 1991).

Bookings for 1992 from the UK were strong, with Majorca increasing its share of the market. Tour Operator Philip Pattison of Sunset Holidays has been quoted in the trade press as considering that the Balearics have become fashionable again, boosted by their spending programme and PR coverage. 'One thing they have got right is that they are not frightened of spending money.' In contrast to his earlier remarks, Charles Newbold of Thomson has also shown optimism: 'The Balearics were written off by many as victims of their own success. *In less than two years, the trans-formation has set an example which other countries could follow'* (emphasis added) (*Travel Weekly*, 1 April 1992).

Future prospects

Observers with less of a vested interest may qualify this optimism by pointing out that the Balearics and the western Mediterranean in general are benefiting because other destinations, most obviously Yugoslavia and the Middle East, but also African countries like Kenya, are currently seen as too dangerous. In a crisis security is a more basic need than discovery or adventure. The familiarity of the established resort becomes an asset again.

Latent in Newbold's remarks is a more long-term problem. The trans-formation of the Balearics has indeed set an example which other countries are very likely to follow. Good parks, precincts, street furniture and promenades may give a short-term competitive advantage, but are not in themselves the basis of a long-term product differentiation strategy. Success is very quickly copied and what works in Magaluf or Benidorm today will soon be available everywhere else. Will the new homogeneity of palm-tree lined precincts, golf courses and marinas in turn be perceived as characterless and unfashionable?

The pressures on resorts to develop on similar lines to each other still exist, even if the dangers – aesthetic, social and commercial – are now better appreciated. The challenge for any resort is to provide the facili-ties, accommodation and attractions of a standard demanded by the international tourist market while retaining and developing its unique character. This character, this image which differentiates it from its many competitors, often depends on geographical, historical and cultural fea-tures that predate tourism and are vulnerable to being obliterated by tourism. This paradox, whereby we simultaneously demand all the advantages and economies of modern life while deploring the resulting bland homogeneity, is an issue which is not confined to tourism. Like all aspects of consumer behaviour, it is both a threat and an opportunity.

References

Astles, R. (1989) Overseas package holidays, where next? *Leisure Intelligence*, **2**, p. 43

Barrett, F. (1989) On the Algarve road to ruin. *The Independent*, 22 July

British Tourist Authority (1991) *Digest of Tourism Statistics*, BTA, London, December, p. 50

East, M. (1990) Business update. *Travel News*, 7 December

Economist Intelligence Unit (1989) *International Tourism Reports*, No. 1

Engel, J. Blackwell, R. and Miniard, P. (1990) *Consumer Behaviour*, 6th ed, Dryden Press, Orlando, Fla, p. 474

Farrell, B. (1982) *Hawaii, the Legend that Sells*, University of Hawaii Press, Honolulu, p. 36

Fayos Sola, E. (1992) A strategic outlook for regional tourism policy – the White Paper on Valencian Tourism. *Tourism Management*, **13**, March, pp. 45–9

Goodall, B. and Bergsma, J. (1990) Destinations as marketed in tour operators' brochures. In *Marketing Tourism Places* (ed. G. Ashworth and B. Goodall), Routledge, London, p. 173

Haywood, K.M. (1986) Can the tourist area life cycle be made operational? *Tourism Management*, **7** September, pp. 154–67

Kotler, P. (1991) *Marketing Management, Analysis, Planning, Implementation and Control*, 7th edn, Simon and Schuster, Englewood Cliffs NJ, pp. 5–6, 365

Lavery, P. (1971) *Recreational Geography*, David and Charles, Newton Abbott, pp. 177–95

Levitt, T. (1988) The globalisation of markets. *Havard Business Review*, May/June, pp. 92–102

Middleton, V.T.C. (1988) *Marketing in Travel and Tourism*, Heinemann, Oxford, pp. 209–25

Mitchell, A. (1990) Marketing out of the down-turn. *Marketing*, 26 April, pp. 25–6

Morgan, M. (1991) Dressing up to survive. Marketing Majorca anew. *Tourism Management*, March **12**, pp. 15–20

Parasuraman, A., Zeithaml, V. and Berry, L. (1985) A conceptual model of service quality. *Journal of Marketing*, Fall, p. 44

Plog, S.C. (1973) Why destination areas rise and fall. *Cornell Hotel and Restaurant Administration Quarterly*, pp. 13–16

Rogers, E.M. (1962) *The Diffusion of Innovation*, Free Press of Glencoe, NY, p. 162

Stansfield, C. A. and Rickert, J.E. (1970) The recreational business district. *Journal of Leisure Research*, **2**(4), pp. 213–25

Stiles, R. and See-Tho, W. (1991) Integrated resort development in the Asia Pacific region. *Travel and Tourism Analyst*, no. 3, pp. 22–37

World Tourism Organisation (1990) *World Tourism Statistics*, WTO, Madrid

Index

Name

Abernathy, William J., 339
Adventure Atlas, 271
Adventure Book, 270
Adventure Society, 271
Adventure Travel, 270
Adventure Vacation Catalog, 270
Ahmed, Z. U., 110
Air Vanuata, 317
Ali Bhutto, Prime Minister Zulfiqar, 155
Allan, C., 367
Allen, L., 110, 115
Almanza, Barbara A., 342
Altman, J. C., 107, 140–1
Alvarez Valdes, Jesus, 249
American Airlines, 338
American Association of Retired Persons (AARP), 368
American Automobile Association, 164
American Demographics, 363
American Express Company, 50, 368
American Institute of Architects Committee on the Environment, 268
Amir, Y., 109
Anderson, B. B., 363
Andropov, Yuri, 62
Annals of Tourism Research, 146
Anscombe, J., 87
Ap, John, 2
Aquino, Louis Felipe, 249
Aquino, President, 153
Archer, Brian, 69, 73, 75
Argyle, M., 113
Ascher, F., 126–7
Ash, John, 102, 106, 109, 112, 126
Ashley, Laura, 55
Ashworth, G., 348

Ashworth, G. H., 331
Astles, R., 387
Astor, Lord, 59
Audubon Society, 52
Auster E. R., 276
Australian Bureau of Tourism Research, 242
Australian Tourist Commission, 243
Austrian National Guest Survey, 199
Austrian National Tourist Office, 199

Bacal, Sarah, 256
Baedekers, 100
Bagozzi, R. P., 199
Balearic Islands Tourism Council, 394
Bananas, Beaches and Bases, 146
Barkham, J. P., 88, 282
Barlow, M., 28
BarOn, Raymond, 10
Barrett, F., 383
Barry, Tom, 149
Basis Research, Ltd, 192
Belisle, F., 31
Bell, Daniel, 336
Benny, Jack, 55
Berger, J., 65
Bergsma, J., 380
Bernard, M., 199
Bingham, Hiram, 251
Binks, G., 321
Blackwell, R., 385
Blake, George, 62
Blank, Uel, 338
Bloomstrom, R., 30
Bochner, S., 105, 109, 112
Bodlender, J. A., 293, 296
Boeing Commercial Airplane Group, 262

Subject